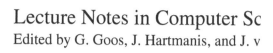

Lecture Notes in Computer Sc

Edited by G. Goos, J. Hartmanis, and J. v

Springer

Berlin
Heidelberg
New York
Barcelona
Hong Kong
London
Milan
Paris
Tokyo

Fabio Roli Josef Kittler (Eds.)

Multiple Classifier Systems

Third International Workshop, MCS 2002
Cagliari, Italy, June 24-26, 2002
Proceedings

 Springer

Series Editors

Gerhard Goos, Karlsruhe University, Germany
Juris Hartmanis, Cornell University, NY, USA
Jan van Leeuwen, Utrecht University, The Netherlands

Volume Editors

Fabio Roli
University of Cagliari, Dept. of Electrical and Electronical Engineering
Piazza D'Armi, 09123 Cagliari,Italy
E-mail:roli@diec.unica.it

Josef Kittler
University of Surrey, Centre for Vision, Speech and Signal Processing
Guilford, Surrey GUZ 7XH, UK
E-mail:j.kittler@eim.surrey.ac.uk

Cataloging-in-Publication Data applied for

Die Deutsche Bibliothek - CIP-Einheitsaufnahme

Multiple classifier systems : third international workshop ; proceedings /
MCS 2002, Cagliari, Italy, June 24 - 26, 2002. Fabio Roli ; Josef Kittler
(ed.). - Berlin ; Heidelberg ; New York ; Barcelona ; Hong Kong ; London ;
Milan ; Paris ; Tokyo : Springer, 2002
    (Lecture notes in computer science ; Vol. 2364)
    ISBN 3-540-43818-1

CR Subject Classification (1998): I.5, I.4, I.2.10, I.2, F.1

ISSN 0302-9743
ISBN 3-540-43818-1 Springer-Verlag Berlin Heidelberg New York

Springer-Verlag Berlin Heidelberg New York
a member of BertelsmannSpringer Science+Business Media GmbH

http://www.springer.de

© Springer-Verlag Berlin Heidelberg 2002
Printed in Germany

Typesetting: Camera-ready by author, data conversion by Boller Mediendesign
Printed on acid-free paper   SPIN 10870300   06/3142   5 4 3 2 1 0

Foreword

More than a decade ago, combining multiple classifiers was proposed as a possible solution to the problems posed by the traditional pattern classification approach which involved selecting the best classifier from a set of candidates based on their experimental evaluation. As no classifier is known to be the best for all cases and the selection of the best classifier for a given practical task is very difficult, diverse research communities, including Machine Learning, Neural Networks, Pattern Recognition, and Statistics, addressed the engineering problem of how to exploit the strengths while avoiding the weaknesses of different designs. This ambitious research trend was also motivated by empirical observations about the complementarity of different classifier designs, natural requirements of information fusion applications, and intrinsic difficulties associated with the optimal choice of some classifier design parameters, such as the architecture and the initial weights for a neural network. After years of research, the combination of multiple classifiers has become a well established and exciting research area, which provides effective solutions to difficult pattern recognition problems. A considerable body of empirical evidence supports the merit of designing combined systems whose accuracy is higher than that of each individual classifier, and various methods for the generation and the combination of multiple classifiers have become available. However, despite the proved utility of multiple classifier systems, no general answer to the original question about the possibility of exploiting the strengths while avoiding the weaknesses of different classifier designs has yet emerged. Other fundamental issues are also a matter of on-going research in different research communities. The results achieved during the past years are also spread over different research communities, and this makes it difficult to exchange such results and promote their cross-fertilization. The acknowledgment of the fundamental role that the creation of a common international forum for researchers of the diverse communities could play for the advancement of this research field motivated the present series of workshops on multiple classifier systems. Following its predecessors, Multiple Classifier Systems 2000 (Springer ISBN 3-540-67704-6) and 2001 (Springer ISBN 3-540-42284-6), this volume contains the proceedings of the Third International Workshop on Multiple Classifier Systems (MCS 2002), held at the Grand Hotel Chia Laguna, Cagliari, Italy, on June 24-26, 2002. The 29 papers selected by the scientific committee have been organized in sessions dealing with bagging and boosting, ensemble learning and neural networks, combination strategies, design methodologies, analysis and performance evaluation, and applications. The workshop program and this volume are enriched with three invited talks given by Joydeep Ghosh (University of Texas, USA), Trevor Hastie (Stanford University, USA), and Sarunas Raudys (Vilnius Gediminas Technical University, Lithuania). Papers were submitted from researchers of the four diverse communities, so confirming that this series of workshops can become a common forum for exchanging views and reporting latest research results. As for the previous editions, the significant number of papers dealing with real pattern recognition applications are proof of the practical utility of multiple classifier systems. This workshop was supported by the University of Cagliari, Italy, the University of Surrey, Guildford, United Kingdom, and the Department of Electrical and Electronic Engineering of the University of Cagliari. All these supports are gratefully acknowledged. We also thank the International Association for Pattern Recognition and its Technical Committee TC1 on Statistical Pattern Recognition Techniques for sponsoring MCS 2002. We wish to express our appreciation to all those who helped to organize MCS 2002. First of all, we would like to thank all the members of the Scientific Committee whose professionalism was instrumental in creating a very interesting technical program. Special thanks are due to the members of the Organizing Committee, Giorgio Fumera, Giorgio Giacinto, and Gian Luca Marcialis for their indispensable contributions to the MCS 2002 web site management, local organization, and proceedings preparation.

April 2002   Fabio Roli and Josef Kittler

Workshop Chairs

F. Roli (Univ. of Cagliari, Italy)
J. Kittler (Univ. of Surrey, United Kingdom)

Scientific Committee

J. A. Benediktsson (Iceland)
H. Bunke (Switzerland)
L.P. Cordella (Italy)
B.V. Dasarathy (USA)
R.P.W. Duin (The Netherlands)
C. Furlanello (Italy)
J. Ghosh (USA)
T.K. Ho (USA)
S. Impedovo (Italy)
N. Intrator (Israel)
A.K. Jain (USA)

M. Kamel (Canada)
L.I. Kuncheva (UK)
L. Lam (Hong Kong)
D. Landgrebe (USA)
Dar-Shyang Lee (USA)
D. Partridge (UK)
A.J.C. Sharkey (UK)
K. Tumer (USA)
G. Vernazza (Italy)
T. Windeatt (UK)

Local Committee

G. Fumera (Univ. of Cagliari, Italy)
G. Giacinto (Univ. of Cagliari, Italy)
G.L. Marcialis (Univ. of Cagliari, Italy)

Organized by

Dept. of Electrical and Electronic Engineering of the University of Cagliari
University of Surrey

Sponsored by

University of Cagliari
University of Surrey
Dept. of Electrical and Electronic Engineering of the University of Cagliari
The International Association for Pattern Recognition

Supported by

University of Cagliari
Dept. of Electrical and Electronic Engineering of the University of Cagliari
University of Surrey

Table of Contents

Design Methodologies

Combination Strategies

Analysis and Performance Evaluation

Applications

Multiclassifier Systems: Back to the Future

Joydeep Ghosh

Department of Electrical and Computer Engineering
University of Texas, Austin, TX 78712-1084
ghosh@ece.utexas.edu
http://www.lans.ece.utexas.edu/~ghosh

Abstract. While a variety of multiple classifier systems have been studied since at least the late 1950's, this area came alive in the 90's with significant theoretical advances as well as numerous successful practical applications. This article argues that our current understanding of ensemble-type multiclassifier systems is now quite mature and exhorts the reader to consider a broader set of models and situations for further progress. Some of these scenarios have already been considered in classical pattern recognition literature, but revisiting them often leads to new insights and progress. As an example, we consider how to integrate multiple *clusterings*, a problem central to several emerging distributed data mining applications. We also revisit output space decomposition to show how this can lead to extraction of valuable domain knowledge in addition to improved classification accuracy.

1 A Brief History of Multilearner Systems

Multiple classifier systems are special cases of approaches that integrate several data-driven models for the *same* problem. A key goal is to obtain a better composite global model, with more accurate and reliable estimates or decisions. In addition, modular approaches often decompose a complex problem into subproblems for which the solutions obtained are simpler to understand, as well as to implement, manage and update.

Multilearner systems have have a rather long and interesting history. For example, Borda counts for combining multiple rankings are named after its 18th century French inventor, Jean-Charles de Borda. Early notable *systems* include Selfridge's Pandemonium [1], a model of human information processing involving multiple demons. Each demon was specialized for detecting specific features or classes. A head-demon (the combiner) would select the demon that "shouted the loudest", a scheme that is nowadays called a "winner-take-all" solution. Nilsson's committee machine [2] combined several linear two-class models to solve a multiclass problem.

A strong motivation for multilearner systems was voiced by Kanal in his classic 1974 paper [3]:

> "It is now recognized that the key to pattern recognition problems does not lie wholly in learning machines, statistical approaches, spatial, filtering,..., or in any other particular solution which has been vigorously

F. Roli and J. Kittler (Eds.): MCS 2002, LNCS 2364, pp. 1–15, 2002.

advocated by one or another group during the last one and a half decades as the solution to the pattern recognition problem. No single model exists for all pattern recognition problems and no single technique is applicable to all problems. Rather what we have is a bag of tools and a bag of problems."

This inspired much work in the late seventies on combining linguistic and statistical models, and on combining heuristic search with statistical pattern recognition. Subsequently, similar sentiments on the importance of multiple approaches were also voiced in the AI community, e.g., by Minsky [4]:

" To solve really hard problems, we'll have to use several different representations.....It is time to stop arguing over which type of pattern-classification technique is best .....Instead we should work at a higher level of organization and discover how to build managerial systems to exploit the different virtues and evade the different limitations of each of these ways of comparing things."

In the 80's, integration of multiple data sources and/or learned models was considered in several disciplines, for example, the combining of estimators in econometrics [5] and evidences in rule-based systems. Especially noteworthy are consensus theoretic methods developed in statistics and management science, including how to produce a single probability distribution that summarizes multiple estimates from different Bayesian experts [6,7]. The area of decision fusion and multi-sensor data fusion [8] has a rich literature from this era that can be useful for modern day multiclassifier problems as well. Multiple model systems are also encountered in some large engineering systems such as those that demand fault tolerance or employing control mechanisms that may need to function in different operating regimes [9]. In particular, multiple models for nonlinear control has a long tradition [10].

In the data analysis world, hybridization in a broader sense is seen in efforts to combine two or more of neural network, Bayesian, GA, fuzzy logic and knowledge-based systems. The goal is to incorporate diverse sources and forms of information and to exploit the somewhat complementary nature of different methodologies. Since in real-life applications, classification is often not a stand-alone problem but rather a part of a larger system involving optimization, explanation and evaluation of decisions, interaction with the environment, etc., such hybrid approaches will be increasingly relevant as we expand the scope of studies involving multiple classifiers.

2   Some Lessons from Multiclassifier Design

Figure 1 shows a generic diagram of the most popular type of multilearner systems studied in the past decade. While data ultimately originates from an underlying universal set X, each learner may receive somewhat different subsets of the data for "training" or parameter estimation (as in bagging and boosting), and

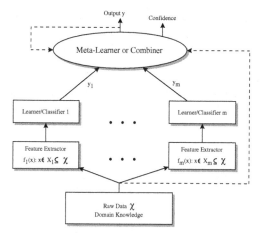

Fig. 1. Generic architecture of a multilearner system

may apply different feature extractors (fs) on the same raw data. Along with selection of training samples and feature extractors, one needs to decide how many and what types of learners to use, and finally, how to design the meta-learner. There are also larger issues of how to train the components given that they are part of a bigger system, and to estimate the overall gains achievable.

Ensembles. The simplest meta-learner is the ensemble or combiner, where the output y is determined solely by the outputs of the individual learners, each trying to solve the same classification or regression problem. The path indicated by the right-most dotted line in Fig. 1 is not used. In the past few years, a host of experimental results from both the neural network and machine learning communities show that combining the outputs of multiple models via voting, (weighted) averaging, order statistics, product rule, entropy, stacking etc., provides a statistically significant improvement in performance along with tighter confidence intervals [11,12]. A notable study [13] shows that if perfect Bayesian classifiers are learned on distinct sets of extracted features, then a weighted product rule is the optimal combination scheme. The study used sensitivity analysis to show that the product rule is more susceptible to imperfections in the individual classifiers, and a sum (or median) rule turns out to be more reliable in practical situations. An extensive listing of both theoretical and practical works on ensembles or committees circa 1996 is in [14].

Analytical expressions have been developed for both regression [15,16] and classification[17,18], to quantitatively estimate the extra accuracy achieved by an ensemble. The seminal work of Hansen and Salamon [17] recognised that the unstable nature of certain neural networks was helpful for ensembles, though it was perhaps too optimistic in anticipating the amount of independence achievable among different networks given a shared training set. An extensive analysis of the gains provided by plurality voting was provided in this paper. In contrast, the analysis of [18] assumes that the individual classifiers provide estimates of the *a posteriori* class probabilities[1]. These estimates are combined by simple averaging. By focussing on the distributions of the *estimated a posteriori* probability functions about the true *a posteriori* probabilities, and how these distributions (and hence the decision boundaries obtained using Bayes rule) are affected when the averaging combiner is used, the following expression was derived under mild assumptions:

$$E_{model}^{ave} = \frac{1 + \delta(m-1)}{m} E_{model} , \qquad (1)$$

where E_{model}^{ave} and E_{model} are the expected values of the *added* [2] classification error rate for the average-based combiner and for the individual classifiers respectively, m is the number of classifiers combined, and δ is the average correlation of the errors (in estimating the *a posteriori* probabilities; not to be confused with classification error rate) among the individual classifiers. Note that if $\delta = 0$, signifying that the errors in approximating the *a posteriori* functions are uncorrelated, then the added error can be reduced by a factor of m if an ensemble of m classifiers is used. The Bayes error of course cannot be changed once the input feature space has been selected. In practice, δ tends to be closer to 1 than to 0 because of (partially) shared training sets and overlapping inductive biases [19], so the gains are not as much.

Dietterich [20] provides an accessible and informal reasoning, from statistical, computational and representational viewpoints, of why ensembles can improve results. Combining is primarily a way of reducing model variance, though in certain situations it also reduces bias. It works best when each learner is well trained, but different learners generalize in different ways, i.e., there is diversity in the ensemble [16].

The impact of diversity is quantified explicitly via the correlation measure δ in Eq. 1. Diversity may be induced through different presentations of the input data, as in bagging, variations in learner design, or by adding a penalty to the ouputs to encourage diversity. Interestingly, while pre-90's work mostly concentrated on design of the individual learners and the combination scheme, the most spectacular gains have come from smart input selection, as this has the most noticeable impact on diversity.[3] Another point of note is that ensembles are most popular in the machine learning and neural network communities, where the favorite classification models, namely decision trees and MLPs, are relatively unstable - hence leading to greater diversity! In constrast, ensembles are not that commonly applied, for example, to combine multiple robust logistic regression models or other more stable techniques. Finally, given adequately powerful constituent classifiers, there is a sweet spot of training data size for which diversity

---

[1] for example, using MLP and RBF based classifiers trained with "1-of-C" desired output vectors and a mean squared error or cross-entropy cost function.

[2] i.e., extra error due to imperfect classifiers, incurred in addition to the Bayes error.

[3] This has prompted studies on why bagging and boosting approaches work so well. Attempts to relate them to established statistical approaches are resulting in more sophisticated input selection techniques [21].

through input variation is most effective. For example, if there is too little data, the gains achieved via a bagged ensemble cannot compensate for the decrease in accuracy of individual models, each of which now sees an even smaller training set. On the other end, if the data set is extremely large and computation time is not an issue, even a single flexible classifier can be quite adequate.

My own "discovery" of ensembles was quite serendipitous. In the late 80's, I participated in the DARPA program of sonar signal classification using neural networks. It was soon evident that many different types of features, including Fourier, wavelet and autoregressive coefficients, could be extracted from a given preprocessed time series. Each type of features provided useful discriminatory information, but was not comprehensive by itself. At the same time, it was clear that networks with global hidden units such as sigmoidal functions, generalized quite differently from those with localized hidden units such as gaussian functions. So our solution was to use multiple feature sets as well as multiple classification models [11]. The results from individual classifiers were combined in several ways, including sum, entropy, majority vote and evidential reasoning based approaches [22]. This multiclassifier system gave the best results among all the solutions in this program and was subsequently selected for further development and deployment. Clearly, an ensemble approach was a good idea, and good ideas tend to pre-exist and get re-invented! Indeed, our subsequent literature study turned up much of the historical work described in the introduction, in addition to more contemporaneous use of ensembles for other applications [23,24]. By now, ensembles are being regarded among the most significant advances in pattern classification in the 90's, and the successful series of international workshops on Multiple Classifier Systems started in 2000 is a solid testimony to this fact [25].

Modular Networks. If the dotted line on the far right in Fig. 1 is used so that the combining action now depends on the current input, we obtain (soft) modular solutions. In these divide-and-conquer approaches, relatively simple learners get specialized in different parts of the input-output space during the training phase. This specialization enables the use of simpler as well as better models tailored to their localized domain of expertise. The total model is a (possibly soft) union of such simpler models. Techniques of modular learning include "mixtures-of-experts" (MOE), local linear regression, CART/MARS, adaptive subspace models, etc.[26,27,28]. Note that, in contrast to ensembles, the individual models do not need to perform well across all inputs, but only for their regions of expertise. Modular learning systems are based on the precept that learning a large number of simple local concepts is both easier and more useful than learning a single complex global concept. They are often found to learn concepts more effectively (better performance) and more efficiently (faster learning). Using simpler local models have several added advantages such as easier interpretability, better local tuning or adaptation, easier incorporation of prior knowledge, and less susceptibility to the curse of dimensionality.

Modular approaches till now have been largely confined to regression problems. A good beginning for classification applications is made in [29], where the authors dynamically select one classifier out of an ensemble based on the estimated accuracy in the neighborhood of the test point under consideration. However, unlike in mixtures-of-experts, the procedure does not specialize different classifiers for different regions of the input space during the training process. Rather, all classifiers are trained on the entire input space and selection of a specific model is only made during the test phase. Thus there is scope for further work in specializing classifiers based on soft decomposition of the input space.

(Back to) The Future. While there seems more scope for investigating modular multiclassifiers, overall I feel that the understanding of multilearner systems for *static* regression and classification is now quite mature. It is time to use this solid foundation to extend the multilearner framework to qualitatively new and more ambitious domains. There are several promising directions that can be taken. In the next sections, I examine two such directions: consensus clustering and output space decomposition. Both topics have been studied in the past to some extent, but recent application demands and theoretical progress makes it worthwhile to revisit them and expand their scope.

3   Combining Multiple Clusterings

Unlike classification problems, there are no well known approaches to combining multiple clusterings. This problem is more difficult than designing *classifier ensembles* since cluster labels are symbolic and so one must also solve a correspondence problem. In addition, the number and shape of clusters provided by the individual solutions may vary based on the clustering method as well as on the particular view of the data presented to that method. Moreover, the desired number of clusters is often not known in advance. In fact, the 'right' number of clusters in a data-set depends on the *scale* at which the data is inspected, and sometimes, equally valid (but substantially different) answers can be obtained for the same data [30].

History. A substantial body of largely theoretical work on *consensus classification* exists from the mid-80's and earlier [31]. These studies used the term 'classification' in a very general sense, encompassing partitions, dendrograms and n-trees as well. In consensus classification, a profile is a set of classifications which is sought to be integrated into a single consensus classification. A representative work is that of [32], who investigated techniques for strict consensus. Their approach is based on the construction of a lattice over the set of all partitionings by using a refinement relation. Such work on strict consensus works well for small data-sets with little noise and little diversity and obtains solution on a *different* level of resolution. The most prominent application of strict consensus is for the computational biology community to obtain phylogenetic trees [33]. A set of DNA sequences can be used to generate evolutionary trees using criteria such as maximum parsimony, but often one obtains several hundreds of trees with the same score function. In such cases, biologists look for the strict *consensus tree*, the 'infimum', which has lower resolution but is compatible with all the individual trees. Note that such consensus approaches are very domain specific. In particular, (i) they combine non-rooted but hierarchical clusterings, (ii) they use domain specific metrics (e.g. Robinson-Foulds distance) and evaluation criteria such as parsimony, specificity and density, and (iii) *strict* consensus is a requirement.

More general approaches to combining multiple clusterings have started to emerge recently. For example, in [34] a feasible approach to combining distributed agglomerative clusterings is introduced, motivated by distributed data mining scenarios. Another innovative approach is encountered in [35], where multiple, fine-grain k-means clusterings are used to determine a co-association matrix of patterns. This matrix represents a derived similarity measure that is then used by an MST algorithm for identifying arbitrary shaped clusters.

3.1 Motivations for a Revisit

Why should the problem of integrating multiple clusterings be revisited? First, the works on strict consensus are narrow in scope. They were not meant for large datasets, and these approaches indeed do not scale well. Moreover, in presence of strong noise the results can be trivial, namely the supremum is the monolithic clustering (one cluster) and the infimum is the set of singletons. Another drawback is that the strict consensus is not at the same level of resolution as the original groupings. Second, there are several emerging applications that can benefit from cluster ensembles. We briefly describe three application scenarios below.

Quality and Robustness. Combining several clusterings can lead to *improved quality* and robustness of results. As compared to classification one often finds even more variability in clustering results for difficult data sets. This increased level of diversity means that the potential gains from employing ensembles is higher than that for classification problems of comparable difficulty. In the clustering context, diversity can be created in numerous ways, including: (i) using different features to represent the objects, (ii) varying the number and/or location of initial cluster centers in iterative algorithms such as k-means, (iii) varying the order of data presentation in on-line methods such as BIRCH, and (iv) using a portfolio of very different clustering algorithms.

A different but related motivation for using a cluster ensemble is to build a *robust*, diverse clustering portfolio that can perform well over a wide range of data-sets with little hand-tuning.

Knowledge Reuse. Another important consideration is the *reuse of existing clusterings*. In several applications, a variety of clusterings for the objects under consideration may already exist. For example, on the web, pages are categorized e.g., by Yahoo! (according to a manually-crafted taxonomy), by your Internet service provider (according to request patterns and frequencies) and by your personal bookmarks (according to your preferences). Can we reuse such pre-existing knowledge to create a single consolidated clustering? Knowledge reuse [36] in this context means that we exploit the information in the provided cluster labels *without* going back to the *original features* or the algorithms that were used to create the clusterings.

Distributed Computing. The ability to deal with clustering in a distributed fashion is becoming increasingly important since real applications nowadays often involve distributed databases. In several situations it may not be feasible to collect all the data into a single flat file, because of the computational, bandwidth and storage costs, or because of a variety of practical reasons including security, privacy, proprietary nature of data, need for fault tolerant distribution of data and services, real-time processing requirements, statutory constraints imposed by law, etc [37]. So, in a distributed computing scenario, each clusterer may have access to only some of the objects, or see only a limited number of features or attributes of each object. How can one perform distributed clustering and combining of results under such situations?

3.2   Cluster Ensembles: A Knowledge Reuse Framework

Clearly, there are many approaches and issues in combining multiple clusterings. In this section, we summarize some results from our recent work [38] on one specific formulation: the *combination* of multiple *partitionings* of the same underlying set of objects *without accessing the original features*. Since only cluster labels are available to the combiner, this is a framework for knowledge reuse [36].

If we number the k clusters as $1, .., k$, then a given clustering can be denoted by a label vector $\lambda \in \mathbb{N}^n$, after imposing an arbitrary order on the n objects that are being clustered. The first issue to address is how to evaluate a consensus clustering. Note that there is no ground truth to measure against. Intuitively, if there is no other apriori knowledge, then the best one can do is to extract the commonalities among the different clusterings. This suggests that mutual information, a symmetric measure that quantifies the statistical information shared between two distributions, is the natural measure of the consensus quality. Suppose there are two labelings $\lambda^{(a)}$ and $\lambda^{(b)}$. Let there be $k^{(a)}$ groups in $\lambda^{(a)}$ and $k^{(b)}$ groups in $\lambda^{(b)}$. Let $n^{(h)}$ be the number of objects in cluster $\mathcal{C}_h$ according to $\lambda^{(a)}$, and n_ℓ the number of objects in cluster $\mathcal{C}_\ell$ according to $\lambda^{(b)}$. Let $n_\ell^{(h)}$ denote the number of objects that are in cluster h according to $\lambda^{(a)}$ as well as in group ℓ according to $\lambda^{(b)}$. Then, a $[0,1]$-normalized mutual information criterion $\phi^{(\mathrm{NMI})}$ is computed as follows [39]:

$$\phi^{(\mathrm{NMI})}(\lambda^{(a)}, \lambda^{(b)}) = \frac{2}{n} \sum_{\ell=1}^{k^{(a)}} \sum_{h=1}^{k^{(b)}} n_\ell^{(h)} \log_{k^{(a)} \cdot k^{(b)}} \left(\frac{n_\ell^{(h)} n}{n^{(h)} n_\ell} \right) \tag{2}$$

We propose that the optimal combined clustering be defined as the one that has maximal average mutual information with all individual labelings, given that the number of consensus clusters desired is k.

Efficient Consensus Functions. In [38], three efficient heuristics are proposed to solve the cluster ensemble problem. All algorithms approach the problem by first transforming the set of clusterings into a hypergraph representation. Simply put, each cluster is considered as a hyperedge connecting all its members (vertices). The hyperedges obtained from different clusterings are all added to a common graph, which thus has n vertices and $\sum_{q=1}^{r} k^{(q)}$ hyperedges.

The simplest heuristic is to define a similarity measure between two objects as the fraction of clusterings in which these objects are in the same cluster. The resulting matrix of pairwise similarities can be used to recluster the objects using any reasonable similarity-based clustering algorithm. The second heuristic looks for a hyperedge separator that partitions the hypergraph into k unconnected components of approximately the same size, using a suitable hypergraph partitioning package such as HMETIS. The idea behind the third heuristic is to group and collapse related hyperedges into k meta-hyperedges. The hyperedges that are considered related for the purpose of collapsing are determined by a graph-based clustering of hyperedges. Finally, each object is assigned to the collapsed hyperedge in which it participates most strongly.

It turns out that the first and third approaches typically do better than the second. Since the third approach is much faster than the first, it is preferred. However, note that our objective function has an added advantage that it allows one to add a stage that selects the best consensus function without any supervision information, by simply selecting the one with the highest NMI. So, for the results reported later, we simply use this 'supra'-consensus function Γ, obtained by running *all three* algorithms, and selecting the one with the greatest score.

Applications and Results. For brevity, we just illustrate one application of cluster ensembles, namely how it can be used to boost quality of results by combining a set of clusterings obtained from partial views of the data. This scenario is motivated by certain distributed data mining situations in which it is not feasible to collect all the features at one central location. Results on a wider range of application scenarios and data sets can be found in [38].

For our experiments, we simulate such a scenario by running several clusterers, each having access to only a restricted, small subset of features. The clusterers find groups in their views/subspaces. In the combining stage, individual results are integrated to recover the full structure of the data (without access to any of the original features). Results are provided on two real data sets: (i) PENDIG from the UCI ML repository, is for pen-based recognition of handwritten digits from 16 spatial features. There are ten classes of roughly equal size corresponding to the digits 0 to 9. (ii) YAHOO represents 2340 documents from 20 news categories, and is available from `ftp://ftp.cs.umn.edu/dept/users/boley/`. After standard preprocessing, each document is represented by a 2903-dimensional vector. These two data sets are partitioned into 10 and 40 clusters respectively by each clustering algorithm. For this experiment, the individual clusterers are all graph-partitioning based (as they are quite robust and give comparable sized clusters), using a domain-appropriate similarity function, namely, Euclidean distance for PENDIG and cosine similarity for YAHOO. Table 1 summarizes the results, averaged over 10 runs. For example, in the YAHOO case, 20 clusterings were performed in 128-dimensions (occurrence frequencies of 128 randomly chosen words) each. The average quality amongst the results was 0.17 and the best quality was 0.21. Using the supra-consensus function to combine all 20 labelings results in a quality of 0.38, or 124% higher mutual information than the average individual clustering. The results indicate that, when processing on the all features is not possible but multiple, limited views exist, a cluster ensemble can significantly boost results compared to individual clusterings.

data	subspace #dims	#models r	quality of consensus $\phi^{(\text{NMI})}(\kappa, \lambda)$	max. individual quality $\max_q \phi^{(\text{NMI})}(\kappa, \lambda^{(q)})$	ave. individual quality $\text{avg}_q \phi^{(\text{NMI})}(\kappa, \lambda^{(q)})$
PENDIG	4	10	**0.59009**	0.53197	0.44625
YAHOO	128	20	**0.38167**	0.21403	0.17075

Table 1. Effectiveness of consensus clustering for integrating multiple clusterings based on partial feature views.

4   Output Space Decomposition [40]

When one is faced with a $C > 2$ class problem, it is often preferable to break it down into multiple sub-problems, each involving less than C classes or meta-classes, where a metaclass, Ω, is formed by the union of two or more of the original classes. This approach entails a decomposition of the output space, i.e., the space of target classes, and has to deal with the issue of how to combine the answers from the sub-problems to yield a solution for the original C-class problem. A major motivation for this approach is that the sub-problems are typically much simpler to solve. In addition, feature selection/extraction can be tailored to each individual sub-problem. We shall see later that output space decomposition can also lead to extraction of valuable domain knowledge such as the relationships and natural hierarchies among different classes, the most discriminative features for a given pair of classes, etc.

Brief History. Both the Pandemonium (1958) and the Learning Machine (1965) models mentioned in the introduction involve output space decomposition. Nilsson's machine trained one linear discriminant function per class. For a given test input, the class with the highest discriminant value was assigned as the predicted label. This machine partitions the input space using hyperplanes that all intersect at a point. This approach has since been extended to include quadratic discriminants and kernel discriminants. Note that they all involve C two-class problems with a simple "max" combination function, and are attractive when the individual classifiers are simple. Even with the advent of more general classifiers, this methodology is helpful if either C is large or the class boundaries are quite complex. For example, it has been shown that in several cases, building C MLP-based models, one each for discriminating a specific class from all the rest, outperforms a single complex model for discriminating all the classes simultaneously [41].

In the 70's and 80's, there were some works in the pattern recognition community that used multiclassifiers arranged in tandem or as a tree-structured hierarchy, and exploited output space decomposition[42]. One interesting technique was to decompose a C-class problem into $\binom{C}{2}$ two-class problems, one for each unique pair of classes. A naive way of labeling a test sample is to let each of the $\binom{C}{2}$ vote for the more likely of its two classes, and then sum up all the votes to determine the winner. A more sophisticated approach [43] iteratively re-estimates the overall posterior probabilities from the $\binom{C}{2}$ pairwise posterior probabilities. We have used this technique to address a 14 feature, 26-class digit recognition problem and a 14 feature, 11-class remote sensing problem [44]. What was most remarkable was that, in both applications, certain pairs of classes could be distinguished by only using 2 or 3 features, even though the entire C-class problem needed all the input features. But a drawback of this approach is that $O(C^2)$ classifiers are needed, which becomes impractical if the number of classes is in the tens or more.

In the machine learning community, a seminal work involving output space decomposition is called error-correcting output coding [45]. Each member of an ensemble solves a 2-class problem obtained by partitioning the original classes into two groups (meta-classes) either randomly or based on error correcting codes. A simple voting scheme is then used by the ensemble to label a test input. This technique has the advantage that the number of classifiers required can be varied and need not be quadratic in C. It also retains another advantage of output decomposition, namely that feature selection can be tailored for each 2-class problem [46]. However, the output partitioning, being random, fails to detect or exploit any natural affinities among different classes. Consequently, some of the two-class problems may be quite complicated as very different classes can get grouped together.

Prognosis. A very promising direction to explore is the design of multiple classifiers organized as a hierarchy. A good example of the benefits of this approach is provided in [47], where a hierarchical topic taxonomy is used to effectively organize large text databases. Recently, we introduced a hierarchical technique to recursively decompose the output space into a binary tree [48]. The resulting architecture is illustrated in Fig. 2. It requires that only $C - 1$ two-(meta) class problems need to be solved.

The hierarchical ensemble is built using a top-down approach based on a generalized associative modular learning approach. Initially, a randomly selected class is fully associated with a metaclass (to seed the partitioning) while all other classes are equally associated with both metaclasses. An EM type iterative procedure is used to update the metaclass parameters for the current class associations, and then update the associations based on the new metaclass parameter values. Note that the selection of features that best discriminate the resulting meta-classes can be concurrently updated as well. Using ideas from deterministic annealing, a temperature parameter can be used to slowly converge the associations to hard partitions in order to induce specialization and decoupling among the modules. The overall approach produces class groupings that are more natural in the sense of being highly likely to conform well with human domain experts' opinions.

The hierarchical ensemble technique described above was applied to the important remote sensing problem of determining the types of land-cover from

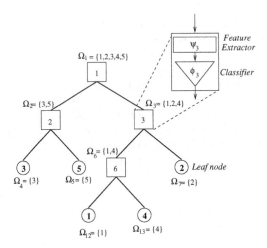

Fig. 2. Hierarchical decomposition of a 5 class problem into four 2-(meta)class problems. All the feature extractors (ψs) as well as the classifiers (ϕs) are automatically determined as part of the decomposition process.

$\sim$200 dimensional hyperspectral images. These are typically about $\sim$10 class problems. In coastal regions, we found that the first split would invariably separate land classes from water classes, the land classes would get further split between uplands and wetlands, and so on. Equally important, custom discriminatory features were obtained for the sub-problems, adding to our domain knowledge.

The real payoff of such extracted knowledge will come as more and more of the earth's surface get mapped. Currently, hyperspectral classification is done based on training and test samples drawn from the same image, since even a single image generates megabytes of data. In a given image, not all classes are present, and there are different mixtures of classes in different images. Due to such changing compositions, when one attempts to apply a classfier to a new image, the results are often much weaker since a fundamental assumption of data-driven modeling, namely that the training and test samples are drawn uniformly from a common distribution, is violated. The extracted domain knowledge from hierarchical ensembles suggests a way out of this dilemma. If one organizes this information properly, then, given data from a new area, one can quickly estimate what features to extract and examine, and what classes to anticipate, even with very little data from this new region. This can greatly reduce the amount of data (both labelled and unlabelled) needed, with little compromise in the results. It also provides a nice platform for integrating semi-supervised learning ideas into a multiclassifier framework, yet another topic worth exploring!

5   Concluding Remarks

Besides the two directions described in this article, there are several more venues worthy of exploration for scholars interested in multilearner systems. For example, virtually all the work on ensembles and mixture of experts to date is on static problems, where the output is solely a function of the current input. Suppose we are interested in classifying variable length sequences of vectors, for example, those representing gene expressions or acoustic signals. Does temporal information have to be dealt with at the pre-processing step since our ensembles cannot handle them directly, or can memory mechanisms be incorporated into the meta-learner? What if one member of an ensemble is ready to make a decision after observing a subsequence while others want to see more of the sequence?

Another interesting situation arises when one has to solve a series of different but related classification tasks, either simultaneously or over time, rather than a single task. This issue is becoming increasingly relevant due to the ever increasing and continual generation of data and problems thanks to the growing Internet, advances in the human genome project, evolving financial markets, etc. Some advances on this topic have already been made under categories such as 'life-long learning', 'learning to learn', and 'knowledge reuse' [49,36]. From a multiclassifier point of view, in this case the individual members of an "ensemble" may not be trying to solve the same task or be trained simultaneously, both *significant departures* from the traditional framework. Clearly there are enough venues that can be fruitfully explored, and I look forward to a continued stream of exciting research on multiclassifier systems in the near future.

Acknowledgements: Parts of this article reflect joint work with Kagan Tumer, Shailesh Kumar and Alexander Strehl, and I thank them for their inputs. This research was supported by the NSF Grant ECS-9900353, and by Intel and IBM.

References

1. Selfridge, O.G.: Pandemonium: a paradigm for learning. Proc. of Symp. held at the National Physical Lab. (1958) 513–526
2. Nilsson, N.J.: Learning Machines: Foundations of Trainable Pattern-Classifying Systems. McGraw Hill, NY (1965)
3. Kanal, L.: Patterns in pattern recognition. IEEE Trans. Information Theory **IT-20** (1974) 697–722
4. Minsky, M.: Logical versus analogical or symbolic versus connectionist or neat versus scruffy. AI Magazine **12** (1991) 34–51
5. Granger, C.W.J.: Combining forecasts–twenty years later. Journal of Forecasting **8** (1989) 167–173
6. French, S.: Group consensus probability distributions: A critical survey. In Bernardo et al., J.M., ed.: Bayesian Statistics 2. North Holland, New York (1985)
7. Benediktsson, J.A., Swain, P.H.: Consensus theoretic classification methods. IEEE Transactions on Systems, Man, and Cybernetics **22** (1992) 688–704

8. Luo, R.C., Kay, M.G.: Multisensor integration and fusion in intelligent systems. IEEE Transactions on Systems, Man, and Cybernetics **19** (1989) 901–931

9. Narendra, K., Balakrishnan, J., Ciliz, K.: Adaptation and learning using multiple models, switching and tuning. IEEE Control Systems Magazine (1995) 37–51

10. Murray-Smith, R., Johansen, T.A.: Multiple Model Approaches to Modelling and Control. Taylor and Francis, UK (1997)

11. Ghosh, J., Deuser, L., Beck, S.: A neural network based hybrid system for detection, characterization and classification of short-duration oceanic signals. IEEE Jl. of Ocean Engineering **17** (1992) 351–363

12. Sharkey, A.: On combining artificial neural networks. Connection Science **8** (1996) 299–314

13. Kittler, J., Hatef, M., Duin, R., Matas, J.: On combining classifiers. IEEE Trans. Pattern Analysis and Machine Intelligence **20** (1998) 226–239

14. Tumer, K.: Linear and order statistics combiners for reliable pattern classification. PhD thesis, Dept. of ECE, Univ. of Texas at Austin, Dec. (1996)

15. Perrone, M.P.: Improving Regression Estimation: Averaging Methods for Variance Reduction with Extensions to General Convex Measure Optimization. PhD thesis, Brown University (1993)

16. Krogh, A., Vedelsby, J.: Neural network ensembles, cross validation and active learning. In G. Tesauro, D.T., Leen, T., eds.: Advances in Neural Information Processing Systems-7. (1995) 231–238

17. Hansen, L.K., Salamon, P.: Neural network ensembles. IEEE Transactions on Pattern Analysis and Machine Intelligence **12** (1990) 993–1000

18. Tumer, K., Ghosh, J.: Analysis of decision boundaries in linearly combined neural classifiers. Pattern Recognition **29** (1996) 341–348

19. Tumer, K., Ghosh, J.: Ensemble correlation and error reduction in ensemble classifiers. Connection Science **8** (1996) 385–404

20. Dietterich, T.G.: Ensemble methods in machine learning. In Kittler, J., Roli, F., eds.: Multiple Classifier Systems. LNCS Vol. 1857, Springer (2001) 1–15

21. Friedman, J., Hastie, T., Tibshirani, R.: Additive logistic regression: a statistical view of boosting. Technical Report Dept. of Statistics, Stanford University. (1998)

22. Ghosh, J., Beck, S., Chu, C.: Evidence combination techniques for robust classification of short-duration oceanic signals. In: SPIE Conf. on Adaptive and Learning Systems, SPIE Proc. Vol. 1706. (1992) 266–276

23. Xu, L., Krzyzak, A., Suen, C.Y.: Methods of combining multiple classifiers and their applications to handwriting recognition. IEEE Transactions on Systems, Man and Cybernetics **22** (1992) 418–435

24. Ho, T.K., Hull, J.J., Srihari, S.N.: Decision combination in multiple classifier systems. IEEE Transactions on Pattern Analysis and Machine Intelligence **16** (1994) 66–76

25. Kittler, J., Roli (Eds.), F.: Multiple Classifier Systems. LNCS Vol. 1857, Springer (2001)

26. Jordan, M., Jacobs, R.: Hierarchical mixture of experts and the EM algorithm. Neural Computation **6** (1994) 181–214

27. Holmstrom, L., Koistinen, P., Laaksonen, J., Oja, E.: Neural and statistical classifiers - taxonomy and two case studies. IEEE Transactions on Neural Networks **8** (1997) 5–17

28. Ramamurti, V., Ghosh, J.: Structurally adaptive modular networks for nonstationary environments. IEEE Transactions on Neural Networks **10** (1999) 152–60

29. Woods, K., Kegelmeyer, W.P., Bowyer, K.: Combination of multiple classifiers using local accuracy estimates. IEEE Transactions on Pattern Analysis and Machine Intelligence **19** (1997) 405–410

30. Jain, A.K., Dubes, R.C.: Algorithms for Clustering Data. Prentice Hall, New Jersey (1988)

31. Barthelemy, J.P., Laclerc, B., Monjardet, B.: On the use of ordered sets in problems of comparison and consensus of classifications. Jl. of Classification **3** (1986) 225–256

32. Neumann, D.A., Norton, V.T.: Clustering and isolation in the consensus problem for partitions. Journal of Classification **3** (1986) 281–298

33. Kim, J., Warnow, T.: Tutorial on phylogenetic tree estimation. In: Intelligent Systems for Molecular Biology, Heidelberg. (1999)

34. Johnson, E., Kargupta, H.: Collective, hierarchical clustering from distributed, heterogeneous data. In Zaki, M., Ho, C., eds.: Large-Scale Parallel KDD Systems. Volume 1759 of LNCS., Springer-Verlag (1999) 221–244

35. Fred, A.L.N., Jain, A.K.: Data clustering using evidence accumulation. In: Proc. ICPR. (2002) to appear

36. Bollacker, K.D., Ghosh, J.: Effective supra-classifiers for knowledge base construction. Pattern Recognition Letters **20(11-13)** (1999) 1347–52

37. Kargupta, H., Chan, P., eds.: Advances in Distributed and Parallel Knowledge Discovery. AAAI/MIT Press, Cambridge, MA (2000)

38. Strehl, A., Ghosh, J.: Cluster ensembles – a knowledge reuse framework for combining partitionings. In: Proceedings of AAAI 2002, Edmonton, Canada, AAAI (2002) in press.

39. Strehl, A., Ghosh, J., Mooney, R.: Impact of similarity measures on web-page clustering. In: Proc. AAAI Workshop on AI for Web Search (AAAI 2000), Austin, AAAI (2000) 58–64

40. Kumar, S.: Modular learning through output space decomposition. PhD thesis, Dept. of ECE, Univ. of Texas at Austin, Dec. (2000)

41. Anand, R., Methrotra, K., Mohan, C.K., Ranka, S.: Efficient classification for multiclass problems using modular neural networks. IEEE Transactions on Neural Networks **6** (1995) 117–125

42. Berenstein, C., Kanal, L.N., Lavine, D.: Consensus rules. In Kanal, L.N., Lemmer, J.F., eds.: Uncertainty in Artificial Intelligence. North Holland, New York (1986)

43. Hastie, T., Tibshirani, R.: Classification by pairwise coupling. In Jordan, M.I., Kearns, M.J., Solla, S.A., eds.: Advances in Neural Information Processing Systems. Volume 10., The MIT Press (1998)

44. Kumar, S., Crawford, M.M., Ghosh, J.: A versatile framework for labelling imagery with a large number of classes. In: Proc. IJCNN. (1999)

45. Dietterich, T.G., Bakiri, G.: Solving multiclass learning problems via error-correcting output codes. Jl. of Artificial Intelligence Research **2** (1995) 263–286

46. Ricci, F., Aha, D.: Extending local learners with errorcorrecting output codes. Technical report, Technical Report 9701-08, IRST (1997)

47. Chakrabarti, S., Dom, B., Agrawal, R., Raghavan, P.: Scalable feature selection, classication and signature generation for organizing large text databases into hierarchical topic taxonomies. VLDB Journal **7** (1998) 163–178

48. Kumar, S., Ghosh, J., Crawford, M.M.: Hierarchical fusion of multiple classifiers for hyperspectral data analysis", Pattern Analysis and Applications, spl. Issue on Fusion of Multiple Classifiers **5** (2002) In Press

49. Thrun, S., Pratt, L.: Learning To Learn. Kluwer Academic, Norwell, MA (1997)

Support Vector Machines, Kernel Logistic Regression and Boosting

Ji Zhu and Trevor Hastie

Department of Statistics
Stanford University
Stanford, CA 94305
{jzhu,hastie}@stat.stanford.edu

Abstract. The support vector machine is known for its excellent performance in binary classification, i.e., the response $y \in \{-1, 1\}$, but its appropriate extension to the multi-class case is still an on-going research issue. Another weakness of the SVM is that it only estimates $sign[p(x) - 1/2]$, while the probability $p(x)$ is often of interest itself, where $p(x) = P(Y = 1 | X = x)$ is the conditional probability of a point being in class 1 given $X = x$. We propose a new approach for classification, called the import vector machine, which is built on kernel logistic regression (KLR). We show on some examples that the IVM performs as well as the SVM in binary classification. The IVM can naturally be generalized to the multi-class case. Furthermore, the IVM provides an estimate of the underlying class probabilities. Similar to the "support points" of the SVM, the IVM model uses only a fraction of the training data to index kernel basis functions, typically a much smaller fraction than the SVM. This can give the IVM a computational advantage over the SVM, especially when the size of the training data set is large. We illustrate these techniques on some examples, and make connections with boosting, another popular machine-learning method for classification.

Keywords: classification, kernel methods, logistic regression, multi-class learning, radial basis, reproducing kernel Hilbert space (RKHS), support vector machines.

1 Introduction

In standard classification problems, we are given a set of training data (x_1, y_1), $(x_2, y_2), \ldots (x_N, y_N)$, where the output y_i is qualitative and assumes values in a finite set $\mathcal{C}$. We wish to find a classification rule from the training data, so that when given a new input x, we can assign a class c from $\mathcal{C}$ to it. Usually it is assumed that the training data are an independently and identically distributed sample from an unknown probability distribution $P(X, Y)$.

The support vector machine (SVM) works well in binary classification, i.e. $y \in \{0, 1\}$, but its appropriate extension to the multi-class case is still an on-going research issue. Another weakness of the SVM is that it only estimates

F. Roli and J. Kittler (Eds.): MCS 2002, LNCS 2364, pp. 16–26, 2002.

$sign[p(x) - 1/2]$, while the probability $p(x)$ is often of interest itself, where $p(x) = P(Y = 1 | X = x)$ is the conditional probability of a point being in class 1 given $X = x$. In this paper, we propose a new approach, called the import vector machine (IVM), to address the classification problem. We show that the IVM not only performs as well as the SVM in binary classification, but also can naturally be generalized to the multi-class case. Furthermore, the IVM provides an estimate of the probability $p(x)$. Similar to the "support points" of the SVM, the IVM model uses only a fraction of the training data to index the kernel basis functions. We call these training data *import points*. The computational cost of the SVM is $O(N^3)$, while the computational cost of the IVM is $O(N^2 q^2)$, where q is the number of import points. Since q does not tend to increase as N increases, the IVM can be faster than the SVM, especially for large training data sets. Empirical results show that the number of import points is usually much less than the number of support points.

In section (2), we briefly review some results of the SVM for binary classification and compare it with kernel logistic regression (KLR). In section (3), we propose our IVM algorithm. In section (4), we show some simulation results. In section (5), we generalize the IVM to the multi-class case.

2   Support Vector Machines and Kernel Logistic Regression

The standard SVM produces a non-linear classification boundary in the original input space by constructing a linear boundary in a transformed version of the original input space. The dimension of the transformed space can be very large, even infinite in some cases. This seemingly prohibitive computation is achieved through a positive definite reproducing kernel K, which gives the inner product in the transformed space.

Many people have noted the relationship between the SVM and regularized function estimation in the reproducing kernel Hilbert spaces (RKHS). An overview can be found in Evgeniou, Pontil, and Poggio (1999), Hastie, Tibshirani, and Friedman 2001) and Wahba, Lin, and Zhang (2000). Fitting an SVM is equivalent to minimizing:

$$\frac{1}{N} \sum_{i=1}^{N} (1 - y_i f(x_i))_+ + \lambda \|f\|_{\mathcal{H}_K}^2. \tag{1}$$

with $f = b + h$, $h \in \mathcal{H}_K$, $b \in \mathcal{R}$. $\mathcal{H}_K$ is the RKHS generated by the kernel K. The classification rule is given by $sign[f]$.

By the representer theorem (Kimeldorf and Wahba 1971), the optimal $f(x)$ has the form:

$$f(x) = b + \sum_{i=1}^{N} a_i K(x, x_i). \tag{2}$$

It often happens that a sizeable fraction of the N values of a_i can be zero. This is a consequence of the truncation property of the first part of criterion (1). This seems to be an attractive property, because only the points on the wrong side of the classification boundary, and those on the right side but near the boundary have an influence in determining the position of the boundary, and hence have non-zero a_i's. The corresponding x_i's are called support points.

Notice that (1) has the form *loss + penalty*. The loss function $(1 - yf)_+$ is plotted in Figure 1, along with several traditional loss functions. As we can see, the negative log-likelihood (NLL) of the binomial distribution has a similar shape to that of the SVM. If we replace $(1 - yf)_+$ in (1) with $\ln(1 + e^{-yf})$, the NLL of the binomial distribution, the problem becomes a KLR problem. We expect that the fitted function performs similarly to the SVM for binary classification.

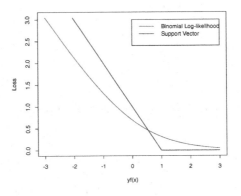

Fig. 1. *The binomial log-likelihood and* hinge *loss function,* $y \in \{-1, 1\}$

There are two immediate advantages of making such a replacement: (a) Besides giving a classification rule, the KLR also offers a natural estimate of the probability $p(x) = e^f/(1 + e^f)$, while the SVM only estimates $sign[p(x) - 1/2]$; (b) The KLR can naturally be generalized to the multi-class case through kernel multi-logit regression, whereas this is not the case for the SVM. However, because the KLR compromises the hinge loss function of the SVM, it no longer has the "support points" property; in other words, all the a_i's in (2) are non-zero.

KLR has been studied by many researchers; see Wahba, Gu, Wang, and Chappell (1995) and references there; see also Green and Silverman (1994) and Hastie and Tibshirani (1990).

The computational cost of the KLR is $O(N^3)$; to save the computational cost, the IVM algorithm will find a sub-model to approximate the full model (2) given by the KLR. The sub-model has the form:

$$f(x) = b + \sum_{x_i \in \mathcal{S}} a_i K(x, x_i) \tag{3}$$

where $\mathcal{S}$ is a subset of the training data $\{x_1, x_2, \ldots x_N\}$, and the data in $\mathcal{S}$ are called import points. The advantage of this sub-model is that the computational cost is reduced, especially for large training data sets, while not jeopardizing the performance in classification.

Several other researchers have investigated techniques in selecting the subset $\mathcal{S}$. Lin, Wahba, Xiang, Gao, Klein, and B. (2001) divide the training data into several clusters, then randomly select a representative from each cluster to make up $\mathcal{S}$. Smola and Schölkopf (2000) develop a greedy technique to sequentially select q columns of the kernel matrix $[K(x_i, x_j)]_{N \times N}$, such that the span of these q columns approximates the span of $[K(x_i, x_j)]_{N \times N}$ well in the Frobenius norm. Williams and Seeger (2001) propose randomly selecting q points of the training data, then using the Nystrom method to approximate the eigen-decomposition of the kernel matrix $[K(x_i, x_j)]_{N \times N}$, and expanding the results back up to N dimensions. None of these methods uses the output y_i in selecting the subset $\mathcal{S}$ (i.e., the procedure only involves x_i). The IVM algorithm uses both the output y_i and the input x_i to select the subset $\mathcal{S}$, in such a way that the resulting fit approximates the full model well.

3 Import Vector Machine

Following the tradition of logistic regression, we let $y_i \in \{0, 1\}$ for the rest of this paper. For notational simplicity, the constant term in the fitted function is ignored.

In the KLR, we want to minimize:

$$H = -\sum_{i=1}^{N} [y_i f(x_i) - \ln(1 + \exp(f(x_i)))] + \frac{\lambda}{2} \|f\|_{\mathcal{H}_K}^2$$

From (2), it can be shown that this is equivalent to the finite dimensional form:

$$H = -\boldsymbol{y}^T (K_a \boldsymbol{a}) + \mathbf{1}^T \ln(1 + \exp(K_a \boldsymbol{a})) + \frac{\lambda}{2} \boldsymbol{a}^T K_q \boldsymbol{a} \tag{4}$$

where $\boldsymbol{a} = (a_1, \ldots a_N)^T$; the regression matrix $K_a = [K(x_i, x_j)]_{N \times N}$; and the regularization matrix $K_q = K_a$.

To find $\boldsymbol{a}$, we set the derivative of H with respect to $\boldsymbol{a}$ equal to 0, and use the Newton-Raphson method to iteratively solve the score equation. It can be shown that the Newton-Raphson step is a weighted least squares step:

$$\boldsymbol{a}^{(k)} = (K_a^T W K_a + \lambda K_q)^{-1} K_a^T W \boldsymbol{z} \tag{5}$$

where $\boldsymbol{a}^{(k)}$ is the value of $\boldsymbol{a}$ in the kth step, $\boldsymbol{z} = (K_a \boldsymbol{a}^{(k-1)} + W^{-1}(\boldsymbol{y} - \boldsymbol{p}))$. The weight matrix is $W = diag[p(x_i)(1 - p(x_i))]_{N \times N}$.

As mentioned in section 2, we want to find a subset $\mathcal{S}$ of $\{x_1, x_2, \ldots x_N\}$, such that the sub-model (3) is a good approximation of the full model (2). Since it is impossible to search for every subset $\mathcal{S}$, we use the following greedy forward strategy:

3.1 Basic Algorithm

(B1) Let $S = \emptyset$, $\mathcal{R} = \{x_1, x_2, \ldots, x_N\}$, $k = 1$.
(B2) For each $x_l \in \mathcal{R}$, let

$$f_l(x) = \sum_{x_j \in S \cup \{x_l\}} a_j K(x, x_j)$$

Find $\boldsymbol{a}$ to minimize

$$H(x_l) = -\sum_{i=1}^{N}[y_i f_l(x_i) - \ln(1 + \exp(f_l(x_i)))] + \frac{\lambda}{2}\|f_l(x)\|^2_{\mathcal{H}_K}$$

$$= -\boldsymbol{y}^T(K_a^l \boldsymbol{a}^l) + \boldsymbol{1}^T \ln(1 + \exp(K_a^l \boldsymbol{a}^l)) + \frac{\lambda}{2}\boldsymbol{a}^{lT} K_q^l \boldsymbol{a}^l \quad (6)$$

where the regression matrix $K_a^l = [K(x_i, x_j)]_{N \times (q+1)}$, $x_i \in \{x_1, x_2, \ldots x_N\}$, $x_j \in S \cup \{x_l\}$; the regularization matrix $K_q^l = [K(x_j, x_l)]_{(q+1) \times (q+1)}$, $x_j, x_l \in S \cup \{x_l\}$; $q = |S|$.
(B3) Let

$$x_{l*} = \operatorname{argmin}_{x_l \in \mathcal{R}} H(x_l).$$

Let $S = S \cup \{x_{l*}\}$, $\mathcal{R} = \mathcal{R} \setminus \{x_{l*}\}$, $H_k = H(x_{l*})$, $k = k + 1$.
(B4) Repeat steps (B2) and (B3) until H_k converges.

We call the points in S import points.

3.2 Revised Algorithm

The above algorithm is computationally feasible, but in step (B2) we need to use the Newton-Raphson method to find $\boldsymbol{a}$ iteratively. When the number of import points q becomes large, the Newton-Raphson computation can be expensive. To reduce this computation, we use a further approximation.

Instead of iteratively computing $\boldsymbol{a}^{(k)}$ until it converges, we can just do a one-step iteration, and use it as an approximation to the converged one. To get a good approximation, we take advantage of the fitted result from the current "optimal" S, i.e., the sub-model when $|S| = q$, and use it as the initial value. This one-step update is similar to the score test in generalized linear models (GLM); but the latter does not have a penalty term. The updating formula allows the weighted regression (5) to be computed in $O(Nq)$ time.

Hence, we have the revised step (B2) for the basic algorithm:

(B2*) For each $x_l \in \mathcal{R}$, correspondingly augment K_a with a column, and K_q with a column and a row. Use the updating formula to find $\boldsymbol{a}$ in (5). Compute (6).

3.3 Stopping Rule for Adding Point to $\mathcal{S}$

In step $(B4)$ of the basic algorithm, we need to decide whether H_k has converged. A natural stopping rule is to look at the regularized NLL. Let $H_1, H_2, \ldots$ be the sequence of regularized NLL's obtained in step $(B4)$. At each step k, we compare H_k with H_{k-r}, where r is a pre-chosen small integer, for example $r = 1$. If the ratio $\frac{|H_k - H_{k-r}|}{|H_k|}$ is less than some pre-chosen small number α, for example, $\alpha = 0.001$, we stop adding new import points to $\mathcal{S}$.

3.4 Choosing the Regularization Parameter λ

So far, we have assumed that the regularization parameter λ is fixed. In practice, we also need to choose an "optimal" λ. We can randomly split all the data into a training set and a tuning set, and use the misclassification error on the tuning set as a criterion for choosing λ. To reduce the computation, we take advantage of the fact that the regularized NLL converges faster for a larger λ. Thus, instead of running the entire revised algorithm for each λ, we propose the following procedure, which combines both adding import points to $\mathcal{S}$ and choosing the optimal λ:

$(C1)$ Start with a large regularization parameter λ.
$(C2)$ Let $\mathcal{S} = \emptyset$, $\mathcal{R} = \{x_1, x_2, \ldots, x_N\}$, $k = 1$.
$(C3)$ Run steps $(B2^*)$, $(B3)$ and $(B4)$ of the revised algorithm, until the stopping criterion is satisfied at $\mathcal{S} = \{x_{i1}, \ldots, x_{iq_k}\}$. Along the way, also compute the misclassification error on the tuning set.
$(C4)$ Decrease λ to a smaller value.
$(C5)$ Repeat steps $(C3)$ and $(C4)$, starting with $\mathcal{S} = \{x_{i1}, \ldots, x_{iq_k}\}$.

We choose the optimal λ as the one that corresponds to the minimum misclassification error on the tuning set.

4 Simulation

In this section, we use a simulation to illustrate the IVM method. The data in each class are generated from a mixture of Gaussians (Hastie, Tibshirani, and Friedman 2001). The simulation results are shown in Figure 2.

4.1 Remarks

The support points of the SVM are those which are close to the classification boundary or misclassified and usually have large weights $[p(x)(1 - p(x))]$. The import points of the IVM are those that decrease the regularized NLL the most, and can be either close to or far from the classification boundary. This difference is natural, because the SVM is only concerned with the classification $sign[p(x) - 1/2]$, while the IVM also focuses on the unknown probability $p(x)$.

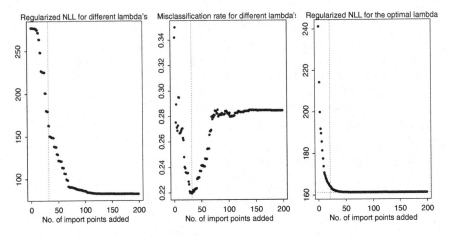

Fig. 2. *Radial kernel is used. $N = 200$. The left and middle panels illustrate how to choose the optimal λ. $r = 1$, $\alpha = 0.001$, λ decreases from e^{10} to e^{-10}. The minimum misclassification rate 0.219 is found to correspond to $\lambda = 0.135$. The right panel is for the optimal $\lambda = 0.135$. The stopping criterion is satisfied when $|\mathcal{S}| = 21$.*

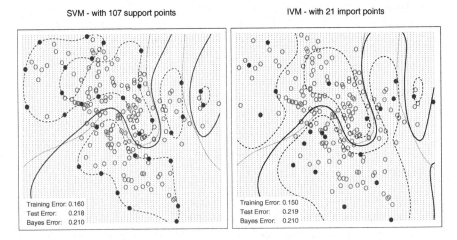

Fig. 3. *The solid black lines are the classification boundaries; the dashed purple lines are the Bayes rule boundaries. For the SVM, the dashed black lines are the edges of the margin. For the IVM, the dashed black lines are the $p(x) = 0.25$ and 0.75 lines, and the black points are the import points.*

Though points away from the classification boundary do not contribute to determining the position of the classification boundary, they may contribute to estimating the unknown probability $p(x)$. Figure 3 shows a comparison of the SVM and the IVM. The total computational cost of the SVM is $O(N^3)$, while the computational cost of the IVM method is $O(N^2q^2)$, where q is the number of import points. Since q does not tend to increase as N increases, the computational cost of the IVM can be smaller than that of the SVM, especially for large training data sets.

5   Multi-class Case

In this section, we briefly describe a generalization of the IVM to multi-class classification. Suppose there are $M + 1$ classes. We can write the response as an M-vector $\boldsymbol{y}$, with each component being either 0 or 1, indicating which class the observation is in. Therefore $y_k = 1$, $y_j = 0$, $j \neq k$, $j \leq M$ indicates the response is in the kth class, and $y_j = 0, j \leq M$ indicates the response is in the $M + 1$th class. Using the $M + 1$th class as the basis, the multi-logit can be written as $f_1 = \ln(p_1/p_{M+1})$, $\ldots$, $f_M = \ln(p_M/p_{M+1})$, $f_{M+1} = 0$. Hence the Bayes classification rule is given by:

$$c = \mathrm{argmax}_{k \in \{1,2,\ldots,M+1\}} f_k$$

We use i to index the observations, j to index the classes, i.e. $i = 1, \ldots N$, $j = 1, \ldots M$. Then the regularized negative log-likelihood is

$$H = -\sum_{i=1}^{N} [\boldsymbol{y}_i^T \boldsymbol{f}(x_i) - \ln(1 + e^{f_1(x_i)} + \cdots + e^{f_M(x_i)})] + \frac{\lambda}{2} \|f\|_{\mathcal{H}_K}^2 \qquad (7)$$

where $\boldsymbol{y}_i = (y_{i1}, y_{i2}, \ldots, y_{iM})^T$, $\boldsymbol{f}(x_i) = (f_1(x_i), f_2(x_i), \ldots, f_M(x_i))^T$, and

$$\|f\|_{\mathcal{H}_K}^2 = \sum_{j=1}^{M} \|f_j\|_{\mathcal{H}_K}^2$$

Using the representer theorem (Kimeldorf and Wahba 1971), the jth element of $\boldsymbol{f}(x)$, $f_j(x)$, which minimizes H has the form

$$f_j(x) = \sum_{i=1}^{N} a_{ij} K(x, x_i). \qquad (8)$$

Hence, (7) becomes

$$H = -\sum_{i=1}^{N} [\boldsymbol{y}_i^T (K_a(i,)A)^T - \ln(1 + \mathbf{1}^T e^{(K_a(i,)A)^T})] + \frac{\lambda}{2} \sum_{j=1}^{M} a_j^T K_q a_j \qquad (9)$$

where $A = (a_1 \ldots a_M) = (a_{ij})$, K_a and K_q are defined in the same way as in the binary case; and $K_a(i,)$ is the ith row of K_a.

The multi-class IVM procedure is similar to the binary case, and the computational cost is $O(MN^2q^2)$. Figure 4 is a simulation of the multi-class IVM. The data in each class are generated from a mixture of Gaussians.

Multi-class IVM - with 32 import points

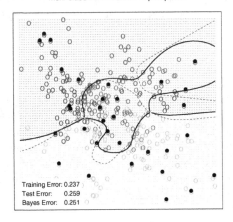

Training Error: 0.237
Test Error: 0.259
Bayes Error: 0.251

Fig. 4. *Radial kernel is used.* $M + 1 = 3$, $N = 300$, $\lambda = 0.368$, $|\mathcal{S}| = 32$.

6   Discussion

Although the intuitive motivation of the SVM is via separating hyperplanes, this intuition gets a murky when the classes overlap. In this case it is perhaps more intuitive to pose the problem as that of regularized function estimation with a loss function particularly suited to classification. Furthermore, the "magic" of the kernel finds its proper home when this function estimation takes place in reproducing kernel Hilbert spaces. We have argued in this paper that the binomial loss function offers several advantages over the hinge loss, in particular that it estimates class probabilities, and generalizes naturally to problems with more than two classes. Although KLR lacks the "support vector" property of SVMs, we propose the IVM, a simple and attractive compromise with performance similar to that of the SVM. The computational cost of the IVM is $O(N^2q^2)$ for the binary case and $O(MN^2q^2)$ for the multi-class case, where q is the number of import points.

The loss function representation of the SVM and KLR encourages a comparison with *boosting* (Freund and Schapire 1996; Hastie, Tibshirani, and Friedman 2001). Figure 5 is similar to Figure 1, and includes the exponential loss function that drives the boosting procedures. Boosting has been shown to fit a logistic regression model by a form of non-parametric gradient descent (Friedman, Hastie, and Tibshirani 2000) using this exponential loss function. It is also motivated as a means for generating a classifier that creates a wide margin between the classes (Schapire and Freund 1997). The comparisons in Figure 5 make it clear that all three methods are similar in this regard, although the exponential left tail in boosting suggests a non-robustness to clumps of observations far from their parent class.

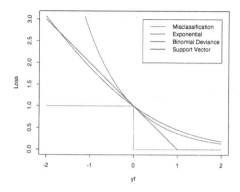

Fig. 5. *The two loss functions from Figure 1, along with the exponential loss function implicit in boosting.*

Acknowledgments We thank Dylan Small, John Storey, Rob Tibshirani, and Jingming Yan for their helpful comments. Ji Zhu is partially supported by the Stanford Graduate Fellowship. Trevor Hastie is partially supported by grant DMS-9803645 from the National Science Foundation, and grant ROI-CA-72028-01 from the National Institutes of Health.

References

Evgeniou, T., M. Pontil, and T. Poggio (1999). Regularization networks and support vector machines. *Advances in Computational Mathematics (to appear)*.

Freund, Y. and R. E. Schapire (1996). Experiments with a new boosting algorithm. In *Machine Learning: Proceedings of the Thirteenth International Conference*, pp. 148–156. Morgan Kauffman, San Francisco.

Friedman, J., T. Hastie, and R. Tibshirani (2000). Additive logistic regression: a statistical view of boosting (with discussion). *Annals of Statistics 28*, 337–307.

Green, P. and B. Silverman (1994). *Nonparametric Regression and Generalized Linear Models*. Chapman and Hall.

Hastie, T. and R. Tibshirani (1990). *Generalized Additive Models*. Chapman and Hall.

Hastie, T., R. Tibshirani, and J. Friedman (2001). *The Elements of Statistical Learning; Data mining, Inference and Prediction*. New York: Springer Verlag.

Kimeldorf, G. and G. Wahba (1971). Some results on tchebycheffian spline functions. *J. Math. Anal. Applic. 33*, 82–95.

Lin, X., G. Wahba, D. Xiang, F. Gao, R. Klein, and K. B. (2001). Smoothing spline anova models for large data sets with bernoulli observations and the randomized gacv. Technical Report 998, Department of Statistics, University of Wisconsin.

Schapire, R. E. and Y. Freund (1997). Boosting the margin: A new explanation for the effectiveness of voting methods. *Proceedings of the Fourteenth International Conference on Machine Learning.*

Smola, A. and B. Schölkopf (2000). Sparse greedy matrix approximation for machine learning. In *Proceedings of the Seventeenth International Conference on Machine Learning.* Morgan Kaufmann.

Wahba, G., C. Gu, Y. Wang, and R. Chappell (1995). *The Mathematics of Generalization.*, Chapter Soft Classification, a.k.a. Risk Estimation, via Penalized Log Likelihood and Smoothing Spline Analysis of Variance. Santa Fe Institute Studies in the Sciences of Complexity. Addison-Wesley.

Wahba, G., Y. Lin, and H. Zhang (2000). Gacv for support vector machines. In A. Smola, P. Bartlett, B. Schölkopf, and D. Schuurmans (Eds.), *Advances in Large Margin Classifiers*, Cambridge, MA, pp. 297–311. MIT Press.

Williams, C. and M. Seeger (2001). Using the nystrom method to speed up kernel machines. In T. K. Leen, T. G. Diettrich, and V. Tresp (Eds.), *Advances in Neural Information Processing Systems*, Volume 13. MIT Press.

Multiple Classification Systems
in the Context of Feature Extraction and Selection

Šarūnas Raudys

Vilnius Gediminas Technical University, Saulėtekio 11, Vilnius, Lithuania
raudys@das.mii.lt

Abstract. Parallels between Feature Extraction / Selection and Multiple Classification Systems methodologies are considered. Both approaches allow the designer to introduce prior information about the pattern recognition task to be solved. However, both are heavily affected by computational difficulties and by the problem of small sample size / classifier complexity. Neither approach is capable of selecting a unique data analysis algorithm.

1. Introduction

The continuing increase in computing power emphasizes the importance of the complexity/sample size problem in pattern recognition. The "scissors effect" [1, 2], the structural risk minimization inductive principle [3], the bias-variance dilemma [4], all suggest that when the sample size is small, classification rules should be as simple as possible. In the large sample case, complex rules can be applied.

The complexity/sample size relation of a statistical classifier depends on the dimensionality of the feature space and on explicit or implicit assumptions that enter into the classifier's training algorithm. Furthermore, the relations considered depend on the data, i.e. on the pattern recognition problem to be solved, and on the features extracted [5].

In many pattern recognition (PR) tasks, we have too many "potentially good" features, and too few training vectors to be used to train the pattern classification system. Thus, one obvious way to resolve the complexity/sample size problem is to reduce the number of features. Here one assumes *a priori* that only a limited number of "relevant" features are important, other features either do not contain useful discriminative information or repeat the information contained in the relevant ones. Two types of dimensionality reduction techniques exist: feature selection and feature extraction.

In feature selection (FS), the designer chooses a small number of most informative features from a pool of candidates. Examples: forward selection, backward elimination, branch and bound approaches and a dozen of others. In feature extraction (FE), the designer performs a linear or non-linear transformation on the original feature space in order to obtain a small number of new, informative features. To extract new features, one introduces some performance measure and optimises it. A common requirement for performance measures is that they should be differentiable in order to apply simple and fast optimisation algorithms.

During the last three decades, a new approach to simplify the decision-making system emerged. It is based on designing a number of simpler classifiers and then fusing their

F. Roli and J. Kittler (Eds.): MCS 2002, LNCS 2364, pp. 27–41, 2002.
© Springer-Verlag Berlin Heidelberg 2002

decisions. Thus, first a number of "simple" expert classifiers categorize the unknown pattern vectors. A "boss" aggregates the outputs of the first level experts and makes the final decision. This approach, known as Multiple Classification Systems (MCS), provides an important tool to solve complex pattern classification, data mining and artificial neural networks problems [6].

In MCS design, the expert classifiers submit their outputs to the fusion (boss) rule. If the fusion rule is a trainable classifier, the experts can be considered as feature extractors [7]. Obviously, each such feature extractor relies on explicit or implicit assumptions regarding the design of the classifier and its training rule. As in conventional feature extraction, we need to distinguish the criterion used to extract new features (outputs of the expert classifiers) and the optimisation algorithm utilized to minimize each expert's cost function. This paper is inspired by a point of view expressed in [7], and its main objective is to consider both feature extraction/selection and MCS from the same viewpoint, paying particular attention to complexity/sample size considerations.

2. Feature Extraction Algorithms

To extract a small number, say r, of informative features (vector $\mathbf{y} = (y_1, \dots, y_r)^T$) one needs to choose [8]:

1) A cost function, i.e. the feature quality criterion,
2) The type of transformation $\mathbf{y}=f(\mathbf{x})$ of input vector, $\mathbf{x} = (x_1, \dots, x_p)^T$,
3) The optimisation criterion.

In many formulations of feature extraction, the probability of misclassification (PMC) is considered as the principal criterion to be minimized. Unfortunately, the PMC is directly related to the type of classification rule to be used later. Moreover, a strict definition of PMC requires computing discontinuous functions, a problem which is mathematically difficult for simple optimisation algorithms. Therefore, many simplifications were introduced.

Feature extraction algorithms can be either supervised or unsupervised. Examples of unsupervised techniques are principal component analysis, and auto-associative neural networks (AA-NNs). AA-NN has the same number, p, of inputs and outputs. In the training phase, all training vectors are supplied to network inputs and outputs together, and the result is obtained as outputs of r units in neural network's hidden layer. The auto-associative neural network minimizes data representation error. No information about the class membership is used.

Supervised FE algorithms utilize parametric or non-parametric estimates of PMC as the performance criterion. The parametric estimates rely explicitly or implicitly on assumptions about the probability density function. E.g., the popular Sammon-Foley optimal discriminant set of vectors implicitly assumes that the pattern classes are multivariate Gaussian, with a common two-class covariance matrix. The Karhunen-Loéve expansion (KLE) is a supervised FE technique that assumes common *within-class* $\mathbf{S}_w$ and *between-class* $\mathbf{S}_b$ covariance matrices [9]. The *signal-to-noise ratio is optimise*d. The solution can be found explicitly:

$$J(j) = \phi_j^T \mathbf{S}_b \phi_j / \lambda_j, \tag{1}$$

where ϕ_j and λ_j are the j-th eigenvector and eigenvalue of $\mathbf{S}_w$, (j=1, ... ,p),

$$\mathbf{S}_w = \frac{1}{N_1 + N_2 + ... + N_K - K} \sum_{i=1}^{K} \sum_{j=1}^{N_i} (X_j^{(i)} - \hat{M}_i)(X_j^{(i)} - \hat{M}_i)^T,$$

$$\mathbf{S}_b = \sum_{i=1}^{K} \frac{N_i}{N_1 + N_2 + ... + N_K} (\hat{M}_i - \hat{M})(\hat{M}_i - \hat{M})^T, X_j^{(i)} \text{ is } j\text{-th training vector}$$

of the i-th class, $\hat{M}_i$ is the sample mean of the N_i training vectors of the i-th class ($i = 1,..., K$), $\hat{M}$ is a mean vector of all training vectors,.

If the indices $J(j)$ are ranked according to their magnitude, then the last r eigenvectors $\mathbf{F}_r = [\phi_{p-r+1}, \phi_{p-r+2}, \ldots, \phi_p]^T$ constitute a matrix of projective axis to make the linear feature extractor $y = \mathbf{F}_r X$. It is assumed that the signal-to-noise ratio minimizes the classification error, however, it is only true for two Gaussian pattern classes with common covariance matrix. The feature extraction method is linear, the optimisation procedure follows directly from the definition of the signal-to-noise ratio and does not require complex iterative calculations. It is claimed that in pattern classification tasks, KLE outperforms the principal component FE [9].
If the patterns are multivariate Gaussian, and the covariance matrices differ, then in the multi-category case, there exist a linear feature extractor [10] that rigorously minimizes the probability of misclassification of a quadratic discriminant function, which, for the assumed data model is an asymptotically optimal classification rule. Similarly to criterion (1), this procedure also requires finding the eigenvectors and eigenvalues of certain matrices, however, it is somewhat more complex. The divergence and the Bhattacharia distance [16] are much simpler criteria, frequently used in feature extraction and selection. According to their definition, these criteria are only indirectly related to the probability of misclassification. However, for the multivariate Gaussian case thy both have rather simple analytical expressions. E.g. the divergence between the i-th and j-th pattern classes is

$$Div(i, j) = \tfrac{1}{2} \operatorname{tr} [(\Sigma_i - \Sigma_j)(\Sigma_i^{-1} - \Sigma_j^{-1})] + \tfrac{1}{2} \operatorname{tr} [(\Sigma_i^{-1} + \Sigma_j^{-1})(M_i - M_j)(M_i - M_j)^T], \quad (2)$$

where M_i is the mean, and Σ_i is the covariance matrix of the i-th class. In the multi-category case one uses the double sum of $Div(i, j)$ over the indexes i and j.

The divergence criterion can be used both for linear and non-linear feature extraction, as well as for feature selection. If the simple parametric expression (2) is used, the divergence does not require complex optimisation methods. Among non-linear criteria utilized to extract informative features is the classification error of a k-NN classifier, estimated by the leave-one-out method [16]. Unfortunately, in terms of optimisation, it requires fairly large computational resources.

An interesting argument is presented in [8] concerning the use of the multilayer perceptron (MLP) for supervised linear feature extraction. The perceptron with p inputs, K outputs and r hidden units is trained to classify the training set; r weighted sums calculated in r hidden neurons comprise a system of r newly extracted features.

In Fig. 1, we present the information processing scheme of an MLP-based linear feature extraction that will be useful later in examining the decision- making process in MCS.

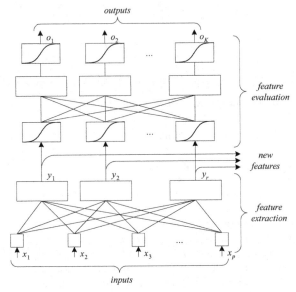

Fig. 1. Linear feature extraction by MLP with one hidden layer.

For the MLP, used as the feature extractor, the feature performance criterion is the classification error that can be evaluated by a scheme composed of r non-linear activation functions, and K output non-linear single-layer perceptrons (SLP). Hence the performance criterion depends on the number of new features extracted. If $K=2$ and $r=2$, then the performance is evaluated by a non-linear decision boundary in a new two-variate feature space. With 3 neurons ($r=3$) a more complex non-linear decision boundary in 3-variate space is possible. Although the feature extraction is linear, the minimization criterion is non-linear and its proximity to the classification error criteria changes with r, the number of new features [8, 24].

Another feature definition procedure frequently used for very small training sets is the introduction of new types of features – similarities to training vectors or cluster centroids [11, 12]. The similarity to a certain vector serves as a single new feature. The similarity concept is popular in potential function classifiers, support vector machines, featureless classification, etc. In this approach, to create new features, the vectors specific to all pattern classes are used. Thus, this approach could be assigned to the group of supervised feature extraction methods. The similarity can be measured as the Euclidean or Mahalonobis distance between vector X and training pattern $X_j^{(i)}$,

or the correlation coefficient between X and $X_j^{(i)}$. In [13], a SLP-based prediction rule was created for a set of short segments formed from a single high-dimensional training vector $X_j^{(i)}$ composed of components representing a single realization of a time series. The SLP was trained to predict the middle elements of each segment. The mean *prediction error*, averaged over all segments in vector X was used as the similarity measure (the ij-th new feature) between vectors X and $X_j^{(i)}$.

3. Multiple Classification Systems as Feature Extractors

As the above review suggests, the choice of available supervised feature extraction methods is limited. The multiple classification systems, however, also can be regarded as feature extractors [7]. Each expert submits to the fusion rule continuous or discrete outputs, and the fusion rule makes the final decision. Currently, non-trainable fusion rules are the most popular algorithms to make the final decision. However, an example of a trainable fusion rule is Wolpert's stacked generalizer [23]. It has been used with considerable success in biomedical classification problems [24]. If a trainable fusion rule is used, then it plays the role of a new classifier, and the set of experts act as the feature extractors. Typical classifiers frequently utilized in MCS design are the Euclidean distance (template matching), the standard Fisher linear discriminant function (DF), the quadratic DF, k-NN, Parzen window classifiers, MLP, stacked generalizer and decision tree classifiers [5, 6, 9, 14–16].

Typically, the cost function utilized to design the expert classifier is the probability of misclassification estimated by one of the methods. In parametric error estimation, the functional form of multivariate density functions of the feature vectors is assumed known. E.g., the assumption of different multivariate Gaussian distributions of the pattern classes leads to quadratic DF. If, in addition, one supposes that classes share a common covariance matrix, then we have the standard Fisher discriminant function where the Mahalonobis distance is a sufficient characteristic of feature quality. In the first case, we have a quadratic performance criterion (quadratic DF is used to estimate the error rate). For the second data model, the linear DF evaluates the overlap of the pattern classes and the performance criterion is linear. The local Parzen window and k-NN classifiers utilize their own non-parametric non-linear performance measures closely related to the Bayes classification error. The cost functions utilized in SLP and MLP training, also are closely associated with the training set's classification error. If the number of training vectors is very large, it is worthwhile to augment the standard sum of squares cost function by an additional anti-regularization term that helps obtain large weights. Then the standard cost function expresses the number of training vectors misclassified [5]. The decision-tree classifier also utilizes the number of training errors as the performance criterion.

The feature extractors obtained by utilizing the Euclidean distance classifier, the standard Fisher DF or SLP are linear. It is quadratic if the quadratic DF is used. The Parzen window and k-NN classifiers perform non-linear FE that relies on all training vectors. The outputs of the decision-tree classifier are obtained by a piece-wise linear function. The feature extraction is piece-wise linear too.

Solutions obtained in the Euclidean distance classifier (EDC), Fisher and quadratic DF are straightforward, and do not require complex optimisation techniques. In SLP and MLP training, one typically utilizes the standard gradient descent or various modification of the Newton optimisation method. The Parzen window and k-NN classifiers do not require training.

The classification rules used as feature extractors expand the set of alternative supervised feature extraction methods. Note that in some classical supervised feature extraction algorithms, the new features are orthogonal. If all experts employ the same features and the same training vectors, then in general, the experts' outputs are statistically dependent. This fact makes the fusion rule design more difficult. If, however, the experts utilize different and slightly correlated features, or different subsets of the training data, then the correlations between the experts' outputs can be small. In difficult PR tasks, the designer of the fusion rule ought to take into account the fact that the distribution density functions of the experts' output vectors are complex and may be multi-modal. It is unrealistic to assume that simple fusion rules will work perfectly in such situations. In simple PR tasks, with considerably overlapping classes and moderately sized training set sizes, often simple non-trainable rules such as the sum rule or majority voting outperform more complex fusion strategies [17].

4. Small Sample Size Problems in Feature Extraction and Selection

In feature selection (extraction) the following factors may affect the accuracy:
- The criterion used to define new features differs from the Bayes error, or from the asymptotic error of the particular classifier used as the fusion rule,
- The size of the training set used in the feature extraction procedure is finite and the set is not representative of the data (the general population),
- One realizes the optimisation procedure imperfectly.

Suppose that in order to estimate the quality of the feature subset one utilizes exact performance criteria appropriate for the classifier that will be used later, and the sample size is infinitely large. Then the optimal subset of features will be selected. Denote this feature subset by the letter j and its true error rate by P_j. We will refer to this error rate as the *ideal error in feature selection*.

In practice, the performance criterion characterizes the classification error only approximately. The sample size is finite. Therefore, a non-optimal subset of features is selected. Denote this feature subset by the letter e. In general, $e \neq j$. We will refer to the error rate of the e subset, P_e as the *true error in feature selection*. The true classification error of the e subset is larger than that of the j subset, i.e. $P_e \geq P_j$. Hence a non-optimal FE criterion leads to an increase in PMC.

To illustrate the influence of the criteria and sample size on the performance of classification error in feature selection, we performed *a special experiment* with an artificial 36-variate Gaussian data. If the data is multivariate Gaussian, the asymptotically optimal classification rule is the standard quadratic DF [5, 16]

$$g_s^Q (X) = (X - \hat{M}_s)^T \, \hat{\Sigma}_s^{-1} (X - \hat{M}_s) + \ln|\hat{\Sigma}_s|, \quad (s = 1, 2, ..., K) \quad (3)$$

where $\hat{\Sigma}_s$ is sample estimate of the covariance matrix of the s-th class.

Our task was to select the best subset composed of 8 features from 1000 subsets of features created by utilizing a random number generator. In order to make the experiment more realistic, mean vectors and covariance matrices of the artificial data were calculated from the real-world data in Satimage ftp.dice.ucl.ac.be/pub/neural-nets/ELENA/databases frequently used for classifier comparison. A scatter diagram of the artificial data (6×100 vectors, K=6) is presented in Fig. 2. In order to see more details in the scatter diagram, we show only a subset of the samples: we remove half of classes π_1 (stars, bottom) and π_3 (hexagons, on the right). Data is presented in the space of the two "best" directions (according to the Karhunen-Loève Expansion criterion (1)). The scatter diagram of the artificial data resembles the analogous scatter diagram of the real data.

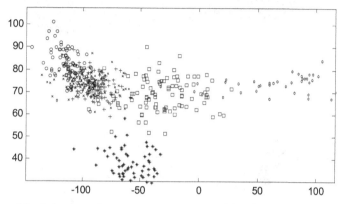

Fig. 2. A scatter diagram of projection of 6×100 36-variate training vectors used onto the space of first two "best" directions found by KLE.

To estimate the quality of the feature subset, we used divergence (2). As an alternative criterion, we employed the error-counting resubstitution estimate of PMC. In the resubstitution method, the training set is used twice. First, it is used to train the classifier. Then it is used to find the misclassification error for the training vectors. In the experiment, we considered two sizes of training set, n_{train} = 6×100 and n_{train} = 6×2000. To estimate the generalization error, we used a test set composed of 6×1000 vectors. In Fig. 3 we present the scatter diagrams of these 1000 vectors: (*a*) the true classification error, P, versus divergence, *div*, and (*b*) P versus the resubstitution error estimate. Each dot in the scattergrams   represents one of the 1000 8-feature subsets. The scatter diagrams show that the ideal classification errors (P_{ideal} = 0.1597 for n_{train}=6×100 and P_{ideal}= 0.1455 for n_{train} = 6×2000) are smaller than the true errors (P_{true} = 0.175/0.188 for n_{train} = 6×100 and P_{true} = 0.182/0.153 for n_{train} = 6×2000. The upper panels correspond to the divergence criterion and the lower ones to the resubstitution error. We see that the divergence is a less effective criterion than the resubstitution error rate. An increase in sample size does not practically affect the upper scatter diagram and the true error rate selected when using the divergence criterion. An increase in the sample size, however, is very effective if the resubstitution error is utilized.

The numerical values presented above were obtained from one collection of M=1000 randomly generated subsets of features. Consequently, the variability of the numerical values is high. It would be desirable to have average values. Suppose the number of feature subsets is equal to 100 (m=100). Then the experimental data of 1000 subsets can be used to create $C_M^m = \dfrac{M!}{(M-m)!\,m!}$ different collections of the feature subsets.

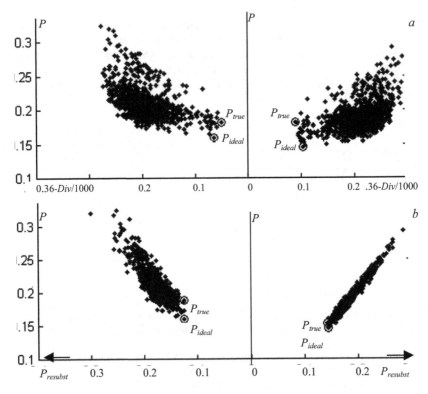

Fig. 3. True classification error, P, versus divergence, div, (a) and versus resubstitution estimate of the classification error, P_{resub} (b). Training set sizes: n_{train} = 6×100 (left scatter diagrams), n_{train} = 6×2000 (right scatter diagrams). Test set size n_{test} = 6×1000.

In Fig. 4 we present curves of average values of C_M^m such collections. The averages were calculated with the fast algorithm presented in [18] (see also Appendix A4 in [5]).

In addition to the true and ideal errors, we also depicted curves for the *apparent error in FS*. It is the average of the minimal values among m resubstitution error estimates in the C_M^m collections of the feature subsets. The curves suggest, that for the feature selection problem in multivariate Gaussian patterns, the divergence is considerably less effective than the resubstitution error counting estimate. Initially, with an increase in m, the true classification error decreases, however, later the decrease slows down. In some cases, the true error actually begins to increase, and we have a situation similar to the overfitting phenomenon observed in neural networks training. The origin of both phenomena is the same: inaccurate criteria used for training and optimization. The experimental curves and conclusions agree with an earlier theoretical analysis of the accuracy problems in the FS process [19]. The curves "true error versus m, the number of the feature subsets" are obtained for a random search feature selection procedure. In practice it does not important which FS strategy is used. Both theory and experiments show that in cases where the sample size is small and/or inaccurate criteria are used, we have an increase in the true classification error due to inaccurate feature selection [19, 25]. Thus, in such situations, there is no need to utilize complex, sophisticated features selection procedures that require substantial computer time.

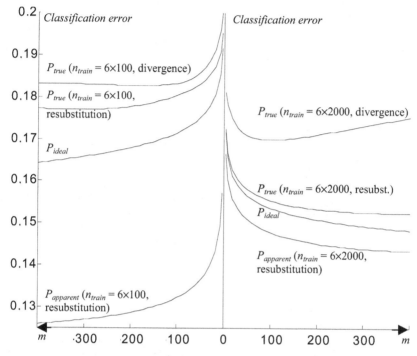

Fig. 4. Classification errors in feature selection versus m, the number of feature subsets compared experimentally.

The experimental curves of the averages show that an increase in the classification error due to inaccurate feature selection is rather high. The increase is caused by two factors: inaccurate feature selection, and non-ideal training of the classification algorithm. As a rule of thumb, one can assume that the increase due to inaccurate feature selection is approximately equal to the standard deviation of the hold-out error-counting estimate, $\sqrt{\hat{P}(1-\hat{P})/n}$. Here n stands for the total number of training vectors and $\hat{P}$ stands for an estimate of the generalization error [5].

Thus, it is worth considering FS accuracy more thoroughly, and distinguishing between the contributions by the two factors just mentioned. Therefore, we reevaluated the data obtained in the previous experiment. We calculated the "ideal classification errors in feature selection" when training sets of different sizes were used to perform feature selection. Curve 1 in Fig. 5 corresponds to the ideal feature selection when a very large training set was used to perform FS and to train quadratic classifier. Theoretical analysis shows that in the eight-variate feature space, a set of

6×2000 vectors is sufficient to train quadratic classifier and to estimate its performance (see Sections 3.5.1 and 6.3.1.2 in [5]).

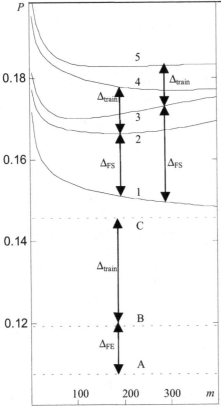

Fig. 5. The increase in classification errors due to non-ideal feature selection / extraction, and due to imperfect training of the classifier (R stands for resubstitution and D indicates the divergence criterion):

1 - n_{train} = 6×2000 for FS (R) and n_{train} = 6×2000 for training.
2 - n_{train} = 6×100 for FS (R) and n_{train} = 6×2000 for training.
3 - n_{train} = 6×100 for FS (D) and n_{train} = 6×2000 for training.
4 - n_{train} = 6×100 for FS (R) and n_{train} = 6×100 for training.
5 - n_{train} = 6×100 for FS (D) and n_{train} = 6×100 for training.
A - n_{train} = 6×2000 for KLE FE and n_{train} = 6×2000 for training.
B - n_{train} = 6×100 for KLE FE and n_{train} = 6×2000 for training.
C - n_{train} = 6×100 for KLE FE and n_{train} = 6×100 for training.

Curve 2 corresponds to imperfect FS. Here, a comparatively small training set was used to perform FS, based on the resubstitution error. A large data set was used to train the classifier. Curve 4 corresponds to imperfect feature selection, when a small training set was used to select features and to train the classifier. The difference between curves 2 and 1, Δ_{FS}, shows an increase in the classification error due to inaccurate feature selection. The difference between curves 2 and 4, Δ_{train}, points to an increase in the classification error due to imperfect training. For the divergence criteria, curves 3 and 1 (Δ_{FS}) and curves 5 and 3 (Δ_{train}) indicate analogous differences. For large m, $\Delta_{FS} > \Delta_{train}$. Thus, if inaccurate criteria are used for FS, there is no need to utilize complicated feature selection algorithms.

Similar differences can be found in *feature extraction*. Here the sample size is also finite, and one uses an inexact, simplified performance criterion. The line A in Fig. 5 corresponds to the classification error if the "ideal" feature extraction was performed. To extract eight features, we used the Karhunen-Loève expansion criteria. The sample size was 6×2000 vectors both in feature extraction and in training a quadratic classifier in the eight-variate feature space. Line B shows the classification error when 6×100 vectors were used for the Karhunen-Loève expansion-based feature extraction and 6×2000 vectors for training. The difference between these two values, Δ_{FE}, shows an increase in the classification error due to inaccurate feature extraction. Line C specifies classification error when 6×100 vectors were used both for KLE FE and classifier training. The difference between classification error values depicted by C and B, Δ_{train}, shows an increase in the classification error due to imperfect training.

For artificial Gaussian data for which means and covariance matrices were calculated from real-world Satimage data, we found that KLE was notably more effective than the feature selection procedures. The differences between efficacy of the FS and FE methods could vanish if non-Gaussian data were considered.

5. Small Sample Size Problems in Multiple Classifier Systems Design

In the analysis of FS and FE accuracy, we identified two causes for the increase in the classification error: inaccurate dimensionality reduction and imperfect training of the classifier. In MCS design, the outputs of single experts serve as input features of the trainable fusion rule. The experts' information processing algorithms are not based on exact performance measures. The data size is finite. Thus, one may assume that a similar increase in the classification error, caused by inaccurate dimensionality reduction and by imperfect training also exists in MCS design.

Consider the case when the training set is used to train both the experts and the fusion rule. It corresponds to a typical solution of the pattern recognition task when the training set is used to extract/select new features and to train the classifier. In small sample situations, the s-th expert presents to the fusion rule incorrect, optimistically biased resubstitution estimates of DF $g_s(X_j^{(i)})$. This means that the experts "boast" to the boss, the fusion rule. In this formulation of the MCS problem, the experts' "self-assessments" correspond to resubstitution classification error estimates.

As a result, the fusion rule is trained with the incorrect outputs of the expert classifiers. If several experts boast in different ways, the incorrect outputs may cause additional increase in the classification error of the MCS. Consequently, we obtain an increase in the classification error due to the experts' "boasting bias". It can be viewed equivalent to inaccurate dimensionality reduction. Fig. 6 illustrates the experts' boasting effect. Here we have two different training subsets (3+3 and 3+3 vectors) used to train two standard linear Fisher classifiers used as experts. Discriminant boundary 5 separates its own training subset with one error and boundary 6 makes no error. In Fig. 6 we depict projections of *true* distribution density functions (solid curves) of the pattern classes on discriminant directions of both experts, $g_1^F(X)$ and $g_2^F(X)$.

The density curves show that in the new space the pattern classes overlap noticeably. We depict also analogous projections of *apparent* distribution density functions of the pattern classes calculated from the sample means and the covariance matrix (dotted curves). The dotted curves show significantly smaller overlap of the pattern classes.

The decreased overlap of the apparent densities suggests the reason of the experts' boasting effect.

In principle, the experts' boasting effect can be reduced. Suppose that standard Fisher discriminant functions are used as expert classifiers:

$$g_s^F (X_s) = (X - \tfrac{1}{2}(\hat{M}_{s1} + \hat{M}_{s2}))^T \hat{\Sigma}_s^{-1} (\hat{M}_{s1} - \hat{M}_{s2}) \quad (s = 1, ..., L) \quad (4)$$

where $\hat{M}_{si}$ is the sample mean of the i-th class, $\hat{\Sigma}_s$ is the sample estimate of common covariance matrix of the s-th expert and L is a number of experts.

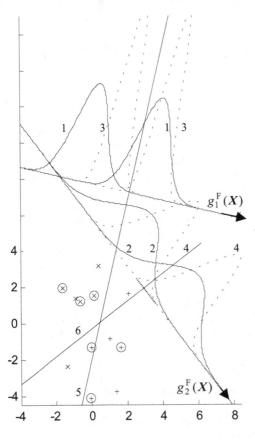

Fig. 6. Classification errors of two-sample-based expert classifiers:
1- true probability density functions (p.d.f.) of projection of the outputs of the first DF (first expert),
2 - true p.d.f. of projection of the outputs of the second DF (second expert),
3 - apparent p.d.f. of projection of the outputs of the first DF,
4 - apparent p.d.f. of projection of the outputs of the second DF.
5 - discriminant boundary of the first expert (DF).
6 - discriminant boundary of the second expert.
The first expert is trained with the six (3+3) circled vectors. Decreased overlap of the apparent densities indicates the need to shift outputs of expert classifiers.

If the number of training vectors and the number of dimensions are large, then expected generalization error of the linear Fisher classifier is [5]

$$EP_N^F \approx \Phi(-\delta/2\,(T_{\mu\Sigma})^{-1/2}) \quad (5)$$

where δ is the Mahalonobis distance, $\Phi(c)$ the cumulative distribution function of the standard N(0,1) Gaussian random variable, and $T_{\mu\Sigma} = (1 + 2p/(N\delta^2))2N/(2N - p)$. Note that for the multivariate Gaussian data model, $\Phi(-\delta/2) = P_\infty^F$, the asymptotic classification error that can be obtained theoretically if $N \to \infty$ (we suppose that $N_2 = N_1 = N$).

Both theoretical and experimental analyses have shown that if the number of training vectors in each pattern class is large enough compared to the number of dimensions, then for many statistical classification rules the expected value of the resubstitution error estimate is approximately symmetric to generalization error with respect to asymptotic classification error. For the resubstitution error of the standard linear Fisher classifier we have

$$E\,P_{resubst} \approx \Phi(-\delta/2\,(T_{\mu\Sigma})^{+1/2}).\qquad(6)$$

The difference between Equations (5) and (6) suggests a shift term that can be used to correct for the decreased overlap of the apparent densities discussed in Fig. 6. Let us use the outputs of the expert classifiers, "normalized" by the learning-set-based standard deviation, $g_j^*(X_j^{(i)}) = g_s(X_j^{(i)})/(\text{stand.dev.}(g_s\ (X_j^{(i)}))$. In order to reduce expert bias, instead of the outputs $g_j^*(X_j^{(i)})$, one ought to use the *shifted values*

$$g_j^*\ (X_j^{(i)}) - (-1)^i\ (T_{\mu\Sigma})^{-1}),\qquad (i = 1, 2).\qquad(7)$$

If (1) standard linear Fisher classifiers are used as experts, (2) the data is approximately multivariate Gaussian, (3) both the sample size and the number of dimensions are high, while $EP_N^F \gg P_\infty^F$, then variances of experts resubstitution error estimates are small in comparison with the bias [5]. Such correction terms gave positive results when the standard linear Fisher rule [20] or a Multinomial classifier (Behaviour-Knowledge Space method) [21] were used to build trainable fusion rule. The correction term (7) explains the principal possibility to reduce the negative effect of experts' boasting bias. Term (7), however, is useful only in a limited context (Gaussian high-variate data, etc.). A more general way to reduce both the experts' boasting effect and the complexity of the fusion rule is to **add randomly generated noise** to training pattern vectors. Accuracy is improved since some informal prior information (actually, the researcher's hypothesis) is introduced into the classifier design process: the multivariate space in the neighbourhood of each training pattern vector is filled with vectors of the same category. For the multiple classification systems design, the noise injection approach was utilized in [17, 20–22] and gave encouraging results.

6. Concluding Remarks

For multiple classification systems with trainable fusion rules, the experts can be considered as individual feature extractors. In conventional supervised FE, one often minimizes performance criteria related to *the set of r new features* to be obtained in the feature acquisition process. In MCS, however, each single feature is obtained *independently* of the others. In MCS design, the criteria most frequently used to develop the experts' information processing algorithm are closely related to the classification error. In contrast, in feature extraction, often the criteria are only indirectly related to classification error.

Feature selection and extraction are affected by inadequate performance measures and finite training set size. These factors lead to an undesired increase in the classification error, due to imperfect dimensionality reduction. Analysis shows that such an increase may become larger than that caused by an insufficient training set size. Therefore, for classification system design, the accuracy of dimensionality reduction is of special concern. As a rule of thumb, the increase in error is approximately equal to the standard deviation of the hold out classification error estimate, $\sqrt{\hat{P}(1-\hat{P})/n}$, where n stands for a total number of training vectors and $\hat{P}$ is an estimate of the generalization error.

Just as for feature extraction, the experts' development process is also affected by limited sample set size. Instead of the increase in classification error due to inexact dimensionality reduction, in multiple classification systems we have to contend with the consequences of the experts' boasting.

Dimensionality reduction and MCS should complement, not compete with each other. For certain PR tasks, both approaches could, and perhaps should be used. Both in dimensionality reduction and in MCS, we are trying to use explicit or implicit prior information available to the designer on the PR problem to be solved. MCS is only one of many possible ways to utilize such additional information. Therefore, in practice one should always bear in mind other approaches [26]. Certain characteristic aspects of feature selection/extraction procedures may suggest new ideas to MCS designers that should not be ignored.

Acknowledgments

The author thanks Dr. Ray Somorjai, Dr. Tin Kam Ho and Aistis Raudys for useful suggestions and friendly aid in preparing a final version of the paper.

References

1. Raudys S. On the problems of sample size in pattern recognition. In: Pugatchiov V.S. (editor) *Detection, Pattern Recognition and Experiment Design*, Proceedings of the 2nd All-Union Conference Statistical Methods in Control Theory. Nauka, Moscow. 2:64–76 (in Russian), 1970.

2. Kanal L. and Chandrasekaran B. On dimensionality and sample size in statistical pattern classification. *Pattern Recognition* 3:238–55, 1971.

3. Vapnik V.N. and Chervonenkis D.Ya. *Theory of Pattern Recognition: Statistical learning problems*. Nauka, Moscow (in Russian), 1974.

4. Geman S.L., Bienenstock E., Doursat R. Neural networks and bias/variance dilemma. *Neural Computation* 4:1–58, 1992.

5. Raudys S. *Statistical and Neural Classifiers: An integrated approach to design*. Springer, London, 2001.

6. Kittler J. and F. Roli (eds.). *Multiple Classifier Systems*. Springer Lecture Notes in Computer Science, Springer Vol. 1857 (2000), Vol. 2096, 2001.

7. Ho T.K. Data complexity analysis for classifier combination. *Multiple Classifier Systems*. Springer Lecture Notes in Computer Science, Springer Vol. 2096(2001): 53-67.

8. Raudys A., Long J. A.. MLP based linear feature extraction for nonlinearly separable data, *Pattern Analysis & Applications*, 4(4): 227-34, 2001.

9. Ripley B.D. *Pattern Recognition and Neural Networks*. Cambridge University press, Cambridge, 1996.

10. Tubbs J.D., Coberley W.A., Young D.M. (1982) Linear dimension reduction and Bayes classification with unkown parameters. *Pattern Recognition* 14(3):167–172, 1982.

11. Haykin S. *Neural Networks: A comprehensive foundation*. 2nd edition. Prentice-Hall, Englewood Cliffs, NJ, 1999.

12. Duin R.P.W. Classifiers for dissimilarity-based pattern recognition. *Proc. 15th Int. Conf of Pattern Recognition*. IEEE press, Los Alamitos, 2: 1-7, 2000.

13. Raudys S and Tamosiunaite M. Biologically inspired architecture of feedforward networks for signal classification. *Advances in Pattern Recognition*. Ferri F, Pudil P (eds). Springer Lecture Notes in Computer Science. Vol. 1876, pp. 727-736, 2000.

14. Giacinto G. and Roli F. Dynamic classifier selection based on multiple classifier behaviour. *Pattern Recognition*, 34(9):179-181, 2001.

15. Kuncheva L.I., Bezdek J.C. Duin and R.P.W. Decision templates for multiple classifier fusion: and experimental comparison. *Pattern Recognition* 34: 299-314, 2001.

16. Fukunaga K. *Introduction to Statistical Pattern Recognition*. 2nd edition. Academic Press, New York, 1990.

17. Roli F., Raudys S. and Marcialis G.L. An experimental comparison of fixed and trained fusion rules for crisp classifiers. In: Kittler J. and F. Roli (eds.). *Multiple Classifier Systems*. Springer Lecture Notes in Computer Science, Springer, 2002.

18. Pikelis V. Calculating statistical characteristics of experimental process for selecting the best version. In: Raudys S. (ed.) *Statistical Problems of Control*, 93:46–56. Institute of Mathematics and Informatics, Vilnius (in Russian), 1991.

19. Raudys S. Influence of sample size on the accuracy of model selection in pattern recognition. In: S Raudys S.(ed.), *Statistical Problems of Control*, 50:9–30. Institute of Mathematics and Informatics, Vilnius (in Russian), 1981.

20. Janeliunas A. and Raudys S. Reduction of the boasting bias of linear experts. In: Kittler J. and F. Roli (eds.). *Multiple Classifier Systems*. Springer Lecture Notes in Computer Science, Springer, 2002.

21. Raudys S. Experts' bias in trainable fusion rule. *IEEE Transactions on Pattern Analysis and Machine Intelligence* (2001, submitted).

22. Güler C., Sankur B., Kahya Y., Skurichina M., Raudys S. Classification of respiratory sound patterns by means of cooperative neural networks. In: G.Ramponi, G.L.Sicuranza, S. Carrato, S.Marsi (editors), *Proceedings of 8th European Signal Processing Conference* (isbn 88-86179-83-9). Edizioni Lint, Trieste, 1996.

23. Wolpert D.H. Stacked generalization. *Neural Networks* 5: 240-259, 1992.

24. Somorjai R.L., Dolenko B., Nikulin A., Nickerson P., Rush D., Shaw A., de Glogowski M., Rendell J., Deslauriers R. Distinguishing normal allografts from biopsy - proven rejections: application of a three - stage classification strategy to urine MR and IR spectra. *Vibrational Spectroscopy* 28: (1) 97-102, 2002.

25. Schulerud H. The influence of feature selection on error estimates in linear discriminant analysis. *IEEE Transactions on Pattern Analysis and Machine Intelligence* (2002, accepted).

26. Somorjai R.L, Janeliūnas A, Baumgartner R., Raudys S. Comparison of two classification methodologies on a real-world biomedical problem: A feature-extraction-based 3-stage strategy vs. the strategy of classifier complexity regularization and multiple classifier systems. *Advances in Pattern Recognition* (Proc. SPR+SSPR'2002, Duin R.P.W. and Kamel M., eds.). Springer, Lecture Notes in Computer Science, 2002.

Boosted Tree Ensembles for Solving Multiclass Problems

Terry Windeatt and Gholamreza Ardeshir

Centre for Vision, Speech and Signal Processing (CVSSP)
University of Surrey, Guildford, Surrey, GU2 5XH, U.K.
T.Windeatt,G. Ardeshir @eim.surrey.ac.uk

Abstract. In this paper we consider the combination of two ensemble techniques, both capable of producing diverse binary base classifiers. Adaboost, a version of Boosting is combined with Output Coding for solving multiclass problems. Decision trees are chosen as the base classifiers, and the issue of tree pruning is addressed. Pruning produces less complex trees and sometimes leads to better generalisation. Experimental results demonstrate that pruning makes little difference in this framework. However, on average over nine benchmark datasets better accuracy is achieved by incorporating unpruned trees.

1 Introduction

Traditionally, the approach that has been used in the design of pattern classification systems is to experimentally assess the performance of several classifiers with the idea that the best one will be chosen. However, the theory of ensemble classifiers represents a departure from the traditional strategy and has been developed to address the problem of designing a system with improved accuracy. Recognising that each classifier may make different and perhaps complementary errors, the aim is to pool together the results from all classifiers in such a way that the ensemble outperforms any constituent (also called base) classifier. There are several categories of techniques capable of producing diversity among base classifiers, which is a necessary condition for improvement by combining. In the first category are methods that reduce dimension of training set to give different feature sets. The second category includes methods that incorporate different types of base classifier or different base classifier parameters. In the third category, which includes Boosting, are techniques that resample the training set and thereby specialise each classifier on a different subset. Finally in the fourth category are Output Coding methods that create complementary two-class problems from multiclass problems.

Ensemble methods from these four categories have been developed and tuned over the past decade. In principle, the problem of creating a good ensemble is solved by jointly optimising the design and fusion of base classiers. However this is a difficult optimisation, and frequently a relatively simple fusion strategy is applied, such as majority or weighted vote. Base classifiers are then designed to

F. Roli and J. Kittler (Eds.): MCS 2002, LNCS 2364, pp. 42–51, 2002.

match the fusion rule. In this paper, two ensemble design strategies are combined. Adaboost which is from category three is combined with Output Coding from category four. The idea is to convert a multiclass problem into complementary binary sub-problems and at the same time concentrate on difficult-to-classify patterns by reweighting; the idea was first reported in [20]. In this study, decision trees are chosen as base classifer and the effect of tree pruning on ensemble performance is investigated. An advantage of using decision trees over other base classifiers is that the decision to prune is the only parameter to set. Pruning reduces the complexity of base classifiers, but does not necessarily lead to improved accuracy.

Boosting adaptively changes the distribution of the training set based upon the performance of sequentially constructed classifiers. Each new classifier is used to adaptively filter and re-weight the training set, so that the next classifier in the sequence has increased probability of selecting patterns that have been previously mis-classified. Boosting is a general method for converting a weak learner into one with high accuracy, but it requires that the weak learning algorithm produce hypotheses with accuracy better than random guessing. For a k-class problem, $k >> 2$, it may be difficult to achieve the required accuracy. One solution proposed by Freund and Schapire, referred to as AdaBoost.M2, is based on a pseudo-loss measure in which the weak learner chooses from a set of plausible labels [20]. AdaBoost.M2 not only divides the training set into hard and easy patterns, but also forces the learning algorithm to concentrate on patterns whose labels are hard to distinguish from each other. Another solution is to combine Boosting with Output Coding (Adaboost.OC), in which the weak learner is rerun on the training patterns while reweighting and relabelling on each round [20]. Output Coding is an ensemble method in which a binary code matrix defines the decomposition of the multiclass into binary sub-problems. Each classifier operates on the same training set but the patterns are relabelled according to the columns of the Output Coding matrix. This process of relabelling was referred to as colouring of the patterns in the context of Adaboost.OC. By introducing colouring into Boosting the weak learner no longer uses the same training set on each round. The main advantage is that Adaboost is then only required to solve a two-class problem.

There have been some previous studies that have compared pruned and unpruned ensembles. In [12], ECOC with C4.5 showed no significant difference on pruned versus unpruned ensembles on six out of eight datasets. In [10] over thirty-three datasets, significant difference due to pruning was observed in ten of the datasets for both C4.5 and randomised C4.5, in four of the datasets for Bagged C4.5 and in none for Boosted C4.5. In [23], six pruning strategies were compared and Error-Based Pruning (EBP) performed better overall than any other strategy for both Bagging and Boosting. Similarly in [21] six methods were compared for Output Coding with C4.5 and overall EBP performed better than any other strategy. In this paper the purpose is to study the effect of pruning in the context of output coded ensembles of boosted trees, rather than to compare boosted ensembles with other techniques.

The structure of this paper is as follows: in Section 2 we review the Output Coding method, followed by a review of AdaBoost.OC in Section 3. In section 4 we briefly explain the Error-based Pruning method (EBP), the default strategy for C4.5. EBP has been used for the experiments in Section 5 in which the performance of unpruned and pruned Adaboost.OC is compared with Adaboost.M2.

2   Output Coding and Diverse Binary Classifiers

Output Coding is a two-stage method, the first being the relabelling stage which can be defined as follows. Let Z be the $k \times b$ code matrix with binary elements, where K is the number of classes and b is the number of binary classifiers. Each column provides a map to convert the multi-class problem to binary sub-problems. Specifically, for the jth sub-problem, a training pattern with target class w_i ($i = 1...k$) is re-labelled either as class Ω_1 or as class Ω_2 depending on the value of Z_{ij} (typically zero or one). Therefore for each column the k classes can be considered to be arranged into two *super-groups* of classes Ω_1 and Ω_2. (The second stage of Output Coding is the decision rule which is based on finding distance to each row of Z that acts as a b-dimensional code word to represent a class).

The Output Coding method was introduced in [11, 12] and named Error-Correcting Output Coding (ECOC). The idea was to base the code on error-correcting principles to facilitate a robust fusion strategy. Various coding strategies have since been proposed, but most code matrices that have been investigated previously are binary and problem-independent, that is pre-designed. Optimal properties of the code matrix for producing diverse classifiers are believed to be maximum Hamming Distance between pairs of columns [12, 24]. Random codes have received much attention, and were first mentioned in [11] as performing well in comparison with error-correcting codes. In [12] random, exhaustive, hill-climbing search and BCH coding methods were used to produce ECOC code matrices for different column lengths. Random codes were also shown in [14] to give Bayesian performance if pairs of code words were equidistant, and it was claimed that a long enough random code would not be outperformed by a pre-defined code. In [25] it is shown that an optimal code performs better than random code as code word length is reduced. Recent developments include investigation of three-valued codes [2], and problem-dependent continuous and discrete codes [8].

The output coding concept has been successfully applied to problems in several domains [1, 3, 4, 15]. It has also been shown to improve performance with different kinds of base classifier including decision tree, multi-layer perceptron, SVM and k-nearest-neighbour.

3   AdaBoost.OC Algorithm

AdaBoost.OC reruns the weak learning algorithm many times and trains it over a new distribution of examples, relabelled as in Output Coding. As can be seen in figure 1, given a training set with the size m, the weights of patterns are initialised as in AdaBoost.M2, that is

$$\tilde{D}_1(i, \ell) = [\![\ell \neq y_i]\!]/(m(k-1)) \qquad (1)$$

where k is the number of classes and $[\![x]\!]$ is 1 when x is true otherwise 0. On each round, patterns are relabelled according to the colouring (μ_t). To minimise the training errors, a colouring scheme should be chosen to maximise U_t, which is defined in step two of figure 1. We have used the scheme from [20] which uses a random assignment of $k/2$ labels to 0 and $k/2$ labels to 1. The weak learner is trained according to D_t and then by calculating the weak hypothesis h_t, all of the labels satisfying $h_t(x) = \mu_t(\ell)$ receive a vote. The weight of this weak hypothesis (α_t), is found from the weighted training error, $\tilde{\epsilon}_t$, is which includes penalty terms for failing to include the correct label in plausible label set and for including any incorrect labels. The weights of patterns are updated so that the learning algorithm is forced to concentrate on hardest patterns and on the labels that are hard to distinguish from each other. Finally the generated hypotheses are combined according to weighted voting so that a test pattern is assigned to the class whose label has received the most votes.

4 Decision Tree Pruning

In the past much effort has been directed toward developing effective tree pruning methods (for a review see [13]) in the context of a single tree. For a tree ensemble, besides base classifier pruning, it is also possible to consider ensemble pruning. In [9], five ensemble pruning methods used with Adaboost are proposed, but the emphasis there is on efficiency, i.e. finding a minimal number of base classifiers without significantly degrading performance.

Decision tree pruning is a process in which one or more subtrees of a decision tree are removed. The need for pruning arises because the generated tree can be large and complex, so it may not be accurate or comprehensible. Complexity of a univariate decision tree is measured as the number of nodes, and the reasons for complexity are mismatch of representational biases and noise [7]. It means that the induction algorithm is unable to model some target concepts, and also that in some algorithms, (e.g. C4.5), subtree replication causes the tree to be too large and to overfit [17].

According to [13] there are different types of pruning methods but post-pruning is more usual [7]. The disadvantage of pre-pruning methods is that tree growth can be prematurely stopped, since the procedure estimates when to stop constructing the tree. A stopping criterion that estimates the performance gain expected from further tree expansion is applied, and tree expansion terminates when the expected gain is not accessible [13], [18]. A way around this problem is to use a post-pruning method which grows the full tree and retro-spectively prunes, starting at the leaves of the tree. Post-pruning methods remove one or more subtrees and replace them by a leaf or one branch of that subtree. One class of these algorithms divides the training set into a growing set and pruning set.

The growing set is used to generate the tree as well as prune, while the pruning set is used to select the best tree [6]. In the case of shortage of training set, the cross-validation method is used i.e. the training set is divided into several equal-sized blocks and then on each iteration one block is used as pruning set and the remaining blocks used as a growing set. Another class of post-pruning algorithm uses all the training set for both growing and pruning [19]. However it is then necessary to define an estimate of the true error rate using the training set alone.

EBP was developed by Quinlan for use in C4.5. It does not need a separate pruning set, but uses an estimate of expected error rate. A set of examples covered by the leaf of a tree is considered to be a statistical sample from which it is possible to calculate confidence for the posterior probability of mis-classification. The assumption is made that the error in this sample follows a binomial distribution, from which the upper limit of confidence [16] is the solution for p of

$$CF = \sum_{x=0}^{E} \binom{N}{x} p^x (1-p)^{N-x} \tag{2}$$

where N is number of cases covered by a node and E is number of cases which is covered by that node erroneously (As C4.5 we have used an approximate solution for equation 2). The upper limit of confidence is multiplied by the number of cases which are covered by a leaf to determine the number of predicted errors for that leaf. Further the number of predicted errors of a subtree is the sum of the predicted errors of its branches. If the number of predicted errors for a leaf is less than the number of predicted errors for the subtree in which that leaf is, then the subtree is replaced with the leaf. We tried changing the confidence level to vary the degree of pruning but found that this is not a reliable way of varying tree complexity [22]. In the experiments in Section 5 the default confidence level of 25% is used.

5   Experiments

The number of patterns, classes and features for the datasets used in these experiments are shown in table 1. These data sets can be found on UCI web site [5]. The data has been randomly split 70/30% into training/test set and the experiment repeated ten times. C4.5, with Error-Based Pruning, has been used as base classifier and in these experiments ensemble of unpruned and pruned trees built by AdaBoost.M2 and AdaBoost.OC have been compared. In the experiments reported in [20] for comparing AdaBoost.M2 and AdaBoost.OC pruning was turned on.

As figures 2 and 3 show, the test error of AdaBoost.OC for both pruned and unpruned trees reduces as number of classifier increases over all datasets. However, the test error of AdaBoost.M2 appears somewhat insensitive to number of rounds although error increases slightly for Car, Glass and Soybean-Large. This appears to show that the pseudo-loss based algorithm AdaBoost.M2 with

C4.5, in contrast to the error-based Adaboost.M2 with C4.5, only takes a few rounds to learn the training set and in some cases overfits as number of rounds increases.

For AdaBoost.OC the performance of pruned ensembles is similar to the performance of unpruned ensembles, although appears slightly better for Anneal, Audiology, Glass, Iris. However the difference did not show up as significant (McNemar 5%). For AdaBoost.M2, the pruned ensemble outperforms the unpruned ensemble except for Dermatology.

In an attempt to see overall performance the composite curve over all datasets is plotted in figure 4. The plot is normalised with respect to the best classification rate for each particular dataset as follows. The best classification rate is the mean over the last x rounds, where x is judged to be the number of classifiers above which there is no further improvement. ¿From the composite performance we see that the mean classification rate over the nine datasets for Adaboost.OC is higher for unpruned than pruned. For AdaBoost.M2, ensemble of unpruned decision trees outperforms pruned ensemble.

6   Discussion

As explained in Section 2 the choice of code matrix may affect performance of Output Coding. In AdaBoost.OC, we have used a random approach to dividing the labels on each round. This may mean that diversity is not as great as it could be, since the Hamming Distance between columns has not been maximised. Providing that the code matrix has enough columns random code may perform as well as an optimal code. However, since each round of Boosting depends on the previous round it may be important for efficiency reasons to minimise the total number of rounds. Pursuing optimal codes is a possible way forward in this regard and would likely modify the curves shown in figure 4 at the low end. AdaBoost.M2 is a time-consuming algorithm because on each round it constructs classifiers according to the same number of classes and in comparison AdaBoost.OC has removed this complexity.

7   Conclusion

In this paper, we have applied two multi-class versions of Boosting to nine datasets by using pruned and unpruned decision trees as base classifiers, and we have seen that AdaBoost.OC outperforms AdaBoost.M2. For AdaBoost.OC, the performance of pruned ensemble is similar to the unpruned ensemble but on average over all datasets it is better not to prune if accuracy is the main consideration.

Table 1. Specification of Datasets

Name	Data size	Class	Attributes	
			Cont.	Disc.
Anneal	898	6	9	29
Audiology	200	24		69
Car	1728	4		6
Dermatology	366	6	1	33
Glass	214	6	9	
Iris	150	3	4	
Segmentation	2310	7	19	
Soybean-Large	683	19		35
Vehicle	846	4	18	

$Given (x_1, y_1), ..., (x_m, y_m) where x_i \in X, y_i \in Y.$
For $t = 1, ..., T$

1. Compute colouring $\mu_t : Y \to \{0, 1\}$.
2. Let $U_t = \sum_{i=1}^{m} \sum_{\ell \in Y} \tilde{D}_t(i, \ell) [\![\mu_t(y_i) \neq \mu_t(\ell)]\!]$
3. Let $D_t(i) = \frac{\sum_{\ell \in Y} \tilde{D}_t(i, \ell) [\![\mu_t(y_i) \neq \mu_t(\ell)]\!]}{U_t}$
4. Train weak learner on $(x_1, \mu_t(y_1)), ..., (x_m, \mu_t(y_m))$ weighted according to D_t
5. Get weak hypothesis $h_t : X \to \{0, 1\}$.
6. Let $\tilde{h}_t = \{\ell \in Y : h_t(x) = \mu_t(\ell)\}$.
7. Let $\tilde{\epsilon}_t = \frac{1}{2} \sum_{i=1}^{m} \sum \tilde{D}_t(i, \ell) \cdot ([\![y_i \notin h(\tilde{x}_i)_t]\!] + [\![\ell \in h(\tilde{x}_i)_t]\!])$
8. Let $\alpha_t = \frac{1}{2} \ln(\frac{1 - \tilde{\epsilon}_t}{\tilde{\epsilon}_t})$
9. $\tilde{D}_{t+1}(i, \ell) = \frac{\tilde{D}_t(i,\ell) \cdot exp(\alpha_t([\![y_i \notin \tilde{h}_t(x_i)]\!] + [\![\ell \in \tilde{h}_t(x_i)]\!]))}{Z_t}$
   where Z_t is a normalisation factor chosen so that $\tilde{D}_{t+1}$ will sum to 1

Output the final hypothesis:

$$H_{final}(x) = arg \max_{l \in Y} \sum_{t=1}^{T} \alpha_t [\![h_t(x) = \mu_t(\ell)]\!].$$

Fig. 1. The AdaBoost.OC algorithm

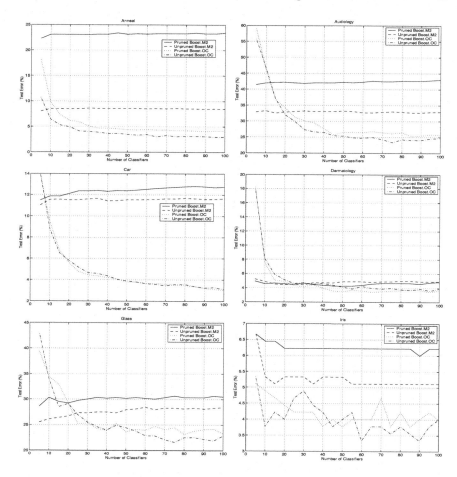

Fig. 2. Test Error of AdaBoost.M2 and AdaBoost.OC

References

[1] D.W. Aha and R. L. Bankert. Cloud classification using error-correcting output codes. *Artificial Intelligence Applications: Natural Resources, Agriculture, and Environmental Science*, 11(1):13–28, 1997.

[2] E.L. Allwein, R.E. Schapire, and Y. Singer. Reducing multi-class to binary: A unifying approach for margin classifiers. *Machine learning research*, 1:113–141, 2000.

[3] G. Bakiri and T. Dietterich. Achieving high-accuracy text-to-speech with machine learning, 1999.

[4] A. Berger. Error-correcting output coding for text classification. In *IJCAI'99, Workshop on machine learning for information filtering*, 1999.

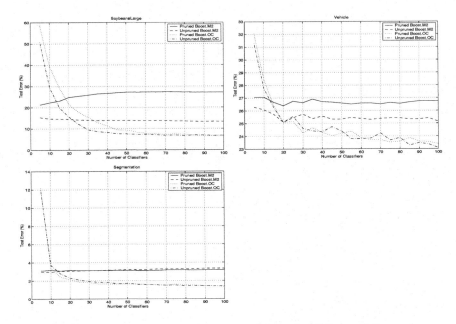

Fig. 3. Test Error of AdaBoost.M2 and AdaBoost.OC

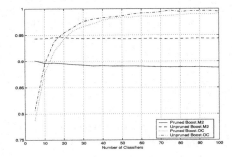

Fig. 4. Composite correct Classification of AdaBoost.M2 and AdaBoost.OC for pruned and unpruned decision trees

[5] C.L. Blake and Merz C.J. Uci repository of machine learning databases. Technical report, Irvine, Univ. of Calif., Inf. and Comp. Scienc, 1998.

[6] Leo Breiman, J. H. Freidman, R. A. Olshen, and C.J. Stone. Classification and regression trees. *Wadsworth International Group*, 1984.

[7] L. A. Breslow and D. W. Aha. Simplifying decision trees: A survey. *Knowledge Engineering Review*, pages 1–40, 1997.

[8] K. Crammer and Y. Singer. On the learnability and design of output codes for multiclass problems. *Machine Learning*, to appear.

[9] T. G. Dietterich D. Margineantu. Pruning adaptive boosting. In *International Conference on Machine Learning*, pages 211–218. Morgan Kaufmann, 1997.

[10] T. G. Dietterich. An experimental comparison of three methods for constructing ensembles of decision trees: Bagging, boosting, and randomization. *Machine Learning*, 40(2):139–158, 2000.

[11] T.G Dietterich and G. Bakiri. Error-correcting output codes: A general method for improving multiclass inductive learning programs. In *Proceedings of the Ninth National Conference on Artificial Intelligence (AAAI-91)*, pages 572–577. AAAI Press, 1991.

[12] T.G. Dietterich and G Bakiri. Solving multi-class learning problems via error-correcting output codes. *Journal of Artificial Intelligence Research*, 2:263–286, 1995.

[13] F. Esposito, D. Malerba, and G. Semeraro. A comparative analysis of methods for pruning decision trees. *IEEE Transactions on Pattern Analysis and Machine Intelligence*, 19(5):476–491, May 1997.

[14] G. M. James and T. Hastie. The error coding method and PICT's. *Computational and Graphical Statistics*, 7:377–387, 1998.

[15] J. Kittler, R. Ghaderi, T. Windeatt, and G. Matas. Face verification using error correcting output codes. In *Computer Vision and Pattern Recognition CVPR01*, volume 1, pages 755–760, Hawaii, December 2001. IEEE Press.

[16] J. Ross Quinlan. Personal communication from Quinlan.

[17] R. Quinlan. Induction of decision tree. *Machine Learning*, 1:81–106, 1986.

[18] R. Quinlan. *C4.5: Programs for Machine Learning*. Morgan Kaufmann, San Mateo,California, 1993.

[19] R.J. Quinlan. Simplyfying decision trees. *International Journal of Man-Machine Studies*, 27:221–234, 1987.

[20] R.E. Schapire. Using output codes to boost multiclass learning problems. In *14th International Conf. on Machine Learning*, pages 313–321. Morgan Kaufman, 1997.

[21] T. Windeatt and A. Ardeshir. Tree pruning for output coded ensembles. In *International Conference of Pattern Recognition*, Quebec, Canada, 2002. submitted.

[22] T. Windeatt and G. Ardeshir. Boosting unpruned and pruned decision trees. In *Applied Informatics, Preceedings of the IASTED International Symposia*, pages 66–71, 2001.

[23] T. Windeatt and G. Ardeshir. An empirical comparison of pruning methods for ensemble classifiers. In *IDA 2001*. Springer-Verlag, Lecture notes in computer science, 2001.

[24] T. Windeatt and R. Ghaderi. Multi-class learning and error-correcting code sensitivity. *Electronics Letters*, 36(19):1630–1632, Sep 2000.

[25] T. Windeatt and R. Ghaderi. Binary labelling and decision level fusion. *Information Fusion*, 2(2):103–112, 2001.

Distributed Pasting of Small Votes

N.V. Chawla[1], L.O. Hall[1], K.W. Bowyer[2], T.E. Moore, Jr.[1], and
W.P. Kegelmeyer[3]

[1] Department of Computer Science and Engineering, University of South Florida
4202 E. Fowler Avenue, Tampa, Florida 33620, USA
{chawla,hall,tmoore4}@csee.usf.edu
[2] Department of Computer Science and Engineering, University of Notre Dame
384 Fitzpatrick Hall, Notre Dame, IN 46556, USA
kwb@cse.nd.edu
[3] Sandia National Labs, Biosystems Research Department, P.O. Box 969, MS 9951,
Livermore, CA 94551-0969, USA
wpk@ca.sandia.gov

Abstract. Bagging and boosting are two popular ensemble methods
that achieve better accuracy than a single classifier. These techniques
have limitations on massive datasets, as the size of the dataset can
be a bottleneck. Voting many classifiers built on small subsets of data
("pasting small votes") is a promising approach for learning from massive datasets. Pasting small votes can utilize the power of boosting and
bagging, and potentially scale up to massive datasets. We propose a
framework for building hundreds or thousands of such classifiers on small
subsets of data in a distributed environment. Experiments show this approach is fast, accurate, and scalable to massive datasets.

1 Introduction

The last decade has witnessed a surge in the availability of massive datasets.
These include historical data of transactions from credit card companies, telephone companies, e-commerce companies, and financial markets. The relatively
new bioinformatics field has also opened the doors to extremely large datasets
such as the Protein Data Bank [16]. The size of these important datasets poses a
challenge for developers of machine learning algorithms and software — how to
construct accurate *and* efficient models. The machine learning community has
essentially focused on two directions to deal with massive datasets: data subsampling [14,17], and the design of parallel or distributed algorithms capable of
handling all the data [5,15,10,6]. The latter approaches try to bypass the need for
loading the entire dataset into the memory of a single computer by distributing
the dataset across a group of computers.

Evaluating these two directions leads to the compelling question: "Do we
really need all the data?" The KDD-2001 conference [20] conducted a panel on
subsampling, which overall offered positive views of subsampling. However, given
100 GB of data, subsampling at 10% can itself pose a challenge. Other pertinent

F. Roli and J. Kittler (Eds.): MCS 2002, LNCS 2364, pp. 52–61, 2002.

issues with subsampling are: What subsampling methodology to adopt? What is the right sample size? To do any intelligent subsampling, one might need to sort through the entire dataset, which could take away some of the efficiency advantages. Ideally, one might want to use the existing computational resources to handle the flood of training data.

Our claim is that distributed data mining can mitigate, to a large extent, the scalability issues presented by massive training sets. The datasets can be partitioned into a size that can be efficiently managed on a group of processors. Partitioning the datasets into random, disjoint partitions will not only overcome the issue of exceeding memory size, but will also lead to creating diverse classifiers (each built from a disjoint partition, but the aggregate processing all of the data) [7]. This can result in an improvement in performance that might not be possible by subsampling.

To implement this idea, we divide the training set into n disjoint partitions, and then paste $Rvote^1$ or $Ivote^2$ respectively [4] on each of the disjoint subsets independently. We call our distributed approaches of pasting Ivotes and Rvotes $DIvote$ and $DRvote$ respectively. Breiman has shown that pasting together Ivotes gives accuracy comparable to Adaboost. Our experimental results with Ivote using C4.5 release 8 [18] agree with Breiman's results using CART. We also show that DIvote is comparable to Ivote for small or moderate datasets, while performing better for a large dataset. One major advantage of DIvote is a *significant reduction in training time as compared to Ivote*. We ran the distributed experiments on a 24-node Beowulf cluster, though DIvote and DRvote can be easily applied on a cluster of workstations. Each workstation could build classifiers on disjoint subsets of data at the same time.

2   Related Work

The machine learning community has generally addressed the problem of massive datasets by a "divide and conquer approach" — break a dataset into subsets, learn models on the subsets, and combine them. Chawla et al. [6] studied various partition strategies and found that an intelligent partitioning methodology — clustering — is generally better than simple random partitioning, and generally performs as well as C4.5 learning on the entire dataset. They also found that applying bagging to the disjoint partitions, and making an ensemble of many C4.5 decision trees, can yield better results than building a decision tree by applying C4.5 on the entire dataset.

Bagging, boosting, and their variants have been shown to improve classifier accuracy [9,3,1,8,12]. According to Breiman, bagging exploits the instability in the classifiers, since perturbing the training set produces different classifiers using the same algorithm. However, creating 30 or more bags of 100% size can be problematic for massive datasets [7]. We observed that for datasets too large to handle practically in the memory of a typical computer, a committee created

---

[1] In pasting Rvotes, each small training set is created by random sampling.

[2] In pasting Ivotes, each small training set is created by importance sampling.

using disjoint partitions can be expected to outperform a committee created using the same number and size of bootstrap aggregates ("bags"). Also, the performance of the committee of classifiers can be expected to exceed that of a single classifier built from all the data [7].

Boosting [9] also creates an ensemble of classifiers from a single dataset by looking at different training set representations of the same dataset, focusing on misclassified cases. Boosting is essentially a sequential procedure applicable to datasets small enough to fit in a computer's memory. Lazarevic and Obradovic proposed a distributed boosting algorithm to deal with massive datasets or very large distributed homogeneous datasets [13]. In their framework, classifiers are learned on each distributed site, and broadcast to every other site. The ensemble of classifiers constructed from each site is used to compute the hypothesis, $h_{j,t}$, at the jth site at iteration t. In addition, each site also broadcasts a vector comprising a sum of local weights, reflecting its prediction accuracy.

They achieved the same or slightly better prediction accuracy than standard boosting, and they also observed a reduction in the costs of learning and the memory requirements, for their datasets [13].

Our work is built on Breiman's pasting votes approach [4], which will be discussed further in the following sections.

3   Pasting Votes

Breiman proposed pasting votes to build many classifiers from small pieces or "bites" of data [4]. He proposed two strategies of pasting votes: Ivote and Rvote. Ivote sequentially generates datasets (and thus classifiers) by sampling, so each new train dataset has more instances that were more likely to be misclassified by the ensemble of classifiers already generated. In the Ivote approach, the small training set (bite) of each subsequent classifier relies on the combined hypothesis of the previous classifiers, and the sampling is done with replacement. The sampling probabilities rely on the out-of-bag error, that is, a classifier is only tested on the instances not belonging to its training set. This out-of-bag estimation gives good estimates of the generalization error [4], and is used to determine the number of iterations in the pasting votes procedure. Ivote is, thus, very similar to boosting, but the "bites" are much smaller in size than the original dataset. Rvote requires the creation of many bags of a very small size (bites), and is a fast and simple approach. Breiman found that Rvote was not competitive in accuracy with Ivote or Adaboost. The detailed algorithms behind both the approaches are presented in Section 4 as part of DIvote and DRvote.

Pasting Ivotes entails multiple random disk accesses, which could swamp the CPU times. So Breiman proposed an alternate scheme: a sequential pass through the dataset. In this scheme, an instance is read, and checked to see if it will make the training set for the next classifier in the aggregate. This is repeated in a sequential fashion until all N instances (size of a bite) are accumulated. The terminating condition for the algorithm is a specified number of trees or epochs, where an epoch is one sequential scan through the entire dataset. However, the sequential pass through the dataset approach led to a degradation in accuracy for a majority of the datasets used in the paper. Breiman also pointed out that this approach of sequentially reading instances from the disk will not work for highly skewed datasets. Thus, one important component of the power of pasting Ivotes is random sampling with replacement.

Breiman also noted that the approach of pasting Ivotes is scalable with memory. The memory requirement to keep track of which instance belongs in which small training set and the number of times the instance was given a particular class is $2JN_B$ bytes, where J is the number of classes and N_B is the number of instances in the entire dataset. The memory requirement for a dataset with 10^5 records and $J = 2$ will be close to a gigabyte; the only increase in the memory will be number of trees stored [4].

In our distributed approach pasting small votes, we divide a dataset into T disjoint subsets, and assign each disjoint subset to a different processor. On each of the disjoint partitions, we follow Breiman's approach of pasting small votes.

4   Pasting DIvotes and DRvotes

The procedure for DIvote is as follows:

1. Divide the dataset into T disjoint subsets.
2. Assign each disjoint subset to a unique processor.
3. On each processor build the first small training set of size N ("bite") by sampling with replacement from its subset, and learn a classifier.
4. For the subsequent bites on each of the processors, an instance is drawn at random from the resident subset of data with all examples having equal probability of selection [4]. If this instance is misclassified by a majority vote of the out-of-bag classifiers (those classifiers for which the instance was not in the training set), then it is selected for the subsequent bite. If not, then the instance is rejected with probability:

   $e(k) = p \times e(k - 1) + (1 - p) \times r(k)$

   $p = 0.75$. the same p value as used by Breiman,

   $k =$ number of classifiers in the aggregate or ensemble so far, and

   $r(k) =$ error rate of the kth aggregated classifiers on a T disjoint subset.

   Repeat until N instances have been selected for the bite.
5. Learn the $(k + 1)th$ classifier on the training set (bite) newly created by step 4.
6. Repeat steps 4 and 5, until the out-of-bag error estimate plateaus, or for a given number of iterations, to produce a desired number of classifiers.
7. After the desired number of classifiers have been learned, combine their predictions on the test data using a voting mechanism. We used simple majority voting.

Pasting DRvotes follows a procedure similar to DIvotes, the only difference being that each bite is a bootstrap replicate of size N. Each instance through all iterations has the same probability of being selected. DRvote is very fast, as no intermediate steps of DIvote — steps 4 and 5 in the above algorithm — are required. However, DRvote does not provide the accuracies achieved by DIvote.

Pasting DIvotes or DRvotes has the advantage of not requiring any communication between the processors, unlike the distributed boosting approach by Lazarevic and Obradovic [13]. Thus, there is no time lost in communication among processors. DIvote can essentially build thousands of trees fast, as on each processor (hundreds of) trees are built independently. Furthermore, dividing the dataset into smaller disjoint subsets can also mitigate the need for gigabyte memory servers. Also, if the disjoint subset size is small compared to the main memory on a computer, the entire dataset can be loaded in the memory and randomly accessed; thus, excessive random disk accesses can be avoided. DIvote reduces the data set size on each processor, hence less examples must be tested by the aggregate classifiers during training, which also significantly reduces the computational time.

5   Experiments

We evaluated DIvote and DRvote by experiments on three small datasets, which were also used by Breiman [4], and one large dataset. We did a 10-fold cross-validation for the small datasets. Since our large dataset has a non-homologous test set, we did not run a 10-fold CV. For the small datasets we set N, the size of each bite, to be 800 examples, while for the large dataset we varied the bite size from 1/256th, 1/128th, and 1/64th of the entire dataset size. For the distributed runs, we divided the smaller datasets into 4 disjoint partitions, and the large dataset into 24 disjoint partitions. We also ran experiments with pasting Ivotes and Rvotes to get a benchmark of sequential performance.

5.1   Datasets

Our three small datasets are from the UCI repository [2]. The large dataset comes from the problem of predicting the secondary structure of proteins. Its training and testing sets ("test set one") were used in developing and validating, respectively, a neural network that won the CASP-3 secondary structure prediction contest [11]. The size of these datasets is summarized in Table 1.

5.2   Base Classifier and Computing Systems

We used the C4.5 release 8 decision tree software for our experiments. The sequential Rvote and Ivote experiments were run on a 1.4 GHz Pentium 4 linux workstation with 2 GB of memory, and an 8-processor Sun-Fire-880 with 32 GB of main memory. We ran DIvote and DRvote experiments on a 24-node Beowulf cluster. Each node on the cluster has a 900 MHz Athlon processor and 512MB of memory. The cluster is connected with 100Bt ethernet.

Table 1. Dataset Sizes, Number of Classes and attributes.

Dataset	Dataset size	Classes	Number of attributes
Satimage	6435	6	36
Pendigits	10992	10	16
Letter	20000	26	16
Jones	Training = 209,529; Testing = 17,731	3	315

5.3   Prediction Accuracy Comparison

To statistically validate the results, we performed a two-tailed paired t-test ($\alpha = 0.05$) on the 10-fold cross validation results of the small datasets. Table 2 shows the confusion matrix for statistical significance comparison. We observed identical statistical significance for our experiments with Satimage and Pendigits, so we have combined the two results. The results are reported at the end of 250 iterations. For instance, consider the first row in Table 2. It shows that DIvote is the same as Ivote, but significantly better than any other approach. The letter dataset differed from Satimage and Pendigits, as DRvote and Rvote performed significantly worse than C4.5. However, for letter also, DIvote and Ivote were comparable, and significantly better than Rvote, DRvote, and C4.5. Figure 1(a) shows the results on letter dataset.

Table 2. Significance Confusion Matrix for Satimage and Pendigits. Same = Not statistically different classification accuracy. Better = Statistically higher classification accuracy.

	DIvote	Ivote	DRvote	Rvote	C4.5
DIvote		Same	Better	Better	Better
Ivote	Same		Better	Better	Better
DRvote	Worse	Worse		Same	Better

For the large dataset, pasting DIvotes is actually more accurate than pasting Ivotes. In addition to pasting DIvotes and Ivotes accuracies, Figure 2(b) also shows that pasting DIvotes produces a more accurate ensemble of classifiers than the ensemble constructed of classifiers learned on the 24 disjoint subsets. It is also interesting to note that the average accuracy of a decision tree learned on bites of size 1/256th of the Jones dataset is below 50%, and the aggregate of all the not-so-good classifiers gives a performance in the range of 66% to 70% for 50 or more learning iterations. Each of the individual DIvote classifiers optimizes the small decision space it is constructed on, so the end result is an ensemble of locally optimum classifiers. Thus, the combined hypothesis of this ensemble of hundreds or thousands of intelligently created classifiers achieves a high accuracy.

We conjecture that the bites (very small training sets) for DRvote are too similar to each other. Creating bites from the disjoint partitions, especially of small datasets, does not provide enough unique instances to each bite. Therefore, it is possible that even an aggregate of all bites is not a good representation of the training set, and the classifiers learned on these bites are not very diverse. For the letter dataset, DRvote and Rvote are significantly worse than C4.5. The letter dataset has 26 classes with 16 dimensions; each 800 sized bite will contain approximately 30 instances for each class. Thus, given the high dimensionality, the 30 examples may not mimic the real distribution of the dataset. To test this model, we created 100% bags on each disjoint partition [6] of the letter dataset, and found that the classification accuracy increased significantly as compared to DRvote or Rvote, but was still not better than DIvote and Ivote. This shows that 100% random bags are introducing more coverage, better individual classifiers, and diversity compared to the DRvote bites (800 instances). Since DIvote and Ivote sample heavily from misclassified instances, after each iteration or series of iterations they focus on different instances, thus creating more diverse classifiers with potentially more coverage.

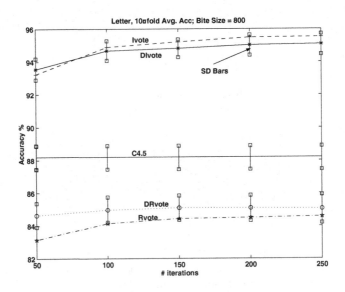

Fig. 1. Accuracy comparisons of DIvote, Ivote, Rvote, DRvote, and C4.5 for the Letter dataset

5.4 Timing

Table 3 show the timing (user and system time during training) ratios of DIvote to Ivote, and DRvote to Rvote on the Beowulf cluster. The experimental

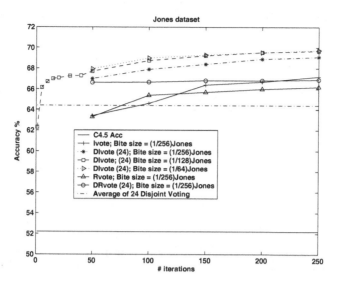

Fig. 2. Accuracy comparisons of DIvote, Ivote, Rvote, DRvote, and C4.5 for the Jones dataset

parameters were: number of iterations $= 100$; bite size $N = 800$ for the small datasets, and bite size $N = (1/256) * $ (Jones dataset size) for the Jones dataset. The time taken for DIvote and DRvote reflects the average of the time taken for 100 iterations on each of the T ($T = 4$ for the small datasets; $T = 24$ for the large dataset) nodes of the cluster. For fair timing comparisons to DRvote and DIvote, we also ran 100 iterations of Ivote and Rvote on a single cluster node. It is noteworthy that we are able to build $T*100$ DIvote classifiers simultaneously.

One significant advantage of the proposed DIvote approach is that it requires much less time than Ivote. Since we divide the original training set into T disjoint subsets, during training the aggregate DIvote classifiers on a processor test many fewer instances than aggregate Ivote classifiers (for the Jones dataset each disjoint partition has only 8730 instances as compared to 209,529 in the entire dataset). Also, a reduction in the training set size implies that the dataset can be more easily handled in main memory. The graphs show that as the dataset size increases, the ratio of DIvote time to Ivote time decreases, which suggests that the time taken for testing the aggregate classifiers, accumulating their votes, computing out-of-bag error, and intelligent sampling increases with dataset size. We would like to note that the same software performs DIvote and Ivote, except that for the distributed runs we wrote an MPI program to load our pasting votes software on different nodes of the cluster, and collect results. So, any further improvement of the software would be applicable across the board.

It is not surprising that the timings for DRvote and Rvote are very similar, as both the approaches essentially build many small bags from a given training set. Nevertheless, DRvote builds T times as many Rvote classifiers in less time.

Table 3. Ratio of time taken by DIvote to Ivote, and DRvote to Rvote, on a cluster node.

Dataset	DIvote/Ivote	DRvote/Rvote
Satimage	0.36	0.91
Pendigits	0.29	0.95
Letter	0.23	0.89
Jones	0.048	0.90

6   Conclusion

The overall conclusion of our work is that pasting DIvotes is a promising approach for very large datasets. Datasets too large to be handled practically in the memory of a typical computer are appropriately handled by simple partitioning into disjoint subsets, and adding another level of learning by pasting DIvotes or DRvotes on each of the disjoint subsets. Our experiments show that DIvote is a fast, accurate, and scalable framework. We show that pasting DIvotes is very comparable in classification accuracy to Ivotes on the small datasets, and is the best for the large dataset. Our results support the theory that given an ensemble of diverse classifiers, an improvement in the accuracy can be observed. Pasting DIvotes is much faster than pasting Ivotes; pasting DIvotes on a processor takes less time compared to pasting Ivotes on a processor. Each processor works independently, without requiring communication at any stage of learning; the end result is an ensemble of thousands of DIvote classifiers. DIvote is able to build a representative model of the dataset through this ensemble of hundreds or thousands of classifiers.

We also conclude that pasting DIvotes is more accurate than pasting DRvotes. We believe that the combined effects of diversity, good coverage, and importance sampling are helping DIvote and Ivote. We wish to understand this more completely, however, and some of our future work is devoted to experiments designed to separate and illustrate these effects.

The DIvote framework is naturally applicable to the scenario in which datasets for a problem are already distributed. At each of the distributed sites multiple classifiers can be built, and the only communication required is the learned classifiers at the end of training. A section of our future work is also devoted to experiments on the ASCI Red supercomputer [19].

Acknowledgments

This work was supported in part by the United States Department of Energy through the Sandia National Laboratories LDRD program and ASCI VIEWS Data Discovery Program, contract number DE-AC04-76DO00789, and the National Science Foundation under grant EIA-0130768.

References

1. Bauer, E., Kohavi, R.: An empirical comparison of voting classification algorithms: Bagging, boosting, and variants. *Machine Learning*, Vol 36, 105 – 139. Kluwer (1999).
2. Blake, C.L., Merz, C.J.: UCI Repository of machine learning databases. *http://www.ics.uci.edu/~mlearn/MLRepository.html*, University of California, Irvine, Dept. of Information and Computer Sciences (1998).
3. Breiman, L. Bagging predictors. *Machine Learning*, Vol 24. Kluwer (1996) 123 – 140.
4. Breiman, L.: Pasting small votes for classification in large databases and on-line. *Machine Learning*, Vol 36. Kluwer (1999) 85–103.
5. Chan, P., Stolfo, S.: Towards parallel and distributed learning by meta-learning. *AAAI Workshop on Knowledge Discovery and Databases.* (1993) 227 – 240.
6. Chawla, N., Eschrich, S., Hall, L.O.; Creating ensembles of classifiers. *First IEEE International Conference on Data Mining.* (2000).
7. Chawla, N.V., Moore, T.E., Bowyer, K.W., Hall, L.O., Springer, C., Kegelmeyer, W.P.: Bagging is a small dataset phenomenon. *International Conference of Computer Vision and Pattern Recognition (CVPR).* (2000) 684 – 689.
8. Dietterich, T.: An experimental comparison of three methods for constructing ensembles of decision trees: Bagging, boosting, and randomization. *Machine Learning*, Vol 40. Kluwer (2000) 139 – 158.
9. Freund, Y., Schapire, R.: Experiments with a new boosting algorithm. *Thirteenth International Conference on Machine Learning.* (1996).
10. Hall, L.O., Chawla, N.V., Bowyer, K.W., Kegelmeyer, W.P.: Learning rules from distributed data. *Workshop of Fifth ACM SIGKDD International Conference on Knowledge Discovery and Data Mining.* (1999).
11. Jones, D.: Protein secondary structure prediction based on decision-specific scoring matrices. *Journal of Molecular Biology*, Vol 292. (1999) 195 – 202.
12. Latinne, P., Debeir, O., Decaestecker, C.: Different ways of weakening decision trees and their impact on classification accuracy of DT combination. *First International Workshop on Multiple Classifier Systems.* Lecture Notes in Computer Science, Vol 1857. Springer-Verlag, (2000) 200 – 210.
13. Lazarevic, A., Obradovic, Z.: The distributed boosting algorithm. *Seventh ACM SIGKDD International Conference on Knowledge Discovery and Data Mining,* (2000).
14. Musick, R., Catlett, J., Russell, S.. Decision theoretic subsampling for induction on large databases. *Tenth International Conference on Machine Learning*, Amherst, MA. (1993) 212 – 219.
15. Provost, F.J., Hennessy D.N.: Scaling up: Distributed machine learning with cooperation. *Thirteenth National Conference on Artificial Intelligence.* (1996) 74 – 79.
16. Protein Data Bank. *http://www.rcsb.org/pdb/*
17. Provost, F., Jensen D., Oates, T.: Efficient progressive sampling. *Sixth ACM SIGKDD International Conference on Knowledge Discovery and Data Mining.* (1999) 23 – 32.
18. Quinlan, J.R.: C4.5: Programs for machine learning. Morgan Kaufman San Mateo, CA (1992).
19. Sandia National Labs.: ASCI RED, the world's first TeraFLOPS supercomputer. *http://www.sandia.gov/ASCI/Red.*
20. *Seventh ACM SIGKDD International Conference on Knowledge Discovery and Data Mining.* http://www.acm.org/sigkdd/kdd2001/ (2001).

Bagging and Boosting for the Nearest Mean Classifier: Effects of Sample Size on Diversity and Accuracy

Marina Skurichina[1], Liudmila I. Kuncheva[2] and Robert P.W. Duin[1]

[1] Pattern Recognition Group, Department of Applied Physics, Faculty of Applied Sciences, Delft University of Technology, P.O. Box 5046, 2600GA Delft, The Netherlands
{marina,duin}@ph.tn.tudelft.nl
[2] School of Informatics, University of Wales, Bangor, Gwynedd, LL57 1UT, United Kingdom
l.i.kuncheva@bangor.ac.uk

Abstract. In combining classifiers, it is believed that diverse ensembles perform better than non-diverse ones. In order to test this hypothesis, we study the accuracy and diversity of ensembles obtained in bagging and boosting applied to the nearest mean classifier. In our simulation study we consider two diversity measures: the Q statistic and the disagreement measure. The experiments, carried out on four data sets have shown that both diversity and the accuracy of the ensembles depend on the training sample size. With exception of very small training sample sizes, both bagging and boosting are more useful when ensembles consist of diverse classifiers. However, in boosting the relationship between diversity and the efficiency of ensembles is much stronger than in bagging.

1   Introduction

Some pattern recognition problems cannot be solved by a single classification rule. This happens when the data distribution is very complex or/and data are high dimensional, having small training sample sizes compared to the data dimensionality [1]. In this case, the combined decision of the ensemble of classifiers can be used in order to improve the performance of a single classification rule [2]. However, it is still quite unclear what classifiers the ensemble should consist of in order to be the most effective. An intuitively desirable characteristic of a classifier team is diversity (orthogonality, complementarity, independence etc.) [2, 3]. Theoretically, combining independent classifiers by majority voting will outperform the single classifier. Combining dependent classifiers may be either better or worse than the single classification rule [4]. Therefore, diverse ensembles seem to have a better potential for improving the accuracy than non-diverse ensembles.

In this paper we intend to test this hypothesis on bagging [5] and boosting [6] applied to the Nearest Mean Classifier (NMC) [7]. We choose these combining techniques for our study because they show a good performance on various data sets [8, 9, 10] and provide useful algorithms for constructing ensembles of classifiers. The NMC is chosen for its simplicity, and because both bagging and boosting have been found to be successful for this linear classifier [11]. The performance and the stability of the combined decision in bagging and boosting, applied to linear classifiers, strongly depend on the training sample size [11]. Therefore, in this paper we will study the relationship between accuracy and diversity of ensembles in bagging and boosting with respect to the training sample size.

F. Roli and J. Kittler (Eds.): MCS 2002, LNCS 2364, pp. 62-71, 2002.
© Springer-Verlag Berlin Heidelberg 2002

The paper is organized in the following way. Section 2 shortly describes bagging and boosting. The two diversity measures used are introduced in section 3. The data sets and the experimental setup are described in section 4. The results of our simulation study are discussed in section 5. Conclusions are summarized in section 6.

2   Combining Techniques

Bagging and boosting are ensemble design techniques that allow us to improve the performance of weak classifiers. Originally, they were designed for decision trees [5, 6]. However, they were found to perform well for other classification rules: neural networks [12], linear classifiers [11] and k-nearest neighbour classifiers [5]. It was shown that for linear classifiers, the performance of bagging and boosting is affected by the training sample size, the choice of the base classifier and the choice of the combining rule [11]. Bagging is useful for linear classifiers constructed on critical training sample sizes, i.e., when the number of training objects is about the data dimensionality. On the other hand, boosting is effective for low-complexity classifiers constructed on large training sample sizes [11, 13]. Both bagging and boosting modify the training data set, build classifiers on these modified training sets and then combine them into a final decision. Usually the simple majority voting is used to get a final decision. However, the weighted majority voting used in boosting [6] is preferable because it is more resistant to overtraining than other combining rules when increasing the number B of combined classifiers [14]. Therefore, we use the weighted majority vote in both studied combining techniques.

Bagging is proposed by Breiman [5] and based on bootstrapping [15] and aggregating concepts thereby benefiting from both approaches. Bootstrapping is based on random sampling with replacement. We take B bootstrap replicates $X^b = (X_1^b, X_2^b, ..., X_n^b)$ of the training set $X = (X_1, X_2, ..., X_n)$ and build a classifier on each of them. *Aggregating* actually means combining the classifiers. Often a combined classifier gives better results than individual classifiers. In bagging, bootstrapping and aggregating techniques are implemented in the following way.

1. Repeat for $b = 1, 2, ..., B$.
   a) Take a bootstrap replicate X^b of the training data set X.
   b) Construct a classifier $C^b(x)$ on X^b with a decision boundary $C^b(x) = 0$ [1].
   c) Compute combining weights $c_b = \frac{1}{2}\log\left(\frac{1 - err_b}{err_b}\right)$, where $err_b = \frac{1}{n}\sum_{i=1}^{n} w_i^b \xi_i^b$
   and $\xi_i^b = \begin{cases} 0, & \text{if } X_i \text{ is classified correctly} \\ 1, & \text{otherwise} \end{cases}$.
2. Combine classifiers $C^b(x)$, $b = 1, ..., B$, by the weighted majority vote with weights c_b to a final decision rule $\beta(x) = \begin{cases} +1, & \text{if } \sum_b c_b \text{sgn}(C^b(x)) > 0 \\ -1, & \text{otherwise} \end{cases}$.

Boosting, proposed by Freund and Schapire [6], is another technique to combine weak classifiers having a poor performance in order to get a classification rule with a better performance. In boosting, classifiers and training sets are obtained in a strictly *deterministic* way. Both, training data sets and classifiers are obtained

---

[1] We note that both bagging and boosting were originally defined for two classes. The class labels for the objects are therefore encoded as -1 and +1, with $C^b(x) = 0$ being the decision boundary.

sequentially in contrast to bagging, where training sets and classifiers are obtained *randomly* and *independently* (in parallel) from the previous step of the algorithm. At each step of boosting, training data are reweighted in such a way that incorrectly classified objects get larger weights in a new, modified training set. By that, one actually maximizes the margins of the training objects (the distance of the training object to the decision boundary). By this, boosting is similar Vapnik's Support Vector Classifier (SVC) [16]. However, in boosting, margins are maximized locally for each training object, while in the support vector classifier, global optimization is performed.

In this study, boosting is organized in the following way. It is based on the "arc-fs" algorithm described by Breiman [17], where we reweight the training set instead of resample it. The "arc-fs" algorithm is the improved version of the standard AdaBoost algorithm [13]. Additionally, we set initial weight values w_i^1, $i = 1, ..., n$, to 1 instead of $1/n$, in order to be independent of data normalization. Therefore, boosting is implemented by us as follows.

1. Repeat for $b = 1, ..., B$.

   a) Construct a base classifier $C_b(x)$ (with a decision boundary $C_b(x)=0$) on the weighted version $X^* = (w_1^b X_1, w_2^b X_2, ..., w_n^b X_n)$ of training data set $X = (X_1, X_2, ..., X_n)$, using weights w_i^b, $i = 1, ..., n$ (all $w_i^b = 1$ for $b = 1$).

   b) Compute combining weights $c_b = \frac{1}{2}\log\left(\frac{1 - err_b}{err_b}\right)$, where $err_b = \frac{1}{n}\sum_{i=1}^{n} w_i^b \xi_i^b$ and $\xi_i^b = \begin{cases} 0, if \ X_i \ is \ classified \ correctly \\ 1, otherwise \end{cases}$.

   c) If $0 < err_b < 0.5$, set $w_i^{b+1} = w_i^b \exp(c_b \xi_i^b)$, $i = 1, ..., n$, and renormalize so that $\sum_{i=1}^{n} w_i^{b+1} = n$. Otherwise, restart the algorithm with weights $w_i^b = 1$, $i = 1, ..., n$.

2. Combine base classifiers $C_b(x)$, $b = 1, ..., B$, by the weighted majority vote with weights c_b to a final decision rule $\beta(x) = \begin{cases} +1, & if \ \sum_b c_b \operatorname{sgn}(C^b(x)) > 0 \\ -1, & otherwise \end{cases}$.

3   Diversity Measures

Different diversity measures are introduced in the literature [18]. In our study, we consider the Q statistic and the disagreement measure.

The Q statistic is the pairwise symmetrical measure of diversity proposed by Yule [19]. For two classifiers C_i and C_j, Q statistic is defined as

$$Q_{ij} = \frac{ad - bc}{ad + bc},$$

where
a is the probability that both classifiers C_i and C_j make the correct classification,
b is the probability that the classifier C_i is correct and the classifier C_j is wrong,
c is the probability that the classifier C_i is wrong and the classifier C_j is correct,
d is the probability that both classifiers C_i and C_j are wrong,
and $a + b + c + d = 1$.

For a set of B classifiers, the averaged statistic Q of all pairs (C_i, C_j) is calculated. Q varies between -1 and 1. For statistically independent classifiers, it is 0. So, the higher the absolute value of Q the less diverse the team of classifiers (denoted $\downarrow$).

The disagreement measure (used in [20, 21]) is defined as

$$D_{ij} = b + c \quad .$$

It is also a pairwise symmetrical measure of diversity. For a set of B classifiers, the averaged statistics D of all pairs is calculated. The higher the value of D the more diverse the team of classifiers (denoted $\uparrow$).

4   Data

In our experimental investigations we considered one artificial and three real data sets representing two-class problems.

The artificial data set, called the *80-dimensional Gaussian correlated data*, was chosen for the many redundant features. The set consists of two classes with equal covariance matrices. Each class is constituted by 500 vectors. The mean of the first class is zero for all features. The mean of the second class is equal to 3 for the first two features and equal to 0 for all other features. The common covariance matrix is diagonal with a variance of 40 for the second feature and unit variance for all other features. This data set is rotated in the subspace spanned by the first two features using a rotation matrix $\begin{bmatrix} 1 & -1 \\ 1 & 1 \end{bmatrix}$. The intrinsic class overlap, found by Monte Carlo experiments (an estimate of the Bayes error) is 0.07.

The three real data sets are taken from the UCI Repository [22]. They are the 8-dimensional *pima-diabetes* data set, the 34-dimensional *ionosphere* data set and the 60-dimensional *sonar* data set.

Training sets are chosen randomly and the remaining data are used for testing. All experiments are repeated 50 times on independent training sets. So all the figures below show the averaged results over 50 repetitions. The standard deviations of the mean generalization errors for the single and combined decisions are around 0.01 for each data set.

For both bagging and boosting, we choose $B=250$ classifiers. As explained earlier, the classifiers were combined by the weighted majority voting to reach a final decision.

5   Diversity and Accuracy of Ensembles in Bagging and Boosting

Let us now consider the accuracy and diversity of ensembles in bagging and boosting when the combining techniques are applied to the nearest mean classifier. It has been shown [11] that the performance of bagging and boosting is affected by the training sample size. This is nicely demonstrated by Fig. 1, 2a,b and 3a,b. Bagging is mainly useful for critical training sample sizes when the number of training objects is comparable with the data dimensionality. Boosting performs best for large training sample sizes. Fig. 2c-f and 3c-f show that diversity of classifiers in the ensembles obtained by bagging and boosting also depends on the training sample size.

In bagging, the classifiers are constructed on bootstrap replicates of the training set. Bootstrapping is most effective when the training sample size is smaller or comparable with the data dimensionality. In this case, one obtains bootstrap replicates with the most dissimilar statistical characteristics. Classifiers constructed on such bootstrap replicates will be also diverse. When the training sample size increases, bootstrapping the training set becomes less effective. Bootstrap replicates of large and very large training sets have similar statistical characteristics, because such training sets represent the real data distribution well and perturbations in their composition barely affect these characteristics. Classifiers constructed on such bootstrap replicates are also similar. Thus, *in bagging, classifiers in the ensemble become less diverse when the number of training objects increases.*

In boosting, the training set is modified in such a way that training objects incorrectly classified at the previous step get larger weights in a new, modified training set. The larger the training set, the higher the number of borderline objects. Consequently, larger training sets are more sensitive than smaller ones to changes in the discriminant function (see example in Fig. 4). In large training sets, more training objects can be classified differently even after a small change in the discriminant function. Consequently, at each step of boosting, more changes in weights for training objects occur. By this, we obtain more diverse training sets and, therefore, more diverse classifiers for large training sample sizes. So, *in boosting, diversity of classifiers in the ensemble increases with an increase in the training sample size.*

Before studying the relationship between accuracy and diversity in bagging and boosting, let us note that the accuracy of the ensemble always depends on the training sample size. Usually the accuracy of statistical classifiers increases with an increase in the number of training objects. Therefore, combining classifiers of a higher accuracy (obtained on larger training sets) may also result in a better combined decision (with a higher accuracy) than when worse performing classifiers (obtained on smaller training sets) are combined. By this, increasing the training sample size, ensembles may perform better whatever the diversity of the ensemble is. As an illustration of this phenomenon let us consider the sonar data set, where bagging is inefficient, i.e., does not improve on the single classifier (see Fig. 3b). We observe, however, that the accuracy of bagging

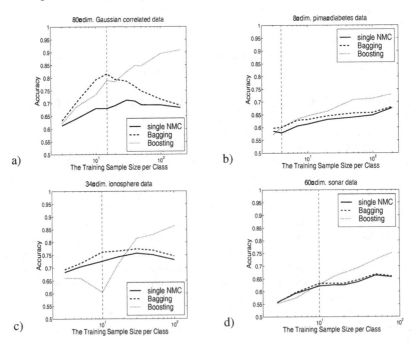

Fig. 1. The accuracy of the single NMC, bagging and boosting applied to the NMC versus the training sample size for the Gaussian correlated, pima-diabetes, ionosphere and sonar datasets.

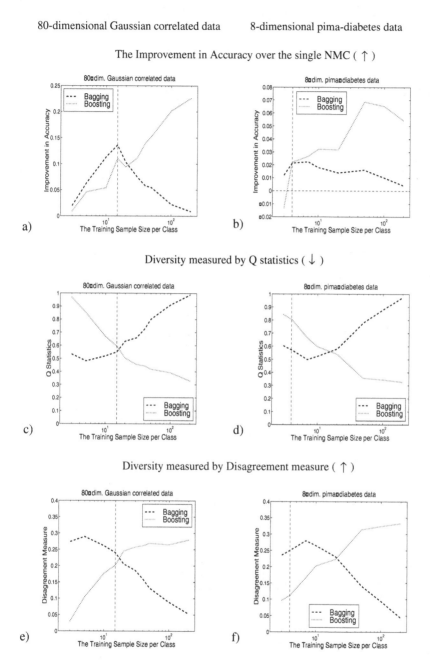

Fig. 2. The efficiency (the improvement in accuracy over the single NMC) and diversity of ensembles (with the NMC as the base classifier) in bagging and boosting versus the training sample size for the 80-dimensional Gaussian correlated data and the 8-dimensional pima-diabetes data (↑ - the larger the better, ↓ - the smaller the better).

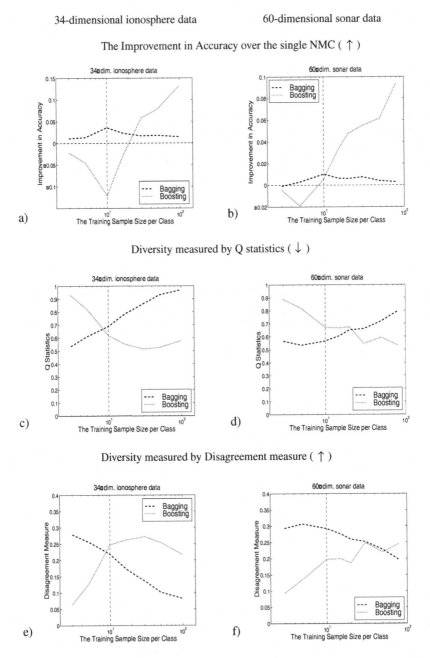

Fig. 3. The efficiency (the improvement in accuracy over the single NMC) and diversity of ensembles (with the NMC as the base classifier) in bagging and boosting versus the training sample size for the 34-dimensional ionosphere data and the 60-dimensional sonar data (↑ - the larger the better, ↓ - the smaller the better).

(see Fig. 1d) increases with an increase in the number of training objects, because the accuracy of the base classifier increases when the number of training objects becomes larger. Boosting also improves when increasing the training sample size. Diversity of the ensembles obtained in bagging and boosting gives us a different insight into the problem (see Fig. 3d,f). We are interested in how the diversity of the ensembles affects the usefulness of the combining techniques. Thus, in our study, instead of studying the accuracy of the combining techniques with respect to diversity of the ensembles, we consider the relationship between the improvement over the performance of the single classifier. The plots in Fig. 2 and 3 help us assess this relationship by eye.

Both diversity and the usefulness of the combining techniques depend on the training sample size. When the training sample size is very small (much smaller than the data dimensionality), the training set is usually non-representative. Modifications by sampling or reweighting of a small and inadequate data set hardly ever give a better representation of the real data distribution. As a result, inaccurate classifiers are obtained all the way through bagging or boosting [1]. Combining these classifiers, be they diverse or non-diverse, is meaningless (see Fig. 1, 2a,b and 3a,b). Therefore, we will exclude very small training sample sizes from our study. Below we discuss only training sample sizes that are not very small: approximately larger than 10 training objects per class for the 80-dimensional Gaussian correlated, the 34 dimensional ionosphere and the 60-dimensional sonar data sets and larger than 4 training objects per class for the 8-dimensional pima-diabetes data set.

Let us now consider diversity of ensembles in bagging and boosting and the efficiency of these combining techniques. Fig. 2 and 3 show that, with exception of very small training sample sizes, *bagging and boosting are more useful (they give a larger improvement over the performance of the single classifier) when they construct diverse ensembles.* When increasing the training sample size, both the efficiency of bagging and diversity of ensembles constructed by bagging decrease. Bagging constructs more diverse ensembles and, therefore, is more useful for the Gaussian correlated and the

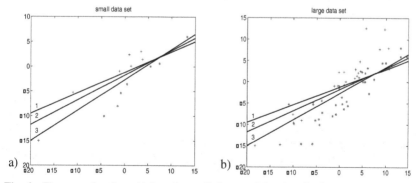

Fig. 4. The example of sensitivity of a small data set (plot a) and a large data set (plot b) to changes in the discriminant function. The classification of the small data set is robust: when the discriminant function changes from 1 to 3, the classification of the data set remains the same. The large training set is more sensitive: when discriminant function changes from 1 to 3, bordeline objects are classified differently. In boosting, when the training set is small (plot a), at each step (1, 2 and 3) the same 2 objects get large weights in a new, modified data set. When the training set is large (plot b), different training objects get large weights at steps 1, 2 and 3. By this, in boosting, we obtain more diverse training sets when the training set is large than when it is small.

pima-diabetes data sets (see Fig. 2) than for the ionosphere data set (see Fig. 3a,c,e). However, the usefulness of bagging does not depend only on diversity of the ensemble. The quality of the constructed base classifier in solving a problem is also important. The sonar data set has a complex data distribution with a non-linear boundary between data classes. Bagging constructs quite diverse classifiers on this data set, but it is not useful (see Fig. 3b,d,f). Boosting constructs more diverse classifiers and becomes more useful when the training sample size increases. Boosting has an advantage to bagging, because by overweighting the borderline objects it constructs classifiers focused on the neighbourhood of a border between data classes. When increasing the training sample size, the border between data classes becomes better defined, which is why boosting constructs more diverse classifiers. Thus, boosting of linear classifiers can be useful even when solving complex problems like in the sonar data set (see Fig, 3b).

As it was mentioned before, the efficiency of the combining techniques depends not only on the diversity of the constructed ensemble but also on the "quality" of the obtained classifiers. Boosting takes special care about the "quality" of classifiers: they are constructed to account for the important regions of the data space, these around the border between classes. Bagging does not take such special care and, therefore, is less efficient for the type of problems considered here. Thus, *in boosting, the relationship between the efficiency and diversity of classifiers is much stronger than in bagging.*

6   Conclusions

In this paper we have studied the relationship between diversity of ensembles in bagging and boosting and the efficiency of these combining techniques applied to the NMC. The accuracy of the ensembles has been obtained by the weighted majority voting. The efficiency of the combining techniques has been measured by the difference between the accuracy of the combined classifier and the accuracy of the single classifier. In our study we have considered two diversity measures: the Q-statistic and the disagreement measure. The simulation study performed on four data sets has shown the following.

Diversity of ensembles in bagging and boosting is affected by the training sample size. In bagging, diversity of ensembles decreases with an increase in the number of training objects. In boosting, the classifiers in the ensemble become more diverse, when the number of training objects increases.

With exception of very small training sample sizes, both bagging and boosting perform better when classifiers in the ensemble are diverse. However, for boosting, the correlation between the efficiency and diversity of ensembles is much stronger than for bagging, because in boosting special care is taken about constructing the classifiers in regions around the borders between data classes.

As the efficiency of the combining techniques is correlated with diversity (especially for boosting), diversity might be useful as a possible criterion for predicting a potential efficiency of the ensemble, for selecting a proper combining rule to aggregate classifiers in the ensemble, or as a stopping criterion against overtraining in bagging and/or boosting.

Acknowledgment

This work is supported by the Dutch Technology Foundation (STW).

References

1. Jain, A.K., Chandrasekaran, B.: Dimensionality and Sample Size Considerations in Pattern Recognition Practice. In: Krishnaiah, P.R., Kanal, L.N. (eds.): Handbook of Statistics, Vol. 2. North-Holland, Amsterdam (1987) 835-855
2. Lam, L.: Classifier Combinations: Implementations and Theoretical Issues. In: Kittler, J., Roli, F. (eds.): Multiple Classifier Systems (Proc. of the First Int. Workshop MCS, Cagliari, Italy). Lecture Notes in Computer Science, Vol. 1857, Springer-Verlag, Berlin (2000) 78-86
3. Cunningham, P., Carney, J.: Diversity versus Quality in Classification Ensembles Based on Feature Selection. Tech. Report TCD-CS-2000-02, Dept. of Computer Science, Trinity College, Dublin (2000)
4. Kuncheva, L.I., Whitaker, C.J., Shipp, C.A., Duin, R.P.W.: Is Independence Good for Combining Classifiers? In: Proc. of the 15th Int. Conference on Pattern Recognition, Vol. 2, Barcelona, Spain (2000) 169-171
5. Breiman, L.: Bagging predictors. In: Machine Learning Journal 24(2) (1996) 123-140
6. Freund, Y., Schapire, R.E.: Experiments with a New Boosting Algorithm. In: Machine Learning: Proc. of the 13th Int. Conference (1996) 148-156
7. Fukunaga, K.: Introduction to Statistical Pattern Recognition. Academic Press (1990) 400-407
8. Bauer, E., Kohavi, R.: An Empirical Comparison of Voting Classification Algorithms: Bagging, Boosting, and Variants. In: Machine Learning 36 (1999) 105-142
9. Dietterich, T.G.: Ensemble Methods in Machine Learning. In: Kittler, J., Roli, F. (eds.): Multiple Classifier Systems (Proc. of the First Int. Workshop MCS, Cagliari, Italy). Lecture Notes in Computer Science, Vol. 1857, Springer-Verlag, Berlin (2000) 1-15
10. Quinlan, J.R.: Bagging, Boosting, and C4.5. In: Proc. of the 14th National Conference on Artificial Intelligence (1996)
11. Skurichina, M.: Stabilizing Weak Classifiers. PhD thesis, Delft University of Technology, Delft, The Netherlands (2001)
12. Avnimelech, R., Intrator, N.: Boosting Regression Estimators. In: Neural Computation 11 (1999) 499-520
13. Freund, Y., Schapire, R.E.: A Decision-Theoretic Generalization of On-line Learning and an Application to Boosting. In: Journal of Computer and System Sciences 55(1) (1997) 119-139
14. Skurichina, M., Duin, R.P.W.: The Role of Combining Rules in Bagging and Boosting. In: Ferri, F.J., Inesta, J.M., Amin, A., Pudil, P. (eds.): Advances in Pattern Recognition (Proc. of the Joint Int. Workshops SSPR and SPR, Alicante, Spain). Lecture Notes in Computer Science, Vol. 1876, Springer-Verlag, Berlin (2000) 631-640
15. Efron, B., Tibshirani, R.: An Introduction to the Bootstrap. Chapman&Hall, New York (1993)
16. Cortes, C., Vapnik, V.: Support Vector Networks. In: Machine Learning 20 (1995) 273-297
17. Breiman, L.: Arcing Classifiers. In: Annals of Statistics 26(3) (1998) 801-849
18. Kuncheva, L.I., Whitaker, C.J.: Measures of Diversity in Classifier Ensembles (submitted)
19. Yule, G.U.: On the Association of Attributes in Statistics. In: Phil. Transactions A(194) (1900) 257-319
20. Ho, T.K.: The Random Subspace Method for Constructing Decision Forests. In: IEEE Transactions on Pattern Analysis and Machine Intelligence 20(8) (1998) 832-844
21. Skalak, D.B.: The Sources of Increased Accuracy for Two Proposed Boosting Algorithms. In: Proc. of American Association for Artificial Intelligence, AAAI-96, Integrating Multiple Learned Models Workshop (1996)
22. Blake, C.L., Merz, C.J.: UCI Repository of Machine Learning Databases [http://www.ics.uci.edu/~mlearn/MLRepository.html]. Irvine, CA: University of California, Department of Information and Computer Science (1998)

Highlighting Hard Patterns
via AdaBoost Weights Evolution

Bruno Caprile, Cesare Furlanello, and Stefano Merler

ITC-irst,
38050 Trento, Italy
{caprile,furlan,merler}@itc.it
http://mpa.itc.it

Abstract. The dynamical evolution of weights in the AdaBoost algorithm contains useful information about the rôle that the associated data points play in the built of the AdaBoost model. In particular, the dynamics induces a bipartition of the data set into two (easy/hard) classes. Easy points are ininfluential in the making of the model, while the varying relevance of hard points can be gauged in terms of an entropy value associated to their evolution. Smooth approximations of entropy highlight regions where classification is most uncertain. Promising results are obtained when methods proposed are applied in the Optimal Sampling framework.

1   Introduction

Since the time it was first proposed, the AdaBoost algorithm [1] has been the subject of extensive investigations – either theoretical [2, 3, 4] and empirical [5, 6]. Various authors have focused on the margin maximization properties of the algorithm, and on its capability of discovering relevant training patterns [7]. In this context, Rätsch et al. [8] have shown how certain training patterns exist that asymptotically have the same (large) margin; these consistently match with the Support Vectors as found by a Support Vector Machine [9].

In this paper, we investigate the dynamics of weights associated to sample points as resulting from application of the AdaBoost algorithm. More specifically, it is argued that such dynamics contains relevant information for highlighting training points and regions of uncertain classification. While a subset of training points can be identified whose weights tend to zero, empirical evidence exist that the weights associated to the remaining points do not tend to any asymptotic value. For the latter, however, the cumulative distribution over boosting iterations is asymptotically stable. These two types of weight dynamics lead to the notion of "easy" and "hard" points in terms of an associated entropy measure – the easy points being those having very low entropy values.

In this framework, we can thus answer questions as: do easy point play any role in building the AdaBoost model? For hard points, can different degrees of "hardness" be identified which account for different degrees of classification

F. Roli and J. Kittler (Eds.): MCS 2002, LNCS 2364, pp. 72–80, 2002.

uncertainty? Do easy/hard points show any preference about where to concentrate? The first two questions are clearly connected to equivalent results in the framework of Support Vector Machines. These issues have been around for some time in the Machine Learning community; here we propose a method to address them which is based on the analysis of the weight histograms.

In the second part of this paper, the smooth approximation (by kernel regression) of the weight entropy at training data is employed as an indicator function of classification uncertainty, thereby obtaining a region highlighting methodology. As an application, a strategy for optimal sampling in classification tasks was implemented: as compared to uniform random sampling, the entropy-based strategy is clearly more effective. Moreover, it compares favorably with an alternative margin-based sampling strategy.

2   The Dynamics of Weights

In the present section, the dynamics that the AdaBoost algorithm sets over the weights is singled out for study. In particular, the intuition is substantiated that the evolution of weights yields information about the varying relevance that different data points have in the built of the AdaBoost model.

Let $D \equiv \{\mathbf{x}_i, y_i\}_{i=1}^N$ be a two-class set of data points, where the $\mathbf{x}_i$s belong to a suitable region, X, of some (metric) feature space, and y_i takes values in $\{1, -1\}$, for $1 \leq i \leq N$. The AdaBoost algorithm iteratively builds a class membership estimator over X as a thresholded linear superposition of different realizations, M_k, of a same base model, M. Any model instance, M_k, resulting from training at step k depends on the values taken at the same step by a set of N numbers (in the following, the *weights*), $\mathbf{w} = w_1, \ldots w_N$ – one for each data point. After training, weights are updated: those associated to points misclassified by the current model instance are increased, while decreased are those for which the associated point is classified correctly. An interesting variant of this basic scheme consists in training the different realizations of the base model, not on the whole data set, but on Bootstrap replicates of it [5]. In this second scheme, samplings are extracted according to the discrete probability distribution defined by the weights associated to data points, normalized to sum one.

In Fig. 1a the plots are reported of the evolution of the weights associated to 3 data points when the AdaBoost algorithm is applied to a simple binary classification task on synthetic two-dimensional data (experiment A-Gaussians as described in Sec. A.1). Classification trees are used as base classifiers for AdaBoost in this paper. Except for occasional bursts, the weight associated to the first point goes rapidly to zero, while the weights associated to the second and third point keep on going up and down in a seemingly chaotic fashion. Our experience is that these two types of behaviour are not specific of the case under consideration, but can be observed in any AdaBoost experiment. Moreover, *tertium non datur*, i.e., no other qualitative behaviour is observed (as, for example, that some weight tends to a strictly positive value).

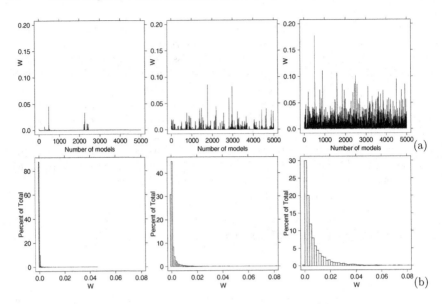

Fig. 1. *Evolution of weights in the AdaBoost algorithm. (a) The evolutions over 5000 steps of the AdaBoost algorithm are reported for the weights associated to 3 data points of experiment* **A-Gaussians**. *From left to right: an "easy" data point (the weight tends to zero), and two "hard" data points (the weight follows a seemingly random pattern). (b) The corresponding frequency histograms.*

2.1   Easy Vs. Hard Data Points

The hypothesis therefore emerges that the AdaBoost algorithm sets a partition of data points into two classes: on one side the points whose weight tends rapidly to zero; on the other, the points whose weights show an apparently chaotic behaviour. In fact, the hypothesis is perfectly consistent with the rationale underlying the AdaBoost algorithm: weights associated to those data points that several model instances classify correctly even when they are *not* contained in the training sample follow the first kind of behaviour. In practice independently of which bootstrap sample is extracted, these points are classified correctly, and their weight is consequently decreased and decreased. We call them the "easy" points. The second type of behaviour is followed by the points that, when not contained in the training set, happen to be often misclassified. A series of misclassifications makes the weight associated with any such point increase, thereby increasing the probability for the point to be contained in the following bootstrap sample. As the probability increases and the point is finally extracted (and classified correctly), its weight is decreased; this in turn makes the point less likely to be extracted – and so forth. We call this kind of points "hard".

In Fig. 1b, histograms are reported of the values that the weights associated to the same 3 data points of Fig. 1a take over the same 5000 iterations of the AdaBoost algorithm. As expected, the histogram of (easy) point 1 is very much squeezed towards zero (more than 80% of weights lies below 10^{-6}). Histograms of (hard) points 2 and 3 exhibit the same Gamma-like shape, but differ remarkably for what concerns average and dispersion. Naturally, the first question is whether any limit exists for these distributions. For each data point, two unbinned cumulative distributions were therefore built by taking the weights generated by the first 3000 steps of the AdaBoost algorithm, and those generated over the whole 5000 steps. The same-distribution hypothesis was then tested by means of the Kolmogorov-Smirnov (KS) test [10]. Results are reported in Fig. 2a, where p-values are plotted against the mean value of all 5000 values. It is interesting to notice that for mean values close to 0 (easy points) the same-distribution hypothesis is always rejected, while it is typically not-rejected for higher values (hard points). It seems that easy points may be confidently identified by simply considering the average of their weight distribution. A binary LDA classifier was therefore trained on the data of Fig. 2a. By setting a p-value threshold equal to 0.05, the resulting *precision* (the complement to 1 of the fraction of false negative) was equal to 0.79 and *recall* (the complement to 1 of the fraction of false positive) was equal to 0.96.

2.2   Entropy

Can we do any better at separating easy points from hard ones? For hard points, can different degrees of "hardness" be identified which account for different degrees of classification uncertainty? What we are going to show is that by associating a notion of *entropy* to the evolutions of weights both questions can be answered in the positive. To this end, the interval $[0, 1]$ is partitioned into L subintervals of length $1/L$, and the entropy value is computed as $\sum_{i=1}^{L} f_i \, log_2 f_i$, where f_i is the relative frequency of weight values falling in the i-th subinterval ($0 \, log_2 0$ is set to 0). For our cases, L was set to 1000.

Qualitatively, the relationship between entropy and p-values of the KS test is similar to the one holding for the mean (Fig. 2a-b). Quantitatively, however, a difference is observed, since the LDA classifier trained on these data performs much better in precision and slightly worse in recall (respectively, 0.99 and 0.90, as compared to 0.79 and 0.96). This implies that the class of easy points can be identified with higher confidence by using the entropy in place of the mean value of the distribution. Further support to the hypothesis of a bipartite (easy/hard) nature of data points is gained by observing the frequency histogram of entropies for the 400 points of experiment A-Gaussians (Fig. 2c), from which two groups of data points emerge as clearly separated. The first is the zero entropy group of easy points, and the second is the group of hard points.

Do easy/hard points show any preference about where to concentrate? In Fig. 3a hard and easy points are shown as determined for the experiment A-Sin (see Sec. A.1 for details). Hard points are mostly found nearby the two-class boundary; yet, their density is much lower along the straight segment of the boundary

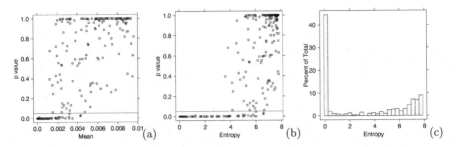

Fig. 2. *Separating easy form hard points. (a) p-values of the KS test Vs. mean values of frequency histograms. (b) p-values of the KS test Vs. entropy of frequency histograms. As in (a), the horizontal line marks the threshold value for the LDA classifier. (c) Histogram of entropy values for the 400 data points of experiment* A-Gaussians.

(where the boundary is smoother), and appear therefore to concentrate where the classification uncertainty is highest. Easy points to the opposite. Considering that easy points stay well clear of the boundary (i.e., hard points typically interpose between them and the boundary), what one may then question is whether they play any rôle in the built of the AdaBoost model. The answer is no. In fact, the models built disregarding the easy points are practically the same as the models built on the complete data set. In the experiment of Fig. 3 only the 0.55% of 10000 test points were classified differently by the two models, as contrasted to reduction of the training set from 400 to only 111 (hard) points.

2.3 Smoothing the Entropy

In the previous section, the entropy of the weight frequency histogram was introduced as an indicator of the uncertainty of classifying the associated data point as belonging to class -1 or 1. By defining a smooth approximation to the punctual entropy values associated to data points, we now extend the notion of classification uncertainty to the whole domain of our binary classifier. For simplicity sake, kernel regression was employed – i.e., the entropy values at data points are convolved with a Gaussian kernel of fixed bandwidth [11]. In so doing, a scalar entropy function, $H = H(\mathbf{x})$, is defined on A. In Fig. 3b, the grey levels encode the values of H (increasing from black to white) for the experiment A-Sin.

The method appears capable of highlighting regions where classification turns out uncertain – due to the distribution of data points, the morphology of the class boundary or both. Of course, function H depends on the geometric properties specific of the base model adopted, and its degree of smoothness depends on the size of the convolution kernel. It should be noticed, however, that the bias/variance balance can be controlled by suitably tuning the convolution parameters. Finally, more sophisticated local smoothing techniques may be em-

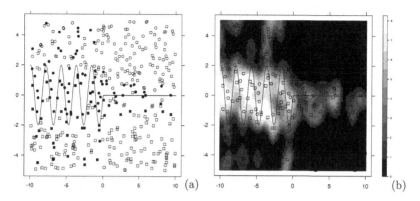

Fig. 3. *(a) Easy (white) and hard (black) data points of experiment A-Sin obtained by thresholding the histogram of entropy. Squares and circlets express the class. (b) Level-plot of the H function. Grey levels encode H values (see scale on the right).*

ployed as well (e.g., Radial Basis Functions) which may adapt to directionality, known morphology of the boundary or local density of sample points.

3   An Application to Optimal Sampling

To illustrate the applicability of notions developed above to practical cases, we refer to the framework of optimal sampling [12]. In general, an optimal sampling problem is one in which a *cost* is associated to the acquisition of data points, in such a way that solving the problem consists not only in minimizing the classification (or regression) error but also in keeping the sampling cost as low as possible. In a typical setting for this class of problems we start from an assigned set of (sparse) data points, and we then incrementally add points to the training set on the basis of certain information extracted from intermediate results.

For the experiments reported below, which are based on the same settings as Sin and Spiral of Sec. A.1 (see also Sec. A.2 for details), we started from a small set of sparse two-dimensional binary classification data. High-uncertainty areas are identified by means of the method described in Sec. 2.3, and additional training points are chosen in these areas. Assuming a unitary cost for each new point, performance of the procedure is finally evaluated by analyzing the sampling cost against the classification error.

In Fig. 4, two plots are reported of the classification error as a function of the number of training points. Comparison is made with a blind (randomly uniform) sampling strategy, and with a specialization of *uncertainty sampling strategy* as recently proposed in [13]. The latter consists in adding training points where the

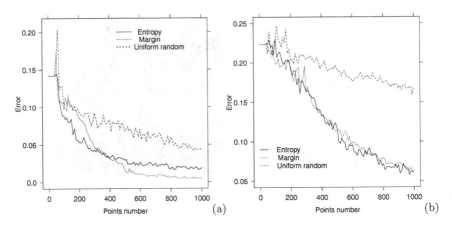

Fig. 4. *Misclassification error as a function of the number of training points for the entropy based scheme is compared to the uniform random sampling and the margin sampling strategy. (a) Experiment* B-Sin. *(b) Experiment* B-Spiral.

classifier is less certain of class membership. In particular, the classifier was the AdaBoost model and the uncertainty indicator was the margin of the prediction.

Results reported in Fig. 4 show that in both experiments the entropy sampling method holds a definite advantage on the random sampling strategy. In the first experiment, an initial advantage of entropy over the margin based sampling is also observed, but the margin strategy takes over as the number of samplings goes beyond 400. It should be noticed, however, that the margin sampling automatically adapts its spatial scale to the increased density of sampling points, while our entropy method does not (the size of the convolution kernel is fixed). In fact, in the experiment B-Spiral (Fig. 4b) where the boundary has a more complex structure and the convolution kernel has a smaller size, 1000 samplings are not sufficient for the margin based method to exhibit an advantage on the entropy method (but the latter loses the initial advantage exhibited in the first experiment).

4 Final Comments

Within the many possible interpretations of learning by boosting, it is promising to create diagnostic indicator functions alternative to margins [2] by tracing the dynamics of boosting weights for individual points. We have used entropy (in the punctual and then smoothed versions) as a descriptor of classification uncertainty, identifying easy and hard points, and designing a specific optimal sampling strategy. The strategy needs to be further automated: for example, adaptive selection of smoothing parameters may be implemented as a function of spatial variability. A direct numerical relationship with the weights of Support

Vector expansions is also clearly needed. On the other hand, it would be also interesting to associate the main types of weight dynamics (or point hardness) to the regularity of the boundary surface and of the noise structure.

Acknowledgment

The authors thank G. Jurman for careful proof reading and comments.

References

[1] Y. Freund and R. E. Schapire, "A Decision-theoretic Generalization of Online Learning and an Application to Boosting," *Journal of Computer and System Sciences*, vol. 55, pp. 119–139, August 1997.

[2] R. E. Schapire, Y. Freund, P. Bartlett, and W. S. Lee, "Boosting the Margin: A New Explanation for the Effectiveness of Voting Methods," *The Annals of Statistics*, vol. 26, no. 5, pp. 1651–1686, 1998.

[3] J. Friedman, T. Hastie, and R. Tibshirani, "Additive logistic regression: a statistical view of boosting," *The Annals of Statistics*, 2000.

[4] R. E. Schapire, "The boosting approach to machine learning: An overview," in *MSRI Workshop on Nonlinear Estimation and Classification*, 2002.

[5] J. Quinlan, "Bagging, Boosting, and C4.5," in *Thirteenth National Conference on Artificial Intelligence*, (Cambridge), pp. 163–175, AAAI Press/MIT Press, 1996.

[6] T. G. Dietterich, "An experimental comparison of three methods for constructing ensembles of decision trees: Bagging, boosting, and randomization," *Machine Learning*, vol. 40, no. 2, pp. 139–157, 2000.

[7] A. J. Grove and D. Schuurmans, "Boosting in the limit: Maximizing the margin of learned ensembles," in *AAAI/IAAI*, pp. 692–699, 1998.

[8] G. Rätsch, T. Onoda, and K. Müller, "Soft margins for Adaboost," *Machine Learning*, vol. 42, pp. 287–320, 2001.

[9] V. Vapnik, *The nature of statistical learning theory*. Statistics for Engineering and Information Science, Springer Verlag, 2000.

[10] W. H. Press, S. A. Teukolsky, W. T. Vetterling, and B. P. Flannery, *Numerical Recipes in C – The Art of Scientific Computing*. Cambridge University Press, second ed., 1992.

[11] W. Härdle, *Applied Nonparametric Regression*, vol. 19 of *Econometric Society Monographs*. Cambridge University Press, 1990.

[12] V. Fedorov, *Theory of Optimal Experiments*. Academic Press, New York, 1972.

[13] D. D. Lewis and J. Catlett, "Heterogeneous Uncertainty Sampling for Supervised Learning," in *Eleventh International Conference on Machine Learning* (Cohen and Hirsh, eds.), (San Francisco), pp. 148–156, Morgan Kaufmann, 1994.

[14] Y. Raviv and N. Intrator, "Variance Reduction via Noise and Bias Constraints.," in *Combining Artificial Neural Nets: Ensemble and Modular Multi-Net Systems* (A. Sharkey, ed.), (London), pp. 163–175, Springer-Verlag, 1999.

A   Data

Details are given on the data employed in experiments of Sec. 2 and 3. Full details and data are accessible at http://mpa.itc.it/mcs-2002/data/.

A.1   Experiment A

Gaussians: 4 sets of points (100 points each) were generated by sampling 4 two-dimensional Gaussian distributions, respectively centered in $(-1.0, 0.5)$, $(0.0, -0.5)$, $(0.0, 0.5)$ and $(1.0, -0.5)$. Covariance matrices were diagonal for all the 4 distributions; variance was constant and equal to 0.4. Points coming from the sampling of the first two Gaussians were labelled with class -1; the others with class 1.

Sin: The box in R^2, $R \equiv [-10, 10] \times [-5, 5]$, was partitioned into two class regions R_1 (upper) and R_{-1} (lower) by means of the curve, C of parametric equations:

$$C \equiv \begin{cases} x(t) = t \\ y(t) = 2sin(3t) \text{ if } -10 \le t \le 0; 0 \text{ if } 0 \le t \le 10. \end{cases}$$

400 two-dimensional data were generated by randomly sampling region R, and labelled with either -1 or 1 according to whether they belonged to R_{-1} or R_1.

Spiral: As in the previous case, the idea was to have a bipartition of a rectangular subset, S, of R^2 presenting fairly complex boundaries ($S \equiv [-5, 5] \times [-5, 5]$). Taking inspiration from [14], a spiral shaped boundary was defined. 400 two-dimensional data were then generated by randomly sampling region S, and were labelled with either -1 or 1 according to whether they belonged to one or the other of the two class regions.

A.2   Experiment B

This group of data was generated in support to the optimal sampling experiments described in Sec. 3. More specifically, two initial data sets, each containing 40 points, were generated for both the Sin and Spiral settings by employing the same procedures as above. At each round of the optimal sampling procedure, 10 new data points were generated by uniformly sampling a suitable, high entropy subregion of the domain. Data points were then labelled according to their belonging to one or the other of the two class regions.

Using Diversity with Three Variants of Boosting: Aggressive, Conservative, and Inverse

Ludmila I. Kuncheva and Christopher J. Whitaker

School of Informatics, University of Wales, Bangor
Bangor, Gwynedd, LL57 1UT, United Kingdom
{l.i.kuncheva,c.j.whitaker}@bangor.ac.uk

Abstract. We look at three variants of the boosting algorithm called here Aggressive Boosting, Conservative Boosting and Inverse Boosting. We associate the diversity measure Q with the accuracy during the progressive development of the ensembles, in the hope of being able to detect the point of "paralysis" of the training, if any. Three data sets are used: the artificial Cone-Torus data and the UCI Pima Indian Diabetes data and the Phoneme data. We run each of the three Boosting variants with two base classifier models: the quadratic classifier and a multi-layer perceptron (MLP) neural network. The three variants show different behavior, favoring in most cases the Conservative Boosting.[1]

1 Introduction

Boosting algorithms are amongst the most popular methods for constructing classifier ensembles [5,3,1,13]. They build the ensemble incrementally, placing increasing weights on those objects in the data set, which appear to be "difficult". The presumption is that this introduces diversity into the ensemble, and therefore enhances the performance. It has been found however, that boosting might get "paralyzed" in the sense that adding more classifiers does not lead to further improvement of the performance [17] and the ensemble testing error might start to increase again.

In this study we are interested in how the diversity of the ensemble progresses when new classifiers are added, one at a time, and how the pattern of diversity is related to the training and testing errors. Section 2 introduces the concept of diversity in classifier ensemble and the Q measure of diversity. In Section 3, three variants of ADAboost (with resampling) are described: Aggressive Boosting, Conservative Boosting and Inverse Boosting. Section 4 gives an illustration of the relationship between the three methods on the one hand, and the measure of diversity Q on the other hand.

2 Diversity in Classifier Ensembles

Several authors have pointed out the importance of diversity for the success of classifier ensembles [11,2,7,6,16,12]. So far there is no diversity measure accepted

---

[1] © Springer-Verlag

F. Roli and J. Kittler (Eds.): MCS 2002, LNCS 2364, pp. 81–90, 2002.
© Springer-Verlag Berlin Heidelberg 2002

by consensus, perhaps owing to the lack of a clear-cut relationship between the measures of diversity and the accuracy of the ensemble [10, 14]. Our previous studies led us to the choice of the Q statistic for measuring diversity [9]. The calculation of Q [18] is based on a pairwise table for each pair of classifiers in the ensemble.

Let $\mathcal{D} = \{D_1, \ldots, D_L\}$ be the ensemble, built on the data set Z, such that $D_i : \Re^n \to \Omega$ for $\mathbf{x} \in \Re^n$. For each classifier D_i, we record whether it correctly classifies $\mathbf{z}_j$ (the label it produces matches the true label) or not. Consider two classifiers D_i and D_k, and a 2×2 table of probabilities that summarizes their combined outputs as in Table 1.

Table 1. The 2×2 relationship table with probabilities

	D_k correct (1)	D_k wrong (0)
D_i correct (1)	a	b
D_i wrong (0)	c	d

$$Q_{i,k} = \frac{ad - bc}{ad + bc}. \qquad (1)$$

Total, $a + b + c + d = 1$

Many pairwise statistics have been proposed as measures of similarity in the numerical taxonomy literature (e.g., [15]). The Q statistic is designed for categorical data with the same intuition as the correlation coefficient for continuous-values data. It is calculated from Table 1 as shown.

For independent D_i and D_k, $Q_{i,k} = 0$. Since independence is important in classifier combination, although not necessarily the best scenario [10], the zero value of Q is a practical target to strive for. We have found that negative values of Q are even better but such ensembles are unlikely to be developed. If we calculate the correlation coefficient between the values 0 (incorrect) and 1 (correct), using the distribution in Table 1, the resultant formula will have the same numerator as Q and a positive (but more cumbersome to calculate) denominator. As with Q, the correlation coefficient will give a value 0 for independence. For none of the other 9 diversity measures researched by us, is there any fixed value for independence [9].

3   The Three Boosting Variants

The general boosting idea is to develop the classifier team $\mathcal{D}$ incrementally, adding one classifier at a time. The classifier that joins the ensemble at step k is trained on a data set selectively sampled from the training data set Z. The sampling distribution starts from uniform, and progresses towards increasing the likelihood of "difficult" data points. Thus the distribution is updated at each step, increasing the likelihood of the objects misclassified by the classifier at step $k - 1$. The basic algorithm implementing this idea is shown in Figure 1. We use the data set $Z = \{\mathbf{z}_1, \ldots, \mathbf{z}_N\}$ to construct and ensemble of L classifiers.

1. Initialize all coefficients as $W_1(i) = \frac{1}{N}$, $i = 1, \ldots, N$. We start with an empty classifier ensemble $\mathcal{D} = \emptyset$ and initialize the iterate counter $k = 1$.
2. For $k = 1, \ldots, L$

   2.1. Take a sample S_k from Z using distribution W_k.
   2.2. Build a classifier D_k using S_k as the training set.
   2.3. Calculate the weighted ensemble error at step k by

$$\epsilon_k = \sum_{i=1}^{N} W_k(i)(1 - y_{i,k}), \qquad (2)$$

   where $y_{i,k} = 1$, if D_k correctly recognizes $z_i \in Z$, and $y_{i,k} = 0$, otherwise. If $\epsilon_k = 0$ or $\epsilon_k \geq 0.5$, the weights $W_k(i)$ are reinitialized to $\frac{1}{N}$.
   2.4. Next we calculate the coefficient

$$\beta_k = \sqrt{\frac{1 - \epsilon_k}{\epsilon_k}}, \quad \epsilon_k \in (0, 0.5), \qquad (3)$$

   to be used in the weighted voting, and subsequently update the individual weights

$$W_{k+1}(i) = \frac{W_k(i)\beta_k^{\xi(y_{i,k})}}{\sum_{j=1}^{N} W_k(j)\beta_k^{\xi(y_{j,k})}}, \quad i = 1, \ldots, N. \qquad (4)$$

   where $\xi(y_{i,k})$ is a function which specifies which of the three Boosting variants we use.

End k.
3. The final decision for a new object $\mathbf{x}$ is made by weighted voting between the L classifiers. First, all classifiers give labels for $\mathbf{x}$ and then for all D_k that gave label ω_t, we calculate the support for that class by

$$\mu_t(\mathbf{x}) = \sum_{D_k(\mathbf{x}) = \omega_t} \ln(\beta_k). \qquad (5)$$

The class with the maximal support is chosen for $\mathbf{x}$.

Fig. 1. A general description of the Boosting algorithm for classifier ensemble design

The three variants of Boosting are as follows:

1. Aggressive Boosting. In this version, the weights for the incorrectly classified objects are increased *and* the weights of the correctly classified objects are decreased at the same step k. Note that even if we do not decrease the weights of the correctly classified objects, they will be decreased anyway by the normalization step. This will happen because we have increased some of the $W_k(i)$'s, and for the sum to be 1, all the remaining weights must go down. The adjective "aggressive" expresses the fact that we force this difference even further. For this case, $\xi(y_{i,k}) = 1 - 2y_{i,k}$. Aggressive Boosting is the versions of ADAboost in [4, 13].

2. Conservative Boosting. Here the weights are changed only in one direction: either the weights of the correctly classified objects are decreased, as for example in [1], *or* the weights of the misclassified objects are increased, e.g. [5]. For the latter case, we use $\xi(y_{i,k}) = 1 - y_{i,k}$.

3. Inverse Boosting. This variant is similar to the "hedge" algorithm described in [5]. The philosophy is completely opposite to that of Boosting. Instead of increasing the likelihood of the "difficult" objects, we decrease it, thereby gradually filtering them out. Thus the classifiers will tend to be more and more similar, eliminating any diversity in the process. The idea for this inverse boosting originated by a missprint (we believe) in [5] by which it turns out that the weights of the misclassified objects were actually decreased. We were curious to see whether the opposite strategy lead anywhere, so we brought this variant into the study as well. For the inverse boosting, $\xi(y_{i,k}) = y_{i,k} - 1$.

In a way, variants 1 and 3 are the two extremes, and 2 is a softer version of 1. Note that although all three variants appear in the literature, no particular distinction has been made between them, most of the time all being called AdaBoost.

4   Experiments

The two data sets used are the Cone-torus data[2], and the Pima Indian Diabetes data set from the UCI Machine Learning Repository[3]

Figure 2 (left) displays the averaged results from 10 runs of the three variants on the Cone-Torus data, using quadratic discriminant classifiers as the base classifiers. The training and testing accuracies are plotted versus the number of the classifiers, as they are added one at a time. Underneath each of these plots, the training and testing diversity Q is shown. On the right in Figure 2 are the point likelihoods found through the three Boosting variants. The light gray color corresponds to the higher likelihood.

The following observations can be made

- The three methods give different performance patterns. The Aggressive Boosting shows overtraining after $L = 13$ while the other two methods gradually decrease both training and testing errors in a close correspondence between the two.
- Training and testing diversities are approximately identical for all three methods and have minima indicating a good place to stop the training. In this example, an early stopping is especially important for the Aggressive Boosting because of the overtraining. The Q has a characteristic 'tic'-shape,

---

[2] available at http://www.bangor.ac.uk/~mas00a/Z.txt and Zte.txt, for more experimental results see [8]

[3] available at http://www.ics.uci.edu/~mlearn/MLRepository.html

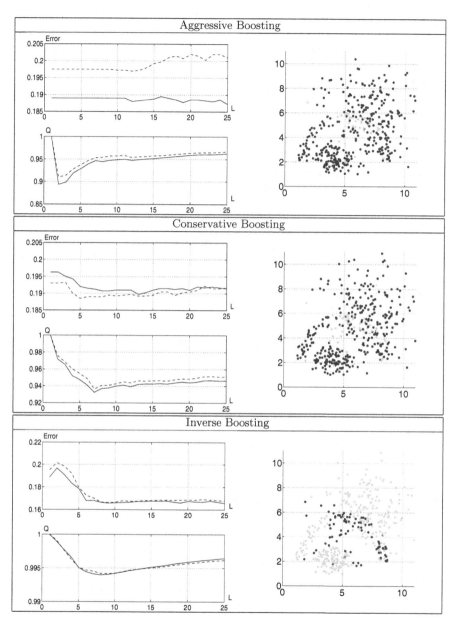

Fig. 2. Results from the three variants of ADAboost and the Cone-Torus data. On the left, for each variant, we show: *top plots*: The training error rate (solid line) and testing error rate (dashed line); *bottom plots*: The training Q (solid line) and the testing Q (dashed line). The corresponding point likelihoods are plotted on the right. Light gray points have highest weights (highest likelihood).

showing that there is a small L for which the classifiers are most diverse, and with L increasing the ensemble loses this diversity.

- For this particular example, "proper" Boosting was not the most successful ensemble building strategy. Inverse Boosting gave better results (lower error rates), although not much lower than the starting error rate.
- As could be expected, the Aggressive and the Conservative Boosting concentrate on the boundary points (see the scatterplots), and the Inverse Boosting does the opposite.
- Note the large difference between the Q values. Even though all training and testing curves had minima, judging by the absolute values of Q, the diversity for the Inverse Boosting is nonexistent. Still, the minimum, however shallow it is, indicates a reasonable place to stop the training.

It is curious to find out how the methods compare to each other in terms of both diversity and performance. We plotted the improvement on the single classifier (the starting classifier for $\mathcal{D}$) versus the diversity Q. To study the differences in the performances we used two basic classifier models: the quadratic discriminant classifier, and an MLP neural network with one hidden layer consisting of 15 nodes. For each classifier, the training was performed for 300 epochs using the fast backpropagation algorithm from the Matlab Neural Network Toolbox. Ten random splits of the data into halves were used for training and for testing, respectively, and the results were averaged. We used $L = 25$ as the final number of classifiers. The figures in the rest of this paper show results on unseen testing data only. Within this set-up, we have four combinations: 2 data sets × 2 base classifier models. The three Boosting methods for the four cases are plotted in Figure 3. The successive points for k from 1 to 25 are joined by lines. The y-axis in all figures show the testing accuracy minus the accuracy of the first classifier. Thus all ensembles started from $Q=1$, and zero improvement.

The plots prompt the following comments:

1. The patterns of performance are not consistent: there is no "best" Boosting variant amongst the three. Of course we can rate the performances noticing that the Inverse Boosting was only beneficial for the Cone-Torus data with quadratic classifiers where the other two methods were useless there. However, this looks more like a fluke than a serious finding. The improvement is not matched in the Pima Indian data plot for boosting quadratic classifiers. In fact, the performance declines after the first few "healthier" classifiers are added to the team, and purifying the training data further only harms the overall accuracy. From all three Boosting variants, perhaps the Conservative Boosting has the best overall performance, managing some improvement in all cases, notably better than the other two on the Pima Indian data plot with quadratic classifiers.

2. Looking at the scales of the two plots for the quadratic classifier and these for the MLP, there is a dramatic difference in the improvement on the single best classifier. While boosting quadratic classifiers leaves us with maximum 1.5 to 3 % improvement, when we combine neural network classifiers, the improvement goes up to 15 %. This confirms the results found by others that boosting makes

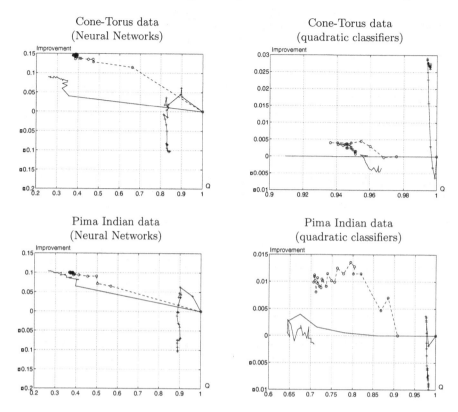

Fig. 3. Plots of improvement versus diversity Q for the two base classifier models and the two data sets. The solid line with the dots corresponds to the Aggressive Boosting, the dashed line with the circles corresponds to the Conservative boosting, and the solid line with the pluses corresponds to the Inverse Boosting.

sense for "capable" classifiers such as neural networks, whereby the possible overtraining is compensated for.

3. Diversity Q is not always a good indicator of the performance. For example, the lowest Q (highest diversity) will fail to detect the highest improvement for the Inverse Boosting (see Figure 3) in all cases except the Cone-Torus data and the quadratic base classifier. Even for that case Q is not too indicative. If we stopped at the lowest Q for the Pima Indian data and the quadratic classifiers, we would have missed the best improvement on all three Boosting methods. However, when the ensembles consist of neural networks, and the improvement is significant, stopping at the lowest Q will lead to the highest improvement both with the Aggressive Boosting and the Conservative Boosting. Notice also that the span of the diversity is much wider than for boosting quadratic classifiers. This indicates that while the relationship between diversity and accuracy might

be blurred when Q spans a short interval of values, when a large improvement on the accuracy is possible, the relationship between diversity and accuracy might become more prominent.

To examine our findings for different sizes of the training data we used the *Phoneme dataset* from UCI. Three training sizes were considered: small, $N = 80$, medium, $N = 350$, and large, $N = 1000$. Ten experiments were carried out with randomly dividing the data set into training and testing. The results are displayed on six Q-error plots in Figure 4 using the same line style as before.

The previous findings were confirmed and we also note that with the Phoneme data Aggressive Boosting gave the most diverse classifiers but Conservative Boosting managed to reach lower testing errors with less diverse classifiers. This suggests that Aggressive Boosting overemphasizes diversity which might result in ensembles with diverse but poor individual members. Conservative Boosting seemed to find a better compromise. The plots also show that Inverse Boosting leads the ensemble in the wrong direction of increasing the testing accuracy. The values of Q were approximately 1, indicating almost identical classifiers. Curiously, we did not find big differences for the different sample sizes with the NN classifiers. The patterns with the small data sets indicated that Aggressive and Conservative Boosting drive the testing error down for both classifier models whereas for larger data sets, the quadratic classifier behaves erratically. The reason for this is probably the fact that for small data sets, the quadratic classifier is no longer "stable". In other words, adding or removing a few data points will cause a sufficient change in the estimates of the covariance matrices to "destabilize" the quadratic classifier thereby making it suitable for boosting. The downside however is that such classifiers might not be accurate enough and therefore the total accuracy of the ensemble might suffer.

5   Conclusions

In this study we distinguish between three models of Boosting: Aggressive, Conservative and Inverse. We use an example of two data sets and two base classifier models to relate diversity in the ensemble and the improvement on the single classifier accuracy. Our results show that this relationship can be useful when the base classifier is flexible, leading to ensembles of high diversity albeit with possible overtraining of the individual members. Figure 2 suggests that the minimum Q identifies a sensible number of classifiers to include in the ensemble. However, paralysis was not induced in our experiments with the neural network classifiers, which are commonly accepted to be one of the more suitable models for Boosting. Therefore we were unable to confirm that Q identifies where paralysis begins. We also found that the Inverse Boosting quickly leads to a decline in the ensemble accuracy, emphasizing again the benefits of trying to produce diverse ensembles. The Conservative Boosting, which can be thought of as a softer alternative of the Aggressive Boosting exhibited better performance than the other two, and we therefore recommend it for practice.

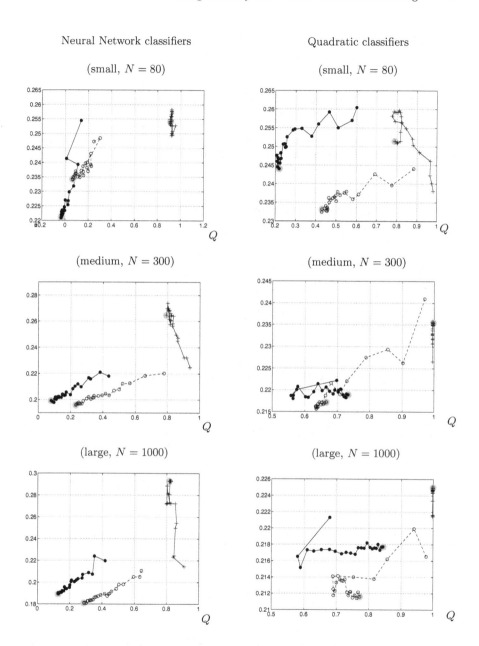

Fig. 4. Plots of error versus diversity Q for the two base classifier models and three sample sizes for the Phoneme data. The gray dot shows the stopping point.

References

[1] E. Bauer and R. Kohavi. An empirical comparison of voting classification algorithms: Bagging, boosting, and variants. *Machine Learning*, 36:105–142, 1999.

[2] P. Cunningham and J. Carney. Diversity versus quality in classification ensembles based on feature selection. Technical Report TCD-CS-2000-02, Department of Computer Science, Trinity College Dublin, 2000.

[3] T.G. Dietterich. Ensemble methods in machine learning. In J. Kittler and F. Roli, editors, *Multiple Classifier Systems*, volume 1857 of *Lecture Notes in Computer Science*, pages 1–15, Cagliari, Italy, 2000. Springer.

[4] R.O. Duda, P.E. Hart, and D.G. Stork. *Pattern Classification*. John Wiley & Sons, NY, second edition, 2001.

[5] Y. Freund and R.E. Schapire. A decision-theoretic generalization of on-line learning and an application to boosting. *Journal of Computer and System Sciences*, 55(1):119–139, 1997.

[6] S. Hashem, B. Schmeiser, and Y. Yih. Optimal linear combinations of neural networks: an overview. In *IEEE International Conference on Neural Networks*, pages 1507–1512, Orlando, Florida, 1994.

[7] A. Krogh and J. Vedelsby. Neural network ensembles, cross validation and active learning. In G. Tesauro, D.S. Touretzky, and T.K. Leen, editors, *Advances in Neural Information Processing Systems*, volume 7, pages 231–238. MIT Press, Cambridge, MA, 1995.

[8] L.I. Kuncheva. *Fuzzy Classifier Design*. Studies in Fuzziness and Soft Computing. Springer Verlag, Heidelberg, 2000.

[9] L.I. Kuncheva and C.J. Whitaker. Ten measures of diversity in classifier ensembles: limits for two classifiers. In *Proc. IEE Workshop on Intelligent Sensor Processing*, pages 10/1–10/6, Birmingham, February 2001. IEE.

[10] L.I. Kuncheva, C.J. Whitaker, C.A. Shipp, and R.P.W. Duin. Is independence good for combining classifiers? In *Proc. 15th International Conference on Pattern Recognition*, volume 2, pages 169–171, Barcelona, Spain, 2000.

[11] L. Lam. Classifier combinations: implementations and theoretical issues. In J. Kittler and F. Roli, editors, *Multiple Classifier Systems*, volume 1857 of *Lecture Notes in Computer Science*, pages 78–86, Cagliari, Italy, 2000. Springer.

[12] B.E. Rosen. Ensemble learning using decorrelated neural networks. *Connection Science*, 8(3/4):373–383, 1996.

[13] R.E. Schapire. Theoretical views of boosting. In *Proc. 4th European Conference on Computational Learning Theory*, pages 1–10, 1999.

[14] C.A. Shipp and L.I. Kuncheva. Relationships between combination methods and measures of diversity in combining classifiers. *Information Fusion*. (accepted).

[15] P.H.A. Sneath and R.R. Sokal. *Numerical Taxonomy*. W.H. Freeman & Co, 1973.

[16] K. Tumer and J. Ghosh. Error correlation and error reduction in ensemble classifiers. *Connection Science*, 8(3/4):385–404, 1996.

[17] J. Wickramaratna, S. Holden, and B. Buxton. Performance degradation in boosting. In J. Kittler and F. Roli, editors, *Proc. Second International Workshop on Multiple Classifier Systems*, volume 2096 of *Lecture Notes in Computer Science*, pages 11–21, Cambridge, UK, 2001. Springer-Verlag.

[18] G.U. Yule. On the association of attributes in statistics. *Phil. Trans.*, A, 194:257–319, 1900.

Multistage Neural Network Ensembles

Shuang Yang[1], Antony Browne[1], and Philip D. Picton[2]

[1] School of Computing, Information Systems and Mathematics, London Guildhall
University, London EC3N 1JY, UK
Tel: (+44) 0207 320 1705, Fax: (+44) 0207 320 1707
syang@lgu.ac.uk
[2] School of Technology and Design, University College Northampton,
Northampton NN2 6JD, UK

Abstract. Neural network ensembles (some times referred to as committees or classifier ensembles) are effective techniques to improve the generalization of a neural network system. Combining a set of neural network classifiers whose error distributions are diverse can lead to generating more accurate results than any single network. Combination strategies commonly used in ensembles include simple averaging, weighted averaging, majority voting and ranking. However, each method has its limitations, dependent either on the application areas it is suited to, or due to its effectiveness. This paper proposes a new ensembles combination scheme called multistage neural network ensembles. Experimental investigations based on multistage neural network ensembles are presented, and the benefit of using this approach as an additional combination method in ensembles is demonstrated.

1 Introduction

Combining the outputs of diverse classifiers can lead to an improved result [1, 2]. Common ensemble combination strategies include simple averaging [8, 9], weighted averaging [10], majority voting [11], and ranking [12,13].

There are no unique criteria on the usage of all the above combination methods. The choice mainly depends on the nature of the application the ensemble is being used for, the size and quality of training data, or generated errors on different regions of the input space. One combination method applied on the ensemble of a regression problem may generate good results, but may not work on a classification problem and vice versa. In addition, different classifiers will have an influence on the selection of the appropriate combination method. However, empirical experiments reported to date cannot find an optimal method for selecting the combination strategy to be used. More theoretical development and experiments are needed to explore in this field. The ensemble combination technique most related to the work reported in this paper is stacking, as the new model outlined here inherits some ideas from stacking and develops them further. In this paper, we will propose a new model for ensemble combination method based on another neural network layer.

F. Roli and J. Kittler (Eds.): MCS 2002, LNCS 2364, pp. 91–97, 2002.

1.1 Stacking

Stacking [6] covers two areas of ensemble construction: preparing data and ensemble combination. Generally, stacking deals with two issues. Firstly, it uses the idea of cross-validation to select training data for ensemble members. Secondly, it explores the notion of using the second level generalizers to combine the results of the first level generalizers (ensemble members). A feature of stacked generalization is that the information supplied to the first-level ensemble members comes from multiple partitioning of the original dataset, which divides that dataset into two subsets. Every ensemble member is trained by one part of the partitions, and the rest of parts are used to generate the outputs of the ensemble members (to be used as the second space generalizers (i.e. combiners) inputs). Then the second level generalizers are trained with the original ensembles outputs and the second level generalizers output is treated as the correct guess. In fact, stacked generalization works by combined classifiers with weights according to individual classifier performance, to find a best combination of ensemble outputs. Based on the idea of the combining method of stacking, we propose a new type of ensemble neural network model called multistage ensemble neural networks.

2 Multistage Neural Network Ensembles

Inspired by stacking, some researchers have realized that it is possible to construct a new combination method using a similar idea.

As early as 1993, some experiments were done in digit recognition [14] by using a single layer network to combine ensemble classifiers. Unfortunately, these experiments did not show any performance gain compared with other combination strategies. It was claimed the failure was due to the very high accuracy of all the classifiers being combined.

In 1995, Partridge and Griffith presented a selector-net approach [5]. The selector-net was defined as a network which used the outputs from a group of different trained nets as its input. The experiments based on this idea delivered that selector-net's performance was better than the populations of networks they were derived from. It clearly confirmed that this kind of ensemble method is better than individual neural networks. But no further exploitation has been done to compare the performance of this strategy with any other ensemble method.

More recently, Kittler [15] stated that:"it is possible to train the output classifier separately using the outputs of the input classifiers as new features".

Very recently, Zeng [7] used a single neural network as an approximator for a voting classifiers. It was claimed that storage and computation could be saved, at the cost of a little less accuracy. However, it is noticed here a neural network being used to approximate the behavior of the ensemble, instead of using it as part of the ensemble components.

This paper extends the idea of stacking and investigates the use of a single neural network model as a combiner to combine the ensemble members results.

The experimental results demonstrate that it is an improved approach which achieves the better generalisation performance of neural network ensembles. The major improvement of this combination method is it offers an alternative neural network ensemble model, which is proved effective after the generalisation improvement obtained, compared with majority voting.

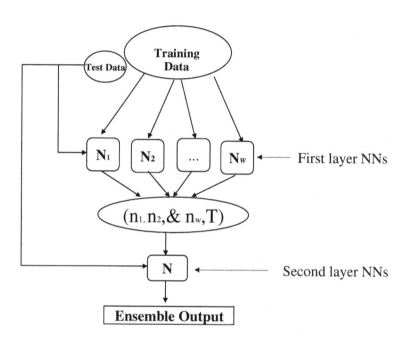

Fig. 1. An illustration of a multistage ensemble neural network.

The experiments on multistage neural network ensembles is based on a well trained group of diverse single neural networks (so called ensemble candidates). A single neural network is trained to combine these well trained neural nets results by concatenating their outputs together as its input. The reason of employing another neural networks to combine ensemble candidates is relying on neural networks capability. A neural network can be trained to prerform complex functions by asjusting the connection weights. Except majority voting, other approaches all adopt weights while combining. If so, why not use neural networks to assign weights to those ensemble members automatically instead of employing some traditional mathematical method manually? The advantage of a neural network is its ability to automatically adjust the connection weights. Therefore, it is very natural to think of using a neural network to combine ensemble results.

Table 1. Summary of UCI machine learning depository data sets, where '*' signifies a multi-class data set.

Data Set	No. of Cases	No. of Input features	No. of Output features
Breast-cancer-w	682	9	2
Bupa-Liver	345	6	2
Glass*	214	9	6
Ionosphere	351	34	2
Iris*	150	4	3
Pima-Diabetes	768	8	2

An illustration of the multistage neural network model described here is shown in Figure 1.

In Figure 1, suppose there is a source data set $S\{s_1, s_2, ...s_n\}$ and its corresponding target data set $T\{t_1, t_2, ...t_n\}$, which are partitioned into two parts: test data and training data. The training data usually will be preprocessed by various methods in order to generate diverse results before they being applied to the first layer's neural network models: $N_1, N_2, ...N_w$. The preprocessing methods on the training data set include distributing sequences randomly, noise injection, bagging, boosting or other methods. After training, the test data set will be applied to these ensemble candidates to access their performance. Afterwards, the whole training data set will be applied and each first layer neural networks' corresponding results $(n_1, n_2, ...n_w)$ are used as the second layer neural network model's inputs. The second layer neural networks, was trained by using the first layers generated results on the whole training data as inputs combined with their target data set. Advantages of multistage ensemble neural networks include:

- Multistage ensemble neural networks can be applied to both classification and regression problems.
- For each ensemble candidate, normal data preparation methods can be applied to them, and ensemble candidates can be trained separately by using various different neural network models and algorithms.
- Generalization of these first layer neural networks when using this model can be tuned to be as diverse as possible, so the choices for the first layer neural network training are very flexible and allow a wide range of selections.

3   Experiments

To investigate the performance of multistage ensembles, six classification data sets are taken from UCI Machine Learning Depository to construct experimental datasets. Details of these data sets are listed in Table 1, where datasets marked with '*' are multi-class datasets.

4   Experiments

4.1   Data Preparation

For each ensemble candidates' training, each data set was randomly partitioned into three parts: training, validation and test data. The sequences of training data were randomly distributed before they were applied to the neural networks model (i.e., steps were taken to prepare the most diverse data among ensemble members for training). There were no overlapping data instances inside the training data sets. For most of the data sets listed in Table 1, this approach was effective in generating diverse training data sets. The exception to this were the Glass and Iris data set, where the bagging [3] method was applied, due to source data's small size.

4.2   Experimental Procedures

Five single hidden layer neural networks trained by the backpropagation algorithm were generated as ensemble candidates for each ensemble. These five candidates were constructed with different sequences of training data, different neural network structures (numbers of hidden neurons) and different initialization. Each neural network model was trained 20 times with random initialization of starting weights. The number of hidden neurons is changed from one to the number of inputs of each data set (time considerations prevented the exploration of networks with hidden layers larger than this). During training, the validation data set was used to prevent overfitting. As the experiments in this paper is concentrated on comparing the performance of two ensemble combination methods. To make the things simpliest, the test data set is applied to the ensemble candidates after their training. Those ensemble candidates with best generalisation performance were kept. Majority voting and multistage neural networks then applied to these same ensemble members to generate the combination results.

After the training of the first layer's ensemble candidates, the whole source data is randomly disturbed again. 10-fold cross-validation [4] is applied to the second layer's neural network training in order to estimate the average performance. First the training data is injected into the ensemble members and their outputs are concatenated together with the corresponding target values as the input of the second layer's neural network. The training procedure and parameter setting for a neural network combiner are the same as an ensemble candidate's training.

The result of the majority voting applied to 3 and 5 ensemble members are then compared with the performance of multistage neural networks by averaging over 10-fold cross-validation.

5   Results

Table 2 shows the results for these different combination strategies when combining the best three ensemble candidates and all five ensemble candidates. In this

Table 2. Percentage correct performance on test set of voting versus multistage networks on UCI datasets. S1..S5 signify single networks, where each '#' indicates one of the three ensemble members selected for three-member combination. V1 and V5 signify combination by voting with three and five ensemble members respectively, whilst M3 and M5 signify combination by multistage neural network with three and five ensemble members respectively.

Data	S1	S2	S3	S4	S5	V3	M3	V5	M5
Breast-cancer-w	97.73#	98.48#	95.45	96.21	96.97#	97.21	97.35	97.35	97.5
Bupa-Liver	75.0#	78.0#	77.0#	77.0	78.0	72.65	73.82	73.53	73.82
Glass	42.19	46.88#	50.0#	45.31#	45.31	58.17	58.50	54.29	54.76
Ionosphere	85.53	94.74#	93.42#	86.84#	86.84	96.0	96.29	96.0	96.29
Iris	93.33#	92.0#	94.67#	90.67	90.67	97.60	98.0	97.6	98.0
Pima-Diabetes	72.02	73.81#	72.02#	75.60#	69.64	74.47	75.13	73.95	74.61

table, the actual ensemble candidates selected for ensembles of three networks are marked with '#'.

From these results, it can be seen that multistage neural networks always perform better than majority voting based on the same ensemble members, regardless the number of ensemble members used in combination is 3 or 5.

6   Conclusions

This paper has demonstrated that, on a wide range of datasets (including simple categorization and multiple categorization), multistage neural network ensembles offer improved performance when compared with majority voting as an ensemble combination method. The experimental results clearly show that statistic improvement can be made by using this new ensemble model on this range data of sets, when compared with another widely used ensemble technique such as majority voting. Currently, experiments are being carried out to investigate the exact theoretical reason for this performance improvement offered by multistage neural networks. The reason probably lies within differences between the kinds of decision surfaces a second layer network can model when compared to those decision surfaces that can be produced by majority voting. However, a clearer analysis and description of this area needs to be developed. In the future the intention is to develop and implement further experiments to investigate if the performance of multistage neural networks can be enhanced by using more ensemble members in the first layer, choice of training, validation and test datasets, and choice of neural network for the second layer combiner. It may be that these factors interact, and will allow this research to push the performance of such ensembles even further.

References

1. Tumer, K., Ghosh, J.: Error correlation and error reduction in ensemble classifiers. Connection Science: Special Issue on Combining Artificial Neural Ensemble Approaches, 8(3&4), 385-404, 1999.
2. Sharkey, A. J. C., Sharkey, N. E., Chandroth, G. O.: Neural nets and diversity. Neural Computing and Applications, 4, 218-227, 1996.
3. Breiman, L.: Bagging predictors. Machine learning, 24 123-140, 1996.
4. Krogh, A., Vedelsby, J. : Neural Network Ensembles, Cross Validation, and Active Learning. Advances in Neural Information Processing Systems, 7, MIT press, Editors: Tesauro, G., Touretzky, D.S. and Leen, T.K. pp.231-238, 1995.
5. Partridge, D., Griffith, N. : Strategies for Improving Neural Net Generalisation. Neural Computing and Applications, 3, 27-37, 1995.
6. Wolpert, D. H.: Stacked generalization. Neural Networks, 5, 241-259, 1992.
7. Zeng, X., Martinez, T. R.: Using a Neural Network to Approximate an Ensemble of Classifiers. Neural Processing Letters, 12, 225-237, 2000.
8. Tumer, K., Ghosh, J.: Order statistics combiners of neural classifiers. In Proceedings of the World Congress on Neural Network, INNS press, Washington DC, 31-34, 1995.
9. Lincoln, W., Skrzypek, J.: Synergy of clustering multiple back propagation networks. Advances in Neural Information Processing Systems-2, Touretzky, D., (ed.), Morgan Kaufmann, 650-657, 1990.
10. Jacobs, R. A.: Methods for combining experts' probability assessments. Neural Computation, 7, 867-888, 1995.
11. Hansen, L., Salamon, P.: Neural network ensembles. IEEE Trans. Pattern Analysis and Machine Intell, 993-1001, 1990.
12. Al-Ghoneim, K., Kumar Vijaya B. V. K.: Learning ranks with neural networks. In Applications and Science of Artificial Neural Networks: Proceedings of the SPIE, 2492, 446-464, 1995.
13. Ho, T. K., Hull, J. J., Srihari, S. N.: Decision combination in multiple classifier systems. IEEE Transactions on Pattern Analysis and Machine Intelligence, 16(1), 66-76, 1994.
14. Lee, D. S., Srihari, S. N.: Handprinted Digit Recognition: A Comparison of Algorithms. Pre-Proc. 3RD International Workshop On Frontiers In Handwriting Recognition, Buffalo, USA, 153-162, 1993.
15. Kittler, J.: Combining Classifiers: A Theoretical Framework. Pattern Analysis and Applications, 1, 18-27, 1998.

Forward and Backward Selection in Regression Hybrid Network

Shimon Cohen and Nathan Intrator

School of Computer Science, Tel Aviv University
www.math.tau.ac.il/~nin

Abstract. We introduce a Forward Backward and Model Selection algorithm (FBMS) for constructing a hybrid regression network of radial and perceptron hidden units. The algorithm determines whether a radial or a perceptron unit is required at a given region of input space. Given an error target, the algorithm also determines the number of hidden units. Then the algorithm uses model selection criteria and prunes unnecessary weights. This results in a final architecture which is often much smaller than a RBF network or a MLP. Results for various data sizes on the Pumadyn data indicate that the resulting architecture competes and often outperform best known results for this data set.

Keywords: Hybrid Network Architecture, SMLP, Clustering, Regularization, Nested Models, Model Selection.

1 Introduction

The construction of a network architecture, which contains units of different types at the same hidden layer is not commonly done. One reason is that such construction makes model selection more challenging, as it requires the determination of each unit type in addition to the determination of network size. A more common approach to achieving higher architecture flexibility is via the use of more flexible units [12, 6]. The potential problem of such a construction is over flexibility which leads to over-fitting.

Analyzing cases where convergence of MLP or RBF networks (as a function of number of hidden units) is slow, reveals that often there is at least one region in input space where an attempt is being made to approximate a function that is radially symmetric (such as a donut) with projection units or vice versa. This suggests that an incremental architecture which chooses the appropriate hidden unit for different regions in input space can lead to a far smaller and more effective architecture.

Earlier approaches, attempted to construct a small network approximation to the desired function at different regions of input space via a "divide and conquer" approach. Rather than reviewing the vast literature on that, we shall point out some approaches which indicate some of the highlights that had motivated our work. Work on trees is reviewed in [1] where the goal is to reach a good

F. Roli and J. Kittler (Eds.): MCS 2002, LNCS 2364, pp. 98–107, 2002.

division of the input space and use a very simple architecture at the terminating nodes. That work suggested some criteria for splitting the input space and provided a cost complexity method for comparing the performance of architectures with different sizes. An approach which constructs more sophisticated architectures at the terminating nodes was proposed in [14, 9], where a gating network performs the division of the input space and small neural networks perform the function approximation at each region separately. Donoho's work [5] has shown that a function can be decomposed into two parts, the radial part and the ridge (projection based) part and that the two parts are mutually exclusive. It is difficult however, to separate the radial portion of a function from its projection based portion.

We have introduced a training methodology for a hybrid MLP/RBF network [4, 3]. This architecture, produced far better classification and regression results compared with advanced RBF methods or with MLP architectures. In this work, we further introduce a novel training methodology, which evaluates the need for additional hidden units, chooses optimally their nature – MLP or RBF – and determines their optimal initial weight values. The determination of additional hidden units is based on an incremental strategy which searches for regions in input space for which the input/output function approximation leads to highest residual error. The last step is to prune unnecessary parameters and to select the best model from the sequence of nested models using Bayesian model selection or Likelihood Ratio Test (LRT). This approach, Forward and Backward Model Selection (FBMS), coupled with optimal determination of initial weight values for the additional hidden units, constructs a computationally efficient training algorithm which appears to scale up with the complexity of the data, better than regular MLP or RBF methods.

2   Parameter Estimation and Model Selection

An incremental architecture with more than one type of building components, requires four decisions at each step; (i) find the next region in input space where a hidden unit might be needed; (ii) decide which unit to add, RBF or a perceptron; (iii) train the network; (iv) prune unnecessary weights. The SMLP [6] network uses both RBF and Perceptron units at each cluster. In higher order networks [12] quadratic and linear terms always exist and strong regularization must be used to avoid over-fitting. Our proposed FBMS selects the proper unit for each region in input space. Thus, the number of hidden units remains minimal and over-fitting is reduced. In order to select the type of units, FBMS divides the space into homogeneous regions and selects the type of hidden unit for each region. During the division of the space into small regions the overall error is estimated and the splitting is stopped when an error goal is reached. Thus, the network size is monitored using the error criterion. When the training data set is small, an over-fitting may occur. Thus, a backward elimination of weights can improve the prediction and reduce the variance of the estimator. The steps in the algorithm include:

– Data clustering and splitting to reduce an error objective function.
– Automatic selection of unit type for each cluster.
– Full gradient descent on the resulting hybrid architecture.
– Pruning of unnecessary weights.

Below, we describe in detail each step.

2.1 Data Clustering

We start by clustering the data based and minimizing the Sum of Square Residual about the mean (SSR):

$$SSR(C_0) = \sum_{y_i \in C_0} (y_i - \bar{y}o)^2,$$

where $\bar{y}o$ is the mean of $y_i \in C_0$. Given a training data set D, we attempt to decompose it into a set $\{C_i\}_{i=1}^k$, such that $\bigcup C_i = D$ and $C_i \bigcap C_j = \phi$ for $i \neq j$. The following algorithm, is similar to the one proposed in CART [1], it splits the cluster with the largest objective function reduction into two clusters. Consider a split for a cluster C_0 into two clusters C_1 and C_2. Let the SSR reduction be defined as follows:

$$\Delta SSR(C_0) = SSR(C_0) - (SSR(C_1) + SSR(C_2)). \tag{1}$$

The splitting is continued until an error goal of the hybrid classifier is reached or a predefined maximum number of clusters is achieved. Since a cluster C with n members has $2^n - 1$ possible number of meaningful splits, an exhaustive search is not feasible. CART [1] solves this problem by considering each axis $1 \leq l \leq d$ of the input space separately and search for the best split of the form $x_i \geq \lambda_i$ for axis x_i. The sorting of the data (by considering each axis separately) reduces the number of possibilities to dn. We seek a similar approach which is not restricted to projections that are parallel to the axes.

Splitting rule We assume that the underlying function to be estimated is continuous. Consider a subset C_0 of the data. Let y_1 be the minimum value of the function in C_0 with a corresponding input x_1. Let y_2 be the maximum value of the function in C_0 with input x_2.

The splitting procedure is defined as follows:

– For-each pattern find the Euclidean distance to x_1 and x_2.
– If the distance to x_1 is smaller, associate the pattern to C_1, otherwise to C_2.
– Choose to split the cluster with the largest reduction in the objective function.

Other distance measures such as Mahalanobis or Manhattan can be considered depending on prior knowledge about the problem.

2.2   Model Selection

FBMS uses a classical statistical approach to select models. We assume that the target function values are corrupted by Gaussian noise with zero mean and equal variance σ^2. In addition we assume that the noise is independent. Thus, the likelihood of the data given the model is:

$$L = \frac{1}{(2\pi)^{\frac{N}{2}}\sigma^N} \exp(-\frac{\sum_{n=1}^{N}(y_n - t_n)^2}{2\sigma^2}). \tag{2}$$

The maximization of the above function is equivalent to the maximization of its *log* value:

$$LL = -\frac{N}{2}\log(2\pi) - N\log(\sigma) - \frac{\sum_{n=1}^{N}(y_n - t_n)^2}{2\sigma^2}. \tag{3}$$

Thus, minimization of the SSE is equivalent to the maximization of the likelihood of the data. To obtain the maximum likelihood value of σ we differentiate 3 with respect to sigma.

$$\frac{\partial LL}{\partial \sigma} = -\frac{N}{\sigma} + \frac{\sum_{n=1}^{N}(y_n - t_n)^2}{\sigma^3}. \tag{4}$$

This leads to the maximum likelihood estimate for σ:

$$\hat{\sigma}^2 = \frac{1}{N}\sum_{n=1}^{N}(y_n - t_n)^2. \tag{5}$$

We use 3 to perform model selection when the type of a hidden unit has to be selected, or when the weights are pruned and thus there are two nested models. The task in this case is to select the best model from a sequence of models. The Bayesian information Criterion (BIC) is used to select the type of unit and either the BIC or LRT is used for the pruning process.

We start by describing the Bayesian approach. Given a data set D, the task is to choose between two (or more) models M_1, M_2. Each model has a parametric family of weights attached to it, with its prior probability $p(w|M)$. The probability of the data under each model is given by:

$$p(D|M) = \int_w p(D, w|M)dw = \int_w p(D|w, M)p(w|M)dw. \tag{6}$$

The Bayes Factors are then defined as:

$$\frac{p(M_1|D)}{p(M_2|D)} = \frac{p(D|M_1)p(M_1)}{p(D|M_2)p(M_2)}. \tag{7}$$

The integration of Eq. 6 can be performed by using Laplace integral [11] which approximates the integrand by a quadratic function. Thus, the value of the integral becomes [11, 16]:

$$p(D|M) \cong (2\pi)^d |H|^{-1/2} p(D|W_{m_0}, M)p(W_{m_0}|M), \tag{8}$$

Where H is the Hessian matrix of the approximation and W_{m_0} is the most probable value of the likelihood $p(D|M)$. With the lack of a-priori knowledge we assume that a model with a RBF or a perceptron as a hidden unit is equally likely, thus: $p(M_1) = p(M_2)$.

This leads to the integrated likelihood ratio: $p(D|M_1)/p(D|M_2)$.

The BIC approximation can be derived from 8 by using Gaussian distribution to the a-priori parameters density [11] to arrive at:

$$BIC \equiv \log(p(D|M)) = \log(p(D, W_{m_0}|M)) - \frac{d}{2}\log(N), \tag{9}$$

where $\log(p(D, W_{m_0}|M))$ is the maximum likelihood estimation of the parameters and d are the number of parameters. Substituting 5 and 3 into 9 we obtain:

$$BIC_i = -\frac{1}{N}\log(2\pi) - N\log(\hat{\sigma}) - \frac{N}{2} - \frac{d_i}{2}\log(N). \tag{10}$$

The first and third terms on the right are constant and can be eliminated when selecting models on the same data set. The truly Bayesian approach then uses the evidence as the weights of the models in order to get a weighted predication for a new value y as follows:

$$p(y|D) = \sum_{i=1}^{m} p(y, M_i|D) = \sum_{i=1}^{m} p(y|M_i, D)p(M_i|D). \tag{11}$$

Equation 11 shows that the evidence of a model can be used as weight when averaging the predications of all models. When the best model gives good predications, the averaging process can be skipped. Then, the FBMS algorithm uses the single best model for predication.

The LRT can be used to select between two nested models. Given two models $M1 \subset M2$ the LRT test is defined as follows [15]:

$$-2\log(\frac{p(D, W_{m_0}|M1)}{p(D, W_{m_0}|M2)}) = \chi^2(d_2 - d_1). \tag{12}$$

This approach uses $P - Values$ to reject the null hypothesis, that is, the simple model is equivalent to the complicated one. The LRT criteria is applicable only when the models are nested. Thus, this process is applicable only for the pruning process. Using the maximum likelihood estimator for σ 5 we arrive at the following test:

$$\chi^2(d2 - d1) = 2N\log(\sigma_1^2) - 2N\log(\sigma_2^2). \tag{13}$$

2.3 Unit Selection

After the decomposition of the input space into more homogeneous subsets, a unit type is selected for each such subset. Since the models are not nested the BIC criterion is applied. The maximum likelihood is computed for each cluster and unit type and the unit type with the higher BIC value is selected. First we set the parameters of hidden units.

The ridge projection is monotonically increasing with the correlation between its weight vector and the data points. It achieves its maximum value when the correlation is maximized (for a unit projection vector). Therefore, the ridge weight vector W_{m_0} should be proportional to the pattern where the function acquires its maximum value.

The RBF function is monotonically decreasing with the distance from the maximum point. Thus, the center of the RBF is located at the function maximum point. To set the forward weights the log-likelihood is computed as follows. Let C_i be the set of points of the current cluster. Let $\phi(x_i)$ be the ridge or RBF values for each $x_i \in C_i$, and let t_i be the targets. We define the objective function:

$$E(w, w_0) = \frac{1}{2} \sum_{i=1}^{N} (w^T \phi(x_i) + w_0 - t_i)^2. \tag{14}$$

The partial derivatives with respect to w and w_0 are:

$$\frac{\partial E}{\partial w} = \sum_{x_i \in C_i} (w^T \phi(x_i) + w_0 - t_i)\phi(x_i) = 0.$$

$$\frac{\partial E}{\partial w_0} = \sum_{x_i \in C_i} (w^T \phi(x_i) + w_0 - t_i) = 0. \tag{15}$$

Thus, we obtain the locally forward weights of the specific unit:

$$w = \frac{n \sum_{x_i \in C_i} \phi(x_i) t_i - \sum_{x_i \in C_i} t_i \sum_{x_i \in C_i} \phi(x_i)}{n \sum_{x_i \in C_i} \phi(x_i)^2 - (\sum_{x_i \in C_i} \phi(x_i))^2}, \tag{16}$$

and

$$w_0 = \frac{\sum_{x_i \in C_i} t_i - w \sum_{x_i \in C_i} \phi(x_i)}{n}. \tag{17}$$

Substituting w and w_0 into Eq. 14 gives the error value of the fit for each unit type. The error is inversely proportional to the likelihood.

The above procedure is repeated for each cluster and using 10, the most probable unit type is selected.

2.4 Pruning

The last step of the algorithm prunes unnecessary weights. This can remove inputs weight to a ridge unit, a feature of a RBF unit or a hidden unit. Using a diagonal approximation to the covariance matrix, the activation of a RBF function is given by:

$$\phi(x) = \exp(-\sum_{i=1}^{N} \frac{(x_i - c_i)^2}{\sigma_i^2}). \tag{18}$$

If we make the substitution: $\frac{1}{\sigma} = r$, we obtain:

$$\phi(x) = \exp(-\sum_{i=1}^{d} \frac{(x_i - c_i)^2 r_i^2}{2}). \tag{19}$$

Consider setting r_j to zero:

$$\phi(x) = \exp(-\sum_{i=1,i \neq j}^{d} \frac{(x_i - c_i)^2 r_i^2}{2}) \exp(0) = \exp(-\sum_{i=1,i \neq j}^{d} \frac{(x_i - c_i)^2 r_i^2}{2}).$$

The partial derivatives with respect to r_i is:

$$\frac{\partial \phi}{\partial r_i} = -\phi(x)(x_i - c_i)^2 r_i. \tag{20}$$

Thus, to prune a feature i it suffices to set r_i to zero. This eliminates two parameters. For the ridge input weights we add a matrix w_{ij} were $w_{ij} \in \{0, 1\}$. If $w_{ij} = 0$, the weight j to projection unit i is pruned. Since the models are nested it is possible to select the model using LRT. On the other hand the best model can be selected by the BIC approximation to its evidence. FMBS uses both criteria when BIC is the default one. Our pruning process is similar to [10, 8]; We start with the full model and at each step we prune the least significant weight. That is, the weight that least contributes to the objective function. When the BIC criterion is used, the search is exhaustive for the best model from a range of possible nested models. When the LRT criterion is used the pruning is stopped when a given threshold is reached. The threshold is derived from the given significance value ($P-value$) of the χ^2 distribution with one or two degrees of freedom. Typically, we use a default value of 95% that matches to $P = 3.841$ of the corresponding distribution for one degree of freedom.

3   Experimental Results

This section describes regression results for the Pumadyn data from the DELEVE archive [2]. The data was generated from a simulation of the dynamics of a Puma robot arm. The target is the angular acceleration of one of the links and the inputs are various joint angles, velocities and torques. The Pumadyn data contains several sets with different noise levels. We have used the data set with the largest noise. This data set is divided into two groups. The first has 8 inputs ($Pumadyn8$) and the second has 32 inputs. There are 5 sizes of the train sample set: 64, 128,256,512,1024. Studying a regressor on all subsets indicates how the method scales with the train sample size.

For these data sets, we compare our results to several other methods that have been used in the past. We thus provide results for the following methods:

- **lin-1** Linear least squares regression.
- **knn-cv-1** K-nearest neighbors for regression. K is selected by using leave-one-out cross-validation.

- **mars3.6-bag-1** Multivariate adaptive regression splines (MARS) [7], version 3.6 with bagging.
- **mlp-ese-1** Multilayer perceptron ensembles, trained with early stopping implemented by conjugate gradient optimization.
- **mlp-mc-1** Multilayer perceptron networks trained by MCMC methods [13].
- **gp-map-1** Gaussian processes for regression, trained using a maximum a-posteriori approach implemented by conjugate gradient optimization.
- **PRBFN-AS-RBF** Using the a regular RBF network with Gaussians units with the pruning algorithm.
- **PRBFN-AS-MLP** Using MLP network with the pruning algorithm.
- **PRBFN-LRT** The PRBFN method with the LRT for the pruning algorithm.
- **PRBFN-FBMS** The hybrid network with BIC for the model selection in the process. Each unit type is selected as described in section 2.3.

Further details can be obtained from the DELVE web site [2].

Pumadyn32nh	64	128	256	512	1024
lin-1	1.98±0.25	1.20±0.05	0.96±0.02	0.89±0.02	0.86±0.02
knn-cv-1	1.00±0.02	1.01±0.03	0.94±0.02	0.92±0.02	0.90±0.02
mlp-ese-1	1.25±0.04	1.13±0.09	0.96±0.02	0.89±0.02	0.86±0.02
gp-map-1	1.01±0.06	0.70±0.12	0.38±0.01	0.36±0.01	0.35±0.01
mlp-mc-1	0.88±0.06	0.58±0.06	0.50±0.09	0.59±0.06	0.35±0.01
mars3.6-bag-1	0.93±0.06	0.53±0.03	0.38±0.01	0.35 ±0.01	0.34±0.01
PRBFN-AS-RBF	1.14±0.2	0.57±0.09	0.40±0.02	0.39 ±0.02	0.38±0.03
PRBFN-AS-MLP	1.11±0.08	0.84±0.06	0.69±0.07	0.54 ±0.06	0.40±0.02
PRBFN-LRT	1.45±0.2	1.14±0.09	0.79±0.07	0.55 ±0.05	0.44±0.03
PRBFN-FBMS	0.75±0.11	0.43±0.02	0.38±0.01	0.37±0.02	0.34±0.01

Table 1. Regression on Pumadyn with 32 input non-linear with high noise

4   Discussion

The work presented in this paper represents a practical step in constructing an incremental hybrid architecture for regression. It was motivated by the success of the original hybrid architecture which was introduced in [3, 4]. Several assumptions were made in various parts of the architecture construction. Our aim was to show that even under these assumptions, an architecture that is smaller in size and better in generalization performance can already be achieved. Furthermore, while this architecture is particularly useful when the data contains ridge and Gaussian parts, its performance were not below the performance of

Pumadyn8nh	64	128	256	512	1024
lin-1	0.73±0.02	0.68±0.02	0.65±0.01	0.63±0.01	0.63±0.02
knn-cv-1	0.79±0.02	0.71±0.02	0.64±0.01	0.58±0.02	0.53±0.02
mlp-ese-1	0.72±0.02	0.67±0.02	0.61±0.01	0.49±0.01	0.41±0.01
gp-map-1	0.44±0.03	0.38±0.01	0.35±0.01	0.33±0.01	0.32±0.01
mlp-mc-1	0.45±0.01	0.39±0.02	0.35±0.01	0.32±0.01	0.32±0.01
mars3.6-bag-1	0.51±0.02	0.38±0.01	0.36±0.01	0.34 ±0.01	0.34±0.01
PRBFN-AS-RBF	0.51±0.03	0.38±0.02	0.36±0.01	0.33 ±0.01	0.32±0.01
PRBFN-AS-MLP	0.57±0.05	0.59±0.14	0.37±0.02	0.33 ±0.08	0.32±0.01
PRBFN-LRT	0.72±0.11	0.60±0.05	0.43±0.02	0.41 ±0.01	0.35±0.02
PRBFN-FBMS	0.48±0.03	0.38±0.01	0.34±0.01	0.33±0.01	0.32±0.01

Table 2. Regression on Pumadyn with 8 input non-linear with high noise

the best known MLP or RBF networks when data that contains only one type of structure was used[1].

In our previous work [4], we have used hard threshold for unit type selection. That algorithm also accepted the number of hidden units in advance. This paper introduces an algorithm that finds automatically the relevant parts of the data and maps these parts onto RBF or Ridge functions respectively. The algorithm also finds the number of hidden units for the network for a given error target. The automatic unit type detection uses the maximum likelihood principle for regression, and the proposed pruning method is applied to individual weights of each hidden unit. Two criteria have been used: BIC and LRT. The BIC criterion can be used for choosing the best model out of a general family of models. The LRT works only with nested models, where the process is terminated when the null hypothesis is rejected.

The tests on the Pumadyn family of data sets suggests that the Bayesian Information Criterion (BIC) is superior to the LRT. Most importantly, the proposed method can achieve better performance for smaller data set sizes. This property is very useful for problems where large training data set is difficult to obtain, e.g., medical data or, most recently, protein and gene expression data.

References

[1] L. Breiman, J. H. Friedman, R. A. Olshen, and C. J. Stone. *Classification and Regression Trees.* The Wadsworth Statistics/Probability Series, Belmont, CA, 1984.

[2] C.E.Rasmussen, R.M. Neal, G.E. Hinton, D. Van Camp, Z. Ghahrman M. Revow, R. Kustra, and R. Tibshirani. The delve manual. 1996.

[3] S. Cohen and N. Intrator. Automatic model selection of ridge and radial functions. In *Second International workshop on Multiple Classifier Systems*, 2001.

---

[1] This finding is based on other data sets which are not included in this paper due to lack of space.

[4] S. Cohen and N. Intrator. A hybrid projection based and radial basis function architecture: Initial values and global optimization. *To appear in Special issue of PAA on Fusion of Multiple Classifiers*, 2001.

[5] D. L. Donoho and I. M. Johnstone. Projection-based approximation and a duality with kernel methods. *Annals of Statistics*, 17:58–106, 1989.

[6] G.W. Flake. Square unit augmented, radially extended, multilayer percpetrons. In G. B. Orr and K. Müller, editors, *Neural Networks: Tricks of the Trade*, pages 145–163. Springer, 1998.

[7] J. H. Friedman. Mutltivariate adaptive regression splines. *The Annals of Statistics*, 19:1–141, 1991.

[8] B. Hassibi and D. G. Stork. Second order derivatives for network pruning: Optimal brain surgeon. In C. L. Giles, S. J. Hanson, and J. D. Cowan, editors, *Advances in Neural Information Processing Systems*, volume 5. Morgan Kaufmann, San Mateo, CA, 1993.

[9] R. A. Jacobs, M. I. Jordan, S. J. Nowlan, and G. E. Hinton. Adaptive mixtures of local experts. *Neural Computation*, 3(1):79–87, 1991.

[10] N. Sugie K. Suzuki, I. Horiba. A simple neural network algorithm with application to filter synthesis. *Neural Processing Letters, Kluwer Academic Publishers, Netherlands*, 13:43–53, 2001.

[11] R. E. Kass and A. E. Raftery. Bayes factors. *Journal of The American Statistical Association*, 90:773–795, 1995.

[12] Y.C. Lee, G. Doolen, H.H. Chen, G.Z.Sun, T. Maxwell, H.Y. Lee, and C.L. Giles. Machine learning using higher order correlation networks. *Physica D*, pages 22–D:276–306, 1986.

[13] R. M. Neal. *Bayesian Learning for Neural Networks*. Springer, New York, 1996.

[14] S. J. Nowlan. Soft competitive adaptation: Neural network learning algorithms basd on fitting statistical mixtures. Ph.D. dissertation, Carnegie Mellon University, 1991.

[15] A. Papoulis. *Probbaility, Random Variables, and Stochastic Process*, volume 1. McGRAW-HILL, New York, third edition, 1991.

[16] D. G. Stork R. O. Duda, P. E. Hart. *Pattern Classification*. John Wiley Sons, INC., New York, 2001.

Types of Multinet System

Amanda J.C. Sharkey

Department of Computer Science, University of Sheffield, UK

Abstract. A limiting factor in research on combining classifiers is a lack of awareness of the full range of available modular structures. One reason for this is that there is as yet little agreement on a means of describing and classifying types of multiple classifier system. In this paper, a categorisation scheme for the identification and description of types of multinet systems is proposed in which systems are described as (a) involving competitive or cooperative combination mechanisms; (b) combining either ensemble, modular, or hybrid components; (c) relying on either bottom-up, or top-down combination, and (d) when bottom up as using either static or fixed combination methods. It is claimed that the categorisation provides an early, but necessary, step in the process of mapping the space of multinet systems: permitting the comparison of different types of system, and facilitating their design and description. On the basis of this scheme, one ensemble and two modular multinet system designs are implemented, and applied to an engine fault diagnosis problem. The best generalisation performance was achieved from the ensemble system.

Introduction

Although the major emphasis in research on multiple classifiers has been on ensemble combinations, there are often considerable gains in performance to be achieved as a result of modularising, or decomposing a task into simpler components. However, currently there is a lack of awareness of the range of modular designs that could be employed. There are also few direct comparisons of different forms of modular architecture, (for exceptions see Auda and Kamel, 1998 and Hansen, 1999). The main aim of this paper is to present a candidate categorisation scheme for types of multiple classifier system, and on the basis of this scheme, to construct three different types of multiple classifier system and compare their performance on an engine fault diagnosis problem.

There have been some previous attempts to identify and compare types of multinet system, but these fall short of a comprehensive categorisation scheme. Auda and Kamel (1998) claim to have covered the range of known MNN designs with the 10 modular structures they consider. They contrast competitive with cooperative decision-making, and identify four possible structures (decoupled, merged, hierarchical and ensemble). However, they do not explicitly categorise the systems they examine in terms of whether they are based on competitive or cooperative relationships, and they seem more concerned to provide a variety

F. Roli and J. Kittler (Eds.): MCS 2002, LNCS 2364, pp. 108–117, 2002.

of structures, than to identify groups or types. Jacobs and colleagues (Jacobs et al 1991; Jordan and Jacobs, 1994) tend to consider only the Mixtures of Experts architecture, and to compare it to a non-modular approach, rather than to other modular architectures. In a more wide-ranging categorisation, Gallinari (1995) distinguishes between systems based on partitions of the input space (ie modular systems), systems based on successive processing, and systems based on combining decisions (i.e. ensemble combinations), but he does not make further discriminations between types of modular or ensemble system.

The starting point for the categorisation proposed here is the distinction between ensemble and modular systems (Sharkey 1996; 1999): whereby in an ensemble, several redundant approximations to the same function are combined by some method to yield a single unified approach, and in a modular approach, the task in question is decomposed into a number of simpler components. Thus, in a classic ensemble combination, any one of the component nets, or classifiers, could be used to provide a solution to the task. By contrast, in a clearly modular combination, individual modules would not be able to provide a solution to the entire task, and a complete solution would require the coordination of all of the modules.

Some researchers (e.g. Hansen, 1999; Giacinto and Roli, 2000) also make a ensemble-modular distinction, whereas others group them together, or make the contrast only indirectly. Avnimelech and Intrator (1999), for example, describe the mixtures of experts algorithm (modular by our definition) as an ensemble. Haykin (1999) contrasts "committee machines" based on static structures that are combined through a mechanism that does not involve the input signal, and dynamic structures in which the input signal is involved in the combination. Here he seems indirectly to contrast ensemble with modular approaches, since the exemplars of the first of his categories are ensemble averaging and boosting, and of the second, Mixtures of Experts and Hierarchical Mixtures of Experts. He does not however, consider the possibility that there could be other kinds of modular structure than that exemplified by the Mixtures of Experts approach.

In the categorisation presented in this paper, we shall retain the distinction between ensemble and modular systems, and also incorporate a selection/fusion contrast made by several researchers. The selection/fusion (or in our terms competitive/cooperative) discriminator refers to the way in which the components of a system are combined. If we ignore sequential or supervisory relationships between modules (Sharkey, 1999), we can see that a set of modules to be concurrently combined can be combined cooperatively or competitively. In a competitive combination, the underlying structure is one in which the aim is to identify the most appropriate module, and switch control to (or take the final output from) that module. In a cooperative combination, by contrast, the outputs of several modules are combined, with or without differential weighting of their contributions. A competitive combination could then be made up of either modular or ensemble components, depending on whether the components do or do not represent decompositions of the task. A cooperative combination on the other hand would seem to imply an ensemble combination, but might, as in the case of sensor fusion, involve building a complete picture from a number of partial solutions.

Several authors make a similar distinction between competitive and cooperative relationships. For example, Nolfi and Floreano (2000) point out, in the context of behaviour-based robotics, that behaviour-based modules may be coordinated "by means of competitive or cooperative methods" (pp 1). Auda and Kamel (1998) distinguish between competitive and cooperative relationships (pp118). Avnimelech and Intrator (1999) contrast systems relying on classifier selection, with those relying on classifier combination. And Kuncheva (in press) makes a distinction between classifier selection and classifier fusion in ensembles.

In addition to the competitive-cooperative and modular-ensemble distinctions, it is also possible to make a distinction between top-down and bottom-up systems, or in other words, between systems that take the outputs of the component modules into account in their combination, and systems that do not. Cooperative combinations are inherently bottom-up, since the outputs of the several modules are taken into account in their combination. By contrast, control switching between modules is often top-down, and accomplished without examining the module outputs. However, competitive combinations can be accomplished by either top-down, or bottom-up means. With a top-down competitive method, module selection is based on something other than the module outputs - as is the case in the gating system used in Mixtures of Experts, (Jacobs, 1991), or the top-down competitive system in Sharkey et al (2000). However, it is also possible to implement a form of control switching in a bottom-up manner, based on a examination of the outputs of the modules as is the case for instance in a winner-takes-all system, or the method employed by Baxt (1992) in which control switching depends on whether the output of one of the modules exceeds an empirically determined threshold.

Related distinctions to the top-down/bottom-up one proposed here are made by other authors. Kuncheva (in press) distinguishes between fusion and selection methods, and then subdivides selection into static and dynamic selection methods. Under a static method, selection is accomplished without considering the output of the modules, and under a dynamic selection method the choice is based on the confidence of the current decision. She does not, however, apply this distinction to the fusion methods she considers. And Haykin's (1999) distinction between *static structures*, and *dynamic structures* is made on the basis of whether or not the components are combined by means of a mechanism that involves the input signal. Static structures are those which are combined without involving the input signal, whilst dynamic structures are combined by means of a mechanism that involves the input signal.

Finally, in this scheme we shall also distinguish between fixed methods of bottom-up combination, (e.g. averaging), and dynamic methods, such as stacking (Wolpert, 1992). In fixed methods, although the outputs are implicated in the computation, the method of combining remains fixed. In dynamic methods, the relative contribution of component classifiers varies as a function of their output. A cooperative bottom-up combination could therefore be either fixed or dynamic, whilst a competitive bottom up system (e.g. winner-takes-all) relies on a fixed decision mechanism that does not vary with the input.

The categorisation scheme proposed here then relies on a description of a system as (a) involving competitive or cooperative combination mechanisms; (b) combining either ensemble, modular, or hybrid components; (c) relying on either bottom-up, or top-down combination, and (d) when bottom up as using either static or fixed combination methods. Illustrations of competitively and cooperatively combined multinet structures can be found in Figure 1. The scheme as such overlaps with distinctions made elsewhere, but attempts to incorporate them within a unified approach.

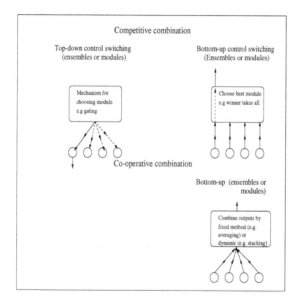

Fig. 1. Types of multinet structure

What is there to gain from a categorisation of modular systems? We suggest that it is an early, and necessary step in the process of mapping the space of possible multinet structures. An important contribution is that it provides us with an initial vocabulary and set of terms with which multinet systems can be described and categorised. For example, we can classify both the Mixture of Experts architecture, and the system presented by Sharkey et al (2000) as examples of a competitive top-down modular multiple classifer system. In addition the scheme opens the way to the construction and description of *new* systems: for instance, instead of a system based on the usual concept of boosting (a bottom-up cooperative ensemble approach), it would be possible to construct a competitively combined boosting system in which the most appropriate component net is selected by means of a (bottom-up) decision mechanism based on their relative confidence (i.e. a bottom-up competitive ensemble version of boosting). And a final advantage is that, as in the present paper, such a scheme can be used to motivate comparisons of exemplars of different types of structure.

On the basis of the categorisation scheme offered here, an ensemble solution to a (five class) engine fault diagnosis problem will be compared to two different modular solutions, one a top-down competitive system, and the other a bottom-up cooperative system. Given the relative lack of comparisons of different systems, it is not obvious *a priori* which might be expected to result in better generalisation performance.

Empirical Research

We shall first provide a necessarily brief overview of the diesel engine application (further details can be found elsewhere in (Chandroth and Sharkey, 1999; Chandroth, 2000; Sharkey et al, 2000). The data on which these studies was based was acquired from a real diesel engine, in which four (subtle) faults were physically induced at different times. The data considered here was based on in-cylinder pressure, sensed by means of a pressure transducer. The engine was a 4 stroke, twin cylinder, air cooled, naturally aspirated diesel engine, with a maximum power output of 10.4 kW at 3000 revolutions per minute (RPM) with a speed range of 1000 to 3000 RPM. Data was acquired under 5 conditions which included 4 fault states, and the normal operating state. Four ranges of engine speed were utilised during the acquisition process (2800 RPM, 2500 RPM, 2100 RPM, and 1800 RPM, all with no load).

The four faults were physically induced in the engine (at separate times), and were (i) leaking exhaust valve (**E**), (ii) leaking air inlet valve (**I**), (iii) worn orifice in injector nozzle (**L**), and (iv) blocked orifice in injector nozzle (**B**). Under each of the five fault conditions (the four described above, and normal operation (**N**), 2400 samples of data representing cylinder pressure were acquired, resulting in a total of 12000 samples. Each of the data samples originally consisted of 7200 points, corresponding to 720 degrees of a 4 stroke cycle. Since the induced faults were all combustion-related, a subset of these points that corresponded to the area of combustion was selected, based on expert knowledge. As a result of this selection, each sample consisted of 200 points. In addition, the complete set of 12000 samples was subdivided into three; 7500 became the training set, 1500 became the validation set, and 3000 became a set reserved for final testing.

Study 1: A unitary solution. Here, the aim was to train a single net to classify the engine data appropriately according to its fault class. In this, as in the other studies reported in this paper, a standard feed-forward Multilayer Perceptron (MLP) trained by means of backpropagation, was used. Since the 200 input points constitute high dimensional data, the number of inputs was reduced still further through the use of an autoencoding network (Baldi and Hornik, 1989). An MLP network was trained on an autoencoding task (reproducing its 200 inputs as outputs), together with the appropriate output classification. Therefore the net was trained with 200 inputs, and 205 outputs; where the last 5 outputs used a 1 of n encoding to indicate the classification of the input in terms of one of the 5 conditions. The autoencoder net, with 50 hidden units, (200-50-205) was trained on the training set for 5000 cycles; not long enough training to reach convergence (only 6566 patterns were learnt), but sufficient to produce an encoding that could be used to train a further net on the 5-class classification.

When the autoencoding net had been trained for 5000 cycles, training was halted. The autoencoding net was tested on the 7500 training examples, and the hidden unit activations for each example extracted, and used to form the inputs for a further net. Each 50 element input vector was paired with a 5 unit output vector (where a 1 of n coding indicated the output classification). Seven nets were trained on this training set, with a variable number of hidden units (varying between 20 and 55 hidden units).

A validation set for testing was similarly created by testing the original pressure examples on the autoencoding net, and replacing the original inputs with the hidden unit activations. When the trained nets were tested on the validation set, the best generalisation was obtained from a net with 50 hidden units, that we shall term Encode1. When tested with a 0.5 tolerance, the Encode1 net generalised correctly to 94.4% of the 1500 examples in the validation set.

In summary: in this first experiment, the best single net trained on the entire fault diagnosis task was able to generalise to 94.4% of the validation set. These results can be found in the first row of Table 1, labelled Study 1: Unitary net.

System	generalisation
Study 1:Unitary net	94.4%
Study 2:Top-down competitive modular system	95.4%
Study 3:Bottom-up cooperative modular system	95.3%
Study 4:Bottom-up cooperative ensemble system	96.6%

Table 1. Validation test set Performance of different Multinet Systems

Study 2: A top-down competitive modular system. A two tier modular structure was constructed. The system consisted of 10 lower level specialist nets, each trained to discriminate between a pair of faults. Control switching to an appropriate module was based on the output of the higher level net trained on all classes of data (the unitary net described in study 1). The system is described as top-down, since the outputs of the specialist nets are not considered by the control switching mechanism.

The lower level specialist modules were each trained on ten different training sets based on subsets of the training set used in study 1. Each dataset consisted of all the examples of a pair of faults from the training set (resulting in 10 pairwise combinations). Effectively, training a net on one of the ten training sets meant training it to discriminate between a pair of faults. After some preliminary experimentation (to establish an appropriate number of training cycles, and of hidden units), one net was trained on each dataset for 10000 cycles (or until convergence, if it occurred in fewer cycles), with 30 hidden units. The same 1 of n output encoding was used, resulting in a 50-30-5 architecture. The specialist nets all produced more accurate results when tested on the pairs of faults on which they had been trained, than did the unitary net. Thus it follows that if it were always possible to correctly identify the most appropriate specialist module, better results would be achieved with this system than with the unitary net described in Study 1.

The control switching method used here relied on an examination of the output of the higher level net: the same net described in Study 1, trained as it was to classify the data into the five fault classes. The decision about which specialist module to switch to was based on identifying the most confident, and the second most confident, or runner-up, output classification of the higher level net. Most of the time, the output activation for the runner-up was very small, but it was still assumed to indicate some doubt about the output classification. Control was then switched to the specialist module trained to discriminate between that pair of faults. For example, the output of the higher level net might indicate that the fault was an example of a Blocked fuel injector (B) and that the second most likely candidate was a leaky Exhaust valve (E). Control would then be switched to the specialist module trained to discriminate between these faults (ie BE in Table 2).

The complete modular system resulted in a generalisation performance of 95.4%, when tested, to a tolerance of 0.5, on the complete validation set of 1500 examples. As can be seen in Table 1, this represents an improvement over the 94.4% of the best unitary net.

Study 3: A bottom-up cooperative modular system: In this study, the same specialist modular nets were used as in Study 2, but this time they were combined in a bottom-up cooperative manner. A stacked system was constructed, in which a higher level net was trained to take the outputs of the ten pairwise specialist modules as input, and to produce the appropriate output classification. The training set was constructed by testing all of the 10 specialist modules on each example in the original training set, and capturing their resulting output values. Thus the training set for the level 1 generaliser consisted of 50 input values (10x5), and 5 output units indicating the classification. A number of ANNs of different topologies were tried, and the best performing net with 20 hidden units was selected. When the lower level modules were combined in this way, the resulting generalisation performance, when tested to 0.5 tolerance on the entire validation set, was 95.3%. As can be seen in Table 1, this again represents a small improvement over the performance of the unitary net, but again, most of the apparent gains due to decomposition seem to have been lost through the combining.

Study 4: A bottom up cooperative ensemble system: In this study, an ensemble solution was constructed. Two further nets were trained on the entire task using different input encodings (an effective method of ensemble creation, (Sharkey and Sharkey 1997). The second encoding was created by taking the original set of inputs from the training set, and training a net to reproduce them as output (autoassociation), as well as producing a further output to indicate the presence or absence of a fault (1 for no fault, and 0 for the other 4 fault conditions), (a 200-30-201 architecture). After training for 16000 cycles, 6550 patterns had been learnt. The net was tested on the training set, and the resulting hidden unit activations captured, and used to form the new input encodings. These new inputs were paired with the original 1 of n output encoding indicating which of the five fault classes was appropriate, and this new training set was used to train several nets with different numbers of hidden units, until the error ceased to decrease. The best performing net (30-30-5) when tested on the validation set generalised to 86.3% of the examples. A third encoding was also created by means of a similar method. The original inputs from the training set were trained in an autoassociative net to reproduce themselves as output, together with a further 3 outputs indicating whether the input was an example of the E class (100), the N class (010) or one of the other classes (001). Again after training, the hidden unit activations produced in response to testing were captured and used to create a new training set in which they were paired with a 1 of n output coding indicating the relevant fault class. A net with 30 hidden units (30-30-5) resulted in the best performance, generalising to 88.1% of the validation set.

The performance of the three nets when tested individually and as an ensemble on the validation set were 94.4%, 86.2% and 88.1% respectively. Although the performance of the nets based on the second and third encodings were less good than other results reported so far, when the three nets were combined by means of a majority vote to form an ensemble, they generalised to 96.6% of the validation set, a better performance than the other modular and unitary nets reported so far in Table 1.

Discussion and Conclusions

In the four studies reported here, three different multinet systems were constructed and their performance compared to that of a unitary net, when tested on the task of discriminating between five fault classes of diesel engine operation. The best performance was obtained from an ensemble of nets, each trained on the entire task, and created through the use of different input encodings. These results lend further support to a widely-held belief in the efficacy of ensemble solutions.

The two modularised designs investigated here did not perform as well as the ensemble system, although they did outperform the unitary net. Performance improvement is not, of course, the only motivation for adopting a modular approach, but it does provide one of the main incentives, and the poorer performance of the modular systems was initially suprising. Nonetheless, it would not be legitimate to conclude on the basis of these results that an ensemble approach will always outperform a system relying on some form of modular decomposition. In the first place, it is clear that only two modular structures were constructed, and that they both relied on the same class-based decomposition; it is quite possible that some other modular structure might have performed better. In the second place, the performance of the best single net was already high (94.4%), and it might well be that a decompositional approach would be more effective in circumstances in which the original task was easier to solve. In addition, it should be noted that the ensemble creation method employed here is one that should be expected to be particularly effective, and that it does not necessarily follow that ensembles constructed by other methods (e.g. varying the topology, or the initial conditions) would do as well.

The finding that, in a direct comparison of ensemble and modular solutions, the ensemble solution resulted the best performance, lends credence to the need to distinguish between ensemble and modular systems in a categorisation of multiple classifier systems. In the empirical research reported here, it made little difference whether modular components were combined cooperatively or competitively. Further research is needed to provide empirical validation for the proposed categorisation scheme, and the scheme itself may require modification in the light of future results. In the meantime, it provides an initial vocabulary and set of descriptors for multiple classifier systems, and as such provides a useful step towards the goal of determining the range and scope of multiple classifier designs.

References

Auda, G., and Kamel, M. (1998) Modular Neural Network Classifiers: A Comparative Study. Journal of Intelligent and Robotic Systems, 21, 117-129.

Avnimelech, R. and Intrator, N. (1999) Boosted mixture of experts: an ensemble learning scheme. Neural Computation, 11, 2, 483-497.

Baldi, P., and Hornik, K. (1989) Neural networks and principal component analysis: learning from examples without local minima. Neural Networks, 2, (1) 53-58.

Baxt, W.G. (1992) Improving the accuracy of an artificial neural network using multiple differently trained networks. Neural Computation, 4, 772-780.

Chandroth, G. and Sharkey, A.J.C. (1999) Utilising the rotational motion of machinery in a high resolution data acquisition system. In Proceedings of Computers and Ships, Organised by The Institute of Marine Engineers in association with The Royal Institution of Naval Architects.

Chandroth, G. (2000) Diagnostic ensembles: enforcing diversity for reliability in the combination. University of Sheffield, Phd Thesis.

Gallinari, P. (1995) Modular neural net systems: training of. In M.A. Arbib (Ed) The Handbook of Brain Theory and Neural Networks, 582-585, Bradford Books, MIT Press.

Giacinto, G. and Roli, F. (2000) Dynamic Classifier Selection, Multiple Classifier Systems 2000, Lecture Notes in Computer Science 1857, pp 177-189.

Hansen, J. (1999) Combining predictors: comparison of five meta machine learning methods, Information Science, 119 (1-2), 91-105.

Haykin, S. (1999) *Neural Networks - A Comprehensive Foundation,* Prentice-Hall, New Jersey, Second Edition.

Jacobs, R.A., Jordan, M.I., Nowlan, S.J. and Hinton, G.E. (1991) Adaptive mixtures of local experts. Neural Computation, 3, 79-97.

Jordan, M.I., and Jacobs, R.A.. (1994) Hierarchical mixtures of expert and the em algorithm. Neural Computation 6(2) 181-214.

Kuncheva, L.I. (in press) Switching between selection and fusion in combining classifiers: An experiment. IEEE Transactions on SMC, Part B.

Nolfi, S. and Floreano, D. (2000) *Evolutionary Robotics: The biology, intelligence and technology of self-organising machines.* A Bradford book: MIT Press.

Sharkey, A.J.C. (1996) On Combining Artificial Neural nets. Connection Science, 8, 3/4, 299-314.

Sharkey, A.J.C. (1999) Multi-Net Systems. In (Ed) A.J.C. Sharkey *Combining Artificial Neural Nets: Ensemble and Modular Multi-Net Systems,* Springer-Verlag, pp 1-30.

Sharkey, A.J.C., Chandroth, G.O, and Sharkey, N.E. (2000) A Multi-Net System for the Fault Diagnosis of a Diesel Engine. Neural Computing and Applications, 9: 152-160.

Sharkey, A.J.C. and Sharkey, N.E. (1997) Combining Diverse Neural Nets, Knowledge Engineering Review, 12, 3, 1-17.

Wolpert, D.H. (1992) Stacked generalization, Neural Networks, 5, 241-259.

Discriminant Analysis and Factorial Multiple Splits in Recursive Partitioning for Data Mining

Francesco Mola[1] and Roberta Siciliano[2]

[1] Dipartimento di Economia, Universitá di Cagliari
Viale Frá Ignazio 17, I-09100 Cagliari, Italia
mola@unica.it

[2] Dipartimento di Matematica e Statistica, Universitá di Napoli Federico II
Via Cintia, Monte S. Angelo, I-80126 Napoli, Italia
roberta@unina.it

Abstract. The framework of this paper is supervised statistical learning in data mining. In particular, multiple sets of inputs are used to predict an output on the basis of a training set. A typical data mining problem is to deal with large sets of within-groups correlated inputs compared to the number of observed objects. Standard tree-based procedures offer unstable and not interpretable solutions especially in case of complex relationships. For that multiple splits defined upon a suitable combination of inputs are required. This paper provides a methodology to build up a tree-based model which nodes splitting is due to factorial multiple splitting variables. A recursive partitioning algorithm is introduced considering a two-stage splitting criterion based on linear discriminant functions. As a result, an automated and fast procedure allows to look for factorial multiple splits able to capture suitable directions in the variability among the sets of inputs. Real world applications are discussed and the results of a simulation study are shown to describe fruitful properties of the proposed methodology.

1 Introduction

1.1 The General Framework

Learning from data and then modelling is the scientific paradigm nowadays [7]. We call this paradigm *Statistical Learning for Information Management*. Modern statistical analysis, based on intelligent and largely automated methods, aims to manage information in order to provide the essential knowledge in decision-making when dealing with large data sets characterized by complexity. This process contributes to define *Data Mining Strategies* within the *Knowledge Discovery Process* [6]. In data mining it becomes crucial to have a prior treatment of the data through some exploratory tools based on heuristic (and thus simple) criteria and feasible (and thus easy) algorithms to be implemented even for huge data sets characterized by complex relations. Such tools should simplify and reduce the dimensionality of the problem so that statistical modelling could be applied and the predictability of the given output improved. Segmentation based

F. Roli and J. Kittler (Eds.): MCS 2002, LNCS 2364, pp. 118–126, 2002.

on partitioning and recursive algorithms are suitable to identify homogeneous sub-populations with respect to the output before a statistical model is applied [5]. Segmentation follows a *supervised learning process*, as it is guided by the presence of an outcome (or response variable). In particular, the measurements of both the outcome and a set of features (inputs or explanatory variables) on a training (or learning) set of objects are observed. The final learner (or predictor) is just a tree-based model to predict or to classify a new unseen object for that the outcome is not known. Applications can be found in various fields, such as finance, medicine, market data analysis, astronomy, manufacturing and education.

1.2   The Real World Tasks

A typical data mining problem is to deal with large sets of within-groups correlated inputs compared to the number of observed objects. Main task is to define few typological predictors. As an example in marketing, questionnaires in survey analysis are often structured into distinct parts, each dedicated to a particular subject of interest. As a result, the number of inputs can be very large with respect to the number of interviews so that any standard procedure might yield to spurious interactions among different types of inputs, describing relations among predictors which might be *not logically related* so that the final interpretation becomes a hard job. A variable reduction criterion needs to be applied in the pre-processing: inputs of a given subject can be combined into one typological predictor describing a given part of the questionnaire. Other examples might concern medical data sets (i.e., the gene expression data) where inputs are partitioned into distinct groups on the basis of its own characteristics. Inputs are correlated within each group and not necessarily correlated among the groups. Furthermore, it might be interesting to analyze how this partition or stratification influence the final outcome. Finally, another typical data mining problem is to deal with more *data marts* within a *data warehouse*. Each data mart includes several within-group correlated inputs which are internally logically related and together externally related to inputs of other data marts. Any statistical analysis might relate typological predictors belonging to different data marts in order to apply statistical tools for the data warehousing.

More generally, in classification problems, every time we analyze a complex and large data set, the objective is not only *to classify* but *to interpret*, too. This is a crucial point; often this is the core for a statistician. The proposed methodology aims contribute to the scientific debate on this important issue.

1.3   The Limits of Standard Approaches

Standard tree-based procedures in this type of data sets do not work well for two main reasons. First, the interpretation of the final decision tree can be very poor: a small sample size implies a very short tree with very few splits deduced from predictors belonging to completely different subjects of interest, thus limiting the interpretation of the variable interactions in the tree. Second, standard tree-based procedures offer unstable solutions especially in case of complex relationships. Indeed, small samples requires cross-validation estimates of the prediction errors [4]. This approach, in presence of too many inputs compared to the sample size, yields to two drawbacks: an unstable selection of the splitting inputs and a computationally expensive greedy searching procedure for the best split to be repeated many times. A possible way to overcome the first of the two drawbacks is bagging estimation procedure, namely an averaging of unstable solutions provides an even better final estimate of the prediction error [3]. But what features have contributed to the prediction? How do they have influenced the final result? Associated to such bagged estimate there is not one decision tree anymore where to derive useful information in terms of splitting variables so to understand the decision-making process!

1.4   This Paper

The approach considered in this paper, in order to overcome both the above mentioned drawbacks of standard procedures, is based on the definition of multiple splits considering suitable combinations of within-groups correlated inputs. In section 2., we introduce a methodology inspired by two-stage segmentation using factorial analysis ([10][12]). The idea is to build up a tree-based model which nodes splitting are given by factorial multiple splits. The latter are understood as linear combinations of observed inputs, namely linear discriminant variables. A recursive partitioning algorithm is proposed and implemented within an automated procedure looking for multiple splits able to capture suitable directions in the variability among the sets of inputs. In section 3., we present some empirical evidence of the advantages of the proposed methodology considering a simulation study and discussing some real world applications. Some concluding remarks end the paper.

2   The Proposed Methodology

2.1   The Key Idea

A standard binary segmentation procedure aims to find at each node the best split of objects into two sub-groups which are internally the most homogeneous and externally the most heterogeneous with respect to the given output. The best split is found among all (or a sufficient set of) possible splits that can be derived from the given inputs, namely partitioning the modalities of the input into two sub-groups so to provide the corresponding binary split of the objects. A similar approach is considered in r-way partitioning procedures (also knows as multiway splits) where the internal homogeneity within the r sub-groups is maximized. Any recursive partitioning procedure is able to deal with large data sets and is particularly suitable for data mining tasks. Some alternatives strategies should be considered in order to deal with large sets of within-groups correlated inputs compared to the sample size.

The key idea of this paper is to approach this problem using an inductive method. Without loss of generality, we consider the case of binary splits although generalizations of the proposed approach can be derived for r-way or multiway splits. First, we define the optimal partition of the objects into two sub-groups which are the most internally homogeneous with respect to the given output without considering the inputs. Then, we look at the observed candidate partitions of the input features (and their combinations) which provide some alternative solutions that best approximate the optimal one. In other words, known the optimal solution we look for the most suitable combination of inputs which has the highest chance to provide nearly the best partition of the objects. Whereas the optimal partition is found in spite of the inputs and it can be just theoretical (in the sense that there might be no input which ensures that partition of the objects into two sub-groups), the observed one is found considering the candidate inputs (or a combination of them) aiming to approximate the optimal solution.

2.2   Notation and Definitions

Let Y be the output and let $\mathbf{X}_g = (X_{1g}, \ldots, X_{d_g g})$ denote the g-th set of inputs, for $g = 1, \ldots, G$ groups and $D = \sum_g d_g$ total inputs. Denote by $\mathcal{L} = \{y_n, \mathbf{x}_n; n = 1, \ldots, N\}$ the training sample of objects in which are measured the output and the G sets of inputs, being the row-vector $\mathbf{x}_n = (\mathbf{x}_{1n}, \ldots, \mathbf{x}_{Gn})$ formed by juxtaposing the G sets of input measurements on the n-the object. Furthermore, assume that within each set, the inputs are strongly correlated. Inputs and output are numerical defined in the real space.

Any binary segmentation procedure can be defined as a recursive partition of the objects into two sub-groups such that at each node the best split of the input features (yielding to the binary partition of the objects) maximizes the between group deviation of the output Y, or minimizes the within groups deviations of the output Y in the two sub-groups. A greedy searching procedure is applied to look for the best split among all possible (or a suitable subset of) splits that can be deduced from the inputs.

We distinguish between prospective and retrospective splits of the objects at a given node[1].

Definition 1: Any split s of the objects induced by splitting the input features is named as a *prospective split*. As an example, an object goes either to the left sub-node if $X \leq c$ or to the right node if $X > c$. Standard tree-growing procedure adopts prospective splits. Let S denote the set of prospective splits.

Definition 2: We define a *retrospective split* any split k of the objects induced by splitting the output: being Y numerical any cut point of the real interval in which the Y is defined yields a retrospective split. Note that in this definition the inputs do not play a role. Let K denote the set of retrospective splits.

This terminology is motivated as follows: a prospective split of the objects is deduced by *looking forward* to the splitting of the input features, whereas a retrospective split of the objects requires *to look backward* to which observed split

---

[1] In the following we omit to indicate the node in order to simplify the notation

of the input features might induce that partition of the objects, so that an inductive approach must be considered.

Property 1: It is worth noting that the set S of prospective splits do not necessarily coincide with the set K of retrospective splits. It can be shown that $S \subseteq K$.

Property 2: There can be retrospective splits which are not admissible, in the sense that for a split of the objects based only on the Y there can be not found any split of the input features yielding to the same partition of the objects. This distinction is important in the proposed methodology because it allows to define upper bounds for the optimality criteria which will be considered.

Let denote $L \equiv Left$ and $R \equiv Right$ the sub-groups of any split k or of any split s. Given a retrospective split k we can calculate within each sub-group the sample mean of Y, denoted by $\bar{y}_k(L)$ and $\bar{y}_k(R)$, the within-group deviations, denoted by $Dev_k(W|L)$ and $Dev_k(W|R)$, or the between class deviation, denoted by $Dev_k(B)$. Similar notation is used for prospective splits.

Definition 3: We define the *optimal theoretical split* of the objects into two sub-groups the split that maximizes the between class deviation of Y over all possible retrospective splits in the set K:

$$k^* \equiv argmax_k\{Dev_k(B)\} \qquad (1)$$

which yields the best discrimination of the objects belonging to the left sub-group of k^* (having an average $\bar{y}_{k^*}(L)$) from the objects belonging to the right sub-group of k^* (having an average $\bar{y}_{k^*}(R)$). This is a theoretical partition since it can be not necessarily produced by any observed split of the input features. Let $\tilde{Y}$ denote a dummy output which discriminates the two sub-groups of objects according to the optimal solution provided by the retrospective split (1).

Definition 4: We define the *best observed split* of the objects into two sub-groups the split s that maximizes the between class deviation of Y over all possible prospective splits in the set S, namely $s^* \equiv argmax_s\{Dev_s(B)\}$.

The set K of all possible retrospective splits can be reduced using the property related to the use of a numerical variable Y. Formally, if Y has N distinct ordered values then there are $N-1$ suitable cut points to divide the values (and thus the objects) into two sub-groups. Although the number of possible splits is in principle $2^{N-1} - 1$, the number of suitable splits reduces to $N-1$ if we consider the ordinal scale of Y and the statistical properties of mean and deviation which is based the optimality criterion on. In other words, the best discrimination of the Y values must simply satisfy the ordering of the Y values by definition. For a node size constraint of say m objects, the cardinality of the set of candidate splits to find the optimal one reduces to $N - 2(m-1) - 1$.

Definition 5: The quantity $Dev_{k^*}(B)$ derived from (1) is the upper limit of the between-group deviation that can be found by any prospective split of the input features, i.e., $Dev_{k^*}(B) \leq Dev_s(B)$.

Definition 6: The ratio $Dev_{s^*}(B)/Dev_{k^*}(B)$, i.e., the between class deviation due to the best observed split over the between class deviation due to the optimal theoretical split, is an efficiency measure of the partition of the objects that is found at a given node. It says how good is the discrimination between the two sub-groups with respect to the given output ranging from zero and one by definition.

2.3 Two-Stage Segmentation

The proposed methodology is inspired by two-stage segmentation and fast splitting algorithm [10] [11]. The general idea was to emphasize the role of the inputs to be globally considered before selecting the best split. According to the two-stage splitting criterion, first we find the best input that provides a good prediction of the given output in order to generate the set of candidate splits, then we find the best split that provides the best partition into two sub-groups. Several two-stage criteria have been proposed considering statistical modelling as also factorial methods for univariate and multivariate output [13].

In the following, we provide an alternative two-stage splitting criterion to overcome the limits of standard procedures.

Our methodology can be viewed as a recursive partitioning which at each node applies the following two stages:

I. Factorial analysis: For each group of within group correlated inputs we find a factorial linear combination of inputs such to maximize the predictability power to get the optimal split of the objects;
II. Multiple splitting criterion: Among the prospective splits that can be deduced from the linear combinations determined in stage one we find the best factorial (multiple) split of the objects.

Stage I allows to reduce the dimensionality of the problem passing from $D = \sum_g d_g$ inputs to G linear combinations of inputs. Stage II provides to define automatically the factorial multiple split of the objects into two sub-groups. Our proposed procedure will be named TS-DIS (*Two-Stage segmentation via DIScriminant analysis*).

In general, main advantage of tree-based models with splits based on factorial linear combinations is to provide better prediction accuracy and shorter trees [9][8]. With respect to the CART use of discriminant analysis, our approach deals with numerical rather than a dummy output.

2.4 Linear Discriminant Functions of Within-Groups Correlated Inputs

Factorial discriminant analysis is applied in stage I. We consider as output the dummy variable $\tilde{Y}$ which summarizes the optimal split of the objects. For each set of inputs, i.e., $\mathbf{X}_g = (X_{1g}, \ldots, X_{d_g g})$ with $g = 1, \ldots, G$, we calculate the within group deviation $\mathbf{W}_g$ and the between class deviation $\mathbf{B}_g$ of the inputs in the g-th group. For each group, we find the linear discriminant variable such that the between class deviation is maximized relative to the within group deviation:

$$Z_g = \sum_{j=1}^{d_g} \alpha_j X_{jg} \qquad (2)$$

where α_j are the values of the eigenvector associated to the largest eigenvalue of the matrix $\mathbf{W}_g^{-1}\mathbf{B}_g$. The (2) is the g-th linear combination of the inputs belonging to the g-th group with weights given by the first eigenvector values. It is obtained maximizing the predictability power of the d_g inputs to explain the optimal split as summarized by the output $\tilde{Y}$. Moreover, the Z_g variables are all normalized such to have mean equal to zero and variance equal to one. In this respect, they will play the same role in the greedy selection of the best split in stage II, thus producing unbiased splits in the procedure.

It is worth noting that the discriminant analysis is applied considering the dummy output $\tilde{Y}$ and each set of inputs separately. In this way, we find the best linear combination within each group of internally correlated inputs.

2.5   Multiple Split Selection

The selection of the best split of the objects into two sub-groups is done in stage II. The linear combinations $Z_1, \ldots, Z_G$ are the candidate splitting variables which generate the set S of prospective splits. These can be interpreted as multiple splits being defined on the basis of a combination of inputs. The best multiple split is found maximizing the between class deviation of the output:

$$s^* \equiv argmax_s\{Dev_s(B)\} \tag{3}$$

for any split s in the set S.

We can also calculate the efficiency measure based on the ratio between the between class deviation due to the best observed split, i.e., $Dev_{s^*}(B)$, and the between class deviation due to the optimal split, i.e., $Dev_{k^*}(B)$. This measure could be also used as a stopping rule for the tree-growing recursive procedure.

2.6   The Recursive Algorithm

In order to summarize the proposed procedure we outline the main steps of the recursive splitting algorithm at any node of the tree:

1. Find the optimal retrospective split of the objects maximizing the between class deviation of the Y and define the dummy output $\tilde{Y}$;
2. Find the discriminant variables $(Z_1, \ldots, Z_G)$ for the G groups according to (2) maximizing the between class deviation of the inputs with respect to the optimal split summarized by $\tilde{Y}$;
3. Using the set of prospective splits generated by the discriminant variables find the best observed split s^* maximizing the between class deviation of the output Y;
4. Calculate statistical measures within each sub-node, providing also interpretation aids and visualization of the splitting process through a factorial axis description[2].

---

[2] For sake of brevity, we have not described the information tools that can be added to our procedure for a better visualization and interpretation of the results

3   The Empirical Evidence

3.1   A Simulation Study

Aim of our simulation study was to analyze the performance of the proposed procedure TS-DIS compared to the standard CART procedure [4].

The planning of our simulation study was the following. We fixed $G = 10$ the number of groups. The experimental design was based on the following parameters: *the sample size*, with levels 100, 500, 1000, 10000, *the number of inputs*, given by 20, 50, 100 partitioned into $G = 10$ groups, *the variance of the inputs and of the output* considering two cases. In the first, the variables were generated from normal distributed functions having mean equal to zero and variance respectively equal to 1, 10, 100, whereas in the second case, the variables were generated from uniform distribution ranging from zero and 10, 100, 1000 respectively. In total, we have generated 36 data sets for normal distributed inputs and 36 for uniform distributed inputs. In order to stress our procedure we have considered the worst conditions assuming within group uncorrelated inputs and checking in particular the performance in the root node of the tree.

We present the results of our simulation study in table 1 and in table 2. For sake of brevity, we have omitted to report the results concerning the last level of the sample size and the first level of the variance.

In the first three columns we indicate the parameters of the experimental design. In the subsequent columns, we report blocks of results concerning respectively the optimal split solution (the optimal retrospective split), the TS-DIS best (observed) solution, the CART best (observed) solution. For each split, we give the average and the standard deviation of the output Y in the left and right subnodes, and for the observed splits, in addition, we give the percentage of errors. The latter is calculated considering the cross-classification of the dummy variable $\tilde{Y}$ with the best observed split of the objects: in this way, we can calculate how many objects were misclassified by the best observed split with respect to the optimal one.

Although we have randomly generated the variables without assuming a dependency data structure the proposed procedure offers better solutions in terms of both misclassification error and within class homogeneity.

3.2   The Real World Applications

Our methodology has been experienced in some applications for *market basket analysis* aiming at identifying associations between a large number of products bought by different consumers in a specific location, such as a hypermarket [1] [2]. TS-DIS has allowed to define hierarchies of the most typological baskets of products which determine high monetary values spent on specific target products. This becomes particularly useful, from a promotional viewpoint: if two products resulted sequentially associated in the final tree, it is sufficient to promote only one to increase sales of both. At the same time, from a merchandizing viewpoint, the products type should be allocated on the same shelf in the layout of a supermarket.

4 Concluding Remarks

This paper has provided a recursive partitioning procedure for a particular data mining problem, that is to find a tree-based model for a numerical output explained by large sets of within group correlated inputs using a small training sample compared to the number of inputs. The procedure is based on two-stage splitting criterion employing linear discriminant analysis and defining factorial multiple splits. New concepts of retrospective and prospective splits were defined and an upper bound of the optimality splitting criterion was in this way defined. The results of our simulation study as well as of real world applications have been very promising, showing that our methodology works much better than CART standard procedure under the above conditions.

Acknowledgments: This work has been supported by MIUR funds. Authors wish to thank three anonymous referees for helpful comments on a previous draft.

References

1. Agrawal, R., Mannila, H., Srikant, R., Toivonen, H. and Verkamo, A.I.: Fast discovery of association rules, (1995), *Advances in Knowledge Discovery and Data Mining*, Chapter 12, pages 307–328, AAAI/MIT Press, Menlo Park, CA.
2. Aria, M., Mola, F., Siciliano, R., Growing and Visualizing Prediction PathsTrees in Market Basket Analysis, *Proceedings of COMPSTAT*, (2002), Berlin (August 24-28), Germany, Physica Verlag.
3. Breiman, L.: Bagging Predictors. *Machine Learning*, *26*, (1996), 46–59.
4. Breiman, L., Friedman, J.H., Olshen, R.A. and Stone, C.J.: *Classification and Regression Trees*, Belmont C.A. Wadsworth, (1984).
5. Conversano, C., Mola, F., Siciliano, R.: Partitioning Algorithms and Combined Model Integration for Data Mining, *Computational Statistics*, (2001), 16, 323-339.
6. Hand, D.J., Mannila, H., Smyth, P.: *Principles of Data Mining*, (2001), The MIT Press.
7. Hastie, T.J., Tibshirani, R.J., Friedman, J.: *The Elements of Statistical Learning*. Springer Verlag, (2001).
8. Kim, H., Loh, W.Y.: Classification Trees with Unbiased Multiway Splits, *Journal of the American Statistical Association*, (2001), 96, 454, 589-604.
9. Loh, W.Y., Vanichsetakul, N.: Tree-Structured Classification Via Generalized Discriminant Analysis, *Journal of the American Statistical Association*, (1988), 83, 403, 715-728.
10. Mola, F., Siciliano, R.: A two-stage predictive splitting algorithm in binary segmentation, in Y. Dodge, J. Whittaker. (Eds.): *Computational Statistics: COMPSTAT '92*, 1, Physica Verlag, Heidelberg (D), (1992), 179-184.
11. Mola, F., Siciliano, R.: A Fast Splitting Procedure for Classification Trees, *Statistics and Computing*, 7, (1997), 208-216.
12. Siciliano, R., Mola, F.: Ternary Classification Trees: a Factorial Approach, in Blasius, J. and Greenacre, M. (Eds.): *Visualization of categorical data* (1998), New York: Academic Press.
13. Siciliano, R., Mola, F: Multivariate Data Analysis through Classification and Regression Trees, *Computational Statistics and Data Analysis*, 32, Elsevier Science, (2000), 285-301.

New Measure of Classifier Dependency in Multiple Classifier Systems

Dymitr Ruta and Bogdan Gabrys

Applied Computational Intelligence Research Unit,
Division of Computing and Information Systems, University of Paisley,
High Street, Paisley PA1-2BE, United Kingdom
{ruta-ci0, gabr-ci0}@paisley.ac.uk

Abstract. Recent findings in the domain of combining classifiers provide a surprising revision of the usefulness of diversity for modelling combined performance. Although there is a common agreement that a successful fusion system should be composed of accurate and diverse classifiers, experimental results show very weak correlations between various diversity measures and combining methods. Effectively neither the combined performance nor its improvement against mean classifier performance seem to be measurable in a consistent and well defined manner. At the same time the most successful diversity measures, barely regarded as measuring diversity, are based on measuring error coincidences and by doing so they move closer to the definitions of combined errors themselves. Following this trend we decided to use directly the combining error normalized within the derivable error limits as a measure of classifiers dependency. Taking into account its simplicity and representativeness we chose majority voting error for the construction of the measure. We examine this novel dependency measure for a number of real datasets and classifiers showing its ability to model combining improvements over an individual mean.

1. Introduction

In many recent works dedicated to pattern recognition the efforts are being shifted towards classifier fusion as a way of further improvement of the recognition rate [1]-[3]. Combining classifiers is now perceived as a universal and obvious advancement of the single–best strategy, often even paraphrased as "gather all and combine" [1]. Very quickly it turned out that "combining all" is expensive and very rarely optimal, which initiated the studies concentrating on the question of what makes some combinations of classifiers work better than others. Individual mean performance was the first indicator to start with. However it has been shown that well performing recognition systems can also be constructed out of weak individually, but strong as a team, classifiers [4]. The system property responsible for the team strength is known under many names in the literature including: disagreement, diversity, independence etc, all denoting certain characteristics among classifier outputs [1]-[9]. More detailed analysis revealed that specific distributions of outputs corresponding to maximum error dispersion account for the optimal performance of the voting systems [10], [11]. In general, however, each combiner has its own characteristic features and phenomena

F. Roli and J. Kittler (Eds.): MCS 2002, LNCS 2364, pp. 127-136, 2002.

explaining successful combination for one combiner may no longer be applicable for others. Nevertheless the classifier diversity, in addition to the individual performances, is believed to explain all the amazing successes of classifier fusion.

The problems with the diversity started to emerge with the attempts of measuring it. Focused mainly on the outputs disagreement, a majority of diversity measures investigated in [12]-[15] showed very weak correlations with combined performances as well as their improvements. In [14] Shipp and Kuncheva illustrated even an apparent conflict between diversity tendencies shown by some measures as falling and by others as rising among AdaBoost generated classifiers as training progressed. An interesting finding emerged from our recent diversity investigations [16]. A substantial gain in the correlation with majority voting error has been observed for measures operating on error coincidences with an asymmetry to change of the individual classifier outputs in their definitions. Our measure ('Fault Majority') built using this principle and additionally exploiting some characteristics of the combiner it was designed for, showed the best average correlation with the majority voting error. In our further investigations into the concept of diversity, the analysis of different error coincidence levels within a pool of classifiers to be combined showed further improvement in the correlation to majority voting error [17]. Consequently the closer the measure to the definition of the combined error, the better its correlation with the combined errors and the better use of the measure.

In this paper we attempt to take a full advantage of these findings and propose to use the normalized combiner error directly as a measure of dependency. This proposition may seem naive but if we confront the properties of such a measure with aims that diversity measures are trying to achieve, this "naive measure" shows superior quality in all aspects. Majority voting combiner is ideal for that purpose as measuring its error is often computationally cheaper than applying complex diversity measures [10]-[17]. We try to explain and illustrate that there is no point of using diversity measures to model majority voting error rather than just using this error itself. Moreover, we show that unlike diversity measures, a measure of combiner error normalized within its limits can be used for modelling the performance improvement of the system. We justify our claims by a number of experiments with majority voting and indicate potential applicability for other combiners.

The remainder of the paper is organized as follows. In Section 2 we raise some doubts about the usefulness of diversity in the context of combining classifiers. Section 3 provides the definition of the novel measure based on the majority voting error. In Section 4 we consider possibility of reducing complexity of the measure. The following section shows the experiments conducted with real datasets and classifiers evaluating the new measure. Finally summary and conclusion are given in Section 6.

2. Problems with Useful Diversity

Diversity perceived as a certain dependency among variables is a well-established statistical concept. More recently, rapid technology development led to rediscovery of the diversity in its entirely new meaning and importance in the context of combining evidences [5]-[8]. In the software development domain, the successful strategy turned out to be designing systems composed of diverse multi-version software implementations preventing from coincident failures [5], [6]. In the pattern recognition domain, diversity is claimed to be the property of the multiple classifier systems deciding about their performance [7], [8]. In general terms diversity is a clear concept of variety, multiplicity and the hope was that diverse (here different) classifiers should produce more reliable and improved classification results. It turned out however that different classifiers are not necessarily diverse and to evaluate the diversity one needs an appropriate measure. We believe that to be called useful with relation to combining classifiers, diversity measure should be:

1. well correlated with combiner performance and/or its improvement;
2. appropriately normalized between extreme values of combined performance;
3. simple or at least less complex than calculating the combined performance.

With respect to these requirements a vast majority of diversity measures completely fail on the first point, some of them fulfil the second and third condition, which additionally depends on a combiner used. The most naive is probably the illusion that a simple measure based on outputs disagreement can be correlated well with a number of different sometimes quite complex combining methods. It is also reflected in many unsuccessful attempts to define a universally useful diversity measure indicating potential benefits of combining [12]-[15]. It is therefore our belief that any measure of diversity, which could be used as a certain criterion for selecting classifiers to be combined, or deciding whether one should use a combination of classifiers in the first instance, should be designed in close connection with the combination method (i.e. majority voting, fuzzy templates, mixture of experts etc.) as indicated in [16] and [17]. In an extreme case, the combination performance, which we advocate in this paper, could be used instead of some kind of "universally useful diversity measure". Trivially, as we intend to show, the measure of combined performance does perfectly everything what diversity measures unsuccessfully try to do and often does it even cheaper, using the same evidence.

3. Majority Voting as Dependency Measure

Majority voting (MV) is an example of a simple fusion operator that can be applied to combine any classifiers as their outputs can always be mapped, if necessary, to the binary representation. Given a system of M trained classifiers: $D = \{D_1,...,D_M\}$ applied for N input data x_i, $i = 1,...,N$ we can represent the system outputs as a binary matrix of outputs $Y^{N \times M}$ (0-correct, 1-error). The decision of majority voting combiner y_i^{MV} for a single i^{th} data sample can be obtained by the following formula:

$$y_i^{MV} = \begin{cases} 0 & \text{if } \sum_{j=1}^{M} y_{ij} < \lceil M/2 \rceil \\ 1 & \text{if } \sum_{j=1}^{M} y_{ij} \geq \lceil M/2 \rceil \end{cases} \tag{1}$$

A more detailed definition of MV including the rejection rule, observed for equal number of opposite votes when M is even, can be found in [9]. However, this work is not concerned with a detailed study of MV itself and in further analysis, without any loss of generality, we assume odd M. In [11] we presented the majority voting error limits assuming that all classifiers perform at the same mean level. Recalling these limits for a specific mean classifier error e we have:

$$E_{MV}^{min} = max\left\{0, \frac{Me - \lceil M/2 \rceil + 1}{M - \lceil M/2 \rceil + 1}\right\} \qquad E_{MV}^{max} = min\left\{\frac{Me}{\lceil M/2 \rceil}, 1\right\} \qquad (2)$$

where E_{MV}^{min} and E_{MV}^{max} stand for the lower and upper limit of MV error respectively.

Now what we propose is that measuring majority voting error (1) and normalizing it within the limits (2) we obtain a very informative measure expressing the relative position of the majority voting error between its limits and call it Relative Error (RE) measure. To get an intuitive norm and relevant interpretation of the specific points of the RE measure we propose the following definition:

$$RE = \begin{cases} (E_{MV} - E_0)/(E_0 - E_{MV}^{min}) & if \quad E_{MV} \leq E_0 \\ (E_{MV} - E_0)/(E_{MV}^{max} - E_0) & if \quad E_{MV} > E_0 \end{cases} \qquad (3)$$

where E_0 is a specific value of the system error, for which the RE measure is equal to 0. The graphical interpretation of the measure with marked components is shown in Figure 1. We consider two possibilities for the value E_0, which is the majority voting error assuming classifier independence or in the second version just mean classifiers error. Note that for both versions of the RE measure, its values range within the limits $\{-1,1\}$ where the worst case: $RE = 1$ corresponds to the maximum majority voting error possible and in the best case: $RE = -1$ the combined error reaches its theoretical minimum. For the case of E_0 being independent error, the measure resembles in its values the concept of negative and positive correlations with the same meaning of the values as discussed in [10]. In the experimental section we evaluate its performance as a dependency measure using real datasets and classifiers.

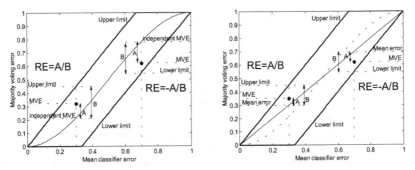

Figure 1. Graphical interpretation of the RE in two versions: with E_0 as independent majority voting error (left), E_0 denoting mean classifier error (right).

4. Complexity Reduction

The classifiers dependency measured by the performance of the combiner may be accused of being too complex and indeed it requires recalculating the majority voting error for different subsets of classifiers taken to the fusion. Applying the RE measure for all classifier combinations from a given pool imposes exponential complexity of the process equal to the exhaustive evaluation of the combiner performance. However the evaluative complexity of non-pairwise measures discussed in [12] is exactly of the same order and the cost of the individual measure is commonly higher. Moreover, seemingly simple pairwise measures in addition to their quadratic evaluative complexity have to add the complexity of measuring the diversity for all pairs within the combination to get the average value, which make them complex even using precalculated matrix of pairwise diversity values. Binary matrix representation of outputs from multiple classifiers is particularly useful for fast calculation of the majority voting. What is required to get the majority vote output for a particular sample is to sum all values within corresponding row of the matrix $Y^{N \times M}$ and check if this sum is greater or equal $\lceil M/2 \rceil$. Given matrix Y the error calculation is equally simple as it is just mean out of all combiner outputs, obtainable by just one line of code in Matlab notation:

$$E_{MV} = \texttt{mean(sum(Y')>M/2);}$$

Further potential reduction of the individual costs of the measure is available through the approximation of the majority voting error. In [17] we showed a decomposition of the majority voting error into levels of general or exclusive coincidences. The kth level of general coincidence L_k^u is just the summing, for all the k-combinations of classifiers, of the sums of cases where all k classifiers fail. In the exclusive version L_k^e additional condition is that all the remaining classifiers should produce correct outputs. Using these definitions majority voting error can be decomposed as:

$$E_{MV} = \frac{1}{N} \sum_{i=\lceil M/2 \rceil}^{M} L_i^E = \frac{1}{N} \sum_{i=\lceil M/2 \rceil}^{M} (-1)^{i-k} \binom{i-1}{k-1} L_i^G \qquad (4)$$

We also showed efficient ways of calculation of these coincidences within the framework of set analysis. Additional savings are potentially available provided it is possible to estimate any of the two types of coincidence levels (see [17] for details). Recalling the experimental results from [17], we observed a substantial loss in the correlation with majority voting error if just one of the required levels is missing. In other words approximation of a number of coincidence levels has to be extremely accurate to produce precise estimations of the overall MV error. A promising phenomenon was observed for the higher levels of general coincidences. Plotted in the logarithmic scale they showed a linear tendency as if the classifiers were independent starting from a certain order of dependency, but with substantially higher mean classifier error. Measuring just 2 points of this line would give the values of all other required levels and potentially the value of majority voting error (4). In the experimental section we examine potential applicability of this option and compare the approximated values with combiner errors.

5. Experiments

The experiments have been carried out in two groups. The first part provides comparative evaluation of the proposed RE measure in two versions discussed in Section

3. Applying a number of classifiers for real datasets, we examine the correlation between the RE and the improvement over individual mean error and compare it against representative diversity measures used so far. In the second experiment we examine the relevance of the components of RE measure. The reliability of the majority voting error limits is examined by comparing the true limits with the ones based just on the information of mean classifier errors. Relating to the majority voting error component of RE measure we show some examples of its modelling implementation discussed in Section 4. To maintain the generality of our findings we chose 11 commonly used classifiers and applied them for a classification of 4 real datasets taken mostly from the UCI Repository[1]. The experiments have been carried out by applying 100 times random splitting into equally populated training and testing sets, the outputs obtained for classification of the testing sets have been hardened and stored in binary matrices.

5.1 Experiment 1

In this experiment both versions of the RE measure have been applied for all the combinations of 3, 5, 7, and 9 out of 11 classifiers. The same has been done with Q statistics measure and Double Fault measure discussed in [12]-[15] for comparison purposes. All these measures have been compared against the difference between the majority voting error and mean classifier error and the quality of a measure was evaluated by calculating correlation coefficients. Table 1 shows the comparative results for all examined datasets and Figure 2 depicts the meaning of the correlation coefficients for the combinations of 3 classifiers. The results clearly show the superior quality of the presented measures in comparison to Q statistics, which only for one dataset showed correlation coefficients reaching 0.9, and even worse Double Fault measure. The first version of the RE_{IMV} measure (with independent MV error as E_0) failed to capture the considered dependency for *Chromo* dataset, whereas in the second version, RE_{ME} (E_0 as a mean classifier error) showed an outstanding correlation with the difference between majority voting error and mean error for all considered datasets.

Table 1. Correlations between the improvement of the majority voting error over the mean classifier error (E_{MV}-E_{ME}) and both versions of the RE measure compared against Q Statistics and Double Fault measures. The correlation coefficients were measured separately for the combinations of 3, 5, 7, and 9 out of 11 classifiers within each dataset.

#Clasf	Iris				Biomed				Satimage				Chromo			
	3	5	7	9	3	5	7	9	3	5	7	9	3	5	7	9
Q	32.8	32.8	30.7	47.4	90.1	95.8	95.4	93.9	79.9	80.7	78.7	76.5	-7.4	13.3	21.2	25.8
DF	27.3	34.7	40.8	38.8	28.8	26.5	23.5	21.0	43.1	48.2	51.9	56.1	32.4	63.4	76.6	78.5
RE_{IMV}	99.0	98.6	98.7	98.7	99.9	99.8	99.8	99.6	98.5	99.3	99.9	99.7	35.8	2.5	-5.9	-6.0
RE_{ME}	96.8	98.2	98.6	98.7	98.8	99.4	99.5	99.6	98.0	97.9	98.0	98.3	99.4	99.8	99.8	99.8

[1] University of California Repository of Machine Learning Databases and Domain Theories, available free at: ftp.ics.uci.edu/pub/machine-learning-databases.

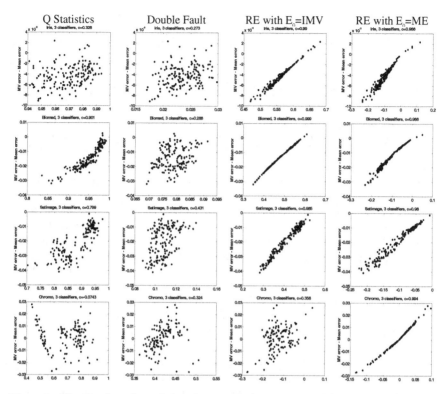

Figure 2. Visualization of correlations between the improvement of the majority voting error and the measures from Table 1. Coordinates of all points represent the measures examined for all 3-element combinations out of 11 classifiers for which the measures were applied.

Very high correlations commonly exceeding 0.98 suggest that the presented measures appropriately model performance improvement that can be obtained by majority voting comparing to mean classifier error. Moreover the quality of the measures does not fall for higher number of classifiers in a team. Nevertheless occasional failures (like for *Chromo* dataset with RE_{IMV}) may suggest that the measures do not deal well with large differences in classifier performances, which for *chromo* dataset exceeds 20% but further experiments are currently conducted to investigate this issue.

5.2 Experiment 2

The definition of the RE measure consists of two major components: majority voting error and the estimates of its limits for given mean classifier error. The derivation of the limits is performed with an assumption that all classifiers to be combined have the same classification performance. Realistically, classifiers perform differently, and there is a limited number of samples which means that realistic boundary distributions of errors in the binary matrix may result in slightly different or substantially different limits if the differences in performances are high. In the example of an extreme case of having 3 classifiers with individual error rates: {0.01, 0.5, 0.99}, as the mean is 0.5, definitions (2) result in the limits {0.25, 0.75} whereas in reality the limits are {0.49, 0.51}. However in realistic situations if the performance differences are high, the worst classifiers are rejected and consequently the final differences are never that extreme. The results in Table 2 showing extremely small absolute discrepancies from the real limits confirm our expectations. The limits component of the RE measure can be therefore considered as a fast and accurate estimation of the true MV error limits.

As discussed in Section 4, the majority voting error component can be calculated in a relatively fast way. Nevertheless definition of majority voting error (4) decomposed into sums of higher coincidence levels makes it tempting to model the error by approximation of the required coincidence levels. Following the observations of linear progression (in a logarithmic scale) of the general coincidence levels, we examine now the accuracy of the approximation based on information of just two boundary coincidence levels. Figure 3-A shows the evolution of the general coincidence levels in the logarithmic scale for four considered datasets. The crucial part of the higher levels is visibly quite close to the linear trend. For all datasets we applied linear regressions for the levels influencing majority voting error defined by (4), resulting in the lines appearing in Figure 3-B. Based on the approximated values of all general coincidence levels we then calculated the majority voting errors according to (4) and compared them with the real error values as shown in Table 3. Although the plots in Figure 3-B show quite satisfactory match for each coincidence level individually, small deviations from the true values result in big differences between the real and approximated majority voting error. It seems that approximation of the MV error by means of error coincidence levels introduced in [17] may not by suitable due to high sensitivity of the combined error to small deviations from the real values of coincidence levels. These results agree in a sense with our findings from error coincidence analysis performed in [17]. Nevertheless the results provide a new interesting characteristic of the multiple classifier system, which is the slope of the falling general coincidence levels. The slope coefficient m, where $f(x)=mx+b$, has a direct equivalence with the error rate of equally performing team of independent classifiers: $p=\exp(m)$. For both cases each consecutive coincidence level falls by multiplying the previous level by the equivalent independent error rate p.

Table 2. Average absolute relative abbreviations (in %) from the real upper limits of majority voting error imposed by applying definitions (2) based only on mean classifier error. Average abbreviations are calculated separately for each dataset out of all combinations of 3 classifers.

Dataset	Iris	Biomed	Satimage	Chromo
Av. Abbrev. [%]	0.4 4	0.19	0.14	0.05

Table 3. Comparison between the real and approximated values of the majority voting error for all datasets and applying all 11 classifiers. The error rates are shown in percentages.

Dataset	Iris	Biomed	Satimage	Chromo
Real MVE [%]	3.6 4	9.97	14.76	56.57
Approx. MVE [%]	1.9 7	6.40	8.01	36.02

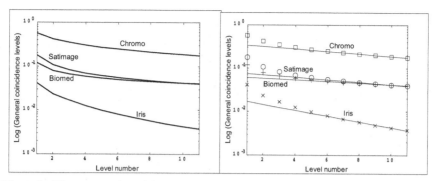

Figure 3. Linear regression of the normalized higher levels of general coincidence. A (left): Evolution of the values for increasing levels in logarithmic scale. B (right): Lines matched in the logarithmic scale to the higher levels (6:11) of general coincidence.

6. Summary and Conclusions

In this paper we attempted to show a new strategy for constructing the classifier dependency measure directly exploiting characteristics of the combining method applied to the classifier team. Inspired by the unsuccessful attempts of finding the relationship between the diversity measures and combining performance, we claim that at the moment it is cheaper and more accurate to measure the combining performance directly rather than using any of a number of existing diversity measures.

As a result we proposed a Relative Error measure which uses majority voting error scaled within accurately approximated error limits. We showed that all components of the RE measure are easy to calculate and its complexity remains of the same order as established diversity measures. Showing two versions of the RE we proved experimentally their very high correlations with the improvement of the majority voting performance over mean classifier error, the indicator commonly used to evaluate the quality of the diversity measures. Both versions have been scaled between -1 and 1 where: -1 indicates a maximum possible improvement while 1 indicates a maximum possible degradation of the performance. The difference between two versions is the meaning of 0 value, which in the first version corresponds to the majority voting error with the assumption of classifier independence, while for the second version means equal values of the majority voting error and average individual classifier error. While the performance of the second version of the measure was extremely good for all four data sets, the first version has failed quite spectacularly for the *Chromo* dataset. The reasons for this failure are not quite clear and require further investigations.

We have also attempted to model the majority voting error using approximated error coincidences which turned out to be inaccurate in predicting the error value though the error coincidences individually are approximated relatively well. However, what is very interesting is the fact that the majority voting error was consistently underestimated for all datasets which might indicate a possibility of using these estimates as lower limits for a given set of classifiers and data sets.

References

1. Sharkey A.J.C.: Combining Artificial Neural Nets: Ensemble and Modular Multi-net Systems. Springer-Verlag, Berlin Heidelberg New York (1999).
2. Gabrys B.: Combining Neuro-Fuzzy Classifiers for Improved Generalisation and Reliability. To be presented at the WCCI'2002 Congress, Honolulu, USA, (2002).
3. Gabrys B. Learning Hybrid Neuro-Fuzzy Classifier Models From Data: To Combine or not to Combine?. In Proceedings of the EUNITE'2001 Conference, Tenerife, Spain (2001).
4. Rogova G.: Combining the results of several neural network classifiers. Neural Networks 7(5) (1994) 777-781.
5. Patridge D., Krzanowski W.J.: Software diversity: practical statistics for its measurements and exploitation. Information & Software Technology 39 (1997) 707-717.
6. Littlewood B., Miller D.R.: Conceptual modeling of coincident failures in multiversion software. IEEE Transactions on Software Engineering 15(12) (1989) 1596-1614.
7. Sharkey A.J.C., Sharkey N.E.: Combining Diverse Neural Nets. The Knowledge Engineering Review 12(3) (1997) 231-247.
8. Partridge D., Griffith N.: Strategies for improving neural net generalisation. Neural Computing & Applications 3 (1995) 27-37.
9. Lam L., Suen C.Y.: Application of majority voting to pattern recognition: an analysis of its behaviour and performance. IEEE Trans. on Sys., Man, and Cyber. 27(5) (1997) 553-568.
10. Kuncheva L.I., Whitaker C.J., Shipp C.A., Duin R.P.W.: Limits on the majority vote accuracy in classifier fusion. Pattern Analysis and Applications, accepted, available at: http://www.bangor.ac.uk/~mas00a/papers/lkpaa.ps.gz.
11. Ruta D., Gabrys B.: A theoretical analysis of the limits of majority voting errors for multiple classifier systems. To appear in the journal of Pattern Analysis and Applications.
12. Kuncheva L.I., C.J. Whitaker.: Measures of diversity in classifier ensembles and their relationship with the ensemble accuracy, submitted, available at: http://www.bangor.ac.uk/~mas00a/papers/lkml.ps.gz.
13. Shipp C.A., Kuncheva L.I.: Relationships between combination methods and measures of diversity in combining classifiers. Information Fusion, accepted, available at: http://www.bangor.ac.uk/~mas00a/papers/csif.ps.gz.
14. Shipp C.A, Kuncheva LI.: An investigation into how ADABOOST affects classifier diversity, submitted, available at: http://www.bangor.ac.uk/~mas00a/papers/csIPMU02.ps.gz
15. Whitaker C.J., Kuncheva L.I.: Examining the Relationship Between Majority Vote Accuracy and Diversity in Bagging and Boosting, submitted, available at: http://www.bangor.ac.uk/~mas00a/papers/cjwst.ps.gz.
16. Ruta D., Gabrys B.: Analysis of the Correlation Between Majority Voting Errors and the Diversity Measures in Multiple Classifier Systems. In Proceedings of the International Symposium on Soft Computing, Paisley, Scotland (2001).
17. Ruta D., Gabrys B.: Set analysis of coincident errors and its applications for combining classifiers, to appear in the upcoming book: Pattern Recognition and String Matching.

A Discussion on the Classifier Projection Space for Classifier Combining

Elżbieta Pękalska, Robert P.W. Duin, and Marina Skurichina

Pattern Recognition Group, Department of Applied Physics,
Faculty of Applied Sciences, Delft University of Technology,
Lorentzweg 1, 2628 CJ Delft, The Netherlands
{ela,duin,marina}@ph.tn.tudelft.nl

Abstract In classifier combining, one tries to fuse the information that is given by a set of base classifiers. In such a process, one of the difficulties is how to deal with the variability between classifiers. Although various measures and many combining rules have been suggested in the past, the problem of constructing optimal combiners is still heavily studied.

In this paper, we discuss and illustrate the possibilities of classifier embedding in order to analyse the variability of base classifiers, as well as their combining rules. Thereby, a space is constructed in which classifiers can be represented as points. Such a space of a low dimensionality is a Classifier Projection Space (CPS). In the first instance, it is used to design a visual tool that gives more insight into the differences of various combining techniques. This is illustrated by some examples. In the end, we discuss how the CPS may also be used as a basis for constructing new combining rules.

1 Introduction

When a pattern classification problem is too complex to be solved by training a single (advanced) classifier, the problem may be divided into subproblems. They can be solved one per time by training simpler base classifiers on subsets or variations of the problem. In the next stage, these base classifiers are combined. Many strategies are possible for creating subproblems as well as for constructing combiners [11]. Base classifiers are different by nature since they deal with different subproblems or operate on different variations of the original problem. It is not useful to store and use sets of classifiers that perform almost identically. If they differ somewhat, as a result of estimation errors, averaging their outputs may be worthwhile. If they differ considerably, e.g. by approaching the problem in independent ways, the product of their estimated posterior probabilities may be a good rule [8]. Other combining rules, like minimum, median or majority voting behave in a similar way. Having significantly different base classifiers in a collection is important since this gives raise to essentially different solutions. The concept of diversity is, thereby, crucial [9]. There are various ways to describe the diversity, usually producing a single number attributed to the whole collection of base classifiers. Later in this paper, we will use it differently.

F. Roli and J. Kittler (Eds.): MCS 2002, LNCS 2364, pp. 137–148, 2002.

A basic problem in classifier combining is the relation between base classifiers. If some are, by accident, identical, and others are very different, what is then the rationale of choosing particular combining rules? The outcomes of these rules depend on the distribution of base classifiers, but there is often no ground for the existence of such a distribution. Other combining rules, like maximum or minimum, are sensitive to outliers. Moreover, most fixed rules heavily rely on well established outputs, in particular, their suitable scaling.

One way to solve the above drawbacks is to use a trained output combiner. If the combiner is trained on a larger set, most of the above problems are overcome. Nevertheless, many architectures remain possible with different output combiners. A disadvantage of a trained combiner is, however, that it treats the outputs of base classifiers as features. Their original nature of distances or posterior probabilities is not preserved. Consequently, trained output combiners need a sufficiently large set of training examples to compensate this loss of information.

What we are looking for is a method of combining base classifiers that is not sensitive to their defects resulting from the way their collection is constituted. We want to use the fact that we deal with classifiers and not with arbitrary functions of the original features. To achieve that, we propose to study the collection of classifier pairwise differences, an $n \times n$ dissimilarity matrix D, before combining them into an output combiner. The dissimilarity value may be based on one of the diversity measures [9], like the disagreement [7]. Such a matrix D can be then embedded into a space $\mathcal{R}^k$, $k < n$, in a (non-)linear way. This means that classifiers are represented as a set of n points in $\mathcal{R}^k$ such that their Euclidean distances are identical to the original dissimilarities, given by D. It is also possible to perform an approximate embedding, where a space of a lower, fixed dimensionality is determined for an optimal approximation of D. We call this a Classifier Projection Space (CPS).

If the CPS is 2-dimensional, it can be visualised. Then, the collection of base classifiers, various combiners and, if desired, also other classifiers can be presented in a single 2D plot. The exact way of visualisation is explained in section 2. In sections 3 and 4, some examples are given for various sets of base classifiers constructed on real data. We will discuss how this illustrates some of the characteristics of the various techniques to generate both base classifiers and some combiners. We see it as a challenge to make use of the CPS for building a new type of combining classifier. This will be a trained output combiner, as it uses the training set. The construction of the CPS will be based on classifiers themselves and not on arbitrary feature functions. The possibilities will be discussed in the final section.

2   Construction of the Classifier Projection Space

Let us assume n classifiers trained on a dataset. For each pair of classifiers, their diversity value is determined, by using an evaluation set. This gives an $n \times n$ symmetric diversity matrix D. To take into account the original characteristics of the base classifier outputs, a suitable diversity measure should be chosen to establish the basic difference between classifiers. A spatial representation of classifiers can be found by a projection to a CPS such that the points correspond to classifiers and the diversities, reflected by Euclidean distances between the points, are preserved as well as possible. Studying the relations between classifiers in the CPS allows us for gaining a better understanding than by using the mean diversity only. The latter might be irrelevant e.g. for an ensemble consisting of both similar and diverse classifiers, where their contributions might average out.

The joint output of two classifiers, C_i and C_j can be related by counting the number of occurrences of correct (1) or wrong (0) classification, e.g. a is the number of correct classifications for both C_i and C_j in Fig. 1. This requires the knowledge of correct labels (e.g. not available for a test set), which can be avoided when the outputs of classifiers are compared and (1) describes the agreement between them. Many known (dis)similarity measures can be used; see e.g. [4, 9]. Here, we will consider a simple diversity measure, the disagreement [7], which for C_i and C_j is defined as (see Fig. 1)

	$C_i(1)$	$C_i(0)$
$C_j[1]$	a	b
$C_j[0]$	c	d

Fig. 1. C_i vs. C_j.

$$D_{i,j} = \frac{b+c}{a+b+c+d}, \qquad i,j = 1, \ldots, n \tag{1}$$

Given the complete diversity matrix D, reflecting the relations between classifiers, the CPS can be found by a (non-)linear projection, a variant of Multidimensional Scaling (MDS) [4]. Such a mapping is insensitive to redundant classifiers and perhaps also to outlier classifiers that do not have much support from the data. It is, however, sensitive to noise in the estimates of the dissimilarities. Below, we explain how from a dissimilarity matrix D one obtains a spatial representation.

2.1   Classical Scaling and Generalization to New Objects

Given an $n \times n$ Euclidean distance matrix D, between the elements of a set T, a configuration X of n points in $\mathcal{R}^m$ ($m \leq n$) can be found, up to rotation and translation, such that the distances are preserved exactly. The process of such a linear mapping is called embedding and it is known as *classical scaling* [4]. Without loss of generality, the mapping is constructed such that the origin coincides with the mean. X is determined, based on the relation between distances and inner products. The matrix of inner products B can be expressed only by using the square distances $D^{(2)}$ [4, 14] as $B = -\frac{1}{2}JD^{(2)}J$, where $J = I - \frac{1}{n}\mathbf{11}^T \in \mathcal{R}^{n \times n}$ (I is the identity matrix) projects the data such that X has a zero mean. By the eigendecomposition of $B = XX^T$, one obtains $B = Q\Lambda Q^T$, where Λ is a diagonal matrix of decreasing positive eigenvalues, followed by zeros. Q is the matrix of the corresponding eigenvectors. Then, X can be represented in an uncorrelated way in the space $\mathcal{R}^m$ as $X = Q_m \Lambda_m^{\frac{1}{2}}$.

To add s novel objects, represented by an $s \times n$ matrix of square distances $D_s^{(2)}$, relating s objects to the set T, a configuration X_s, projected onto $\mathcal{R}^m$, is

Table 1. Disagreement values, $D*100$, between classifiers built on the morphological features of the MFEAT set; since D is symmetric, only the upper part is presented.

	NMSC	LDC	UDC	QDC	1-NN	k-NN	Parzen	SVC1	SVC2	DT	ANN20	ANN50
NMC	47.1	47.3	43.4	50.3	53.5	30.9	24.1	63.1	71.4	50.4	77.5	72.8
NMSC	–	13.7	43.3	30.2	54.0	46.9	46.8	54.7	59.9	21.9	71.5	69.1
LDC	–	–	48.5	24.1	53.9	49.0	48.4	53.0	58.0	24.3	72.1	69.1
UDC	–	–	–	53.8	64.8	54.5	50.5	55.5	76.8	54.7	72.1	75.2
QDC	–	–	–	–	53.8	39.5	39.9	50.3	65.5	31.5	67.5	57.1
1-NN	–	–	–	–	–	48.5	49.5	65.5	78.7	53.9	77.7	77.0
k-NN	–	–	–	–	–	–	7.5	56.5	75.5	48.0	68.1	72.2
Parzen	–	–	–	–	–	–	–	56.7	73.2	48.1	68.8	71.2
SVC-1	–	–	–	–	–	–	–	–	79.1	54.2	36.7	89.9
SVC-2	–	–	–	–	–	–	–	–	–	65.0	84.2	86.7
DT	–	–	–	–	–	–	–	–	–	–	70.1	71.4
ANN20	–	–	–	–	–	–	–	–	–	–	–	100.0

then sought. Based on the matrix of inner products $B_s = -\frac{1}{2}(D_s^{(2)}J - UD^{(2)}J)$, where $U = \frac{1}{s}\mathbf{1}\mathbf{1}^T \in \mathcal{R}^{s \times n}$, X_s becomes $X_s = B_s X \Lambda_m^{-1}$ [6, 14].

In practice, often $m \approx n$, but the intrinsic dimensionality of the data is much smaller. Since X is an uncorrelated representation, the reduced configuration, preserving the distances approximately, is determined by k largest eigenvalues [4, 14]. Therefore, $X^{red} \in \mathcal{R}^k$, $k < m$, is found as $X^{red} = Q_k \Lambda_k^{\frac{1}{2}}$. If D is the matrix of diversities values between classifiers, X^{red} is the configuration in the sought CPS.

For a non-Euclidean distance, B has negative eigenvalues [4, 6] and X cannot be determined. One possibility is to consider a pseudo-Euclidean space, see [6, 14], another one is to skip the directions corresponding to the negative eigenvalues.

2.2   Multidimensional Scaling - A Nonlinear Projection

For an $n \times n$ dissimilarity matrix D, Sammon mapping [4] is a nonlinear MDS projection onto a a space $\mathcal{R}^k$ such that the distances are preserved. For this purpose, an error function, called *stress*, is defined, which measures the difference between the original dissimilarities and Euclidean distances of the configuration X of n objects. Let D be the given dissimilarity matrix and $\tilde{D}$ be the distance matrix for the projected configuration X. A variant of the stress [4] is here considered as

$$S = \frac{1}{\sum_{i=1}^{n-1}\sum_{j=i+1}^{n} d_{ij}^2} \sum_{i=1}^{n-1}\sum_{j=i+1}^{n} (d_{ij} - \tilde{d}_{ij})^2.$$

To find an MDS representation, one starts from an initial representation and proceeds in an iterative manner until a configuration corresponding to a (local) minimum of S is found [4]. Here, for a stable solution, classical scaling is used to initialize the optimization procedure. If D is the matrix of diversities values between classifiers, X is the configuration in the CPS. Since there is no straightforward way of adding new objects to an existing MDS map, a modified version of the mapping has been proposed, which generalizes to new objects; see [3, 13].

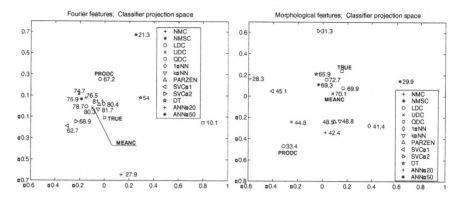

Fig. 2. A 2-dimensional CPS for the MFEAT dataset. Points correspond to classifiers; numbers refer to their accuracy. The 'perfect' classifier is marked as TRUE.

2.3   An Example

To present a 2-dimensional CPS, the 10-class MFEAT digit dataset [12] is considered. For our presentation, Fourier (74D) and morphological (6D) feature sets are chosen with a training set consisting of 50 randomly chosen objects per class. The classifiers considered are: the nearest (scaled) mean classifier NM(S)C, linear/uncorrelated quadratic/quadratic discriminant classifier LDC/UDC/QDC, 1/k-nearest neigbour rule 1-NN/k-NN, Parzen classifier, linear/quadratic support vector classifier SVC-1/SVC-2, decision tree DT and feed-forward neural network with 20/50 hidden units ANN20/ANN50. For each feature set, the disagreement matrix between all classifiers and two combiners, the mean (MEANC) and the product (PRODC) rules, is computed by formula (1); see also Table 1. This is done for the test set of 150 objects per class. The diversity matrix served then for a construction of a 2-dimensional CPS by the MDS procedure, described in section 2.2. Such examples of the CPS can be seen in Fig. 2. Note that the points correspond to classifiers. The distances between them approximate the original pairwise disagreement values, by which we can visually judge the similarities between classifiers. The hypothetical perfect classifier, i.e. given by the original labels, marked as TRUE, is also projected. The numbers in the plots show the accuracy reached on the test set. Let us emphasize that the axes cannot be interpreted themselves; it is simply distances that count.

   In both cases, we can observe that the mean combiner is better than the product combiner. The latter, apparently deteriorates w.r.t. some, although diverse, but very badly performing classifiers. The mean rule seems to reflect the averaged variability of the most compact cloud. Note also that diversity might not be always correlated with accuracy. See, for instance, the right plot in Fig. 2, where the NMSC is more similar (less diverse) to the hypothetical classifier than ANN20, although the accuracy of the latter is higher.

3   Bagging, Boosting, and the Random Subspace Method

Many combining techniques can be used to improve the performance of weak classifiers. Examples are bagging [2], boosting [5] or the random subspace method (RSM) [7, 15]. They modify the training set by sampling the training objects (bagging), or by weighting them (boosting), or by sampling data features (the RSM).

Next, they build classifiers on these modified training sets and combine them into a final decision. Bagging is useful for linear classifiers constructed when the training size is about the data dimensionality. Boosting is effective for classifiers of low-complexity built on large training sets [15]. The RSM is beneficial for small training sets of a relatively large dimensionality, or for data with redundant features (where the discrimination power is spread over many features) [15].

To study the relations within those ensembles, the 34-dimensional, 2-class ionosphere data [1] is considered. The NMC is used for constructing the ensembles of 50 classifiers. The training is done on $T_1 = 100$ and $T_2 = 17$ objects per class (randomly chosen) to observe a different behaviour of base classifiers. The following combining rules are used: (weighted) majority voting, mean, product, minimum, maximum, decision templates and naive bayes (NB). The test set consists of 151 objects for which the disagreement matrix between the base classifiers of the mentioned ensembles and the combiners is com-

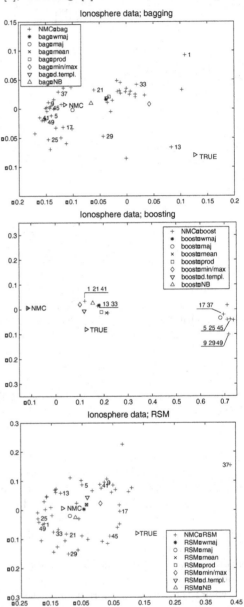

Fig. 3. A 2-dimensional CPS; Ionosphere dataset trained with T_1.

puted. Such a matrix serves for obtaining the CPS by using the MDS mapping, as described in section 2.2. The hypothetical, perfect classifier, representing true labels (marked as TRUE) has been added, as well; see Fig. 3.

To understand better the relation between the diversity and accuracy of the classifiers, while maintaining the clarity of presentation, another plots have been made; see Fig. 4 – 5. They show a 1-dimensional CPS (representing the relative difference in diversity) vs accuracy. So, the differences between classifiers in the horizontal and vertical directions correspond to the change in diversity and accuracy, respectively.

Analysing Fig. 3, 4 and 5, the following conclusions can be made. First of all, in the CPS, the classifiers obtained by bagging and the RSM are grouped around the single (original) NMC, creating mostly a compact cloud. The variability relations between the bagged and RSM classifiers might be very small. On the contrary, the boosted classifiers do not form a single cloud. In terms of both diversity and accuracy, they are reduced to 9 – 14 different ones (depending on the training set). A group of 5 – 8 poor classifiers is then completely separated from the others, as well as from the bagged and RSM classifiers.

Secondly, for a small training size T_2, Fig. 5, the RSM and bagging create classifiers that behave similarly in variability, since the classifier clouds in the 1D CPS are in the same range and of a similar size. For a larger training size T_1, Fig. 4, the diversity for the RSM classifiers is larger.

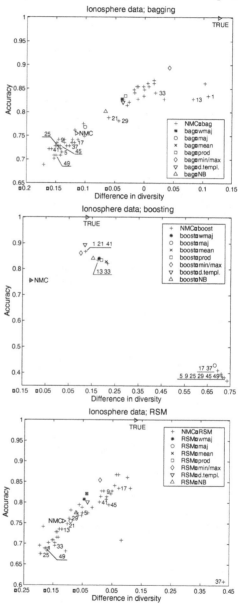

Fig. 4. Accuracy vs. 1D CPS; Ionosphere dataset trained with T_1.

Thirdly, the classifiers in all ensembles, even in boosting, seem to be constructed in a random order w.r.t. the diversity and accuracy.

Concerning the combiners studied here, the minimum rule (equivalent to the maximum rule for a 2-class problem) achieves, in most cases, the highest accuracy. It is even better than the weighted majority, used for the boosting construction. For a small sample size problem, Fig. 5, most of the combining rules for bagging and the RSM are alike, both in diversity and accuracy. A much larger variability is observed for boosting; a collection of diverse both classifiers and combiners is here obtained.

Finally, a striking observation is that nearly all classifiers, as well as their combiners, are placed in the CPS at one side (i.e. not around) of the perfect classifier (this was less apparent for the MFEAT data; compare to Fig. 2).

4   Image Retrieval

In the problem of image database retrieval, images can be represented by single feature vectors or by clouds of points. Usually, given a query image Q, represented by a vector, images in the database are ranked according to their similarity to Q, measured e.g. by the normalized inner product. A cloud of points offers a more flexible representation, but it may suffer from overlap between cloud representations, even for very distinct images. Recently, we have pro-

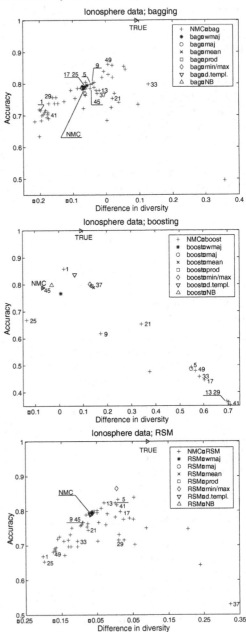

Fig. 5. Accuracy vs. 1D CPS; Ionosphere dataset; trained with T_2

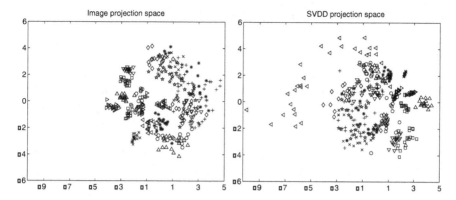

Fig. 6. 2D representations: images (left) and the CPS configuration for the SVDD-classifiers (right); different marks correspond to different classes.

posed a novel approach for describing clouds of points based on support vector data description (SVDD) [16], which try to describe the domain (boundary) of such a cloud. For each image in the database, such a SVDD is trained. The retrieval is based on the fraction of the points rejected by the SVDD's and the lowest ranks are returned. A single SVDD still suffers if the clouds of points between different images are highly overlapping. We have shown, however, that combining of the SVDD classifiers may improve the retrieval precision; see [10] for details.

In our experiment, performed on a dataset of texture images, 23 different images are given. Each original image is cut into 16 128 × 128 non-overlapping pieces. These correspond to a single class. Such pieces are mostly homogeneous and represent one type of a texture. The images are, one by one, considered as queries, and the 16 best ranked images are taken into account. The retrieval precision is computed using all 368 images; see [10] for details.

Each image is represented by a combined profile of all SVDD-classifiers. In our approach to the retrieval problem, a dissimilarity between a profile of the SVDD's for the query Q and the other images is considered. This might be based on the Euclidean distance. In order to see all the relations between images, a distance matrix and the resulting spatial representation of the images can be found, see Fig. 6, left plot. On the other hand, we can build the CPS, now based on the differences between SVDD-classifiers, see Fig. 6, right plot. Remind that in this case classifiers correspond directly to images, since each SVDD is a more conceptual description of an image. Comparing those two graphs, we see that the image space maintains a better separation, which was confirmed by our good retrieval precision [10].

5   Perspective on Possibilities of the CPS

The CPS has been used as a visualisation tool for analysing the differences
between base classifiers and as an argument for the selection of some combining
rules. Let us now discuss whether a CPS can be used for building classifier
combiners. The figures presented in the previous sections contain just classifiers.
If points, corresponding to classifiers, are close in a plot, the classifiers are similar.
This may be an argument to select just one of a cluster of related classifiers or
to average their outputs in order to reduce the noise. Very different classifiers
should be preserved since they may be candidates for the product combiner.
In this way, the relative positions of the classifiers in the CPS may serve for a
construction of the overall system architecture.

In order to train a new classifier, using the CPS space, it is highly desirable to project training objects in such
a space. In case of a linear embedding
(section 2.1), the mapping of new classifiers into an existing CPS is well defined.
In order to project an object into this
space, an equivalent dissimilarity measure between objects and classifiers should
be defined. Here, we face the problem
that an object belongs to a single class
and a classifier is a multi-class entity. In
section 2, the behaviour w.r.t. the distinct classes was averaged, as in the dis-

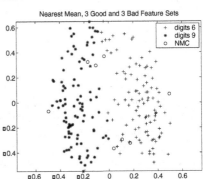

Fig. 7. The CPS with objects.

agreement measure (1), just differences in label assignments are counted, neglect-
ing further class differences. The measure is, therefore, modified into a matrix of
numbers. The disagreement between the classifiers $\mathcal{C}_i$ and $\mathcal{C}_j$ w.r.t. the classes p
and q can be written as

$$D_{p,q}(\mathcal{C}_i,\mathcal{C}_j) = \text{Prob}\left(\mathcal{C}_i = p, \mathcal{C}_j = q\right) + \text{Prob}\left(\mathcal{C}_i = q, \mathcal{C}_j = p\right), \qquad (2)$$

where the probabilities are taken w.r.t. the set of objects x to be classified. For
a c-class problem and n classifiers, the total size of the dissimilarity matrix is
then $nc \times nc$. Now, for an object y, a similar quantity is defined as

$$D_{y,q}(y,\mathcal{C}_j) = \text{Prob}\left(\mathcal{C}_j(q,x) > \mathcal{C}_j(q,y)\right), \qquad (3)$$

resulting in a $1 \times nc$ row vector, since $\mathcal{C}_j(q,x)$ is the support of classifier $\mathcal{C}_j$,
$j=1,\dots,n$ for an object x w.r.t. the class q, $q=1,\dots,c$. The probability is
zero if no other object x exists with more support for the given class q than the
presented object y. This is in agreement with the concept of a dissimilarity since
this implies that this object is very q-like according to $\mathcal{C}_j$.

An example is presented in Fig. 7. We computed six NMC for all six feature
sets of the MFEAT dataset [12] between the classes '6' and '9'. From the 12×12
dissimilarity matrix between the classifiers, a 2-dimensional CPS is found by

classical scaling. 100 objects per class are projected into this space. Classifiers and objects are shown in Fig. 7. The 2 × 3 classifiers at the top and at the bottom correspond to bad feature sets that cannot distinguish between classes '6' and '9' as they are based on rotation invariant properties. The 3 classifiers, corresponding to good feature sets, are projected right on the top of each other on the left and on the right sides.

6   Discussion and Conclusion

We presented a new way of representing classifiers. The classifier projection space (CPS), based on (approximate) embedding of the diversities between the classifiers, offers a possibility to study their differences. This may increase the understanding of the recognition problem at hand and, thereby, offers an analyst a tool based on which he can decide on the architecture of the entire combining system.

We also showed how objects can be mapped into the CPS. It has to be further investigated under what circumstances the construction of a combined output classifier in such a space is beneficial. This will be a trained combiner and its performance has to be compared with the direct use of the base classifier outputs as their features. The advantage of the presented approach is that by the choice of the dissimilarity measure the character of these 'features' as classifier outputs may be preserved.

Acknowledgments

This work is supported by the Dutch Organization for Scientific Research (NWO). The authors thank dr Ludmila Kuncheva for supplying some of the routines.

References

[1] C.L. Blake and C.J. Merz. UCI repository of machine learning databases, 1998.

[2] L. Breiman. Bagging predictors. *Machine Learning*, 24(2):123–140, 1996.

[3] D. Cho and D.J. Miller. A Low-complexity Multidimensional Scaling Method Based on Clustering. *concept paper*, 2002.

[4] T.F. Cox and M.A.A. Cox. *Multidimensional Scaling*. Chapman & Hall, 1995.

[5] Y. Freund and R. E. Schapire. Experiments with a new boosting algorithm. In *Machine Learning: Proc. of the 13th International Conference*, pages 148–156, 1996.

[6] L. Goldfarb. A new approach to pattern recognition. In L.N. Kanal and A. Rosenfeld, editors, *Progress in Pattern Recognition*, volume 2, pages 241–402. Elsevier Science Publishers B.V., 1985.

[7] T.K. Ho. The random subspace method for constructing decision forests. *IEEE Trans. on PAMI*, 20(8):832–844, 1998.

[8] J. Kittler, M. Hatef, R.P.W. Duin, and J. Matas. On combining classifiers. *IEEE Trans. on PAMI*, 20(3):226–239, 1998.

[9] L.I. Kuncheva and C.J. Whitaker. Measures of diversity in classifier ensembles. *submitted*, 2002.

[10] C. Lai, D.M.J. Tax, R.p.W. Duin, P. Paclík, and E. Pękalska. On combining one-class classifiers for image database retrieval. In *International Workshop on Multiple Classifier Systems*, Cagliari, Sardinia, 2002.

[11] L. Lam. Classifier combinations: implementation and theoretical issues. In *Multiple Classifier Systems, LNCS*, volume 1857, pages 78–86, 2000.

[12] MFEAT: ftp://ftp.ics.uci.edu/pub/machine-learning-databases/mfeat/.

[13] E. Pękalska and R.P.W. Duin. Spatial representation of dissimilarity data via lower-complexity linear and nonlinear mappings. In *Joint International Workshop on SSPR and SPR*, Windsor, Canada, 2002.

[14] E. Pękalska, P. Paclík, and R.P.W. Duin. A Generalized Kernel Approach to Dissimilarity Based Classification. *Journal of Mach. Learn. Research*, 2:175–211, 2001.

[15] M. Skurichina. *Stabilizing Weak Classifiers*. PhD thesis, Delft University of Technology, Delft, The Netherlands, 2001.

[16] D.J.M. Tax. *One-class classifiers*. PhD thesis, Delft University of Technology, Delft, The Netherlands, 2001.

On the General Application of the Tomographic Classifier Fusion Methodology

D. Windridge and J. Kittler

Dept. of Electronic and Electrical Engineering,
University of Surrey, Guildford, Surrey, GU2 7XH, U.K.
{D.Windridge,J.Kittler}@surrey.ac.uk

Abstract. We have previously (MCS2001) presented a mathematical metaphor setting out an equivalence between multiple expert fusion and the process of tomographic reconstruction familiar from medical imaging. However, the discussion took place only in relation to a restricted case: namely, classifiers containing discrete feature sets. This, its sequel paper, will therefore endeavour to extend the methodology to the fully general case.

The investigation is thus conducted initially within the context of classical feature selection (that is, selection algorithms that place no restriction upon the overlap of feature sets), the findings in relation to which demonstrating the necessity of a re-evaluation of the role of feature-selection when conducted within an explicitly combinatorial framework. When fully enunciated, the resulting investigation leads naturally to a completely generalised, morphologically-optimal strategy for classifier combination.

1 Introduction

1.1 Synopsis of First Paper

The preceding paper in this series, presented at MCS2001 [1], concerned the attempt to obtain a limited solution-set mathematical optimisation of the process of multiple expert fusion by outlining an analogy with the apparently unrelated subject of tomographic reconstruction.

This was motivated by the observation that classical methods of multiple expert fusion have in common that they are based on fairly intuitive output-dependent techniques for the combination of classifiers [eg 2-7]. Optimisation under these circumstances has therefore typically taken the form of the manipulation of the remaining free parameters, namely: the space of possible PDF parameterisations [eg 8], the training set composition (bagging [9] and boosting [eg 10]), the composition of the feature sets [11], or, more rarely, the manipulation of the output classes [eg 12]. There had not, however, been any attempt to optimise the combination process *per se*. We were thus led to address this deficit by proposing a metaphor for classifier combination in terms of the reconstruction of Radon integral data via tomographic means. By interpreting the

F. Roli and J. Kittler (Eds.): MCS 2002, LNCS 2364, pp. 149–158, 2002.

combination of classifiers with *distinct* feature sets as the implicit reconstruction of the combined pattern space probability density function (PDF), we were able to envisage the problem in geometric terms, and, in consequence, propose an optimal solution within the specifically morphological scope of the investigation.

Very broadly, this involved the reinterpretation of the linearly projective process of feature selection as constituting a *Radon transformation*[1] of the total pattern-space PDF (ie the space of every feature presented to the feature selection algorithm), with combination in its various forms then acting to approximate Radon transformation's inverse operation; *back-projection*. Thus, the act of combination could be interpreted as an attempted reconstruction of the original pattern-space PDF from a series of idealised models of its projections as represented by the classifiers, selected on the basis of their representative abilities via the feature-selection algorithm. Optimisation within this scenario therefore amounted to the application of prior filtration to the Radon data (which is to say, the PDFs of each individual classifier) *before* reconstruction via the Sum Rule combination scheme.

The paper concluded that, to the extent that the features presented to the individual classifiers within a multi-classifier system are distinct, all familiar techniques of classifier combination gained their effectiveness by virtue of being implicit, if only partial, attempts at the reconstruction of the composite pattern-space PDF.

1.2   Aim the Current Paper: The Derivation of a Strategy for the Combination of Non-distinct Feature Sets

We have in the first paper, [1], thus considered tomographic reconstruction theory only in terms of distinct feature sets: the contrary situation must be addressed if we are to arrive at a universally optimised solution to the problem of classifier combination. Before embarking on this investigation we should, however, reiterate just how exceptional it is to find overlapping feature sets amongst the classifiers within a combination when feature selection is explicitly carried out within a combinatorial context (see [13]).

The specific question that we are seeking to address in the second part of this series is therefore what strategy to adopt when presented with overlapping feature sets on attempting our tomographic reconstruction of the complete N-dimensional pattern-space probability density function. This is clearly is not a problem for classical methods of combination, which consider combination in probabilistic, not morphological, terms, and which do not thus consider the implicit ambiguity in PDF representations as presenting any particular difficulty. Indeed, classical techniques such as majority voting may actively assist us in our tomographic endeavour by explicitly eliminating superfluous PDF characterisations, and, as such, are not in any way mutually exclusive to our methodology. In general, though, it will not be obvious whether the current and classical methodologies are of simultaneous applicability.

---

[1] For a full definition of this, and other tomography-related terms, refer to [1].

There is, however, another perspective from which we may view the action of classical combination methods in regard to overlapping feature sets (as opposed to implicit unfiltered tomographic reconstruction, which would only apply to distinct feature sets), and that is as methods for refining the PDF morphology of the particular class under consideration. This is because all such methods of combination will propose a probabilistic output for a given pattern vector input (even if the input and/or output are ostensibly in terms of a class, as opposed to a probability, there is still an underlying PDF that may be straightforwardly reconstructed by exhaustively scanning across the pattern space). If the collective decision making process for overlapping feature sets is then more effective than that for the classifiers individually, then this is because the aggregate PDF is closer to the prior probability density distribution. In terms of one of the more familiar combinatorial methods, the "Weighted Mean" decision system, the mechanics of PDF refinement are fairly intuitive: in this case the PDFs are combined via summing in appropriate ratio, with the final PDF recovered after a later renormalising step; and similarly, though perhaps less obviously, for the other decision schemes that have been discussed.

Thus we see that conventional combination methods, by virtue of not having specified the nature of the feature sets to which they apply, have tended to conflate two absolutely distinct methods of improving classification performance: namely, (in so far as the feature sets are distinct) classifier combination has gained its advantages by being an implicit tomographic reconstruction of the N-dimensional pattern space PDF, and (in so far as the feature sets are overlapping), the advantage is obtained via a refinement of the features' PDF morphology.

If we are to set about obtaining an optimal solution to the problem of classifier combination it is therefore clear that we shall have to apply these two differing mechanisms in their appropriate, and *rigorously distinguished*, domains of operation. That is, we should retain the classical methods of combination, but employ them only within the non-tomographic domain (to which they constitute only an imperfect approximation); that is, solely within the domain of overlapping classifiers, where they can be treated simply as methods of PDF refinement.

It shall therefore be the endeavour of this paper to fully achieve this distinction on an operational level. Prior to this, however, it is illustrative to consider the imperfect situation in which we are presented with overlapping features within a *tomographic* framework, and to consider a concrete case:

2   A Specific Instance of the Tomographic Combination of Classifiers with Non-distinct Feature Sets

Suppose that we have obtained two classifiers (A and B) that contain, respectively, the preferred feature sets $\{1, 2\}$ and $\{2, 3\}$ at the completion of the feature selection process. We then wish to obtain the best possible classification performance from the combination of features and classifiers available. There are a number possibilities open to us, for example we might:

1. Establish which of the two classifiers A or B is the better classifier of feature 2 *alone*, and then apply the filtered inverse Radon transformation to features 1, 2 and 3 separately (feature 1 already being associated with classifier A, and feature 2 with classifier B). Note that we can envisage the first part of this as, in a sense, an implicit weighted majority vote decision scheme applied to both of the classifiers containing feature 2: this observation shall later help us to generalise our differing approaches within a unified framework.

2. Establish which of the two classifiers can least afford, in terms of classification performance, to lose feature 2, and (supposing that this is classifier A) perform the filtered inverse Radon transformation on the data sets A(1,2) and B(3) (the bracketed terms being the features associated with the classier outside the bracket). Note that there is still an implicit majority vote at the outset of this procedure, though not so obviously as in the previous case. We also note, without rigorous proof, that we might expect this to be the better option on intuitive grounds, since it does not involve either the addition of features rejected by the feature selection process (see later), or else the tomographic reconstruction of spaces that are already fully defined (as for 1).

3. Establish whether one of the two classifiers (A or B) is the better classifier of feature 2 *alone*, or whether a weighted mean combination of classifiers A and B sharing feature 2 constitutes the better classifier of that feature, and then deploy the filtered inverse Radon transformation on the three features within their designated classifiers individually. Note that we might consider this a generalisation of strategy 1, permitting the two classical combination methods (majority vote and weighted mean) to vie for the representation of feature 2's PDF prior to inverse Radon transformation. We might similarly have included any of the other classical combination methods.

4. Establish which is the better classifier (either A or B) of the entire pattern space of features 1,2 and 3 and consider only that classifier's output. (An implicit weighted majority vote applied to the two classifiers' output).

5. Generate the two three-dimensional PDFs of the pattern space consisting of the features 1,2 and 3 via classifiers A and B, and then combine through any of the classical methods of classifier combination. This may then be considered simply as a generalisation of the preceding option. Note that we do not expect either of these possibilities to generate particularly good classifications, despite containing the full three-dimensional pattern space within the two classifiers (therefore avoiding a necessarily ambiguous tomographic reconstruction of it), because the space implicitly then includes features rejected by the feature selection process, designed, as it is, specifically to exclude those features that do not lend themselves to the generation of accurate PDFs.

We begin to see that in the above (by no means exhaustive) list of strategies a number of consistent patterns begin to emerge. We should therefore like to generalise all of above into unified framework by giving a formal (and therefore necessarily algebraic) description of the various approaches to the problem.

Suppose, therefore, that we have a battery, T, of techniques for PDF combination *excluding* the Radon method, and a set of features F_A associated with classifier A and a set of features F_B associated with classifier B. Then, in the reconstruction of the pattern space $F_A \cup F_B$, we can set about generalising the combination techniques in each of the above instances in the following manner: We firstly denote the best-performing classical PDF combination technique by $^*\{X\}(F)$ (the star-operator extracting the optimum classifier from the total body of classifiers, X, with that classifier acting on the feature set F): the converse of this, the operator that extracts the worst performing classifier we denote by $^{*'}\{\}$. The filtered inverse Radon combination of classifiers A, B and C containing arbitrary arrangements of *non-overlapping* features we shall then denote by $R_i[A, B, C]$. The additional functional operator $^\mathcal{F}X$ is then introduced, which acts to extract the feature set from a particular classifying entity X (whether it be a single or compound classification scheme, ie a solitary classifier or combination via conventional methods of classifiers with identical feature sets). We shall make the further assumption that the filtered inverse Radon transformation of a single PDF $R_i[A]$ constitutes an identity operation (ie $R_i[A] = A$), as required for algebraic consistency, and further that there exists a 'zero' of the algebra such that A() (ie the classifier A acting on the empty set) produces the value "**0**" such that $R_i[X, \mathbf{0}] \equiv R_i[X]$.

Under the algebraic formalism we have therefore evolved the list above would be written:

1. $R_i[A(F_A \notin F_A \cap F_B), ^*\{A(F_A \cap F_B), B(F_A \cap F_B)\}, B(F_B \notin F_A \cap F_B)]$
2. $R_i[^*T\{A(F_A \notin F_A\cap F_B), B(F_B \notin F_A\cap F_B)\}(^{*\mathcal{F}}T\{A(F_A \notin F_A\cap F_B), B(F_B \notin F_A \cap F_B)\}), ^*T\{A(F_A \notin F_A \cap F_B), B(F_B \notin F_A \cap F_B)\}(^{*'\mathcal{F}}T\{A(F_A \notin F_A \cap F_B), B(F_B \notin F_A \cap F_B)\} \cup (F_A \cap F_B))]$
3. as 1
4. $^*T\{A(F_A \cup F_B), B(F_A \cup F_B)\}$
5. as 4.

With this common framework in place, we may now seek to generalise options 1 and 2 by defining the feature sets F'_A and F'_B such that $F'_A \subset F_A$ and $F'_B \subset F_B$. That is, F'_A and F'_B are subsets of their respective originals *permitting the empty and isomorphic sets* [$\{\}$ and F_X] as appropriate. In conjunction with this, we further generalise the * operator to $^{*O(z)}$ such that it now extracts the optimal classifier with respect to every possible feature set z: that is, $O(z)$ may be considered a function in its own right, although with respect to feature sets rather than classifiers as for *, and which multiplies the number of options instead of reducing them. Thus $^{*O(z)}$ might be considered "$O(z)$ followed by *". This will permit us to exploit a redundancy in relation to * later on.

Within this regard, the generalisation of options 1 and 2 (and therefore 3) would appear:

$$R_i[A(F_A \notin^{*O(F'_A,F'_B)\mathcal{F}} T\{A(F'_A), B(F'_B)\}),$$
$$^{*O(F'_A,F'_B)}T\{A(F'_A), B(F'_B)\}, B(F_B \notin^{*O(F'_A,F'_B)\mathcal{F}} T\{A(F'_A), B(F'_B)\})] \quad (1)$$

However, because we have specified that $R_i[X, \mathbf{0}] \equiv R_i[X]$ and, $R_i[X] = X$ we see that the above formulation can also be made to subsume options 4 and 5 by setting $F'_A = F_A \cup F_B$ and $F'_B = F_A \cup F_B$ (that is, explicitly abandoning the imposed limitation that F'_A and F'_B be subsets of the original feature sets), such that the above form becomes:

$$R_i[A(F_A \notin^{*O(F'_A,F'_B)\mathcal{F}} T\{A(F'_A), B(F'_B)\}),^{*O(F'_A,F'_B)}T\{$$
$$A(F'_A), B(F'_B)\}, B(F_B \notin^{*O(F'_A,F'_B)\mathcal{F}} T\{A(F'_A), B(F'_B)\})]$$
$$= R_i[\mathbf{0},^* T\{A(F_A \cup F_B), B(F_A \cup F_B)\}, \mathbf{0}]$$
$$= R_i[^*T\{A(F_A \cup F_B), B(F_A \cup F_B)\}]$$
$$=^* T\{A(F_A \cup F_B), B(F_A \cup F_B)\}] \quad (2)$$

(equals option 4)

In equation 2 we have then obtained a very general form for the optimal strategy for dealing with overlapping feature sets, one that may be made completely general for the case of two classifiers by noting that the operator *, is in effect, a weighted majority vote combination scheme, which will therefore belong to the total body of non-tomographic combination methods, T. Hence by inverting this consideration, and applying to the above, we see that we can obtain the exhaustive combination strategy:

$$R_i[A(F_A \notin^{O(F'_A,F'_B)\mathcal{F}} T\{\{A(F'_A), B(F'_B)\}),$$
$$^{O(F'_A,F'_B)}T\{A(F'_A), B(F'_B)\}, B(F_B \notin^{O(F'_A,F'_B)\mathcal{F}} T\{A(F'_A), B(F'_B)\})] \quad (3)$$

We might, furthermore, consider no longer restricting the overlap of feature sets to be merely one feature amongst two classifiers, permitting instead α features to overlap amongst β classifiers: however we begin to see that any such process would involve a very major modification of the feature selection algorithm, upon which we are already beginning to encroach. Thus we can begin to appreciate that, in seeking to obtain optimality, there can be no rigorous distinction between the two processes of feature selection and classifier combination.

In fact the difficulty of overlapping feature sets that we have been seeking to address only really arises when we have been failing to rigorously distinguish between the classifier combinations that are, in effect, single classifiers, and the classifier combinations that are tomographically reconstructive in nature. We might therefore suppose that, if this distinction were built into the feature selection process, such that the final combination process were a purely tomographic procedure in relation to distinct feature sets contained within single (or classically combined) classifiers, the difficulty would never have arisen. This is indeed the case, and a morphologically optimal solution to the problem of classifier combination implemented from the level of the feature selection algorithm upwards is outlined in the following section.

3   Morphologically Optimal Solution to the Combination Problem: Implicit Unity of the Feature Selection Process

To summarise our findings thus far: throughout the investigation we have found it necessary to postulate (and clarify the nature of) an apparent double aspect to the functionality of conventional classifier combination, one facet of which may be considered the refinement of PDF morphology, and therefore a form of classification in its own right, and the other being that of tomographic reconstruction, in so far as the feature sets belonging to the classifiers within the combination are distinct. Classical techniques of combination tend to conflate these two disparate aspects through not having made a rigorous distinction between those classifier combinations that, in effect, act as a single classifier and those combinations that may be considered to act on entirely distinct orthogonal projections of a single PDF encompassing the whole of the N-dimensional pattern space. We, in contrast, have found it necessary, in seeking an optimised solution to the combination problem, to make this distinction completely formal. Explicitly separating the two, however, will involve reverting to a stage prior to combination, and addressing the nature of the feature selection process itself. Thus we find we must take a unified perspective on the apparently separate issues of feature selection and classifier combination if we are to achieve our aim of attaining a morphologically idealised solution.

The essence of the unity that we are seeking will lie in ensuring that we exhaust those possibilities of classifier combination that serve only to act as single classifiers at the feature selection stage, with classifier/feature set combinations then being chosen by the feature selector only on the basis of their suitability for tomographic combination by the optimal filtered process. This basis will clearly centre on the principle of supplying classifiers with distinct feature sets to the tomographic combination. The precise methodology of this procedure is therefore as follows:

Besides the classifiers $(a, b, c \ldots n_c)$, we must also consider as being classifiers in their own right every possible combination of these classifiers via the various *non-tomographic* techniques, $(1, 2, 3 \ldots n_0)$, that exist for conventional classifier combination. That is, we require the various combinations ab_1, ac_1, $\ldots$; ab_2, ac_2, $\ldots$; abc_1, $abd_1 \ldots$ etc (with the appropriate combination method indicated by the numeric subscript). We must, however, also consider the possibilities of the form: $\{ab_1\}\{bcd_2\}_3$ (that is, the associative composition by method 3 of the non-tomographically-combined 'pseudo'-classifiers ab_1 and bcd_2), wherein the preceding combinations may *themselves* be combined by any of the conventional combination methods.

Thus the total set of classifiers of the first kind (that is to say, non-associative combinations) now numbers:

$$^{n_c}C_1 + n_0(\sum_{i=2}^{n_c} {}^{n_c}C_i) = {}^{n_c}C_1 + n_0([1+1]^{n_c} - 1 - n_c)$$

(via the binomial theorem)

$$= n_c + n_0(2^{n_c} - 1 - n_c) \qquad (4)$$

By a similar progression we arrive at the total number of higher order associative combinations as being (progressively):

$$n_0\,{}^{n_c+n_0(2^{n_c}-1-n_c)}C_2 + n_0\,{}^{n_c+n_0(2^{n_c}-1-n_c)}C_3 + \ldots,$$

giving an overall total of classifiers of both varieties of the number:

$$^{\mathcal{P}}C_1 + n_0(\sum_{i=2}^{\mathcal{P}} {}^{\mathcal{P}}C_i) = {}^{\mathcal{P}}C_1 + n_0([1+1]^{\mathcal{P}} - 1 - \mathcal{P})$$

(via the binomial theorem)

$$= \mathcal{P} + n_0(2^{\mathcal{P}} - 1 - \mathcal{P}) \qquad (5)$$

where $\mathcal{P} = n_c + n_0(2^{n_c} - 1 - n_c)$.

Note that, in general, there will be tautologies, and consequently simplifications, in the descriptions of the above terms: for instance $\{ab_1\}\{cd_1\}_1$ would be the equivalent of $abcd_1$ if 1 is the (weighted) majority vote scheme. Whether it will be possible in general to exploit such redundancies for the purpose of saving computation time will depend entirely on the nature of the combination scheme.

With all of the compound classifiers that may be legitimately considered to act as single classifiers thus constructed, we may then go on, in a *reverse* of the usual procedure, to specify the appropriate feature selection algorithm. We need not in consequence worry, as we would otherwise have to if we mean to obtain an optimal solution, about selecting features for the original classifiers on the basis of their ability to act in combination (at least in conventional terms), because we have inherently constructed all of their combinations *prior* to feature selection: feature selection can then be conducted on a purely tomographic basis amongst the original classifiers and their composites. Thus we test (exhaustively, if we require optimality) those feature combinations consisting only of *distinct* feature sets distributed amongst the classifiers and pseudo-classifiers, with final feature set selection occurring only on the basis of the features' collective ability to classify within the tomographic regime. It is also possible to exploit this principle *non-optimally*, and within a less computationally intense framework, by utilising conventional feature selection methods such as sequential forward selection in an appropriate manner (see [14]).

As an additional note to conclude this section, we should also like to address the question of the optimality of the filtering procedure. In fact, a complete inversion of the tomographic reconstruction formula (equation 4 of paper [1]) through filtration (that is, construction of an appropriate v function) does not always constitute a mathematically analytic problem, the difficulty (by inspection of equation 7 of [1]) being essentially one of deconvolution; a notoriously ill-posed problem in consequence of convolution being an information destroying procedure when the convolving function is bandwidth limited to any degree (or at least when more so than the data undergoing convolution). However, since we are inherently working with discrete data (due to the computational necessity of sampling the PDF at discrete intervals), this latter point does not apply to our technique, the PDF data being bandwidth limited to exactly the same extent as the filtering function. There is then no fundamental difficulty to obtaining an optimal filtering function via inversion of equation 4 (paper [1]), merely the pragmatic one of establishing whether this can be done by analytic methods, or whether it would be better approached by numeric means. The discrete nature of the computational representation of the filter function, however, will ensure that either of the methods will suffice.

4   Conclusion

We have, in the current and preceding papers, sought to set out a morphologically optimal method of classifier combination via a tomographic analogy of what we now appreciate to be a major aspect of the process, the assemblage of Radon transform data, finding, in delineating this aspect, that classifier combination is inseparable from the feature selection process.

Our assertion of the morphological optimality of our method then centres on it being a full completion of the partial tomographic reconstruction process implicit in all conventional methods of classifier combination, the only other considerations that we need address in this regard being, firstly, that of the remaining aspect of combination as implicit refinement of the PDF morphologies and, secondly, the robustness of the reconstructive procedure in relation to estimation error. The former point is necessarily now addressed at the level of feature selection and hence, within our unified perspective, may now be carried out at an optimal level through having distinguished it from the purely tomographic aspects of classical combination. The latter concern, the robustness of the procedure to estimation error, has been shown [1] to be of the order of that of the Sum Rule, the previously optimal procedure in this regard.

The only remaining directions for the methodology to take in terms of enhancing performance would therefore be in the treatment of incorporated *a priori* knowledge during the PDF reconstruction phase, and in the extension of the range of classifiers that the feature selection algorithm has access to, the latter within the context of our investigation being considered to represent the current extent of human knowledge as to the range of probability density function reconstruction possibilities.

5   Acknowledgement

This research was carried out at the University of Surrey, UK, supported by, and within the framework of, EPSRC research grant number GR/M61320.

References

1. D. Windridge, J. Kittler, "Classifier Combination as a Tomographic Process", (Multiple Classifier Systems, LNCS. Vol. 2096 , 2001.)
2. R A Jacobs, "Methods for combining experts' probability assessments", Neural Computation, 3, pp 79-87, 1991
3. J. Kittler, M. Hatef, R.P.W. Duin, and J. Matas, "On combining classifiers", IEEE Transactions on Pattern Analysis and Machine Intelligence, vol. 20, no. 3, 1998, 226-239
4. L. Lam and C.Y. Suen, "Optimal combinations of pattern classifiers", Pattern Recognition Letters, vol. 16, no. 9, 1995, 945-954.
5. A F R Rahman and M C Fairhurst, "An evaluation of multi-expert configurations for the recognition of handwritten numerals", Pattern Recognition Letters, 31, pp 1255-1273, 1998
6. A F R Rahman and M C Fairhurst, "A new hybrid approach in combining multiple experts to recognise handwritten numerals", Pattern Recognition Letters, 18, pp 781-790, 1997
7. K Woods, W P Kegelmeyer and K Bowyer, "Combination of multiple classifiers using local accuracy estimates", IEEE Trans. Pattern Analysis and Machine Intelligence, 19, pp 405-410, 1997
8. Neal R., Probabilistic inference using Markov chain Monte Carlo methods. Tech. rep. CRG-TR-93-1 1993 , Department of Computer Science, University of Toronto, Toronto, CA.
9. Breiman L., Bagging predictors, Machine Learning 1996; vol. 24, no. 2:123-140.
10. Drucker H., Cortes C., Jackel L. D., Lecun Y., and Vapnik V., Boosting and other ensemble methods, Neural Computation, 1994; vol. 6, no. 6:1289-1301
11. Windridge D., Kittler J., "Combined Classifier Optimisation via Feature Selection", Proceedings "Advances in Pattern Recognition", Joint IAPR International Workshops SSPR 2000 and SPR 2000 Alicante, Spain, August 30 - September 1, 2000; Lecture Notes in Computer Science.VOL. 1876
12. Dietterich T. G., Bakiri G. "Solving Multiclass Learning Problems via Error-Correcting Output Codes." Journal of Artificial Intelligence Research, 1995; Vol 2.: 263-286.
13. D. Windridge, J. Kittler, "Combined Classifier Optimisation via Feature Selection", Proceedings "Advances in Pattern Recognition", Joint IAPR International Workshops SSPR 2000 and SPR 2000 Alicante, Spain, August 30 - September 1, 2000, Lecture Notes in Computer Science.VOL. 1876
14. D. Windridge, J. Kittler, "A Generalised Solution to the Problem of Multiple Expert Fusion", Univ. of Surrey Technical Report: VSSP-TR-5/2000

Post-processing of Classifier Outputs in Multiple Classifier Systems

Hakan Altınçay[1] and Mübeccel Demirekler[2]

[1] Computer Engineering Dept., Eastern Mediterranean University, Gazi Mağusa,
KKTC Mersin 10, TURKEY
hakan.altincay@emu.edu.tr
[2] Electrical and Electronics Engineering Dept., Middle East Technical University,
Ankara, TURKEY
demirek@eee.metu.edu.tr

Abstract. Incomparability in classifier outputs due to the variability in their scales is a major problem in the combination of different classification systems. In order to compensate this, output normalization is generally performed where the main aim is to transform the outputs onto the same scale. In this paper, it is proposed that in selecting the transformation function, the scale similarity goal should be accomplished with two more requirements. The first one is the separability of the pattern classes in the transformed output space and the second is the compatibility of the outputs with the combination rule. A method of transformation that provides improved satisfaction of the additional requirements is proposed which is shown to improve the classification performance of both linear and Bayesian combination systems based on the use of confusion matrix based a posteriori probabilities. ...

1 Introduction

The performance of classification systems based on the use of multiple classifiers are shown to be superior to individual classifiers in many classification experiments [1,2]. There are different combination frameworks proposed in the literature that can be roughly categorized according to the levels of classifier outputs. Abstract level Multiple Classifier Systems (MCS) take into account the most likely pattern class output of each classifier. A well known combination approach for this category is the *majority voting* [1]. Rank level MCS make use of a ranked list of classes where ranking is based on decreasing likelihood. *Borda count* method is the most frequently used rank level combination approach. In the measurement level combination, log likelihood values of the classes provided by the classifiers based on statistical modeling techniques like Gaussian Mixture Models (GMM) or cumulative distance values of each class based on a non-parametric modeling approach like Vector Quantization (VQ) are used in the combination. Linear combination method where the output vectors from different classifiers are added and Bayesian combination with independence assumption where the classifier outputs are multiplied are typical measurement level combination methodologies [3].

F. Roli and J. Kittler (Eds.): MCS 2002, LNCS 2364, pp. 159–168, 2002.
© Springer-Verlag Berlin Heidelberg 2002

Among three different levels of classifier outputs, measurement level is the one conveying greatest amount of information about the relative degree that each particular class may or may not be the correct and, this information can be quite useful during combination. For example, when the measurement values of all classes are very close to each other, the classifier may be considered not to be sure about its most likely pattern class. However, abstract level output errors cannot be differentiated from each other. These discussions mainly emphasize the advantages of using measurement level classifier outputs in combination. However, a major problem in measurement level combination is the *incomparability* of the classifier outputs. In this study, the main objective is to clarify the main reasons for this incomparability, analyze some of the available normalization techniques and then propose a hybrid approach.

2   Incomparability in Classifiers' Outputs

The outputs of different classifiers making use of different feature vectors or modeling techniques are not comparable and hence, they are not suitable for direct use in the combination operation. There are two basic reasons for this. The first is the *scale* of the classifier outputs. For instance, GMM based classifiers provide log likelihood values that are negative and VQ based classifiers may provide distance values of the order 10^3. The second reason is that, for some classifiers like GMMs, the correct class is the one getting the maximum output value whereas in distance based classifiers like VQ, the correct class is selected as the one which gets the minimum measurement value.

In order to tackle with these problems, basically two approaches are proposed. In the first approach, the *distribution* of the actual classifier outputs are estimated either with the use of non-parametric techniques like Parzen windows, k-nearest neighbors, or the distributions are assumed to be multi-dimensional Gaussian [4,5,6,7]. These distributions are later used to convert the actual outputs into probabilities. In this approach, the classifiers can be considered as some preprocessors producing more regular distributions than the original input space or the density estimation can be treated as a statistical post processor [4].

The second approach is based on normalization of the measurement level classifier outputs so that they satisfy the axioms of probability [8,9,10,11]. Let O_i denote the output corresponding to the class w_i and N denote the total number of classes. The most frequently used function for this output normalization approach is [10],

$$F(O_i) = \frac{f(O_i)}{\sum_{j=1}^{N} f(O_j)} \tag{1}$$

where $f(O_i)$ may be selected as $f(O_i) = O_i$, $f(O_i) = 1/O_i$, $f(O_i) = O_i^2$, $f(O_i) = 1/O_i^2$ etc. Some other methods can be found in Ref. [12]. The normalization of classifier outputs can be considered as a *transformation* from the *actual output space* into a new space which may be named as *transformed output space*. We may also consider the abstract or rank level outputs as the transformed outputs spaces from measurements provided by the classifiers. The confusion matrix based a posteriori probability estimation is another form of transformation from the actual classifier outputs. The number of the post-processing techniques for classifier can be further increased.

It has been reported that output transformation of the form given in Eq. (1) may sometimes result in quite undesirable effects where combined systems may have less performance than the individual classifiers [9,13]. In our recent study, it is shown that the dimensionality reduction effect in some transformation methods reduces the *separability* of the pattern classes [14]. As a matter of fact, the exact relation between the transformation itself and the other components of the MCS (e.g. method of combination, classifier) should be clarified. At this stage, some critical questions that should be asked are: Which of the above transformation methods is the best one? Is there any dependence between this best choice and the classifier? Does it have a dependence on the combination rule? The next section is devoted to the answers of these questions

3   Criteria for Selecting the Output Transformation Method

The transformation of classifier outputs is an intermediate stage between classifier development and combination. Because of this, we may consider it as the last step of classifier development. In other words, transformation can be assumed as a part of the classifier itself and classifier dependent. Because of the fact that classifier selection is dependent on the combination rule [15], it can directly be argued that selection of the transformation approach depends on the method of combination as well. In other words, the transformation should be done in such a way that the expectations from the classifiers by the combination rule are satisfied.

A summary of some criteria that should be considered before transformation method selection are given below:

1. The transformation should not reduce the separability of the pattern classes,
2. The classifier outputs should be transformed onto a similar scale,
3. The transformation should provide compatible outputs with the combination rule.

The first item means that originally separable pattern classes should not become overlapping after normalization. The main reason for this is that many of the transformations in the form given in Eq. (1) are *many-to-one mappings* leading to such an undesirable behavior. For instance, if $f(O_i) = O_i$ is considered, for the case of 3 classes the output vectors $O_1 = [1.2, 0.9, 0.9]$ and $O_2 = [0.4, 0.3, 0.3]$ will be transformed to the same point in the transformed output space although O_1 may correspond to a sample of class w_1 and O_2 may correspond to a sample of class w_2. A detailed analysis about this undesirable behavior of some normalization methods can be found in Ref. [14].

The requirement of the scale similarity seems to be a must for most of the basic combination rules like linear or logarithmic opinion pools and learning combination systems which are optimized in some sense. For instance, if a neural network is going to be used, there will be some problems in the selection of the initial values of the weights if the entries in the input vectors have big differences in their dynamic ranges [16]. On the other hand, if linear combination is to be used, correct information coming from one classifier may not be able to compensate misleading information from another classifier if dynamic range of the outputs of the former classifier is much smaller. In general, the similarity in the output scales is achieved by setting the sum of the output vector elements to 1.0 as in Eq. (1). However, as described above this reduces the separability of pattern classes leading to undesirable effects.

The compatibility of classifier outputs and the combination rule is another important aspect in selecting the transformation function. Firstly, if the combination scheme treats a pattern class with larger output value as more likely, then this should be taken into account during the transformation of the outputs of the classifiers like VQ where a larger output value corresponds to a less likely pattern class. Secondly, for the combination rules like linear and logarithmic opinion pools and also in their weighted forms, the relative output values are also important. Hence, the transformation should minimize $(O_n - O_c)$ when the correct class does not get the maximum measurement value and maximize $(O_c - O_n)$ when the correct class gets the maximum value, where O_c and O_n denote the transformed outputs of the correct and any other pattern class respectively. It should be noted that when the confusion matrix based a posteriori probabilities are used, the requirement that $(O_n - O_c)$ is minimized in the cases where the correct class does not get the maximum measurement value is not satisfied.

For a better understanding, consider a pattern classification problem involving three classes. Assume that the trained classifier is validated using 100 samples for each pattern class and the following confusion matrix is obtained [3].

$$conf = \begin{bmatrix} 90 & 0 & 10 \\ 0 & 100 & 0 \\ 2 & 0 & 98 \end{bmatrix} \tag{2}$$

Confusion matrix based a posteriori probabilities can be estimated using

$$P(sample \in w_i | output = w_j) = \frac{n_{ij}}{\sum_{k=1}^{3} n_{kj}}. \tag{3}$$

In the above equation, n_{ij} denotes the number of samples from class w_i that are classified as w_j.

During testing, assume that the output of this classifier is the first class, w_1. According to the confusion matrix, this means that the correct class may be either w_1 or w_3. The transformation represented by the confusion matrix maps some of the samples of w_1 and some samples of w_3 onto the same point into the transformed output space and hence completely removes their separability. For the given confusion matrix, the a posteriori probability vector is approximately calculated as $\mathbf{p} = [90/92, 0, 2/92]$. It is evident from this output vector that, apart from the first, the third class may also be the tested one. However, this is almost completely *masked* by the large probability of the first class. In other words, this transformation does not satisfy the requirement of minimizing $(O_n - O_c)$ when the correct speaker does not get the maximum measurement value. Furthermore, combination of the outputs of more than one classifier may not even solve the problem unless a large amount of classifiers are used since, the support on this class is almost the same as the support on the second class which, according to the confusion matrix, is almost impossible to be the correct one. Because of this, this transformation violates the requirement given in item three above. Actually, this is one of the major reason for close combination performance of abstract level combination schemes like majority voting and confusion based measurement level combination methods like linear combination. In this context, this problem is named as *rare output masking*.

In this study, a transformation is proposed that has better satisfaction for the three requirements described above. It is based on the integration of the measurement level based outputs and the statistical information about the classification behavior of each classifier at the first rank. We defined two distinct modes of operation: *correct classification* and *indecision*. A detailed description of this modeling is given in the next section.

4 Multi-modal Operation by Multiple Confusion Matrices

Let us define the global classifier error as the percentage of the misclassified validation samples when all the samples from all pattern classes are considered. Assume that, by examining the *actual* classifier outputs, we can select a robust measure that can be used to partition the samples into two categories. The first category, corresponding to *correct classification* mode of operation, is made up of the samples for which the value of the measure obtained is larger than an empirically calculated threshold so that the probability of classification error is very small compared to the global classifier error rate. The rest of the outputs with measures less than the threshold forms the *indecision* mode of operation. Naturally, for this category of outputs, the probability of error is much larger than the global classifier error.

The next step is to represent each category of samples by a different confusion matrix. Consider the output categorization represented by the following modes:

$$
conf = \begin{bmatrix} 90 & 0 & 10 \\ 0 & 100 & 0 \\ 2 & 0 & 98 \end{bmatrix} = \begin{bmatrix} 5 & 0 & 9 \\ 0 & 10 & 0 \\ 2 & 0 & 15 \end{bmatrix} \begin{matrix} indecision \\ mode \end{matrix}
$$
$$
+ \begin{bmatrix} 85 & 0 & 1 \\ 0 & 90 & 0 \\ 0 & 0 & 83 \end{bmatrix} \begin{matrix} correct\ classification \\ mode \end{matrix}
\tag{4}
$$

The original confusion matrix on the left is written as the sum of two confusion matrices, each corresponding to different mode of operation. As seen from the first matrix on the right, the rare output masking problem is not available any more for the outputs with measure values less than some threshold and hence the information about the misclassified classes is not completely masked. For instance, the a posteriori probability for the third class which was masked with the value 2/92 is increased to 2/7. Comparing the original and the correct classification confusion matrices, since the second confusion matrix is used for the samples that are considered to be correctly classified using the threshold, it can be argued that there may not be any loss for the class originally having a high a posteriori probability. By this way, the satisfaction of the compatibility require-

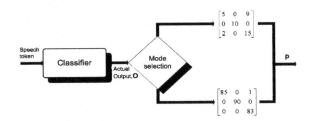

Fig. 1. Multi-modal classifier operation with two modes.

ment is improved. The proposed multi-modal classifier operation improves the separability problem by using multiple confusion matrices as well. For instance, the output vectors of the samples belonging to classes w_1 and w_3 that were transformed to $\mathbf{p} = [90/92, 0, 2/92]$ are now separated into two groups. Using two confusion matrices, samples belonging to a different group are transformed into a different output vector. Perfect separation would be achieved if the number of these confusion matrices could be further increased in a reliable manner so that each group involves actual output space vectors belonging to only one class. For instance, we may define a *reject* mode of operation and represent it with a third confusion matrix.

The block diagram of a classifier with two different modes of operation is given in Figure 1. As seen in the figure, the classifier modes are dynamically selected taking into account the actual classifier output vector denoted by $\mathbf{O}$ in the figure. By this way, integration of actual classifier outputs and confusion based a posteriori probabilities is achieved.

In this approach, it is assumed that the *relative* values of the *actual* classifier outputs for the first ranked class and the rest provide important clue for correct classification or indecision of a classifier. Actually, this is a general assumption used in many studies [13,17]. The details about this mode selection procedure, the measure used and the way of computing its classifier dependent threshold are described in the next section.

5 Measure for Determination of the Mode of Operation

As described in the previous section, a reliable measure is required for identifying the correct classifications of a classifier based on the actual output values. There are several measures that can be used [18,19]. In this study, we used

$$meas = \frac{1/O_{r_1} - 1/O_{r_2}}{\sum_{i=1}^{N} 1/O_i} \tag{5}$$

In order to satisfy the first requirement in item 3 given above for our VQ based classifiers, the reciprocal values of the outputs are used as the measurement level outputs where O_{r_1} and O_{r_2} are the actual values for the first and second ranked (most likely) classes. It can be argued that the larger the value of *meas*, the more likely that the first ranked class is the correct one [13,17]. Some other approaches can also be used like those discussed in [6]. Actually, further experimental research comparing the effectiveness of these measures is necessary for classifier combination studies. Such measures will also be useful for developing better dynamic classifier or classifier subset selection studies.

If the output value of the most likely pattern class is close to the output value of the second ranked, it means that the top two classes are almost equally likely to be the correct class according to the classifier. Hence, the most likely class may or may not be the correct class. In the proposed approach, the samples having low *meas* values are considered in the estimation of *indecision* mode confusion matrix and the samples having high *meas* values are considered in the estimation of *correct classification* mode confusion matrix. Distribution of *meas* values for the classifier e_1 is given in Figure 2. Detailed information about this classifier

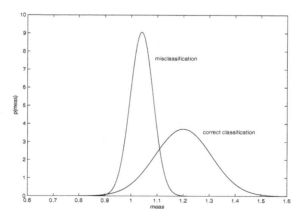

Fig. 2. An example distribution of *meas* values for *indecision* and *correct classification* modes of operation.

is given in Table 1. As seen in the figure, for small values of *meas*, there is a severe overlap in the classification behavior of the classifier. Thus, looking at the *meas* value, we can not decide whether the classification is correct or not. Hence, this region is included in the *indecision* mode of operation. However, a threshold can be selected (around 1.2 for this classifier) above which the classification can be considered as a *correct classification*. In our experiments, the threshold is optimally determined so that the correct classification rate of the combined system is maximized on the validation data.

Consider the classifier e_1 with 3 pattern classes and let $\mathbf{O} = [O_1, O_2, O_3]$ be the actual output vector. Assume that the best fitting threshold was computed to be 1.2 during validation. Let $meas(\mathbf{O}) = 1.4$ and w_1 be the most likely. Then, since $1.4 > 1.2$ the mode of operation is correct classification and hence, using the correct classification confusion matrix in Eq. (4), the corresponding a posteriori probability vector is computed as $[1, 0, 0]$. On the other hand, if $meas(\mathbf{O}) = 0.5 < 1.4$, the mode of operation is indecision and hence the corresponding a posteriori probability vector is computed as $[5/7, 0, 2/7]$.

6   Experimental Setup and Database

The proposed approach is applied to the closed-set text-independent speaker identification problem. In the simulation experiments, four different classifiers are used. Table 1 gives the list of these classifiers. They are based on VQ modeling where the models are trained with the LGB algorithm and each speaker is represented by 32 code vectors. 12 LPC derived cepstral coefficients ($LPCC$) and 12 Mel-frequency cepstral coefficients ($MFCC$) type features are extracted and used in the classifiers [17]. Delta features are also appended to obtain 24 element feature vector for each speech frame. Cepstral Mean Subtraction (CMS) is also used for some classifiers. The experiments are conducted on 25 speakers

Table 1. Classifiers used in the simulation experiments

$Classifier$	$Model$	$Feature$	CMS	$Perf.$
e_1	VQ	LPCC	$\checkmark$	89.4
e_2	VQ	LPCC		84.4
e_3	VQ	MFCC	$\checkmark$	86.3
e_4	VQ	MFCC		79.9

from the POLYCOST database. There are approximately 10 sessions for each speaker. The records are done on telephone lines, sampled at 8kHz and alaw coded. First three sessions are used for training and cross validation. There are totally 6675 training and 17709 test tokens. 200 consecutive frames, each 20ms long, are used to form speech tokens where each speech token is treated as a separate training or test sample. Let x_i denote the ith frame. Then, the set of frames $\{x_1, x_2, \ldots, x_{200}\}$ belongs to the first token, $\{x_{11}, \ldots, x_{211}\}$ belongs to the second token etc.

7 Simulation Results and Discussions

The experimental results are given in Table 2 and Table 3. As seen in the tables, the proposed multi-modal classifier operation approach provided consistent improvement in the classification performance. We believe that the proposed method of classifier combination can be further improved by using more sophisticated measures of classifier mode selection.

The proposed algorithm provided a strong evidence towards the need for improved satisfaction of the criteria described in Section 3. Hence, classifier output transformation should not be considered simply as transforming the classifier outputs onto similar scales. Beside this, separability of the pattern classes in the transformed output space and their compatibility with the combination rule should also be taken into account.

Table 2. Performances of linear combination and multi-modal (MM) linear combination methods.

e_1	e_2	e_3	e_4	Linear combination	MM linear combination
√		√		88.8	89.0
	√		√	83.8	85.5
√	√			87.9	89.5
		√	√	84.9	86.1
√	√	√	√	91.5	91.8

Table 3. Performances of Bayesian and multi-modal (MM) Bayesian combination with independence assumption.

e_1	e_2	e_3	e_4	Bayesian combination	MM Bayesian combination
√		√		87.7	88.0
	√		√	82.4	84.2
√	√			87.3	87.5
		√	√	83.5	84.9
√	√	√	√	90.4	90.6

References

1. T. Ho, J. Hull, and S. Srihari. Decision combination in multiple classifier systems. *IEEE Transactions on Pattern Analysis and Machine Intelligence*, 16:66–75, 1994.

2. L. Xu, A. Krzyzak, and C. Y. Suen. Methods of combining multiple classifiers and their applications to handwriting recognition. *IEEE Transactions on Systems, Man and Cybernetics*, 22:418–435, 1992.

3. H. Altınçay and M. Demirekler. An information theoretic framework for weight estimation in the combination of probabilistic classifiers for speaker identification. *Speech Communication*, 30(4):255–272, April 2000.

4. J. S. Denker and Y. leCun. Transforming neural-net output levels to probability distributions. Technical report, AT&T Bell Laboratories, 1991.

5. R. P. W. Duin and M. J. Tax. Classifier conditional posteriori probabilities. *SSPR/SPR*, pages 611–619, 1998.

6. G. Giacinto and F. Roli. Methods for dynamic classifier selection. *ICIAP'99, 10th international conference on image analysis and processing, Italy*, pages 659–664, September 1999.

7. K. Woods, W. P. Kegelmeyer, and K. Bowyer. Combination of multiple classifiers using local accuracy estimates. *IEEE Transactions on Pattern Analysis and Machine Intelligence*, 19(4):405–410, april 1997.

8. R. Brunelli and D. Falavigna. Person identification using multiple cues. *IEEE Transactions on Pattern Analysis and Machine Intelligence*, 17(10):955–966, 1995.

9. Y. S. Huang and C. Y. Suen. A method of combining multiple classifiers- a neural network approach. *Proceedings of the 12th IAPR international conference*, 2:473–475, 1994.

10. K. Chen, L. Wang, and H. Chi. Methods of combining multiple classifiers with different features and their applications to text-independent speaker identification. *International Journal of Pattern Recognition and Artificial Intelligence*, 11(3):417–445, 1997.

11. D. M. J. Tax, M. Breukelen, R. P. W. Duin, and J. Kittler. Combining multiple classifiers by averaging or by multiplying. *Pattern Recognition*, 33:1475–1485, 2000.

12. B. Achermann and H. Bunke. Combination of face classifiers for person identification. *Proc. 13th International Conference on Pattern Recognition*, pages 416–420, 1996.

13. R. Battiti and A. M. Colla. Democracy in neural nets: Voting schemes for classification. *Neural Networks*, 7(4):691–707, 1994.

14. H. Altınçay and M. Demirekler. Undesirable effects of output normalization in multiple classifier systems. *Submitted to Pattern Recognition Letters*.

15. M. Demirekler and H. Altincay. Plurality voting based multiple classifier systems: statistically independent with respect to dependent classifier sets. *Accepted for publication in Pattern Recognition Journal*.

16. C. M. Bishop. *Neural Networks for Pattern Recognition*. Oxford University press, 1995.

17. H. Gish and M. Schmidt. Text-independent speaker identification. *IEEE Signal Processing Magazine*, pages 18–32, October 1994.

18. K. Yu, X. Jiang, and H. Bunke. Lipreading: A classifier combination approach. *Pattern Recognition Letters*, 18:1421–1426, 1997.

19. X. Lin, X. Ding, M. Chen, R. Zhang, and Y. Wu. Adaptive confidence transform based classifier combination for chinese character recognition. *Pattern Recognition Letters*, 19:975–988, 1998.

Trainable Multiple Classifier Schemes for Handwritten Character Recognition

K. Sirlantzis, S. Hoque, and M.C. Fairhurst

Department of Electronics, University of Kent, Canterbury, Kent CT2 7NT,
United Kingdom.
{ks30,msh4,mcf}@ukc.ac.uk

Abstract. In this paper we propose two novel multiple classifier fusion
schemes which, although different in terms of architecture, share the
idea of dynamically extracting additional statistical information about
the individually trained participant classifiers by reinterpreting their outputs on a validation set. This is achieved through training on the resulting *intermediate feature spaces* of another classifier, be it a combiner
or an intermediate stage classification device. We subsequently implemented our proposals as multi-classifier systems for handwritten character recognition and compare the performance obtained through a series of cross-validation experiments of increasing difficulty. Our findings
strongly suggest that both schemes can successfully overcome the limitations imposed on fixed combination strategies from the requirement of
comparable performance levels among their participant classifiers. In addition, the results presented demonstrate the significant gains achieved
by our proposals in comparison with both individual classifiers experimentally optimized for the task in hand, and a multi-classifier system
design process which incorporates artificial intelligence techniques.

1 Introduction

Handwritten character recognition is still one of the most challenging areas of the
field of pattern recognition. Among the numerous methods proposed to tackle
its intricacies the development of multiple classifier fusion methodology in recent
years has been shown to be among the most successful. The basic idea underlying
multiple classifier systems is to exploit the diverse interpretation of the patterns
to be classified offered by different (relatively simple) classifiers in order to obtain
enhanced performance. The comparative advantages offered by multiple classifier systems are, by now, well appreciated by the pattern recognition community
[1,2]. Although a significant number of theoretical and empirical studies have
been published to date, predicting the likely success of a fusion scheme often
remains an open question. However, both theoretical analysis and empirical evidence suggest that two of the most important requirements for fusion strategies
to achieve performance improvements are that the individual participant classifiers should: *(i) produce uncorrelated errors*, and *(ii) have comparable levels*

F. Roli and J. Kittler (Eds.): MCS 2002, LNCS 2364, pp. 169–178, 2002.
© Springer-Verlag Berlin Heidelberg 2002

of performance. Considerations about the diversity of the properties of different individual classifiers add further levels of complexity to the system design process.

Fusion methods can be broadly categorised as fixed or trainable. Although most work published to date seem to deal with fixed combination rules there is an increasing interest towards trainable combiners. The reason behind this development can be traced to the fact that while fixed rules use *statically* the output of the trained individual classifiers to produce a decision, trainable schemes attempt to *dynamically* extract additional information by reinterpreting this output through training of the combiner. In principle any classifier can serve as a trained combiner. However, taking into account the characteristics of the initial classifiers' output can provide guidelines about the types of classifiers more appropriate to the task in hand, as will be discussed below. An important and open issue when using trainable fusion rules is whether the use of the classifiers' output on their training set is sufficient to allow effective learning in the combiner or whether a separate validation set is needed in order to extract additional information. Preliminary studies suggest that no comparative advantages over the fixed combination schemes can be achieved by using the initial training set outputs to train the combiner, be it one of the conventional classifiers (e.g. a Bayes Linear Discriminant [3]), or an algorithm based on the Machine Learning paradigm such as an Artificial Neural Network [4], or a dynamic multi-classifier system design process based on genetic algorithms [5,6,7]. On the other hand in [8] it is shown that the use of a separate validation set, in the case of a multi-classifier scheme for handwritten character recognition optimised by a genetic algorithm, can provide significant performance enhancements. Finally, Wolpert in [9] takes an intermediate position proposing a leave-one-out cross-validation type process to create the space on which his combiner is trained.

Considering the above discussion we introduce in this paper two types of multiple classifier fusion processes, both based on the use of the output of the *1st stage* classifiers as an *intermediate feature space* to be reinterpreted by trainable *2nd stage* classifiers. Motivated by the requirement of independence and the restriction to comparable performances we use in our experiments two classifiers which, although both belong in the n-tuple based group, utilise different features extracted from the original objects and are expected to present significantly different performances. To investigate the statistical properties of the systems we propose we perform a series of cross-validation experiments on two problems drawn from the field of handwritten character recognition. Finally, we present comparisons with a number of fixed combination schemes and individual classifiers experimentally optimised for the task at hand.

The remainder of the paper is organised as follows. The next section gives a general description of the proposed fusion strategies followed by the presentation of the systems used in our investigations and their components. Subsequently, we define the experimental setup and discuss the results obtained, concluding with some general observations.

2   The Proposed Fusion Scheme

In this paper, we investigate two fusion architectures. In both the systems, the main classification blocks are arranged in a parallel manner. In the first of the proposed architectures, after training the first stage classifiers on a training set, their outputs on a disjoint validation set are used to form a *composite interme-diate feature space* for the 'trainable classifier'. The latter is usually a classifier of a different type. The information flow during the combiner learning phase in this scheme is illustrated in Figure 1. As stated above, a validation data set is needed to generate the intermediate feature vectors, from which information about the bias/variance characteristics of the trained first stage classifiers can be extracted.

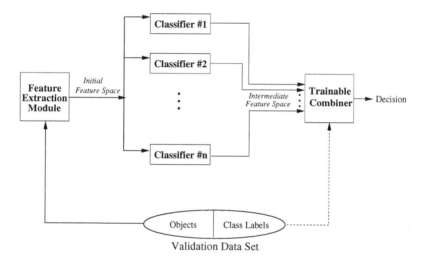

Fig. 1. The Combiner training in the first fusion scheme proposed

The second configuration involves one additional set of classifiers. Each of these '2nd stage' classifiers are independently trained on the separate interme-diate feature space formed from the validation output of the corresponding 1st stage classifier. The outputs of the 2nd stage classifiers are then fused using ei-ther a fixed or trainable combiner to generate the final decision label. Figure 2 shows the information flow of this fusion structure during the 2nd stage classi-fiers learning. Multiple disjoint validation data sets can be used in the training process when a trainable combiner is present. In our experiments we used the validation set to train only the 2nd stage classifiers and then employed a fixed combiner.

It should be noted that although the number and type of the individual 1st stage classifiers in both structures is dependent on the particular task domain and the specific performance requirements to be addressed, the choice of the

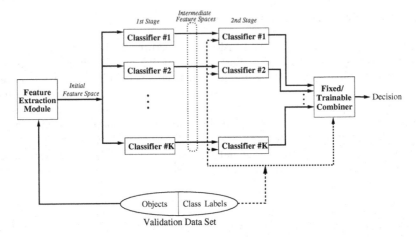

Fig. 2. Training phase of the 2nd stage classifiers and the Combiner (if trainable) in the second fusion scheme proposed.

second stage is dictated by the properties and the geometry of the generated intermediate feature spaces. It has been argued [10] that for similar schemes, such as 'stack generalization', to be successful, the first stage classifiers outputs should be transformed to posterior probabilities. However, we did not find this to be necessary for our schemes, though appropriate scaling of these outputs in our first scheme, where a composite intermediate feature space is used, is obviously necessary.

For investigative study of these configurations, we implemented two networks. The first comprises two classifiers (FWS and sn-tuple) in the first stage and a trainable combiner (Fisher Linear Discriminant, FLD). The second scheme additionally incorporates two FLDs in the second stage and uses a fixed combiner. Descriptions of these classifiers are provided in the following section.

3   Application to Handwritten Character Recognition

We start by describing the components of the systems we propose for the hand-written character recognition task. First, we describe the Frequency Weighted Scheme (FWS) which is an n-tuple based classifier reported to demonstrate reasonable levels of performance while requiring comparatively low memory size. We also describe the Scanning n-tuple scheme (sn-tuple) [11]. This is one of the most successful among the n-tuple based family of classifiers. Unfortunately there is usually a trade-off between high performance and, either increased computational load, or increased memory requirements. The Scanning n-tuple classifier is a typical example of the case where superior recognition rates are often achievable at the expense of significant storage requirements, especially in applications with samples of realistic size. The reason behind the choice of these two classifiers as 1st stage participants in our schemes is exactly the difference in the levels of performance we expect they will present. As will be demonstrated in the following section, the fusion schemes we propose here do not seem to require that the participant classifiers have comparable levels of performance in order to achieve improvements, in contrast to most of the fixed combination rules. We conclude this section discussing briefly the reasoning behind the choice of the Fisher Linear Discriminant as the 2nd stage classifier in our systems.

3.1   The Frequency Weighed Scheme (FWS)

In a basic n-tuple classifier, the n-tuples are formed by selecting multiple sets of n distinct locations from the pattern space. Each n-tuple, thus, sees an n-bit feature derived from the pattern. For classification, a pattern is assigned to that class for which the number of matching features found in the training set is maximum. The training process, therefore, requires counting the number of times different features are seen by individual n-tuples. To ensure equal likelihood of all classes, the counts are normalized so that the maximum possible score remains the same for all classes [12].

The FWS is the simplest enhancement of the basic n-tuple classification system. In the basic scheme, both the common and rare feature occurrences are accorded the same discriminatory weight. Thus, the presence of even one rogue pattern in the training set of a class can reduce the discriminatory power of the n-tuple network significantly. As a remedy, in the FWS, instead of setting the flag to record the occurrence of a certain feature in the training set, the relative frequencies are recorded. The frequency counts need to be normalized when different classes have different numbers of training images. The sum of these frequencies corresponding to a particular test image determine its class label.

3.2   The Scanning n-tuple Classifier (Sn-tuple)

The Scanning n-tuple (or simply sn-tuple) classifier has been introduced as a statistical-syntactic method for high performance OCR applications [11]. This is also a variant of the n-tuple classifier except that instead of using the two dimensional raw images directly, the operation is conducted on a one dimensional gray scale representation of the bitmap image. Another difference between the n-tuple and the sn-tuple is that, whereas each n-tuple samples a set of fixed points in the input space, each sn-tuple defines a set of relative offsets between its input points. Each sn-tuple is then scanned over the entire input space.

The one dimensional representation of the binary pattern image is obtained by tracing the contour edges of the image and representing the path by Freeman chain codes [13]. The sn-tuple algorithm is designed to model only one chain code string per pattern and a difficulty arises for images consisting of more than one contour. This is dealt with by mapping a set of strings to a single string by discarding the positional information (i.e., the start coordinates) and then concatenating the strings together. Also, the length of a chain coded string is dependent on the character class as well as writing style, degree of slant, image quality etc. Since image classes with short chain codes may be adversely affected, all chains are expanded to a predefined fixed length before training and testing.

3.3   The Fisher Linear Discriminant (FLD)

The Fisher Linear Discriminant is probably the most well-known and well studied linear classifier. Although it is also among the simpler to implement and faster to calculate, it is one of the most efficient linear classifiers since it accounts for the within and between classes variances. The multi-class version we use as a 2nd stage classifier in both the implementations of our proposed fusion schemes computes a single linear discriminant between each class and the combined set of all the other classes. This choice is dictated by the particular characteristics of the intermediate feature spaces we use for training, that is the dichotomy every 1st stage classifier induces between the output corresponding to the chosen class for each pattern and the outputs for the rest of the classes.

4   Experiments and Discussion

To observe the behaviour of our system and its statistical properties we performed 10-fold cross validation experiments on two handwritten character recognition problems of increasing difficulty. To this end we employed a database which consists of 34 classes of pre-segmented characters (numerals 0-9, and upper case letters A-Z, without differentiation between the pairs 0/O and 1/I). The database corresponds to handwritten characters, every class has 300 samples (10200 characters in total), and the images are provided at a resolution of 16x24 pixels. The two recognition problems were constructed as follows. The first included only the numerals (a 10-class task), while the second consisted of all the 34 classes (numerals and letters). For each problem randomly defined disjoint partitions in training, validation, and test sets are used to produce the cross-validation estimates of the statistics reported here. The training sets contain 150 samples per class (1500 characters in the digits case and 5100 in the alphanumeric case). The validation and test sets have sizes fixed to 75 samples per class (750 characters for the 10-class task and 2550 characters for the 34-class one).

   We first examine the individual performances of the participants of the multiple classifier system. Table 1 shows the recognition error rates of the FWS as well as the sn-tuple classifiers for the two task domains. It becomes readily apparent that the FWS classifier generates a significantly poorer performance compared to the sn-tuple. In fact, it exhibits, in both cases, approximately double the error rate of sn-tuple.

   Following the suggestions of theoretical analysis and considering such difference in performances between the two classifiers we would reasonably expect that their combination will not improve over the best individual case, a hypothesis which is verified by the results presented in Table 2. The Table includes average

Table 1. Mean Error Rates (%) of the individual components of the proposed system (1st stage).

1st stage classifier	Digits (10 classes)	Digits & Letters (34 classes)
FWS	10.00	22.28
Sn-tuple	4.58	12.42

error rates obtained from the combination of the outputs of the two classifiers on the test sets using five of the most commonly used fixed fusion schemes. Considering the fact that the original sn-tuple algorithm results in error rates of 4.59% and 12.42% for the 10 and 34-class problem respectively, we may safely conclude that none of the fixed combiners achieves improved performance.

Table 2. Mean Error Rates (%) of the multiple classifier systems (from fixed combination rules).

Fusion Rule	Digits (10 classes)	Digits & Letters (34 classes)
SUM	5.15	13.29
PRODUCT	5.09	13.29
MIN	4.82	13.49
MAX	7.84	18.44

The results included in Table 3 allow some interesting observations. In the first two rows we show error rates on the test sets obtained by two serial combination schemes in which, after training the 1st stage classifiers (FWS and sn-tuple) independently on the training set, we used their output on the validation set intermediate spaces to individually train two Fisher Linear Discriminants. It is not difficult to observe that none of these schemes improves over the corresponding 1st stage classifier. However, when the outputs of these two schemes are combined by a fixed combiner (namely the "sum" rule), an architecture which corresponds to the second of our proposed fusion schemes, significant gains can be obtained as demonstrated by the results in the last row of Table 3. In fact, these results are very similar to those shown in the second row of the same Table which correspond to the first of our proposed schemes. In this case the combined outputs on the validation set of the two 1st stage classifiers form the intermediate feature space on which a Fisher Linear Discriminant is trained. We believe that the similarity in the performances of both the fusion strategies we propose and their differences to the outcomes of the schemes represented in the first two rows of Table 3 are worth further investigation, as they may provide a path to understanding the underlying mechanisms of the mappings formed between the original feature spaces to the decisions produced by the final combination schemes.

Table 3. Mean Error Rates (%) of the multiple classifier systems (from trainable combiners).

Fusion scheme	Digits (10 classes)	Digits & Letters (34 classes)
Sn-tuple + FLD	4.91	13.33
FWS + FLD	10.27	23.79
Scheme 1: FLD(Sn-tuple, FWS)	3.01	10.64
Scheme 2: SUM(Sn-tuple+FLD, FWS+FLD)	3.31	10.59

Table 4 provides a comparison of the gains achievable in recognition accuracy by our fusion schemes with respect to a diverse set of classifiers **optimised** and tested on the same database. In addition to the best performing of the proposed architectures (indicated as Best of Proposed, BoP), error rates for three other classifiers are shown. The classifiers included in the Table are briefly described below:

Moment-based Pattern Classifier(MPC): This is a statistical classifier which explores the possible cluster formation with respect to a distance measure calculated on the nth order mathematical moments derived from the binary image [14].

Multilayer Perceptron (MLP): This is the well-known Artificial Neural Network architecture trained using Backpropagation Learning [15].

The MPC and MLP results we use in our comparisons have been initially presented in [16].

Moving Window Classifier (MWC): This is again an n−tuple based scheme which utilizes the idea of a window scanning the binarised image to provide partial classification indices which are finally combined to obtain the overall classification decision. The results presented here have been reported in [17].

Finally, it is worth noting that the schemes proposed in this paper exhibit comparable performance to a multiple classifier system optimised by a genetic algorithm (which is indicated by GA in Table 4), introduced in [8]. The corresponding error rates for the same database achieved by the genetically designed multi-classifier system were 3.40% for the 10-class, and 8.62% for the 34-class tasks. The comparison turns in favour of the systems proposed here if we take into account the computational load overhead which is well-known to be required by the genetic algorithm to produce the final optimised structure. So, when computational resources are at a premium the fusion strategies we propose would be the most attractive choice.

Table 4. A comparative study of error rates from different optimized classifiers.

Classification scheme	Digits (10 classes)	Digits & Letters (34 classes)
BoP	3.01	10.59
MPC	15.0	21.29
MLP	7.20	18.22
MWC	5.84	14.59
GA	3.40	8.62

5   Conclusions

Two multiple classifier architectures have been proposed and investigated in this paper. Experiments were carried out with off-line handwritten character data and results establish that either of the proposed systems is capable of generating improved performance. This establishes that use of a trainable combiner and/or trainable intermediate stage classifiers (provided they are trained on a data set separate from those used for training the 1st stage classifiers) can provide an overall error rate indeed better than the constituent classifiers. In addition, the results presented demonstrate the significant gains achieved by our proposals in comparison with both individual classifiers experimentally optimized for the task in hand, and a multi-classifier system design process which incorporates artificial intelligence techniques. Finally, our findings also suggest that both schemes can successfully overcome the limitations imposed on fixed combination strategies from the requirement of comparable performance levels among their participant classifiers.

6   Acknowledgement

The authors gratefully acknowledge the support of the UK Engineering and Physical Sciences Research Council.

References

1. Kittler, J., Hatef, M., Duin, R., Matas, J.: On combining classifiers. IEEE Transactions on Pattern Analysis and Machine Intelligence **20** (1998) 226–239
2. Dietterich, T.: Machine Learning Research: Four Current Directions. AI Magazine **18** (1997) 97–136
3. Duin, R., Tax, D.: Experiments with classifier combining rules. In Kittler, J., Roli, F., eds.: First International Workshop on Multiple Classifier Systems. Volume 1857 of LNCS. Springer (2000) 16–29
4. Lam, L., Huang, Y.S., Suen, C.Y.: Combination of multiple classifier decisions for optical character recognition. In Bunke, H., Wang, P.S.P., eds.: Handbook of Character Recognition and Document Image Analysis. World Scientific Publishing Company (1997) 79–101

5. Sirlantzis, K., Fairhurst, M.C.: Investigation of a novel self-configurable multiple classifier system for character recognition. In: Proceedings of the 6th ICDAR, Seattle, USA (2001) 1002–1006

6. Rahman, A.F.R., Fairhurst, M.C.: Automatic self-configuration of a novel multiple-expert classifier using a genetic algorithm. In: Proc. Int. Conf. on Image Processing and Applications (IPA'99). Volume 1. (1999) 57–61

7. Kuncheva, L., Jain, L.: Designing classifier fusion systems by genetic algorithms. IEEE Transactions on Evolutionary Computation **4** (2000) 327–336

8. Sirlantzis, K., Fairhurst, M., Hoque, M.S.: Genetic algorithms for multiple classifier system configuration: A case study in character recognition. In Kittler, J., Roli, F., eds.: Multiple Classifier Systems. Volume 2096 of LNCS. Springer (2001) 99–108

9. Wolpert, D.H.: Stacked generalization. Neural Networks **5** (1992) 241–259

10. Ting, K.M., Witten, I.H.: Stacked generalization: when does it work? In: Proceedings of 15th International Joint Conference on Artificial Intelligence (IJCAI-97), Nagoya, Japan (1997) 866–873

11. Lucas, S., Amiri, A.: Recognition of chain-coded handwritten character images with scanning n-tuple method. Electronic Letters **31** (1995) 2088–2089

12. Fairhurst, M.C., Stonham, T.J.: A classification system for alpha-numeric characters based on learning network techniques. Digital Processes **2** (1976) 321–329

13. Freeman, H.: Computer processing of line-drawing images. ACM Computing Surveys **6** (1974) 57–98

14. Rahman, A.F.R., Fairhurst, M.C.: Machine-printed character recognition revisited: Re-application of recent advances in handwritten character recognition research. Special Issue on Document Image Processing and Multimedia Environments, Image & Vision Computing **16** (1998) 819–842

15. Rumelhart, D.E., Hinton, G.E., Williams, R.J.: Learning internal representations by error propagation. In Rumelhart, D.E., McClelland, J.L., eds.: Parallel Distributed Processing. Volume 1. MIT Press, Cambridge, MA (1986) 318–362

16. Rahman, A.F.R.: Study of Multiple Expert Decision Combination Strategies for Handwritten and Printed Character Recognition. Phd thesis, University of Kent at Canterbury, United Kingdom (1997)

17. Fairhurst, M.C., Hoque, M.S.: Moving window classifier: approach to off-line image recognition. Electronics Letters **36** (2000) 628–630

Generating Classifier Ensembles from Multiple Prototypes and Its Application to Handwriting Recognition

Simon Günter and Horst Bunke

Department of Computer Science, University of Bern
Neubrückstrasse 10, CH-3012 Bern, Switzerland
`sguenter,bunke@iam.unibe.ch`

Abstract. There are many examples of classification problems in the literature where multiple classifier systems increase the performance over single classifiers. Normally one of the two following approaches is used to create a multiple classifier system. 1. Several classifiers are developed completely independent of each other and combined in a last step. 2. Several classifiers are created out of one base classifier by using so called classifier ensemble creation methods. In this paper algorithms which combine both approaches are introduced and they are experimentally evaluated in the context of an hidden Markov model (HMM) based handwritten word recognizer.

Keywords: Multiple Classifier System; Ensemble Creation Method; AdaBoost; Hidden Markov Model (HMM); Handwriting Recognition.

1 Introduction

The field of off-line handwriting recognition has been a topic of intensive research for many years. First only the recognition of isolated handwritten characters was investigated [21], but later whole words [19] were addressed. Most of the systems reported in the literature until today consider constrained recognition problems based on vocabularies from specific domains, e.g. the recognition of handwritten check amounts [9] or postal addresses [10]. Free handwriting recognition, without domain specific constraints and large vocabularies, was addressed only recently in a few papers [11,16]. The recognition rate of such systems is still low, and there is a need to improve it.

The combination of multiple classifiers was shown to be suitable for improving the recognition performance in difficult classification problems [12,13]. Also in handwriting recognition, classifier combination has been applied. Examples are given in [1,14,22]. Recently new ensemble creation methods have been proposed in the field of machine learning, which generate an ensemble of classifiers from a single classifier [3]. Given a single classifier, the base classifier, a set of classifiers can be generated by changing the training set [2], the input features [8], the

F. Roli and J. Kittler (Eds.): MCS 2002, LNCS 2364, pp. 179–188, 2002.

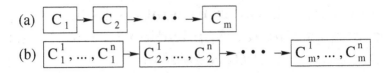

Fig. 1. Graphical illustration of the original version of AdaBoost (a) and the proposed extension (b).

input data by injecting randomness [5], or the parameters and architecture of the classifier [17]. Another possibility is to change the classification task from a multi-class to many two-class problems [4]. Examples of widely used methods that change the training set are Bagging [2] and AdaBoost [7]. Random subspace method [8] is a wel

One common feature of all the ensemble creation methods discussed above is the fact that they start from a single classifier to derive an ensemble. In this paper we propose a more general approach where we initially consider a set of classifier prototypes and apply the ensemble generation algorithms on the whole set. In the first scenario under consideration, we start with n classifier prototypes $C^1, \ldots, C^n$ and derive an ensemble $C^i_1, \ldots, C^i_m$ for each C^i separately. This eventually yields $n \cdot m$ classifiers that are to be combined by an appropriate combination rule. In the second scenario, the generation of C^i_j not only depends on $C^i_1, \ldots, C^i_{j-1}$, but also on all other prototypes C^k_l; $k = 1, \ldots, n$; $l = 1, \ldots, j - 1$. In particular we propose a generalized version of AdaBoost. Given a base classifier C^i, AdaBoost sequentially generates classifiers $C^i_1, \ldots, C^i_m$, where C^i_j is derived from C^i_{j-1} (and some other information). For the first classifi

As a result of the proposed procedure, an ensemble of $n \cdot m$ classifiers are obtained, which are to be combined by an appropriate combination rule.

The rest of this paper is organized as follows. In Section 2, the proposed method for classifier generation, which starts from a set of prototypes, rather than a single base classifier, is introduced. In Section 3 a new version of the AdaBoost algorithm, which is an enhancement of the general method proposed in Section 2, is described. Two prototype classifiers for handwriting recognition used in the experiments are presented in Section 4. Then, in Section 5, results of an experimental evaluation of the proposed approach are given. Finally, some conclusions are drawn in Section 6.

2   Creation of Ensembles from Sets of Prototypical Classifiers

The idea of the proposed ensemble generation method is very simple. Rather than starting with a single classifier, as it is done in Bagging, AdaBoost and the random subspace method, we initially consider a set of classifiers (called prototypes in the following) and use an ensemble creation method to generate

Input: classifiers (prototypes) $C_1, \ldots, C_n$; ensemble creation method ECM; number of classifier per ensemble, m.
Output: $m \cdot n$ classifiers.
CS is an empty set of classifiers;
for(i:=1;i<=n;i++)
    use ECM with classifier C_i to produce m classifiers;
    put all produced classifiers in CS;
return CS;

Table 1. Ensemble creation method starting with a set of prototypes

an ensemble out of each individual prototype. Then we merge all classifiers of these ensembles to get a single ensemble. This procedure is described in Table 1.

The procedure shown in Table 1 is straightforward. Nevertheless, there are two issues that need to be addressed here. First, after an ensemble of classifiers have been generated, a rule is needed to combine their results. A large number of such rules have been proposed in the literature. For a detailed discussion the reader is referred to [6,20]. In the experiments described in Section 5 some of these rules were actually applied, namely maximum rule, voting and weighted voting. Most of these rules need additional information about the results produced by the individual classifiers, for example, score values. Using the algorithm described in Table 1, a combination rule can only be applied if all prototypes $C_1, \ldots, C_n$ provide the information needed by the combination rule.

The second issue that needs to be addressed when implementing the method sketched in Table 1 is the generation of the initial prototype classifiers $C_1, \ldots, C_n$. Sometimes different classifiers for the same task may already exist, but often there is only one classifier. Clearly one could start with this single base classifier C and derive $C_1, \ldots, C_n$ using any of the known ensemble creation methods. The same - or another - ensemble generation method can then be used to produce an ensemble out of each C_i according to the algorithm sketched in Table 1, $i = 1, \ldots, n$. One of the main problems with this procedure is, however, that classifier diversity may be poor. In any multiple classifier system, a high level of classifier diversity and individual classifier performance should be provided. Only if the classifiers of an ensemble are diverse, an improvement of the performance can be expected. It is well known that an ensemble of classifiers with a poor divers

In the experiments described in Section 5, we used only two initial prototypes, C_1 and C_2, which are described in Section 4. From the way C_1 and C_2 are constructed it can be expected that the classifiers have a sufficiently high degree of diversity.

3   New Version of AdaBoost

In the procedure introduced in the last section the diversity of the initial prototype classifiers is not explicitly exploited in the ensemble creation methods. In this section a new version of the AdaBoost algorithm is introduced, which uses the diversity of the classifiers.

In the AdaBoost algorithm we try to create classifiers so that for each pattern there exist some classifiers that classify it correctly. In a two class problem the number of those classifiers should be more than half of all classifiers, while in an n class problem ($n > 2$) it may be sufficient if more than $\frac{1}{n}$ classifiers are correct. AdaBoost tries to construct classifiers, which classify "difficult" patterns correctly. These "difficult" patterns are the ones that are misclassified by a classifier with a training set sampled from the original training data. The "easy" patterns, i.e. the patterns that are correctly classified by a classifier whose training set is sampled from the original training set, are neglected, because there are enough classifiers that handle them correctly.

If we start from a set of various prototype classifiers, some patterns may be "easy" for one prototype, but "difficult" for others. The goal of the AdaBoost algorithm is the ensemble's correct recognition of as many training patterns as possible. There are three possible cases for each training pattern:

- The pattern is "easy" for all classifier prototypes. In this case there are enough classifiers which produce the correct result and new classifiers should not be trained on these patterns.
- The pattern is "easy" for some classifiers, but "difficult" for others. In this case the classifiers for which the pattern is "easy" should be trained on it, but not the classifiers for which the pattern is "difficult'. The reason to do so is an optimization of resources. When the classifiers for which the pattern is "easy" are trained on this pattern then it is very likely that they output the correct result. But if we train a classifier on "difficult" patterns the correct result is still not guaranteed. So it is better to train these classifiers on other patterns. Note that, as mentioned before, only a fraction of all classifiers must output the correct result to achieve a correct decision of the ensemble. Hence correct results from the classifiers for which the pattern is "easy" may be sufficient to make the ensemble result correct.
- The pattern is "difficult" for all classifier prototypes. In this case all prototypes should be trained on it so that at least some of them produce a correct result.

If we have two classifiers, C_1 and C_2, the training set can be split in four parts:

1. patterns that are "difficult" for C_1, but not for C_2.
2. patterns that are "difficult" for C_2, but not for C_1.
3. patterns that are "difficult" for C_1 and C_2.
4. patterns that are not "difficult" for either classifier.

Based on the previous considerations, the following procedure is adopted: Both classifiers concentrate on patterns of the third type. C_1 also takes the patterns of the second type into account, and C_2 the patterns of the first type. This can be summarized by the rule that each classifier is trained on the patterns misclassified by the other.

In the new AdaBoost algorithm a classifier for each prototype is produced in each step. In contrast to the classical AdaBoost algorithm we have now a selection probability for each pattern and each prototype instead of only one per pattern. In the original AdaBoost an error of a classifier is weighted by the selection probability of the misclassified pattern (which signifies its difficulty). In the new algorithm the difficulty of a pattern is estimated for a whole set of classifiers. The error of a classifier is the sum of the weights of the misclassified patterns, where the weight of a pattern is proportional to its difficulty. In the classical AdaBoost algorithm the difficulty of a pattern is defined as the selection probability, but here it is the geometric mean of the selection probabilities of all classifiers, and the error of a classifier is proportional to the sum of the difficulties of all patterns that are misclassified by it. Note that with this definition the error used in the original algorithm

The most important part of the new algorithm is the modification of the selection probabilities. In the original version of AdaBoost, each misclassified pattern gets an increased probability of being selected. By contrast, in the new version the selection probability of a pattern under all *other* classifier prototypes is increased if the pattern is misclassified. So the classifiers are concentrating on those patterns which are "difficult" for the classifiers of other prototypes. The parameters of the new algorithm are chosen so that the ratio of the selection probabilities of a pattern classified correctly by all classifiers and a pattern misclassified by all classifiers is the same as the ratio of the selection probabilities of a correctly classified pattern and a misclassified one in the original AdaBoost algorithm.

4   Handwritten Text Recognizer

In the experiments described in Section 5, two HMM-based handwritten word recognizers are used as base classifiers. The two recognizers, C_1 and C_2, are similar to the one described in [16]. We assume that each handwritten word input to the recognizers has been normalized with respect to slant, skew, baseline location and height (for details of the normalization procedures see [16]). A sliding window of width one pixel is moved from left to right over the word and nine geometric features are extracted at each position of the window. Thus an input word is converted into a sequence of feature vectors in a 9-dimensional feature space. The geometric features used in the system include the fraction of black pixels in the window, the center of gravity, and the second order moment. These features characterize the window from the global point of view. The other features give additional information. They represent the position of the upper and lowermost pixel, the contour direction at the position of the upper and lowermost pixel[1], the number of black-to-white transitions in the window, and the fraction of black pixels between the upper and lowermost black pixel. In [16] a more detailed description of the feature extraction procedures can be found.

---

[1] To compute the contour direction, the windows to the left and to the right of the actual window are used.

For each uppercase and lowercase character, an HMM is build. For all HMMs the linear topology is used, i.e. there are only two transitions per state, one to itself and one to the next state. The character models are concatenated to word models. There is exactly one model for each word from the underlying dictionary. This approach makes it possible to share training data across different words. That is, each word in the training set containing character x contributes to the training of the model of x. Thus the words in the training set are more intensively utilized than in the case where an individual model is build for each word as a whole, and characters are not shared across different models.

The difference of the two classifiers, C_1 and C_2, is the following:

- Each character HMM in C_1 has 14 states. This number of states was found to be optimal for the actual application under the assumption that each character has the same number of states.

- In C_2 the number of states varies from one character to another. For details of the calculation of the number of states see [24]. Because the number of states of the HMMs is adapted to the actual lengths of the characters, C_2 can be expected to perform better than C_1.

The implementation of the system is based on the Hidden Markov Model Toolkit (HTK), which was originally developed for speech recognition [23]. This software tool employs the Baum-Welch algorithm for training and the Viterbi algorithm for recognition [18]. The output of each of the two HMM classifiers is the word with the highest rank among all word models together with its score value.

5   Experiments

For isolated character and digit recognition, a number of commonly used databases exist. However, for the task considered in this paper, there exists only one suitable database to the knowledge of the authors, holding a sufficiently large number of words produced by different writers [15]. Consequently, a subset of this database was used for the experiments. The training set contains 9861 and the test set 1066 words over a vocabulary of size 2296. That is, a classification problem with 2296 different classes is considered in the experiments. The test set was chosen in such a way that none of its writers was represented in the training set. Hence all experiments described in this paper are writer independent. The total number of writers who contributed to the training and test set is 81. The two prototype classifiers, C_1 and C_2, are described in Section 4. The recognition rate for prototype C_1 is 66.22 %, and for prototype C_2 it is 70.17 %.

The following classifier combination schemes are used:

1. Maximum rule (*max*): The word class with the highest score among all word classes and all classifiers is the output of the combined classifier.

algorithm	C	max r.	voting	perf. v.	ga. v.	aboost v.
Bagging	C_1	65.2 %	67.35 %	67.64 %	67.92 %	-
Bagging	C_2	69.04 %	70.64 %	70.45 %	70.63 %	-
AdaBoost	C_1	63.51 %	68.29 %	68.86 %	68.29 %	68.11 %
AdaBoost	C_2	70.26 %	70.64 %	70.17 %	70.45 %	70..08 %
random subspace	C_1	62.1 %	67.54 %	68.11 %	68.67 %	-
random subspace	C_2	64.73 %	70.17 %	70.54 %	70.92 %	-
Bagging	C_1, C_2	69.04 %	71.86 %	71.95 %	71.76 %	-
AdaBoost	C_1, C_2	69.23 %	70.92 %	71.67 %	71.39 %	70.83 %
random subspace	C_1, C_2	64.54 %	71.29 %	71.67 %	71.67 %	-
new AdaBoost	C_1, C_2	69.42 %	70.73 %	70.92 %	71.2 %	69.04%
single classifier	C_1	66.23 %				
single classifier	C_2	70.17 %				

Table 2. Results of the experiments. The recognition rate of prototype classifiers C_1 and C_2 is 66.23 % and 70.17 %, respectively

2. Voting scheme (*voting*): Initially, only the top choice of each classifier is considered. The word class that is most often on the first rank is the output of the combined classifier. Ties are broken by means of the maximum rule, which is only applied to the competing word classes.
3. Weighted voting (*perf. v.*): Here we consider again the top class of each classifier. In contrast with regular voting, a weight is assigned to each classifier. The weight is equal to the classifier's performance (i.e. recognition rate) on the training set. The output of the combined classifier is the word class that received the largest sum of weights.
4. ga weighted voting (*ga v.*): Like weighted voting, but the optimal weights are calculated by a genetic algorithm based on the results of the classifiers on the training set.
5. AdaBoost weighted voting (*aboost v.*): The weights for the weighted voting are those calculated by the AdaBoost algorithm. This combination is only used in conjunction with the AdaBoost algorithm, of course.

The results of the experiments are shown in Table 2. In each experiment 10 classifiers are produced. The entries in column C denote the classifiers used for the experiment. If there is only one classifier then the normal ensemble creation method is used. If the entry contain both classifiers then the algorithm shown in Table 1 is used with the ensemble creation method indicated in the column *algorithm*. In this case 5 classifiers are generated from each prototype C_1 and C_2. The number of features for the random subspace method id set to 6.

The combination scheme *max r.* produces poor results while the other schemes always achieve the same or better recognition rates for the ensemble than for the individual prototype classifiers C_1 and C_2. The values in column *aboost v* are always lower than the values in the columns *perf. v.* and *ga. v.* This observation leads to the conclusion that while the weight calculation of AdaBoost may be appropriate to be used within the algorithm, it is not particularly suited for classifier combination in the considered application. In most of the experiments the weights produced by the genetic algorithm lead to better results than the performance weights.

From rows 1-6 in Table 2 it can be concluded that the classical versions of Bagging, AdaBoost and random subspace ensemble generation lead to an improved performance when compared to the individual classifiers C_1 and C_2, except for the maximum rule. Moreover, rows 7-9 indicate that, expect for the maximum rule, a further improvement can be achieved by means of the new ensemble generation method proposed in Section 2 (see Table 1). As indicated in row 10, the new version of AdaBoost leads also to a performance improvement when compared to the classical ensemble creation methods (see row 1-6). However, the recognition rates in row 10 are lower than those in rows 7-9. One important feature of the new algorithms proposed in Section 2 and 3 is their robustness with respect to the combination rule. The performance improvement discussed above is achieved under any of the considered rules except for the maximum rule.

6   Conclusions

In this paper, the generation of ensembles of classifiers for multiple classifier systems was studied. The contribution of the paper is twofold. First, a general approach to classifier ensemble generation has been proposed. In contrast with similar methods known from the literature, the proposed scheme starts with a set of prototype classifiers rather than a single classifier to derive an ensemble. If the given prototypes are sufficiently diverse, it can be expected that the final ensemble generated by the proposed method has a higher degree of diversity, and a better performance, than an ensemble consisting of the same number of classifiers derived from a single base classifier.

The second contribution of the paper is a new version of the AdaBoost algorithm. The conventional version of AdaBoost derives a sequence of classifiers starting from a single base classifier in a such a way that each classifier C in the ensemble directly depends on the classifier that was generated immediately before C. By contrast, the proposed method starts from a set of classifiers and derives, in each step, a set of new classifiers. Each classifier in this new set doesn't depend on only one, but on all classifiers generated in the last step.

The new ensemble creation methods were experimentally evaluated in the context of a complex handwritten word recognition task involving over 2000 different word classes. Bagging, AdaBoost, and the random subspace method were applied to generate classifier ensembles out of a base HMM handwritten word recognizer. The experiments were conducted with two different base HMM classifiers. In these experiments, the classifier ensembles have shown an improved performance over the base classifiers. The performance could be further improved by starting with two classifiers rather than a single base classifier. This confirms our expectation that starting from a set of (diverse) classifiers rather than a single base classifier results in an ensemble of higher diversity and improved recognition rate. It turns out that the new ensemble creation methods are quite robust with respect to the combination rule applied in the combined system. Out of four combination rules used, only one, the maximum score rule, didn't perfo

Because the experiments described in this paper are very time consuming, no crossvalidation was made. However, such a crossvalidation could be very useful in future to verify the results reported in this paper. Additional future work will include experiments with larger sets of classifiers and with more diverse prototype classifiers. How such prototypes are generated was not addressed in this paper and will also be a future research topic. Another research topic may be the use of dynamic selection of one or more classifiers from the ensemble. However, one reason why such a dynamic selection may be difficult to implement is the rather small amount of information delivered by a classifier (each classifier outputs only the best class with its score value).

Acknowledgment

The research was supported by the Swiss National Science Foundation (Nr. 20-52087.97). The authors thank Dr. Urs-Victor Marti for providing the handwritten word recognizer.

References

1. A. Brakensiek, J. Rottland, A. Kosmala, and G. Rigoll. Off-line handwriting recognition using various hybrid modeling techniques and character n-grams. In *7th International Workshop on Frontiers in Handwritten Recognition*, pages 343–352, 2000.
2. Leo Breiman. Bagging predictors. *Machine Learning*, (2):123–140, 1996.
3. T. G. Dietterich. Ensemble methods in machine learning. In *[12]*, pages 1–15.
4. T. G. Dietterich and G. Bakiri. Solving multiclass learning problems via error-correcting output codes. *Journal of Artifical Intelligence Research*, 2:263–286, 1995.
5. T.G. Dietterich and E.B. Kong. Machine learning bias, statistical bias, and statistical variance of decision tree algorithms. Technical report, Departement of Computer Science, Oregon State University, 1995.
6. R. Duin and D. Tax. Experiments with classifier combination rules. In *[12]*, pages 16–29.
7. Yoav Freund and Robert E. Schapire. A descision-theoretic generalisation of on-line learning and an application to boosting. *Journal of Computer and Systems Sciences*, 55(1):119–139, 1997.
8. T. K. Ho. The random subspace method for constructing decision forests. *IEEE Transactions on Pattern Analysis and Machine Intelligence*, 20(8):832–844, 1998.
9. S. Impedovo, P. Wang, and H. Bunke, editors. *Automatic Bankcheck Processing*. World Scientific Publ. Co, Singapore, 1997.
10. A. Kaltenmeier, T. Caesar, J.M. Gloger, and E. Mandler. Sophisticated topology of hidden Markov models for cursive script recognition. In *Proc. of the 2nd Int. Conf. on Document Analysis and Recognition, Tsukuba Science City, Japan*, pages 139–142, 1993.

11. G. Kim, V. Govindaraju, and S.N. Srihari. Architecture for handwritten text recognition systems. In S.-W. Lee, editor, *Advances in Handwriting Recognition*, pages 163–172. World Scientific Publ. Co., 1999.

12. J. Kittler and F. Roli, editors. *First International Workshop on Multiple Classifier Systems*, Cagliari, Italy, 2000. Springer.

13. J. Kittler and F. Roli, editors. *Second International Workshop on Multiple Classifier Systems*, Cambridge, UK, 2001. Springer.

14. D. Lee and S. Srihari. Handprinted digit recognition: A comparison of algorithms. In *Third International Workshop on Frontiers in Handwriting Recognition*, pages 153–162, 1993.

15. U. Marti and H. Bunke. A full English sentence database for off-line handwriting recognition. In *Proc. of the 5th Int. Conf. on Document Analysis and Recognition*, Bangalore, India, pages 705–708, 1999.

16. U.-V. Marti and H. Bunke. Using a statistical language model to improve the performance of an HMM-based cursive handwriting recognition system. *Int. Journal of Pattern Recognition and Art. Intelligence*, 15:65–90, 2001.

17. D. Partridge and W. B. Yates. Engineering multiversion neural-net systems. *Neural Computation*, 8(4):869–893, 1996.

18. L. Rabiner. A tutorial on hidden Markov models and selected applications in speech recognition. *Proceedings of the IEEE*, 77(2):257–285, 1989.

19. J.-C. Simon. Off-line cursive word recognition. *Special Issue of Proc. of the IEEE*, 80(7):1150–1161, July 1992.

20. C. Suen and L. Lam. Multiple classifier combination methodologies for different output level. In *[12]*, pages 52–66.

21. C.Y. Suen, C. Nadal, R. Legault, T.A. Mai, and L. Lam. Computer recognition of unconstrained handwritten numerals. *Special Issue of Proc. of the IEEE*, 80(7):1162–1180, 1992.

22. L. Xu, A. Krzyzak, and C. Suen. Methods of combining multiple classifiers and their applications to handwriting recognition. *IEEE Transactions on Systems, Man and Cybernetics*, 22(3):418–435, 1992.

23. S. J. Young, J. Jansen, J. J. Odell, D. Ollason, and P. C. Woodland. *The HTK Hidden Markov Model Toolkit Book*. Entropic Cambridge Research Laboratory, http://htk.eng.cam.ac.uk/, 1995.

24. M. Zimmermann and H. Bunke. Hidden markov model length optimization for handwriting recognition systems. Technical Report IAM-01-003, Department of Computer Science, University of Bern, 2001.

Adaptive Feature Spaces for Land Cover Classification with Limited Ground Truth Data

Joseph T. Morgan[1], Alex Henneguelle[2], Melba M. Crawford[1], Joydeep Ghosh[2], and Amy Neuenschwander[1]

[1]Center for Space Research
{JMorgan, Crawford, Amy}@csr.utexas.edu
[2]Department of Electrical and Computer Engineering
The University of Texas at Austin
{Hennegue, Ghosh}@ece.utexas.edu

Abstract. Classification of hyperspectral data is challenging because of high dimensionality (O(100)) inputs, several possible output classes with uneven priors, and scarcity of labeled information. In an earlier work, a multiclassifier system arranged as a binary hierarchy was developed to group classes for easier, progressive discrimination [27]. This paper substantially expands the scope of such a system by integrating a feature reduction scheme that adaptively adjusts to the amount of labeled data available, while exploiting the highly correlated nature of certain adjacent hyperspectral bands. The resulting best-basis binary hierarchical classifier (BB-BHC) family is thus able to address the "small sample size" problem, as evidenced by our experimental results.

1   Introduction

The increasing availability of data from hyperspectral sensors has generated tremendous interest in the remote sensing community because these instruments characterize the response of targets (spectral signatures) with greater detail than traditional sensors and thereby can potentially improve discrimination between targets [7, 28]. A common application is to determine the land cover label of each (vector) pixel using supervised classification where labeled training data (ground truth), X, are used to estimate the parameters of the label-conditional probability density functions, $P(x_1, x_2, ..., x_D | L_i), i = 1, ..., C$, or to directly estimate the *aposteriori* class probabilities. Unfortunately, hyperspectral data also presents special challenges in its analysis. The dimensionality of the data (D) is high (~ 200), and the number of classes C is often at least 10. To handle both issues, Kumar et al. proposed a method at MCS 2000 [27] to decompose a $(C > 2)$-class problem into a binary hierarchy of $(C - 1)$ simpler 2-class problems that could be solved using a corresponding hierarchy of classifiers, each using a simple discriminant (Fisher projection). This top-down Binary Hierarchical Classifier (TD-BHC) provided superior results in terms of test accuracies and yielded valuable domain knowledge.

This paper addresses a different challenge stemming from the scarcity of labeled data, which is often of limited quantity relative to the dimensionality D, at least for

F. Roli and J. Kittler (Eds.): MCS 2002, LNCS 2364, pp. 189-200, 2002.

some poorly represented classes. This leads to well studied "small sample size" problems. For example, a classifier using Fisher's linear discriminant function requires the inversion of the within-class covariance matrix. For the covariance matrix of D-dimensional data, there are $D(D+1)/2$ parameters to estimate and, minimally there must be $D+1$ observations of each class to ensure estimation of non-singular/invertible class specific covariance matrices [1]. There should be at least $5D$ data points/class for adequate estimation of the covariance matrix. Existing hyperspectral classifiers including the BHC are thus susceptible to small sample size issues [2].

This paper introduces a hierarchical, multiclassifier method that is applicable to multiclass problems, while addressing the issue of limited training sets. It utilizes both regularization of covariance estimates and an adaptive feature reduction approach that exploits domain knowledge. Experiments show that it provides substantial improvements over the original BHC when data are scarce, without compromising performance for larger data sets.

2   Previous Work

2.1 Small Sample Size Problems

The substantial methodology in this area can be largely categorized as one of three approaches [8]. Regularization methods, including "shrinkage," try to stabilize the estimated covariance matrix directly by weighting the sample covariance matrix as well as "supplemental" matrices [17]. The covariance matrix can be "shrunk" toward the identity matrix or a pooled covariance matrix. Hybrid approaches assign weights to the sample covariance (normal and diagonal) matrix and a pooled covariance (normal and diagonal) matrix [5, 14]. While this may reduce the variance of the parameter estimates, the bias of the estimates can increase dramatically. Rather than stabilizing the covariance matrix directly, the pseudo-inverse of the covariance matrix can be substituted for the true inverse. Pseudo-inversion utilizes the non-zero eigenvalues of the covariance matrix [15, 17]. However, in addition to poor performance when the ratio of training data to dimensionality is very small, the pseudo-inverse has a "peaking effect" in its performance. It has been shown that the pseudo-inverse performs best when $|X| = \frac{D}{2}$ and that the performance degrades as $|X|$ approaches D [12, 16].

An alternate approach involves transforming the input space into a reduced feature space via feature extraction or selection [10, 15], or artificially adding labeled samples. The transformations may result in some loss of interpretability and may be poorly estimated due to the limited data. Specific techniques for identifying and augmenting the existing training data with unlabeled data already exist and have been shown to enhance strictly supervised classification [3, 9, 18-23]. However, not only can convergence of the updating scheme be problematic, but it is also affected by selection of the initial training samples and by outliers.

A third approach uses an ensemble of "weaker" classifiers. Bagging, Simple Random Sub-sampling, and Arcing involve selecting subset samples of the original data and generating a classifier specific to each sub-sample [13]. When the data set is very small, however, these methods are inadequate because the degradation in individual classifier performance (because of lack of data) cannot be compensated for by the gains from using an ensemble [29].

2.2 Hyperspectral Classification

Among previous work on hyperspectral classification, the method that is most relevant to this research is the top down BINARY HIERARCHICAL CLASSIFIER (TD-BHC) framework that creates a multiclassifier system with C-1 classifiers arranged as a binary tree [27]. The root classifier tries to optimally partition the original set of classes into two disjoint meta-classes while simultaneously determining the Fisher discriminant that separates these two subsets. This procedure is recursed, i.e., the meta-class Ω_n at node n is partitioned into two meta-classes $(\Omega_{2n}, \Omega_{2n+1})$, until the original C classes are obtained at the leaves [4]. The tree structure allows the more natural, easier discriminations to be accomplished earlier [6]. Subsequently, a bottom-up version (BU-BHC) was developed based on an agglomerative clustering algorithm used for merging the two most "similar" meta-classes until only one meta-class remains. Fisher's discriminant was again used as the distance measure for determining the order in which the classes are merged. These two algorithms yielded superior results compared to a variety of other supervised approaches for classifying hyperspectral data. Figure 1 shows an example of a C-class BHC.

2.3 Hyperspectral Feature Reduction

From the domain knowledge in this field, it is known that the original input features - the bands of the hyperspectral data - that are "spectrally close" to one another, tend to be highly correlated. Jia and Richards proposed a Segmented Principal Components Transformation (SPCT) that exploits this characteristic [25, 26]. Edge detection algorithms are used to transform the original D individual bands into subsets of adjacent bands that are highly correlated, based on the estimated population correlation matrix. From each subset, the most significant principal components are selected to yield a feature vector that is significantly smaller in dimension than D. Although this approach exploits the highly correlated adjacent bands in hyperspectral data, it does not guarantee good discrimination capability because PCT preserves variance in the data rather than maximizing discrimination between classes. Additionally, the segmentation approach of SPCT is based on the correlation matrix over all of classes, and thus loses the often-significant variance in the class conditional correlation matrices. Subsequently, Kumar et al. proposed band combining techniques inspired by Best Basis functions [7]. Adjacent bands were selected for merging (alt. Splitting) in a bottom-up (alt. Top down) fashion using the product of a correlation measure and a Fisher based discrimination measure [4]. Although these two methods utilize the ordering of the bands and yield excellent discrimination, they are computationally intensive. Additionally, the quality of the discrimination functions, and thus the structure of the resulting feature space, is affected by the amount of training data, and this critical issue is not addressed.

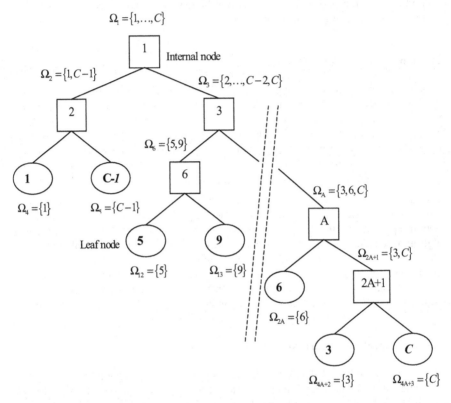

Figure 1. An example of a BINARY HIERACHICAL(multi)-CLASSIFIER for solving a C-class problem. Each internal node n comprises of a feature extractor, a classifier, a left child $2n$, and a right child $2n+1$. Each node n is associated with a meta-class Ω.

3 Adaptive Best-Basis Binary Hierarchical Classifiers

The new approach presented here applies a best-basis band-combining algorithm in conjunction with the BHC framework, while tuning the amount of feature reduction to the quantity of available training data. It also exploits the discovered hierarchy of classes to regularize covariance estimates using shrinkage.

3.1 Integrating Band Combination into Hierarchical, Multi-classifier Systems

The proposed approach can be viewed as a "best-basis" version of BHC (BB-BHC) that performs a band-combining step prior to the partitioning (top down variant) or combining (bottom-up variant) of meta-classes. Band combing is performed on highly correlated AND spectrally adjacent bands as this intuitively leads to the least loss in discrimination power. Because the correlation between bands varies among classes, the band reduction algorithm must be class dependent. In order to estimate the "correlation" for a group of bands (meta-bands) $B = [p:q]$ over a set of classes Ω, we define the correlation measure $Q(B)$ as the minimum of all the correlations within that group:

$$Q(B) = \min_{L_k \in \Omega} \min_{p \le i < j \le q} Q^{L_k}_{i,j} = \min_{L_k \in \Omega} \min_{p \le i < j \le q} \frac{S^{L_k}_{i,j}}{\sqrt{S^{L_k}_{i,i} S^{L_k}_{i,j}}} \tag{1}$$

where $|X|$ is the (i, j)th element of the sample covariance matrix for class L_k. The correlation measure (1) is used to determine which set of adjacent meta-bands should be merged at each successive step of the algorithm. Once the number of group bands is small enough, we maximize the discrimination between classes in the reduced space.

To address small sample sizes, rather than using a threshold on the correlation measure to determine whether bands or group-bands should be merged, our algorithm focuses on preserving as many of the original bands as possible, commensurate with the amount of training data available. Thus the band-combining algorithm ensures that the least amount of discriminatory information is lost while trying to achieve a satisfactory ratio of training data to dimensionality. Because literature recommends different thresholds for the minimum $\alpha_{ratio} \le \dfrac{|X|}{D}$, we allow this to be a user-defined input. Note that $|X|$ represents the number of data points in a child meta-class, and this number decreases as we proceed toward the leaves.

In pseudo-code, the adaptive band-combining algorithm that is performed before partitioning or merging meta-classes is:

1. $D^* = \min\left(D, \dfrac{|X|}{\alpha_{ratio}}\right)$

2. Initialize $l = 0$, $N_0 = D$, and $B^k_l = [k:k]$, $\forall\, k = 1, ..., D$

3. If $N_l > D^*$ then continue. Otherwise, stop.

4. Find the best pair of band to merge: $K = \arg\max_{k=1,...,N_l-1} = Q\left(B^k_l \cup B^{k+1}_l\right)$

5. Update band structure:
    - $l = l+1$, $N_l = N_{l-1} - 1$
    - If $K > 1$ then $B^k_l = B^k_{l-1}$, $\forall\, k = 1, ..., K-1$

- $\mathcal{B}_l^K = \mathcal{B}_{l-1}^K \cup \mathcal{B}_{l-1}^{K+1}$
- If $K < N_l$ then $\mathcal{B}_l^k = \mathcal{B}_{l-1}^{k+1}$, $\forall\ k = K+1, ..., N_l$

6.   Return to step 3.

3.2   Best Basis and Limited Data

When constructing a basis specific to each split in the BB-BHC, the quality of the correlation measure, computed from the class condition covariance matrices, is dependent on the quantity of training data available to estimate the meta-class covariance matrices. This becomes even more critical for the "low branches" of the BB-BHC as the meta-classes become smaller in cardinality, and the amount of training data per meta-class decreases. In particular, the class specific correlation

matrices $Q_{i,j}^{L_i} = \dfrac{S_{i,j}^{L_i}}{\sqrt{S_{i,i}^{L_i} S_{i,j}^{L_i}}}$ are   required   in   (1)   to   estimate   the   correlation

measure $Q(\mathcal{B})$. However, if the label specific S^{L_k} covariance matrices are not suitable for inversion, failure to stabilize their estimation before constructing the basis unsatisfactorily passes the disadvantage of the small sample size from the estimate of Fisher's discriminant and linear discriminant function to the basis construction. Therefore, the label specific sample covariance matrices must be stabilized. We define the ancestor sample covariance matrix S^{Anc} as being the sample covariance matrix which is estimated from at least $\alpha_{\mathrm{ratio}}|X|$ observations and is most closely related to L_k based on the BB-BHC structure. Because the trees are constructed in top-down and bottom-up manners, the search for S^{Anc} is performed uniquely for each type. In the top-down framework, if meta-class Ω_k is being considered for partitioning, than $S^{\Omega_k} = \sum\limits_{L_i \in \Omega_k} P(L_i) S^{L_i}$ is the first candidate for S^{Anc}. However, if $|X_{\Omega_k}| < \alpha_{\mathrm{ratio}} D$, then the BB-BHC tree structure is climbed in search of a meta-class where $|X_{\Omega_k}| \geq \alpha_{\mathrm{ratio}} D$. With the bottom-up framework, if $\{\Omega_{2n}, \Omega_{2n+1}\}$ are being considered   for   agglomeration,   the   first   candidate   for S^{Anc} is $S^{Pooled} = P(\Omega_{2n}) S^{\Omega_{2n}} + P(\Omega_{2n+1}) S^{\Omega_{2n+1}}$. However, because the BB-BHC is being constructed bottom-up, the structure cannot be climbed in search of a suitable S^{Anc}. Therefore, if $|X_{\Omega_i + \Omega_j}| < \alpha_{\mathrm{ratio}} D$, then $S^{\mathrm{Anc}} = \sum\limits_{i=1}^{c} P(L_i) S^{L_i}$. Note that this estimate

for S^{Anc} is used, even when the total quantity of training data available is less than $\alpha_{\mathrm{ratio}} D$. When applicable, the stabilized estimates of the label specific covariance matrices are utilized to estimate the correlation measure (1).

4   Results

Evaluation of the proposed D-BB-BHC algorithm was performed on two sites: Bolivar Peninsula, located at the mouth of Galveston Bay, Texas and NASA's John F. Kennedy Space Center (KSC) at Cape Canaveral, Florida.

4.1   Bolivar Peninsula

Bolivar Peninsula is located at the mouth of Galveston Bay and is part of the low relief barrier island system on the Texas Gulf coast. The area contains two general vegetation types, wetlands and uplands, with the marsh area further characterized in terms of sub-environments. For classification purposes, 11 classes representing the various land cover types were defined for the site (Table 1). HyMap (Hyperspectral Mapper) collected data over Bolivar Peninsula on September 17, 1999, at 5m spatial resolution. Data were acquired in 126 bands with almost contiguous spectral coverage from 440-2480 nm [24]. After removing water absorption and low SNR bands, 122 bands were used in the analysis.

Table 1. Classes for Bolivar Peninsula and the quantity of training data per class

Class	Name	Total Obs
1	Water	1019
2	Low Proximal Marsh	1127
3	High Proximal Marsh	910
4	High Distal Marsh	752
5	Sand Flats	148
6	Ag 1 (pasture)	3073
7	Trees	222
8	General Uplands	704
9	Ag 2 (bare soil)	1095
10	Transition Zone	114
11	Pure Silicornia	214

Multiple experiments were performed using stratified (class specific) sampling at percentages of: 75, 50, 30, 15, 5, and 1.5. Even at the sampling percentage of 75, the amounts of training data for classes 5 and 10 are still less then D (sand flats $|X_{L_5}| = 86$ and transition zone $|X_{L_{10}}| = 111$). We used $\alpha_{ratio} = 5$ for all sampling percentages except for 1.5 ($\alpha_{ratio} = 1.5$). The lower threshold ensured that there were at least two observations per label L_i. Ten experiments, using simple random sampling, were performed at each percentage for the bottom-up and top-down frameworks of the traditional BHC [TD-BHC, BU-BHC], the traditional BHC using the pseudo-inverse for tree construction (estimating Fisher's discriminant) and feature extraction (calculating Fisher's linear discriminant function), [TD-P-BHC, BU-P-BHC], and the adaptive best-basis BHC [TD-BB-BHC, BU-BB-BHC]. The results are presented in Figure 2.

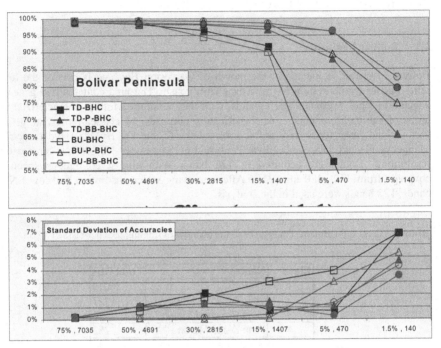

Figure 2. Classification (test set) accuracies for Bolivar Peninsula

By adapting the size of the feature space to reflect the amount of training data available, a high level of classification accuracy is preserved for an extremely low number of observations. At 50% sampling, which is typically used to separate data sets into training and testing, the BB-BHC actually performs slightly better that the BHC. Importantly, even though using the pseudo-inverse does not improve the accuracies at 50% sampling because there are at least $D+1$ observations per L_i, the results indicate that while the covariance matrices are non-singular, they are still poorly estimated. Not only does the BB-BHC perform the best at every sampling percentage with respect to the other TD and BU classifiers, but the accuracies are generally more stable (smaller standard deviation of accuracies) as well. Combating the limited training data by using the correlation matrix for feature reduction helps retain the information necessary for successful land cover prediction. Classification accuracies of >80% can still be achieved with only 140 total labeled samples and only 2 labeled pixels available for classes 5 (sand flats) and 10 (transition zone).

4.2   Cape Canaveral

The wetlands of the Indian River Lagoon system, located on the western coast of the Kennedy Space Center (KSC) at Cape Canaveral, Florida, are a critical habitat for several species of waterfowl and aquatic life. The test site for this research consists of a series of impounded estuarine wetlands of the northern Indian River Lagoon (IRL) that reside on the western shore of the Kennedy Space Center. Classification of land cover for this environment is difficult due to the similarity of spectral signatures for certain vegetation types. For classification purposes, 13 classes representing the various land cover types that occur in this environment have been defined for the site (Table 2).

Table 2. Classes for Kennedy Space Center and the quantity of training data per class

Class	Name	Total Obs
1	Scrub	761
2	Willow Swamp	243
3	CP Hammock	256
4	CP/Oak Hammock	252
5	Slash Pine	161
6	Oak/Broadleaf Hammock	229
7	Hardwood Swamp	105
8	Graminoid Marsh	420
9	Spartina Marsh	520
10	Cattail Marsh	397
11	Salt Marsh	419
12	Mud Flats	447
13	Water	927

The NASA AVIRIS (Airborne Visible/Infrared Imaging Spectrometer) spectrometer acquired data over the KSC, Florida on March 23, 1996. AVIRIS acquires data in 224 bands of 10 nm width from 400 - 2500 nm. The KSC data, acquired from an altitude of approximately 20km, have a spatial resolution of 18 m [19]. After removing water absorption and low SNR bands, D=176 bands were used for the analysis. Again, multiple experiments were performed using stratified (class specific) sampling at percentages of: 75, 50, 30, 15, 5, and 1.5. At 75% sampling rate, the quantity of training data for classes 5, 6, and 7 is less than D and, at 50%, so are classes 2, 3, and 4. Ten experiments, using simple random sampling, were performed at each percentage for the bottom-up and top-down frameworks of the traditional BHC [TD-BHC, BU-BHC], the traditional BHC using the pseudo-inverse for tree construction (estimating Fisher's discriminant) and feature extraction (calculating Fisher's linear discriminant function), [TD-P-BHC, BU-P-BHC], and the adaptive best-basis BHC [TD-BB-BHC, BU-BB-BHC]. The results are presented in Figure 3.

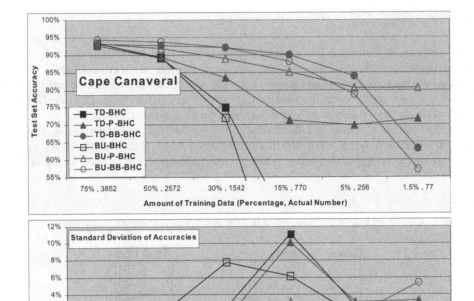

Figure 3. Classification (test set) accuracies for Cape Canaveral

The test set accuracies for Cape Canaveral are very similar to those of Bolivar Peninsula except that the pseudo-inverse classifiers perform better at the 1.5% sampling rate, with the accuracies for the pseudo-inverse BHC classifiers maintaining the accuracy level that had been achieved at the 5% sampling rate. At the lower sampling percentages, the covariance matrices are very poorly estimated in the full dimensional space, yet the accuracies are still fairly high using pseudo-inversion, indicating that the differences in class means is the main reason the level of discrimination is being maintained. This result is also reflected by the standard deviations of the accuracies, which increase dramatically at 15%-30% sampling rate for the pseudo-inverse classifiers where the covariance matrices are still helping maintain a higher level of classification accuracy (than the 1.5%-5% range), though unstable. Also, an explanation for reduced classification accuracies of the BB-BHC at the 1.5% sampling rate is that there might be a minimum requirement, the "intrinsic dimensionality" [11], for the number of bands, after which the results drop off sharply.

5   Conclusions and Future Work

The dependency of classification accuracy upon the ratio of training data size to the dimensionality of the data has been widely noted and needs to be addressed in the design of a classifier. While the advent of hyperspectral sensors has provided unique opportunities in remote sensing, the increased dimensionality of the data necessitates that researchers pay design classifiers that are more tolerant of the quantity of available training data. A multi-classifier framework that utilizes the flexibility gained by transforming the output space and input space simultaneously to combat the small sample size problem is proposed. By reducing the size of the feature space in a directed manner, dependent on the quantity of training data available in the binary hierarchy of meta-classes, a high level of classification accuracy is preserved even when quantities of training data for some classes are low.

Combating the small sample size problem with the dynamic best-basis algorithm helps preserve the interpretability of the data, but using Fisher's linear discriminant function as the feature extractor at each internal node of the BHC diminishes this attractive characteristic. While the discriminant function weights on each band/group-band could be analyzed to determine the respective band's importance, the interpretation and insight would be better if feature selection were performed rather than feature extraction. Therefore, using feature selection rather than feature extraction, and the likely trade-off between classification accuracy and retention of domain knowledge, should be investigated further.

References

1. T.W. Anderson, *An Introduction to Multivariate Statistical Analysis*. New York: John Wiley & Sons, 1984.

2. D. Landgrebe, "Information extraction principles and methods for multispectral and hyperspectral image data," *Information Processing for Remote Sensing*, ed. Chen, C.H., World Scientific Pub. Co, NJ, 1999.

3. S. Tadjudin and D.A. Landgrebe, "Robust parameter estimation for mixture model," *IEEE Trans. Geosci.Rem. Sens.* 38(1): 439-45, 2000.

4. S. Kumar, J. Ghosh and M. M. Crawford, "Hierarchical fusion of multiple classifiers for hyperspectral data analysis," *Pattern Analysis and Applications,* Special Issue on Classifier Fusion (to appear).

5. S. Tadjudin and D.A. Landgrebe, "Covariance estimation with limited training samples," *IEEE Trans.Geosci.Rem. Sens.*, 37(4): 2113-8, 1999.

6. P.A. Devijver and J. Kittler (editors), *Pattern Recognition Theory and Application.* Springer-Verlag, 1987.

7. S. Kumar, J. Ghosh, and M.M. Crawford, "Best basis feature exaction algorithms for classification of hyperspectral data," *IEEE Trans. Geosci.Rem. Sens.*, 39(7): 1368-79, 2001.

8. S.J. Raudys and A.K. Jain, "Small sample size effects in statistical pattern recognition: recommendations for practitioners", *IEEE Trans on PAMI*, 13(3): 252–64, 1991.

9. Qiong Jackson and David Landgrebe, "An adaptive classifier design for high-dimensional data analysis with a limited training data set", *IEEE Trans. Geosci.Rem. Sens*, 39(12): 2664-79, 2001.

10. T.W. Anderson, *An Introduction to Multivariate Statistical Analysis*. New York: John Wiley & Sons, 1984.

11. Andrew Webb, *Statistical pattern recognition*. London: Oxford University Press, 1999.

12. Marina Skurichina, "Stabilizing weak classifiers," Thesis, Vilnius State University, 2001.

13. L. Breiman, "Bagging predictors," *Machine Learning*, 24(2): 123-40, 1996.

14. A. McCallum, R. Rosenfeld, T. Mitchell, and A.Y. Ng, "Improving text classification by shrinkage in a hierarchy of classes," Proc. 15th International Conf. on Machine, Madison, WI, Morgan Kaufmann, San Mateo, CA, 359-67 1998.

15. K. Fukunaga, *Introduction to Statistical Pattern Recognition*, 2nd Ed, Boston, 1990.

16. Sarunas Raudys and Robert P. W. Duin, "Expected classification error of the Fisher linear classifier with pseudo-inverse covariance matrix," *Pattern Recognition Letters*, 19: 385-92, 1998.

17. M. Skurichina and R.P.W. Duin, "Stabilizing classifiers for very small sample sizes", Proc. 13th Int. Conf. on Pattern Recognition (Vienna, Austria, Aug.25-29) Vol. 2, Track B: Pattern Recognition and Signal Analysis, IEEE Computer Society Press, Los Alamitos, 891-6, 1996.

18. A. Blum and T. Mitchell, "Combining labeled and unlabeled data with co-training," *Proc. 11th Annual Conf. Computational Learning Theory*, 92-100, 1998.

19. Webpage. Jet Propulsion Lab, California Institute of Technology, http://makalu.jpl.nasa.gov/.

20. B. Jeon and D. Landgrebe, "Partially supervised classification using weighted unsupervised clustering," *IEEE Trans. Geosci.Rem. Sens.*, 37(2): 1073-9, March 1999.

21. T.M. Mitchell, "The role of unlabeled data in supervised learning," *Proc. Sixth Intl. Colloquium on Cognitive Science*, 8pgs, 1999.

22. V.R. de Sa, "Learning classification with unlabeled data," *Advances in Neural Information Processing Systems 6*, 1994.

23. B.M. Shahshahani and D.A. Landgrebe, "The effect of unlabeled samples in reducing the small sample size problem and mitigating the Hughes phenomenon," *IEEE Trans. Geosci.Rem. Sens.*, 32(5):1087-95, 1994.

24. T. Cocks, R. Jenssen, A. Stewart, I. Wilson, and T. Shields, "The HyMap airborne hyperspectral sensor: the system, calibration and performance", Proc. 1st EARSeL Workshop on Imaging Spectroscopy (M. Schaepman, D. Schläpfer, and K.I. Itten, Eds.), Zurich, EARSeL, Paris, 37-42, 6-8 October, 1998.

25. X. Jia, Classification Techniques for Hyperspectral Remote Sensing Image Data. PhD Thesis, Univ. College, ADFA, University of New South Wales, Australia, 1996.

26. X. Jia and J.A. Richards, "Segmented principal components transformation for efficient hyperspectral remote-sensing image display and classification", *IEEE Trans. Geosci.Rem. Sens.*, 37(1): 538-42, 1999.

27. S. Kumar, J. Ghosh, and M. M. Crawford, "A hierarchical multiclassifier system for hyperspectral data analysis", 1st Intl.Workshop on Multiple Classifier Systems, Sardinia, Italy, 270-9, June 2000.

28. David Landgrebe, "Hyperspectral image data analysis as a high dimensional signal processing problem," (Invited), Special Issue of the *IEEE Signal Processing Magazine*, 19(1), 17-28, 2002.

29. K. Tumer and J. Ghosh, "Error correlation and error reduction in ensemble classifiers" *Connection Science*, Special Issue on Combining, 8(3/4), 385-404, 1996.

Stacking with Multi-response Model Trees

Sašo Džeroski and Bernard Ženko

Department of Intelligent Systems, Jožef Stefan Institute,
Jamova 39, 1000 Ljubljana, Slovenia,
Saso.Dzeroski@ijs.si, Bernard.Zenko@ijs.si

Abstract. We empirically evaluate several state-of-the-art methods for constructing ensembles of classifiers with stacking and show that they perform (at best) comparably to selecting the best classifier from the ensemble by cross validation. We then propose a new method for stacking, that uses multi-response model trees at the meta-level, and show that it outperforms existing stacking approaches, as well as selecting the best classifier from the ensemble by cross validation.

1 Introduction

An ensemble of classifiers is a set of classifiers whose individual predictions are combined in some way (typically by voting) to classify new examples. One of the most active areas of research in supervised learning has been to study methods for constructing good ensembles of classifiers [3]. The attraction that this topic exerts on machine learning researchers is based on the premise that ensembles are often much more accurate than the individual classifiers that make them up.

Most of the research on classifier ensembles is concerned with generating ensembles by using a single learning algorithm [4], such as decision tree learning or neural network training. Different classifiers are generated by manipulating the training set (as done in boosting or bagging), manipulating the input features, manipulating the output targets or injecting randomness in the learning algorithm. The generated classifiers are then typically combined by voting or weighted voting.

Another approach is to generate classifiers by applying different learning algorithms (with heterogeneous model representations) to a single data set (see, e.g., [9]). More complicated methods for combining classifiers are typically used in this setting. Stacking [18] is often used to learn a combining method in addition to the ensemble of classifiers. Voting is then used as a baseline method for combining classifiers against which the learned combiners are compared. Typically, much better performance is achieved by stacking as compared to voting.

The work presented in this paper is set in the stacking framework. We argue that selecting the best of the classifiers in an ensemble generated by applying different learning algorithms should be considered as a baseline to which the stacking performance should be compared. Our empirical evaluation of several recent stacking approaches shows that they perform comparably to the best of the individual classifiers as selected by cross validation, but not better. We then

F. Roli and J. Kittler (Eds.): MCS 2002, LNCS 2364, pp. 201–211, 2002.
© Springer-Verlag Berlin Heidelberg 2002

propose a new stacking method, based on classification by using model trees, and show that this method does perform better than other combining approaches, as well as better than selecting the best individual classifier.

Section 2 first summarizes the stacking framework, then surveys some recent results and finally introduces our stacking approach based on classification via model trees. The setup for the experimental comparison of several stacking methods, voting and selecting the best classifier is described in Section 3. Section 4 presents and discusses the experimental results and Section 5 concludes.

2   Stacking with Model Trees

We first give a brief introduction to the stacking framework, introduced by [18]. We then summarize the results of several recent studies in stacking [9, 13, 14, 12, 15]. Motivated by these, we introduce a stacking approach based on classification via model trees [5].

2.1   The Stacking Framework

Stacking is concerned with combining multiple classifiers generated by using different learning algorithms $L_1, \ldots, L_N$ on a single data set S, which consists of examples $s_i = (x_i, y_i)$, i.e., pairs of feature vectors (x_i) and their classifications (y_i). In the first phase, a set of base-level classifiers $C_1, C_2, \ldots C_N$ is generated, where $C_i = L_i(S)$. In the second phase, a meta-level classifier is learned that combines the outputs of the base-level classifiers.

To generate a training set for learning the meta-level classifier, a leave-one-out or a cross validation procedure is applied. For leave-one-out, we apply each of the base-level learning algorithms to almost the entire data set, leaving one example for testing: $C_k^i = L_k(S - s_i)$. We then use the learned classifiers to generate predictions for s_i: $\hat{y}_i^k = C_k^i(x_i)$. The meta-level data set consists of examples of the form $((\hat{y}_i^1, \ldots, \hat{y}_i^N), y_i)$, where the features are the predictions of the base-level classifiers and the class is the correct class of the example at hand.

In contrast to stacking, no learning takes place at the meta-level when combining classifiers by a voting scheme (such as plurality, probabilistic or weighted voting). The voting scheme remains the same for all different training sets and sets of learning algorithms (or base-level classifiers). The simplest voting scheme is the plurality vote. According to this voting scheme, each base-level classifier casts a vote for its prediction. The example is classified in the class that collects the most votes.

2.2   Recent Advances

The most important issues in stacking are probably the choice of the features and the algorithm for learning at the meta-level. Below we review some recent research on stacking that addresses the above issues.

It is common knowledge that ensembles of diverse base-level classifiers (with weakly correlated predictions) yield good performance. [9] proposes a stacking method called SCANN that uses correspondence analysis do detect correlations between the predictions of base-level classifiers. The original meta-level feature space (the class-value predictions) is transformed to remove the dependencies, and a nearest neighbor method is used as the meta-level classifier on this new feature space.

[13] use base-level classifiers whose predictions are probability distributions over the set of class values, rather than single class values. The meta-level attributes are thus the probabilities of each of the class values returned by each of the base-level classifiers. The authors argue that this allows to use not only the predictions, but also the confidence of the base-level classifiers. Multi-response linear regression (MLR) is recommended for meta-level learning, while several learning algorithms are shown not to be suitable for this task.

[12] propose a method for combining classifiers called grading that learns a meta-level classifier for each base-level classifier. The meta-level classifier predicts whether the base-level classifier is to be trusted (i.e., whether its prediction will be correct). The base-level attributes are used also as meta-level attributes, while the meta-level class values are $+$ (correct) and $-$ (incorrect). Only the base-level classifiers that are predicted to be correct are taken and their predictions combined by summing up the probability distributions predicted.

[14] introduce a new meta-level learning method for combining classifiers with stacking: meta decision trees (MDTs) have base-level classifiers in the leaves, instead of class-value predictions. Properties of the probability distributions predicted by the base-level classifiers (such as entropy and maximum probability) are used as meta-level attributes, rather than the distributions themselves. These properties reflect the confidence of the base-level classifiers and give rise to very small MDTs, which can (at least in principle) be inspected and interpreted.

[15] report that stacking with MDTs clearly outperforms voting and stacking with decision trees, as well as boosting and bagging of decision trees. On the other hand, MDTs perform only slightly better than SCANN and selecting the best classifier with cross validation (SelectBest). [19] report that MDTs perform slightly worse as compared to stacking with MLR. Overall, SCANN, MDTs, stacking with MLR and SelectBest seem to perform at about the same level.

It would seem natural to expect that ensembles of classifiers induced by stacking would perform better than the best individual base-level classifier: otherwise the extra work of learning a meta-level classifier doesn't seem justified. The experimental results mentioned above, however, do not show clear evidence of this. This has motivated us to investigate the performance of state-of-the-art stacking methods in comparison to SelectBest and seek new stacking methods that would be clearly superior to SelectBest.

2.3   Stacking with Multi-response Model Trees

We assume that each base-level classifier predicts a probability distribution over the possible class values. Thus, the prediction of the base-level classifier C when applied to example x is a probability distribution:

$$\mathbf{p}^C(x) = \left(p^C(c_1|x), p^C(c_2|x), \ldots p^C(c_m|x)\right),$$

where $\{c_1, c_2, \ldots c_m\}$ is the set of possible class values and $p^C(c_i|x)$ denotes the probability that example x belongs to class c_i as estimated (and predicted) by classifier C. The class c_j with the highest class probability $p^C(c_j|x)$ is predicted by classifier C. The meta-level attributes are thus the probabilities predicted for each possible class by each of the base-level classifiers, i.e., $p^{C_j}(c_i|x)$ for $i = 1, \ldots, m$ and $j = 1, \ldots, N$.

The experimental evidence mentioned above indicates that although SCANN, MDTs, stacking with MLR and SelectBest seem to perform at about the same level, stacking with MLR has a slight advantage over the other methods. It would thus seem as a suitable starting point in the search for better method for meta-level learning to be used in stacking. Stacking with MLR uses linear regression to perform classification. A natural direction to look into is the use of model trees (which perform piece-wise linear regression) instead of MLR: model trees have namely been shown to perform better than MLR for classification via regression [5].

MLR is an adaptation of linear regression. For a classification problem with m class values $\{c_1, c_2, \ldots c_m\}$, m regression problems are formulated: for problem j, a linear equation LR_j is constructed to predict a binary variable which has value one if the class value is c_j and zero otherwise. Given a new example x to classify, $LR_j(x)$ is calculated for all j, and the class k is predicted with maximum $LR_k(x)$.

In our approach, we use model tree induction instead of linear regression and keep everything else the same. Instead of m linear equations LR_j, we induce m model trees MT_j. M5' [16], a re-implementation of M5 [10] included in the data mining suite Weka [17] is used to induce the trees. Given a new example x to classify, $MT_j(x)$ is calculated for all j, and the class k is predicted with maximum $MT_k(x)$. We call our approach stacking with multi-response model trees and denoted with SMM5 in the tables with experimental results.

3   Experimental Setup

In the experiments, we investigate the following issues:

- The (relative) performance of existing state-of-the-art stacking methods, especially in comparison to SelectBest.
- The performance of stacking with multi-response model trees relative to the above methods.
- The influence of the number of base-level classifiers on the (relative) performance of the above methods.

We look into the last topic because the recent studies mentioned above use different numbers of base-level classifiers, ranging from three to eight.

The Weka data mining suite [17] was used for all experiments, within which all the base-level and meta-level learning algorithms used in the experiments have been implemented.

3.1 Data Sets

In order to evaluate the performance of the different combining algorithms, we perform experiments on a collection of twenty-one data sets from the *UCI Repository of machine learning databases* [2]. These data sets have been widely used in other comparative studies.

3.2 Base-Level Algorithms

We perform two batches of experiments: one with three and one with seven base-level learners. The set of three contains the following algorithms:
- J4.8: a Java re-implementation of the decision tree learning algorithm C4.5 [11],
- IBk: the k-nearest neighbor algorithm of [1], and
- NB: the naive Bayes algorithm of [7].

The second set of algorithms contains, in addition to the above three, also the following four algorithms:
- K*: an instance-based algorithm which uses an entropic distance measure [6],
- KDE: a simple kernel density estimation algorithm,
- DT: the decision table majority algorithm of [8],
- MLR: the multi-response linear regression algorithm, as used by [13] and described in Section 2.3.

All algorithms are used with their default parameter settings, with the exceptions described below. IBk in the set of three learners uses inverse distance weighting and k was selected with cross validation from the range of 1 to 77. (IBk in the set of seven learners uses the default parameter values, i.e., no weighting and $k = 1$.) The NB algorithm in both sets uses the kernel density estimator rather than assume normal distributions for numeric attributes.

3.3 Meta-level Algorithms

At the meta-level, we evaluate the performance of six different schemes for combining classifiers (listed below), each applied with the two different sets of base-level algorithms described above.
- VOTE: The simple plurality vote scheme (see Section 2.1),
- SELB: The SelectBest scheme selects the best of the base-level classifiers by cross validation.
- GRAD: Grading as introduced by [12] and briefly described in Section 2.2.
- SMDT: Stacking with meta decision-trees as introduced by [14] and briefly described in Section 2.2.

- SMLR: Stacking with multiple-response regression as used by [13] and described in Sections 2.2 and 2.3.
- SMM5: Stacking with multiple-response model trees, as proposed by this paper and described in Section 2.3.

3.4 Evaluating and Comparing Algorithms

In all the experiments presented here, classification errors are estimated using ten-fold stratified cross validation. Cross validation is repeated ten times using different random generator seeds resulting in ten different sets of folds. The same folds (random generator seeds) are used in all experiments. The classification error of a classification algorithm C for a given data set as estimated by averaging over the ten runs of ten-fold cross validation is denoted error(C).

For pair-wise comparisons of classification algorithms, we calculate the relative improvement and the paired t-test, as described below. In order to evaluate the accuracy improvement achieved in a given domain by using classifier C_1 as compared to using classifier C_2, we calculate the relative improvement: $1 - \text{error}(C_1)/\text{error}(C_2)$. The average relative improvement across all domains is calculated using the geometric mean of error reduction in individual domains: $1 - \text{geometric\_mean}(\text{error}(C_1)/\text{error}(C_2))$. Note that this may be different from geometric_mean$(\text{error}(C_2)/\text{error}(C_1)) - 1$.

The classification errors of C_1 and C_2 averaged over the ten runs of 10-fold cross validation are compared for each data set (error(C_1) and error(C_2) refer to these averages). The statistical significance of the difference in performance is tested using the paired t-test (exactly the same folds are used for C_1 and C_2) with significance level of 95%: $+/-$ to the right of a figure in the tables with results means that the classifier C_1 is significantly better/worse than C_2.

4   Experimental Results

The error rates of the 3-classifier and 7-classifier ensembles induced as described above on the twenty-one data set and combined with the different combining methods are given in Table 3. However, for the purpose of comparing the performance of different combining methods, Tables 1 and 2 are of much more interest: they give the average relative improvement of X over Y for each pair of combining methods X and Y, as well as the number of significant wins/losses. Below we highlight some of our more interesting findings.

4.1 State-of-the-Art Stacking Methods

Inspecting Tables 1 and 2, we find that we can partition the five combining algorithms (we do not consider SMM5 at this stage of the analysis) into three groups. VOTE and GRAD are at the lower end of the performance scale, SELB and SMDT are in the middle, while SMLR performs best. While SMLR clearly outperforms VOTE and GRAD, the advantage over SELB is slim (3 and 2 more wins than losses, about 4% relative improvement) and the advantage over SMDT even slimmer (1 more win than loss in both cases, 4 and 5% of relative improvement).

Table 1. The relative performance of 3-classifier ensembles with different combining methods. The entry in row X and column Y gives the relative improvement of X over Y in % and the number of wins/loses.

	VOTE	SELB	GRAD	SMDT	SMLR	SMM5	TOTAL
VOTE		-21.53 7+/10-	-4.12 6+/5-	-22.45 6+/11-	-27.43 5+/11-	-47.06 2+/10-	26+/47-
SELB	17.72 10+/7-		14.33 11+/3-	-0.76 0+/2-	-4.85 2+/5-	-21.00 1+/9-	24+/26-
GRAD	3.96 5+/6-	-16.72 3+/11-		-17.60 1+/12-	-22.39 2+/14-	-41.24 1+/13-	12+/56-
SMDT	18.34 11+/6-	0.75 2+/0-	14.97 12+/1-		-4.07 4+/5-	-20.10 2+/8-	31+/20-
SMLR	21.53 11+/5-	4.63 5+/2-	18.29 14+/2-	3.91 5+/4-		-15.40 1+/7-	36+/20-
SMM5	32.00 10+/2-	17.36 9+/1-	29.20 13+/1-	16.73 8+/2-	13.35 7+/1-		47+/7-

Table 2. The relative performance of 7-classifier ensembles with different combining methods. The entry in row X and column Y gives the relative improvement of X over Y in % and the number of wins/loses.

	VOTE	SELB	GRAD	SMDT	SMLR	SMM5	TOTAL
VOTE		-19.21 5+/12-	-6.73 2+/7-	-18.04 4+/9-	-24.40 2+/10-	-42.04 0+/10-	13+/48-
SELB	16.10 12+/5-		10.46 11+/4-	0.97 3+/3-	-4.37 5+/7-	-19.17 2+/7-	33+/26-
GRAD	6.30 7+/2-	-11.68 4+/11-		-10.60 5+/7-	-16.56 2+/12-	-33.09 0+/12-	18+/44-
SMDT	15.29 9+/4-	-0.97 3+/3-	9.59 7+/5-		-5.39 5+/6-	-20.33 0+/11-	24+/29-
SMLR	19.62 10+/2-	4.19 7+/5-	14.21 12+/2-	5.11 6+/5-		-14.18 1+/5-	36+/19-
SMM5	29.60 10+/0-	16.08 7+/2-	24.86 12+/0-	16.89 11+/0-	12.42 5+/1-		45+/3-

4.2   Stacking with Multi-response Model Trees

Returning to Tables 1 and 2, this time paying attention to the relative performance of SMM5 to the other combining methods, we find that SMM5 is in a
league of its own. It clearly outperforms all the other combining methods, with
a wins − loss difference of at least 4 and a relative improvement of at least 10%.
The difference is smallest when compared to SMLR.

4.3   The Influence of the Number of Base-Level Classifiers

Studying the differences between Tables 1 and 2, we can note that the relative
performance of the different combining methods is not affected too much by
the change of the number of base-level classifiers. GRAD and SMDT seem to be
affected most. The relative performance of GRAD improves, while that of SMDT
worsens, when we go from 3 to 7 base-level classifiers: GRAD becomes better
than VOTE, while SMDT becomes ever-so-slightly worse than SELB. SMM5 and
SMLR are clearly the best in both cases.

5   Conclusions and Further Work

We have empirically evaluated several state-of-the-art methods for constructing
ensembles of classifiers with stacking and shown that they perform (at best)
comparably to selecting the best classifier from the ensemble by cross validation. We have proposed a new method for stacking, that uses multi-response
model trees at the meta-level. We have shown that it clearly outperforms existing stacking approaches and selecting the best classifier from the ensemble by
cross validation.

   While this study clearly shows good performance of our method on standard
UCI domains, it would be instructive to perform the same experiments on real
applicative domains. Another issue to investigate is the influence of the parameters of the meta-level learner (M5') on overall performance. While conducting
this study and a few other recent studies [19, 15], we have encountered quite a
few contradictions between claims in the recent literature on stacking and our
experimental results e.g., [9, 13, 12]. A comparative study including the data
sets used in these papers and a few other stacking methods (such as SCANN)
should resolve these contradictions and provide a clearer picture of who's who
in stacking. We believe this is a worthwhile topic to pursue in near-term future
work. We also believe that further research on stacking in the context of base-
level classifiers created by different learning algorithms is in order, despite the
current focus of the machine learning community on creating ensembles with
a single learning algorithm with injected randomness or its application to ma-
nipulated training sets, input features and output targets. This should include
the pursuit for better sets of meta-level features and better meta-level learning
algorithms.

Table 3. Error rates (in %) of the learned ensembles of classifiers.

DATA SET	3 BASE LEVEL CLASSIFIERS						7 BASE LEVEL CLASSIFIERS					
	VOTE	SELB	GRAD	SMDT	SMLR	SMM5	VOTE	SELB	GRAD	SMDT	SMLR	SMM5
AUSTRALIAN	13.81	13.78	14.04	13.77	14.16	14.29	13.99	14.84	14.46	15.06	13.97	14.26
BALANCE	8.91	8.51	8.78	8.51	9.47	4.37	10.14	8.48	10.02	8.45	10.51	4.99
BREAST-W	3.46	2.69	3.69	2.69	2.73	2.82	3.65	2.69	3.65	2.69	2.72	2.70
BRIDGES-TD	15.78	15.78	15.10	16.08	14.12	14.61	15.39	16.47	15.39	17.45	15.59	15.69
CAR	6.49	5.83	6.10	5.02	5.61	1.52	6.73	5.69	5.32	3.72	4.24	1.38
CHESS	1.46	0.60	1.16	0.60	0.60	0.60	1.59	0.60	1.20	0.60	0.60	0.62
DIABETES	24.01	25.09	24.26	24.74	23.78	24.10	24.10	23.11	24.38	24.27	23.70	24.05
ECHO	29.24	27.63	30.38	27.71	28.63	27.63	30.92	28.63	30.92	30.61	29.54	30.23
GERMAN	25.19	25.69	25.41	25.60	24.36	24.97	24.08	24.67	24.39	24.29	23.20	23.25
GLASS	29.67	32.06	30.75	31.78	30.93	31.26	25.79	25.19	26.54	25.56	24.63	25.05
HEART	17.11	16.04	17.70	16.04	15.30	15.67	17.26	16.15	17.48	16.63	16.04	15.85
HEPATITIS	17.42	15.87	18.39	15.87	15.68	14.97	16.39	16.06	17.23	16.71	16.84	16.13
HYPO	1.32	0.72	0.80	0.79	0.72	0.76	1.56	0.76	1.05	1.35	0.77	0.78
IMAGE	2.94	2.85	3.32	2.53	2.84	2.84	1.92	3.03	1.98	2.47	2.02	2.05
IONOSPHERE	7.18	8.40	8.06	8.83	7.35	6.55	8.52	8.43	8.60	8.80	7.12	7.89
IRIS	4.20	4.73	4.40	4.73	4.47	4.47	5.00	4.40	4.87	4.40	4.93	5.20
SOYA	6.75	7.22	7.38	7.06	7.22	6.65	6.71	6.22	6.33	6.34	7.36	6.37
TIC-TAC-TOE	9.24	0.96	6.08	0.96	0.58	0.26	3.58	0.96	2.46	0.96	0.64	0.27
VOTE	7.10	3.54	5.22	3.54	3.54	3.36	6.25	3.93	5.20	3.93	3.75	3.79
WAVEFORM	15.90	14.42	17.04	14.40	14.33	13.69	16.64	14.04	16.78	13.85	15.65	13.48
WINE	1.74	3.26	1.80	3.26	2.87	3.03	1.46	2.30	1.46	2.19	2.08	2.02
AVERAGE	11.85	11.22	11.90	11.17	10.92	10.40	11.51	10.79	11.41	10.97	10.76	10.29

Acknowledgements

This work was supported in part by the METAL project (ESPRIT Framework IV LTR Grant Nr. 26.357). Many thanks to Ljupčo Todorovski for the cooperation on combining classifiers with meta-decision trees and the many interesting and stimulating discussions related to this paper. Thanks also to Alexander Seewald for providing his implementation of grading in Weka.

References

[1] D. Aha, D.W. Kibler, and M. K. Albert. Instance-based learning algorithms. *Machine Learning*, 6:37–66, 1991.

[2] C.L. Blake and C.J. Merz. UCI repository of machine learning databases, 1998.

[3] T. G. Dietterich. Machine-learning research: Four current directions. *AI Magazine*, 18(4):97–136, 1997.

[4] T. G. Dietterich. Ensemble methods in machine learning. In *Proceedings of the First International Workshop on Multiple Classifier Systems*, pages 1–15, Berlin, 2000. Springer.

[5] E. Frank, Y. Wang, S. Inglis, G. Holmes, and I. H. Witten. Using model trees for classification. *Machine Learning*, 32(1):63–76, 1998.

[6] G. C. John and E. T. Leonard. K*: An instance-based learner using an entropic distance measure. In *Proceedings of the 12th International Conference on Machine Learning*, pages 108–114, San Francisco, 1995. Morgan Kaufmann.

[7] G. H. John and P. Langley. Estimating continuous distributions in bayesian classifiers. In *Proceedings of the Eleventh Conference on Uncertainty in Artificial Intelligence*, pages 338–345, San Francisco, 1995. Morgan Kaufmann.

[8] R. Kohavi. The power of decision tables. In *Proceedings of the Eighth European Conference on Machine Learning*, pages 174–189, 1995.

[9] C. J. Merz. Using correspondence analysis to combine classifiers. *Machine Learning*, 36(1/2):33–58, 1999.

[10] J. R. Quinlan. Learning with continuous classes. In *Proceedings of the Fifth Australian Joint Conference on Artificial Intelligence*, pages 343–348, Singapore, 1992. World Scientific.

[11] J. R. Quinlan. *C4.5: Programs for Machine Learning*. Morgan Kaufmann, San Francisco, 1993.

[12] A. K. Seewald and J. Fürnkranz. An evaluation of grading classifiers. In *Advances in Intelligent Data Analysis: Proceedings of the Fourth International Symposium (IDA-01)*, pages 221–232, Berlin, 2001. Springer.

[13] K. M. Ting and I. H. Witten. Issues in stacked generalization. *Journal of Artificial Intelligence Research*, 10:271–289, 1999.

[14] L. Todorovski and S. Džeroski. Combining multiple models with meta decision trees. In *Proceedings of the Fourth European Conference on Principles of Data Mining and Knowledge Discovery*, pages 54–64, Berlin, 2000. Springer.

[15] L. Todorovski and S. Džeroski. Combining classifiers with meta decision trees. *Machine Learning*, In press, 2002.

[16] Y. Wang and I. H. Witten. Induction of model trees for predicting continuous classes. In *Proceedings of the Poster Papers of the European Conference on Machine Learning*, Prague, 1997. University of Economics, Faculty of Informatics and Statistics.

[17] I. H. Witten and E. Frank. *Data Mining: Practical Machine Learning Tools and Techniques with Java Implementations.* Morgan Kaufmann, San Francisco, 1999.

[18] D. Wolpert. Stacked generalization. *Neural Networks*, 5(2):241–260, 1992.

[19] B. Ženko, L. Todorovski, and S. Džeroski. A comparison of stacking with mdts to bagging, boosting, and other stacking methods. In *Proceedings of the First IEEE International Conference on Data Mining*, pages 669–670, Los Alamitos, 2001. IEEE Computer Society.

On Combining One-Class Classifiers for Image Database Retrieval

Carmen Lai[1], David M.J. Tax[2], Robert P.W. Duin[3], Elżbieta Pękalska[3], and Pavel Paclík[3]

[1] DIEE, University of Cagliari, Sardinia, Italy
`carmen@ph.tn.tudelft.nl`
[2] Fraunhofer Institute FIRST.IDA, Berlin, Germany
`davidt@first.fhg.de`
[3] Pattern Recognition Group, TU Delft, The Netherlands
`{duin,ela,pavel}@ph.tn.tudelft.nl`

Abstract. In image retrieval systems, images can be represented by single feature vectors or by clouds of points. A cloud of points offers a more flexible description but suffers from class overlap. We propose a novel approach for describing clouds of points based on support vector data description (SVDD). We show that combining SVDD-based classifiers improves the retrieval precision. We investigate the performance of the proposed retrieval technique on a database of 368 texture images and compare it to other methods.

1 Introduction

In the problem of image database retrieval, we look for a particular image in a huge collection of images. If an example, or a query image is available, we would like to find images, similar to the query, according to our (human) perception. Making an automated system for such a search, would, therefore, require advanced matching methods in order to approximate this. In this paper, we discuss two approaches how images may be represented in an image retrieval system. We propose to represent images by support vector data description (SVDD) for clouds of feature vectors. We show that combining SVDD representations helps to find a good description of the data.

A number of approaches has been investigated how to represent images for image database retrieval [3, 5, 1]. Usually, an image is encoded by a single feature vector containing color-, texture-, or shape-based information about the whole image. This feature vector is computed for all images in the database. To retrieve images resembling the query image, a suitable distance measure between the image feature vectors is needed. The images with smaller distances are then considered to be more similar to the query. This method provides a global description, which does not take into account possible image substructures.

The other, more robust, way to represent images is to encode an image as a set of feature vectors (or a cloud of points). Usually, simple features like average intensities in small image patches are used. Each image patch is again encoded

F. Roli and J. Kittler (Eds.): MCS 2002, LNCS 2364, pp. 212–221, 2002.

by a feature vector, storing information about color and texture. The complete image is then represented by a set of such vectors. We propose to describe this cloud of points by the SVDD method. In order to find the resembling images in the database, a boundary around the cloud is fitted. Images, whose pixel clouds lie within this boundary, are then the most resembling ones. Although in this cloud representation the storage and computation costs are much higher, it is simpler to detect substructures in the original images. Two clearly distinct objects in the image (for instance, a sculpture and a background) will appear as two separate clouds in the feature space. In the 'single-vector' representation it is much harder to detect substructures in the original image.

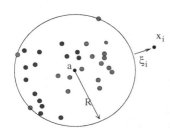

Fig. 1. Graphical representation of the (hyper)sphere around some training data. One object $\mathbf{x}_i$ is rejected by the description (i.e. an error).

Another complication of the cloud representation is a possible overlap between clouds built from different images. It might even happen, that one of the clouds is completely covered by another cloud. Although all the pixels lie within the description of the query image, their distribution is completely different. For similar images, the fraction of pixels lying outside and within the boundary, will be (roughly) the same.

The SVDD method, employed to represent the cloud of points, is explained in section 2. In section 3, we present the image retrieval problem and two approaches to image representation. The first one uses single feature vectors, while the second method is based on a cloud of points. Later, the combination of individual SVDD one-class classifiers is described. In section 4, the experiments on texture images are presented. Conclusion are summarized in section 5.

2   Support Vector Data Description

First, we give a short derivation of the SVDD (for a more extended explanation, see [8]). To describe the domain of a dataset, we enclose the data with a hypersphere with minimum volume. By minimizing the volume of the captured feature space, we hope to minimize the chance of accepting outlier objects. Assume we have a dataset containing M data objects, $\{\mathbf{x}_i, i = 1, .., M\}$ and that the hypersphere is described by the center $\mathbf{a}$ and the radius R. A graphical representation is shown in Figure 1.

To allow the possibility of outliers in the training set, the distance from $\mathbf{x}_i$ to the center $\mathbf{a}$ must not be strictly smaller than R^2, but larger distances should be penalized. Therefore, we introduce slack variables ξ_i which measure the distance to the boundary, if an object is outside the description. An extra parameter C has to be introduced for the trade-off between the volume of the hypersphere and the errors. Now, we minimize an error L containing the volume of the hypersphere and the distance from the boundary of the outlier objects.

We constrain the solution with the requirement that (almost) all data is within the hypersphere:

$$L(R, \mathbf{a}, \boldsymbol{\gamma}) = R^2 + C \sum_i \xi_i \tag{1}$$

$$\|\mathbf{x}_i - \mathbf{a}\|^2 \leq R^2 + \xi_i, \qquad \forall i \tag{2}$$

The constraints (2) can be incorporated in the error (1) by applying Lagrange multipliers [2] and optimizing the Lagrangian. This allows to determine the center in terms of the Lagrange multipliers $\boldsymbol{\alpha}$ and the data $\mathbf{x}_i$ as $\mathbf{a} = \sum_i \alpha_i \mathbf{x}_i$ with $0 \leq \alpha_i \leq C$, $\forall i$ and $\sum_i \alpha_i = 1$ (see [8]).

In practice, it appears that a large fraction of the α_i becomes zero. For a small fraction, $\alpha_i > 0$, and the corresponding objects are called *support objects*. These objects appear to lie on the boundary (in figure 1 these are the three light gray objects on the boundary). Therefore, the center of the hypersphere depends just on a few support objects. The objects with $\alpha_i = 0$ can be disregarded in the description of the data. An object $\mathbf{z}$ is then accepted by the description when:

$$\|\mathbf{z} - \mathbf{a}\|^2 = (\mathbf{z} \cdot \mathbf{z}) - 2 \sum_i \alpha_i (\mathbf{z} \cdot \mathbf{x}_i) + \sum_{i,j} \alpha_i \alpha_j (\mathbf{x}_i \cdot \mathbf{x}_j) \leq R^2, \tag{3}$$

where the radius R can be determined by calculating the distance from the center $\mathbf{a}$ to a support vector $\mathbf{x}_i$ on the boundary.

Here, the model of a hypersphere is assumed and this will not be satisfied in the general case. Analogous to the method of Vapnik [10], we can replace the inner products $(\mathbf{x} \cdot \mathbf{y})$ by kernel functions $K(\mathbf{x}, \mathbf{y})$ which gives a much more flexible method. Especially the Gaussian kernel appears to provide a good data transformation [8]:

$$(\mathbf{x} \cdot \mathbf{y}) \rightarrow K(\mathbf{x}, \mathbf{y}) = \exp(-\|\mathbf{x} - \mathbf{y}\|^2 / s^2). \tag{4}$$

This Gaussian kernel contains an extra free parameter, the width parameter s in the kernel (from definition (4)). For small values of s the SVDD resembles a Parzen density estimation, while for large s the original hypersphere solution is obtained [9]. As shown in [9], this parameter can be set by setting a priori the maximal allowed rejection rate of the target set, i.e. the error on the target set.

Secondly, we also have the trade-off parameter C. We can define a new variable $\nu = \frac{1}{MC}$, which describes an upper bound for the fraction of objects outside the description [7]. When the user specifies beforehand a fraction of the target objects which can be rejected by the description, just one of the parameters s or ν can be determined. In this paper, we choose, therefore, to set ν to a fixed, small value of 1%. The value of s is optimized such that the user-specified fraction of the data is rejected.

3   Image Database Retrieval

Let us denote by I_D an image database with N images I_i, $i = 1, ..., N$. The image retrieval problem is formulated as a selection of a subset of images, similar to a given query image Q. In our application, images in the database can be assigned to classes, which describe images from the same origin, e.g. grain textures, sky images, images with flowers etc. Therefore, whenever we speak about a class, we mean a group of similar images. In this way, an image retrieval strategy can be tested in a more objective way. Such a retrieval strategy is defined in two steps: image representation and a similarity measure between the query image and images stored in the database.

3.1   Image Representation

For the sake of image discrimination, images should be represented in a feature space such that the class differences are emphasized. A convenient way to extract good features is to apply a bank of filters to each image in a database. These filters may be, for example, wavelets, Gabor filters or other texture detectors. In many cases, the filters will give response values which are incomparable to each other. To avoid that one filter with large variance will dominate, the data is preprocessed by weighting individual features on the basis of a dataset mean and standard deviation. We use a scaling that emphasizes differences between individual images in the database.

Assume we have constructed a dataset F containing N K-dimensional feature vectors, representing all images in the database. The weight vector $\mathbf{w}$ is computed element-wise in the following way (see also [6]):

$$w_k = \frac{1}{\text{mean}(F_k)}\, \text{std}\left(\frac{F_k}{\text{mean}(F_k)}\right), \tag{5}$$

where F_k is the k-th feature in the dataset F. All features of all images are rescaled according to this weight vector.

3.2   Single Pixel or Cloud Representation

If we choose to represent one image by one feature vector, the filter responses have to be converted, in one way or another, into a single feature vector. This can be, for example, the average of the filter response over the whole image. All images are then represented by single points in a feature space. The similarity between a query image Q and the image I_i from a database may be defined in various ways. For example, Rui $et\ al.$ [6] proposed to use a cosine similarity:

$$Sim(Q, I_i) = \frac{\boldsymbol{x}_Q^T \boldsymbol{x}_{I_i}}{||\boldsymbol{x}_Q||\,||\boldsymbol{x}_{I_i}||}, \tag{6}$$

where $\boldsymbol{x}_Q$ and $\boldsymbol{x}_{I_i}$ are vector representations of the query and the image I_i respectively and $||\cdot||$ is the L_2-norm. The larger Sim value for two vectors in the feature space, the more similar the corresponding images.

Depending on the conversion from an image to a feature vector, it is very hard to retain the individual characteristics of substructures present in the image.

For instance, when the original image contains sky and sand in two different parts, the image feature vector will represent the average of the sand and sky characteristics. Only for homogeneous images, the single feature will capture the structure well.

A more flexible image representation can be defined by using a cloud of points, instead. A cloud C_i, representing the image I_i, consists of M_i feature vectors, storing the information on patches in the image. The more compact the cloud, the simpler its separation from the other clouds (images). We propose to fit the SVDD around the cloud of points. As explained in section 2, the user has to define the percentage of target objects (points) that will lie on the boundary. Given this fraction, a one-class classifier is constructed for the query cloud. Let B^i_{SVDD} be a one-class classifier constructed for the image I_i. For a vector x, coming from the cloud of points C_i, representing the image I_i, i.e. $x \in C_i$, it is defined as:

$$B^i_{\text{SVDD}}(x) = \begin{cases} 1 & \text{if } x \text{ is accepted by the SVDD} \\ 0 & \text{if } x \text{ is rejected by the SVDD} \end{cases} \tag{7}$$

This classifier is trained such that the fraction of $p = 0.2$ target vectors lie on the boundary, i.e.:

$$\text{Prob}\left(B^i_{\text{SVDD}}(x) = 0 \ \& \ x \text{ is on the boundary} \mid x \in C_i\right) = 0.2, \tag{8}$$

which means that the boundary vectors are here considered as outliers.

An image I_j is classified by the B^i_{SVDD}, taking into account the fraction of vectors from the cloud representation C_j, which are rejected by the description, i.e. the fraction S_i of the retained outliers:

$$S_i(I_j) = \frac{1}{M_j} \sum_{x \in C_j} (1 - B^i_{\text{SVDD}}(x)), \tag{9}$$

where M_j is the number of points in the cloud C_j. So, the clouds representing other images in the database can now be classified by this one-class classifier, counting the number of outliers for each of them. The smaller the percentage of outliers, the more similar the two images.

3.3   Image Similarity by Combining One-Class Classifiers

If only one classifier is used, the performance may suffer from a large overlap between individual clouds of points. For instance, if one cloud completely contains another one, originating from a different class, the percentage of outliers can still be zero. Such an image is then considered to be more similar to the query image than to other images from the same class. This, of course, lowers the performance of the whole image retrieval system.

To prevent such inconvenient situations, we propose to use a set of one-class classifiers, found for the images in the database , i.e. *a combined classifier profile*. The query image Q of a classifier profile is defined as follows:

$$\mathbf{S}(Q) = [S_1(Q), S_2(Q), \dots, S_N(Q)], \tag{10}$$

which is the vector of N individual SVDD's responses S_i, defined by (9) for the image Q (see Figure 2). Of course, this requires a set of SVDD's to be trained in advance.

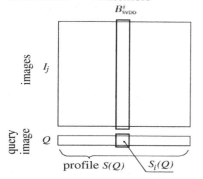

Fig. 2. Classifier combination scheme for image database retrieval.

Our proposal is to compare the query profile with the profiles of the images in the database. For this purpose, different dissimilarity measures can be used, for instance the Euclidean distance:

$$D_E(Q, I_i) = \|\mathbf{S}(Q) - \mathbf{S}(I_i)\|, \; i = 1, \dots, N$$

The other possibility is a cosine distance, based on the inner product between classifier profiles :

$$D_{cos} = \frac{1}{2}\left(1 - Sim(\mathbf{S}(Q), \mathbf{S}(I_i))\right),$$

where Sim is defined by (6). In this way, the responses of the individual one-class classifiers are combined to express the dissimilarity between the query image and the images in the database. The images, most similar to the query image, are then retrieved by ranking the dissimilarities $D_E(Q, I_i)$. This approach is similar to the decision based on multiple classifiers, proposed by Kuncheva *et al.* [4], where the decision templates are created by averaging over all training objects in a class. In our experiments, individual classifiers are constructed for all single images in the database. As a result, the number of classifiers to be combined is as large as the number of images in the database. This is not essential, because a smaller set of classifiers may be used as well. In this way, the computational complexity can be reduced significantly. For the moment, this was not our primary concern.

4 Experiments

In this section, we describe a set of experiments performed on a dataset of texture images. Our dataset is based on 23 images obtained from MIT Media Lab[1]. Each original image is cut into 16 128×128 non-overlapping pieces. These represent a single class. Therefore, we use a database with 23 classes and 368 images. Note that these images are mostly homogeneous and should represent one type of a texture. In this case, it is to be expected that the single feature vector representation performs well.

The images are, one by one, considered as queries. The retrieval precision is computed using all 368 images. The presence of the query image in the training set leads to a slightly optimistic performance estimate. We decided for this

---

[1] `ftp://whitechapel.media.mit.edu/pub/VisTex/`

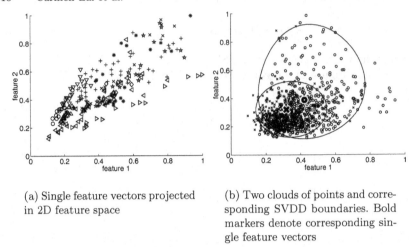

(a) Single feature vectors projected in 2D feature space

(b) Two clouds of points and corresponding SVDD boundaries. Bold markers denote corresponding single feature vectors

Fig. 3. Two different image representations.

approach because it allowed us to work with the complete distance matrices. For each query image, 16 most similar images are found. The retrieval precision for each query is then defined as the percentage of returned images, originating from the same class as the query. The total precision of the retrieval method is then the average precision of all 368 individual queries, i.e.:

$$P = \frac{1}{368} \sum_{I \in I_D} \frac{\# \text{images of the same class as I in the first 16 retrieved}}{16} \cdot 100\%$$

(11)

The absolute values of responses of 10 different Gabor filters are used as features. These 10 features were chosen by a backward feature selection from the larger set of 48 Gabor filters with different smoothing, frequency and direction parameters. We have used the retrieval precision computed on the vector representation as the feature selection criterion. We used the same set of 10 Gabor filters for all experiments presented in this paper.

4.1   Experiment 1: Image Representation by a Single Feature Vector

In this experiment we investigate, as a reference, the performance of the image retrieval system representing images by single feature vectors. Each vector is computed as the average vector of the corresponding Gabor filter responses. The data is weighted as described in section 3.1. For an illustration, the scatterplot of the first two features is shown in Figure 3(a). Each point corresponds to a single image; classes are denoted by different markers. As it can be observed, images of the same class are often grouped together. Two dissimilarity measures: cosine distance (6) and Euclidean distance are used for the image retrieval, for which the total precision is presented in the first two rows of Table 1.

4.2   Experiment 2: Image Representation by a Cloud of Points

In the second set of experiments, we investigate the retrieval system, where the images are represented by clouds of points. An image is described by the average intensities in 9×9 pixel neighborhoods. Each cloud consists of 500 patches randomly selected from the image. The choice of 500 is a compromise between a higher standard deviation (noise sensitive) for small number of patches, and a computational complexity. An example of clouds of points in a 2D space is given in figure 3(b). Different markers are used to denote images originating from different classes.

First, we have computed Mahalonobis distances between clouds of points. The poor performance (19.06%, see Table 1) is probably caused by a large cloud overlap, not normally distributed data and differences in covariance matrices.

We built an SVDD for the cloud of points, setting 20% of points to the boundary; see (8). Exemplar resulting boundaries in the 2D case are shown in figure 3(b), for which a clear difference in distribution characteristics of the two clouds can be observed.

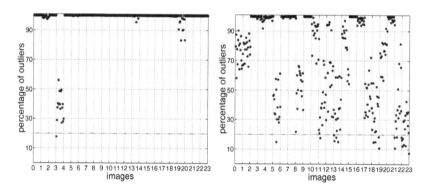

Fig. 4. Percentage of outliers of a query classifier applied to all images. An image from the class 4 is used in the left and image from the class 9 in the right graph.

We use a single SVDD, trained on the query cloud and we apply it to other images, represented by clouds. It follows from the Table 1 that the total precision is 67.85% which is worse than using the single feature vector representation (73.44%), but it still outperforms method using Mahalonobis distance (19.06%). This can be explained by a heavy overlap between clouds of points, as illustrated in Figure 4. This figure shows the percentage of outliers for a classifier trained by a particular query image and applied to all 368 images. The left graph presents the case when a class, containing the query image, is separated from all the other classes. In the right graph, the classifier, trained on the query image (from the class 9), entirely overlaps with several other classes. We judge that, in such cases, combining the responses of a number of one-class classifiers may improve the overall retrieval precision.

The classifier responses form a combined classifier profile, as described in section 3.3 for both distance measures. The images, most similar to the query, may be obtained by a direct ranking of the classifier profile. This approach is comparable to a maximum classifier combination rule. It can be seen in the Table 1 that the profile ranking reaches a low performance (56.76%) because its outcome is again based on single pairs of clouds.

This motivated us to combine these SVDD's further, as described in section 3.3. This leads to a decision based on the (dis)similarities between combined classifier profiles for the query and other images. Two different distance measures are considered here: the Euclidean distance and the cosine distance. Those distance measures are consistent with our first approach, where each image was represented by a 10-dimensional vector of the averaged Gabor responses.

In this paper, classification profiles were built using all SVDD's in a dataset. It allowed us to work with square distance matrices. It should be stressed, that just a subset of database images ('prototype' images) may be described by SVDD's and used to build a profile. Similarity between other images may be still measured as it is based on profile patterns.

Image representation	Method	Precision [%]
Single feature vector	Euclidean distance	67.44
	cosine distance	73.44
Cloud of points	Mahalonobis	19.06
SVDD	target classifier	67.85
SVDD combined	Euclidean distance	79.11
	cosine distance	79.40
	ranking	56.76

Table 1. Experimental results: Precisions of different retrieval methods.

5   Summary and Conclusions

The performance of image retrieval systems depends on the selection of an appropriate representation of image data. Usually, an image is represented by a single feature vector. It is an efficient, but sometimes oversimplifying way of information encoding. This type of representation averages out details in the images. Other, more complex image representations may be used instead, e.g. a cloud of points. This is more robust to noise and, at the same time, sensitive to substructures in the data.

To apply this type of a representation, a convenient way of measuring similarity between images must be defined. It should take into account possible data multimodality. We have found out that simple methods, such as the Mahalonobis distance between clouds of points, suffer since the corresponding assumptions are not fulfilled.

We propose to describe a cloud of points by the support vector data description (SVDD) method. On the contrary to other methods based on the probabilistic approach, SVDD describes the data domain. By this approach, images can be easily matched, based on the fraction of the points rejected by the description (the smaller, the better). It appears that this type of image representation is a flexible tool for image retrieval.

The retrieval performance of a single cloud is, however, worse than for a single vector representation due to a large cloud overlap. To overcome this problem, we propose to combine the one-class classifiers of the database images into a profile of classifiers' responses. Direct ranking in the query profile gives a poor performance, because the outcome is again based on just pairs of clouds. We have found that computing distances between complete classifier profiles is a better strategy.

We have performed a set of experiments on a dataset of 368 texture images. It appears, that a representation by single feature vectors leads to a good retrieval performance, which was expected because of relatively homogeneous images in our database. The proposed method of combining distances between classifier profiles outperforms methods based on a single feature vector.

We think that a similarity criterion based on profile patterns improves the scalability of an image retrieval system. Large image collection may be represented by several SVDD's. Similarity between images may still be computed due to unique patterns in a classifier profile. How a set of images, representing an image database, may be chosen is an interesting point for further research.

References

[1] S. Antani, R. Kasturi, and R. Jain. Pattern recognition methods in image and video databases: past, present and future. In *Advances in Pattern Recognition, Proceedings of SPR'98 and SSPR'98*, pages 31–53, Berlin, 1998. IAPR, Springer-Verlag.

[2] Christopher M. Bishop. *Neural Networks for Pattern Recognition*. Oxford University Press, 1995.

[3] T. Huang, Y. Rui, and S.-F. Chang. Image retrieval: Past, present, and future. In *International Symposium on Multimedia Information Processing*, 1997.

[4] Ludmila I Kuncheva, James C Bezdek, and Robert P W Duin. Decision templates for multiple classifier fusion: an experimental comparison. *Pattern Recognition*, 34(2):299–314, 2001.

[5] K. Messer and J. Kittler. A region-based image database system using colour and texture. *Pattern Recognition Letters*, 20:1323–1330, 1999.

[6] Y. Rui, T. Huang, and S. Mehrotra. Content-based image retrieval with relevance feedback in MARS, 1997.

[7] B. Schölkopf, P. Bartlett, A.J. Smola, and R. Williamson. Shrinking the tube: A new support vector regression algorithm. M. S. Kearns, S. A. Solla, and D. A. Cohn, editors, Advances in Neural Information Processing Systems, 1999.

[8] D.M.J. Tax. *One-class classification*. PhD thesis, Delft University of Technology, http://www.ph.tn.tudelft.nl/~davidt/thesis.pdf, June 2001.

[9] D.M.J. Tax and R.P.W Duin. Support vector domain description. *Pattern Recognition Letters*, 20(11-13):1191–1199, December 1999.

[10] Vladimir N. Vapnik. *Statistical Learning Theory*. John Wiley & Sons, 1998.

Bias–Variance Analysis and Ensembles of SVM

Giorgio Valentini[1,2] and Thomas G. Dietterich[3]

[1] DISI - Dipartimento di Informatica e Scienze dell'Informazione,
Università di Genova, 16146 Genova, Italy
[2] INFM, Istituto Nazionale per la Fisica della Materia, 16146 Genova, Italy
valenti@disi.unige.it
[3] Department of Computer Science,
Oregon State University, Corvallis, OR 97331, USA
tgd@cs.orst.edu

Abstract. Accuracy, diversity, and learning characteristics of base learners critically influence the effectiveness of ensemble methods. Bias–variance decomposition of the error can be used as a tool to gain insights into the behavior of learning algorithms, in order to properly design ensemble methods well-tuned to the properties of a specific base learner. In this work we analyse bias–variance decomposition of the error in Support Vector Machines (SVM), characterizing it with respect to the kernel and its parameters. We show that the bias–variance decomposition offers a rationale to develop ensemble methods using SVMs as base learners, and we outline two directions for developing SVM ensembles, exploiting the SVM bias characteristics and the bias-variance dependence on the kernel parameters.

1 Introduction

The effectiveness of ensemble methods depends on the geometry and topology of the data [8], on the relationship between diversity and accuracy of the base learners [3, 12], on their stability [1], and on their general geometrical properties [2]. The analysis of the features and properties of the base learners used in ensemble methods is crucial in order to design ensemble methods well-tuned to the characteristics of a specific base learner.

SVM are "strong" dichotomic classifiers, well-founded on the Vapnik's Statistical Learning Theory [16], and our aim is to study if and how we can exploit their specific features in the context of ensemble methods. We analysed the learning properties of SVMs using the bias–variance decomposition of the error as a tool to understand the relationships between kernels, kernel parameters, and learning processes in SVM. Historically, the bias–variance insight was borrowed from the field of regression, using squared–loss as the loss function [7]. For classification problems, where the 0/1 loss is the main criterion, several authors proposed bias–variance decompositions related to 0/1 loss [11, 1, 10, 14, 6]. All these decompositions suffer of significant shortcomings: in particular they lose the relationship to the original squared loss decomposition, forcing in most cases bias and variance to be purely additive.

F. Roli and J. Kittler (Eds.): MCS 2002, LNCS 2364, pp. 222–231, 2002.

We consider classification problems and the $0/1$ loss function in the Domingos' unified framework of bias–variance decomposition of the error [4, 5]. In this approach bias and variance are defined for an arbitrary loss function, showing that the resulting decomposition specializes to the standard one for squared loss, but it holds also for the $0/1$ loss [4]. Using this theoretical framework, we tried to answer two main questions:

- Can we characterize bias and variance in SVMs with respect to the kernel and its parameters?
- Can the bias–variance decomposition offer guidance for developing ensemble methods using SVMs as base learners?

In order to answer these two questions, we planned and performed an extensive series of experiments on synthetic and real data sets to evaluate bias variance–decomposition of the error with different kernels and different kernel parameters.

The paper is organized as follows. In Sect. 2, we summarize the main results of Domingos' unified bias–variance decomposition of error. Sect. 3 outlines the main characteristics of the data sets employed in our experiments and the main experimental tasks performed. Then we present the principal results of our experimentation about bias–variance decomposition of the error in SVM. Sect. 4 exploits the knowledge achieved by the bias–variance decomposition of the error to formulate hypotheses about the effectiveness of SVMs as base learners in ensembles of learning machines, and two directions for developing new ensemble models of SVM are proposed. An outline of future developments of this work concludes the paper.

2 Bias–Variance Decomposition of the Error

Consider a (potentially infinite) population U of labeled training data points, where each point is a pair (x_j, t_j), $t_j \in \{-1, 1\}$, $x_j \in \mathbb{R}^d$, $d \in \mathbb{N}$. Let $P(x, t)$ be the joint distribution of the data points in U. Let D be a set of m points drawn identically and independently from U according to P. We think of D as being the training sample that we are given for training a classifier. We can view D as a random variable, and we will let $E_D[\cdot]$ indicate the expected value with respect to the distribution D.

Let $\mathcal{L}$ be a learning algorithm, and define $f_D = \mathcal{L}(D)$ as the classifier produced by $\mathcal{L}$ applied to training set D. The model produces a prediction $f_D(x) = y$. Let $L(t, y)$ be the $0/1$ loss function, that is $L(t, y) = 0$ if $y = t$, and $L(t, y) = 1$ otherwise.

Suppose we consider a fixed point $x \in \mathbb{R}^d$. This point may appear in many labeled training points in the population. We can view the corresponding labels as being distributed according to the conditional distribution $P(t|x)$. (Recall that it is always possible to factor the joint distribution as $P(x, t) = P(x)P(t|x)$.) Let $E_t[\cdot]$ indicate the expectation with respect to t drawn according to $P(t|x)$.

Suppose we consider a *fixed* predicted class y for a given x. This prediction will have an expected loss of $E_t[L(t, y)]$. In general, however, the prediction y is not fixed. Instead, it is computed from a model f_D which is in turn computed from a training sample D. Hence, the expected loss EL of learning algorithm $\mathcal{L}$ at point x can be written by considering both the randomness due to the choice of the training set D and the randomness in t due to the choice of a particular test point (x, t):

$$EL(\mathcal{L}, x) = E_D[E_t[L(t, f_D(x))]],$$

where $f_D = \mathcal{L}(D)$ is the classifier learned by $\mathcal{L}$ on training data D. The purpose of the bias-variance analysis is to decompose this expected loss into terms that separate the bias and the variance.

To derive this decomposition, we must define two things: the optimal prediction and the main prediction. The *optimal prediction* y_* for point x minimizes $E_t[L(t, y)]$: $y_*(x) = \arg\min_y E_t[L(t, y)]$. For 0/1 loss, the optimal prediction is equal to the label t that is observed more often in the universe U of data points. The *optimal model* $\hat{f}(x) = y_*$, $\forall x$ makes the optimal prediction at each point x. Define the noise, $N(x) = E_t[L(t, y_*)]$ to be the remaining loss that cannot be eliminated, even by the optimal prediction.

The *main prediction* y_m at point x is defined as $y_m = \arg\min_{y'} E_D[L(f_D(x), y')]$. This is a value that would give the lowest expected loss if it were the "true label" of x. In other words, it is the label for x that the learning algorithm "wishes" were correct. Foo 0/1 loss, the main prediction is the class predicted most often by the learning algorithm $\mathcal{L}$ when applied to training sets D.

Given these definitions, the *bias* $B(x)$ (of learning algorithm $\mathcal{L}$ on training sets of size m) is the loss of the main prediction relative to the optimal prediction: $B(x) = L(y_*, y_m)$. For 0/1 loss, the bias is always 0 or 1. We will say that $\mathcal{L}$ is *biased at point* x, if $B(x) = 1$.

The *variance* $V(x)$ is the average loss of the predictions relative to the main prediction: $V(x) = E_D[L(y_m, f_D(x))]$. It captures the extent to which the various predictions $f_D(x)$ vary depending on D.

Domingos shows that

$$EL(\mathcal{L}, x) = c_1 N(x) + B(x) + c_2 V(x),$$

where c_1 is $2P_D(f_D(x) = y_*) - 1$ and c_2 is $+1$ if $B(x) = 0$ and -1 if $B(x) = 1$. This can be simplified if we consider the noise free case and if we define the unbiased variance, $V_u(x)$, be the variance when $B(x) = 0$ and the biased variance, $V_b(x)$, to be the variance when $B(x) = 1$. Under these conditions,

$$EL(\mathcal{L}, x) = B(x) + V_u(x) - V_b(x).$$

If we further define $V_n(x) = V_u(x) - V_b(x)$ to be the *net variance*, then we can write

$$EL(\mathcal{L}, x) = B(x) + V_n(x).$$

To gain an understanding of this decomposition, let p_{corr} be the probability that the main prediction is correct: $p_{corr}(x) = P(y_m = t | x)$. If $p_{corr}(x) > 0.5$, then the main prediction is equal to the optimal prediction, and the (unbiased) variance is $V_u(x) = 1 - p_{corr}(x)$. If $p_{corr}(x) \leq 0.5$, then the main prediction is wrong. However, with probability $p_{corr}(x)$, the actual prediction is right (and unequal to the main prediction). The (biased) variance is therefore $V_b(x) = p_{corr}(x)$.

An interesting aspect of Domingos' decomposition is that variance hurts on unbiased points x, but it helps on biased points. Nonetheless, to obtain low overall expected loss, we want the bias to be small, and hence, we see to reduce both the bias and the unbiased variance.

This decomposition for a single point x can be generalized to the entire population by defining $E_x[\cdot]$ to be the expectation with respect to $P(x)$. Then define the *average bias* $E_x[B(x)]$, the *average unbiased variance* $E_x[V_u(x)]$, and the *average biased variance* $E_x[V_b(x)]$. In the noise-free case, the expected loss over the entire population is

$$E_x[EL(\mathcal{L}, x)] = E_x[B(x)] + E_x[V_u(x)] - E_x[V_b(x)].$$

3 Bias–Variance Analysis in SVM

The bias–variance decomposition of error represents a powerful tool to analyze learning processes in learning machines. Our aim consists in characterizing bias–variance decomposition of the error with respect to SVM kernels and their parameters.

3.1 Experimental Tasks

In the experiments, we employed 7 different two-class data sets, both synthetic and "real". Most of them are from the UCI repository [13]. We selected two synthetic data sets (*P2* and *Waveform*) and 5 "real" data sets (*Grey-Landsat, Letter*, reduced to the two-class problem of discriminating between the letters B and R, *Letter* with added 20% noise, *Spam*, and *Musk*). For synthetic data sets, we generated small training sets of 100 examples and reasonably large test sets (10000 examples) to perform a reliable evaluation of bias and variance. We generated 400 different training sets for *P2* and 200 training sets for *Waveform*. For real data sets, we first divided the data into training $\mathcal{T}$ and test $\mathcal{S}$ sets. We then drew 200 data sets from $\mathcal{T}$, each consisting of 100 examples drawn uniformly with replacement. The data were normalized in such a way that for each attribute the mean was 0 and the standard deviation 1.

To evaluate the bias and variance of SVMs, we conducted experiments with different kernels and different kernel parameters. In particular we considered 3 different SVM kernels: *RBF* (Gaussian Radial Basis Functions), *polynomial*, and *dot-product*. In all cases we evaluated bias and variance while varying the parameters of the kernel and the C parameter that controls the trade–off between training error and the margin. In particular we analysed:

1. The relationships between average error, bias, net–variance, unbiased and biased variance and the parameter σ (*RBF-SVM*) or the *degree* (*polynomial SVM*) of the kernel.

2. The relationships between average error, bias, net–variance, unbiased and biased variance and the parameter C (the regularization factor) of the kernel.

Each SVM model (i.e., choice of kernel, setting of kernel parameters, and C) required the training of 200 different SVMs, one for each synthesized or bootstrapped data set, for a total of about one half million training runs. For each SVM model, we computed the main prediction, bias, net-variance, biased and unbiased variance on each example of the test set, and the corresponding average quantities on the overall test set.

In all our experiments we used the *NEURObjects* [15][1] and *SVM-light* [9] programs, and we developed a C++ program `analyze_BV`[2] to perform the bias–variance decomposition of the error.

3.2   Characterization of Bias–Variance Decomposition of the Error

Space limitations preclude full description of the results. Here we present only the main observations about the experiments with *RBF-SVM*. Fig. 1 depicts the average loss, bias net–variance, unbiased and biased variance varying the values of σ and the regularization parameter C in *RBF-SVM* on the *GreyLandsat* data set. We note that σ is the most important parameter: although for very low values of C the SVM cannot learn, independently of the values of σ, (Fig. 1 a), the error, the bias, and the net–variance depend mostly on the σ parameter. In particular for low values of σ, the bias is very high and net-variance is 0, as biased and unbiased variance are equal. Then the bias suddenly drops (Fig. 1b), which lowers the average loss (Fig. 1a), and then stabilizes for higher values σ.

Fig. 2 shows the bias–variance decomposition on different data sets, varying σ, and for a fixed value of C. The plots show that average loss, bias, and variance depend significantly on σ for all the considered data sets, confirming the existence of an "high biased region" for low values of σ. In this region, biased and unbiased variance are about equal (net–variance $V = V_u - V_b$ is low). Then unbiased variance increases while biased variance decreases (Fig. 2 a,b,c and d), and finally both stabilize for relatively high values of σ. Interestingly, the average loss and the bias do not increase for high values of σ, especially if C is high.

Error, bias, net–variance, unbiased and biased variance show a common trend in the 7 data sets we used in the experimentation. Some differences, of course, arise in the different data sets, but we can distinguish three different regions in the error analysis of *RBF-SVM*, with respect to increasing values of σ (Fig. 3):

1. **High bias region.** For low values of σ, error is high: it depends on high bias. Net–variance is about 0 as biased and unbiased variance are equivalent. In this region there are no remarkable fluctuations of bias and variance: both remain constant, with high values of bias and comparable values of unbiased and biased variance, leading to net–variance values near to 0. In some cases biased and unbiased variance are about equal, but different from 0, in other cases they are equal, but near to 0.

---

[1] Download web site: `http://www.disi.unige.it/person/ValentiniG/NEURObjects`.

[2] The source code is available at `http://ftp.disi.unige.it/person/ValentiniG/BV`.

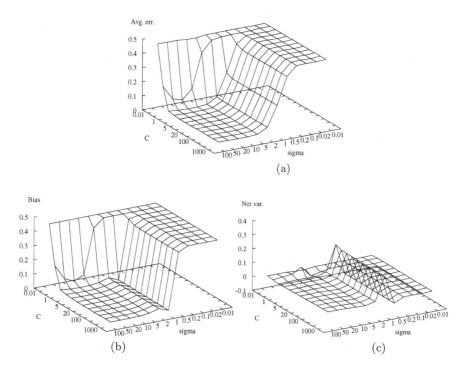

Fig. 1. Grey-Landsat data set. Error (a) and its decomposition in bias (b) and net variance (c) in RBF-SVM, varying both C and σ.

2. **Switching region**. Suddenly, for a critical value of σ, the bias decreases rapidly. This critical value depends also on C: for very low values of C, we have no learning, then for higher values the bias drops. Higher values of C cause the critical value of σ to decrease (Fig. 1 (b) and 2). In this region the increase in net–variance is less than the decrease in bias: so the average error decreases.

3. **Stabilized region**. This region is characterized by small or no variations in bias and net–variance. For high values of σ both bias and net–variance stabilize and the average error is constant.

In the first region, bias rules SVM behavior: in most cases the bias is constant and close to 0.5, showing that we have a sort of random guessing, without effective learning. It appears that the area of influence of each support vector is too small, and the learning machine overfits the data. This is confirmed by the fact that in this region the training error is about 0 and almost all the training points are support vectors.

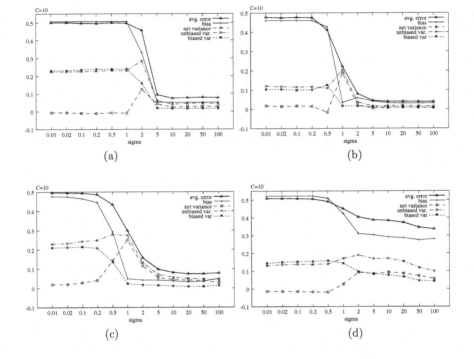

Fig. 2. Bias-variance decomposition of error in bias, net variance, unbiased and biased variance in SVM RBF, varying σ and for $C = 10$: (a) Waveform, (b) Grey-Landsat, (c) Letter-Two, (d) Letter-Two with added noise.

In the switching region, the SVM starts to learn, adapting itself to the data characteristics. Bias rapidly goes down (at the expenses of a growing net–variance), but for higher values of σ (in the second part of the switching region), sometimes net–variance also goes down, working to lower the error.

In the third region for low values of C, the error increases with σ (data not shown), as a result of the bias increment; on the whole RBF-SVMs are sensitive to low values of C: if C is too low, then bias can grow quickly. High values of C lower the bias.

For polynomial and dot–product SVMs, we have also characterized the behavior of the SVM in terms of average error, bias, net–variance, unbiased and biased variance. Here we note only that the average loss curve shows in general a U shape with respect to the polynomial degree, and this shape may depend only on unbiased variance or on both the bias and variance according to the characteristics of the data set.

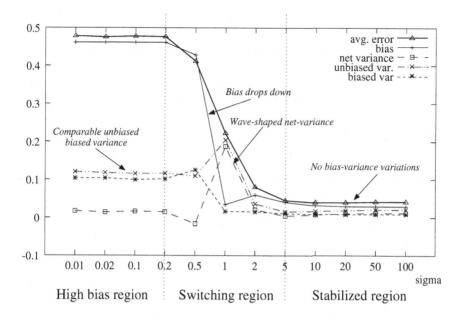

Fig. 3. The 3 regions of error in RBF-SVM with respect to σ. The data refer to Grey-Landsat data set ($C = 100$).

4   Ensembles of SVMs Based on Bias–Variance Analysis

In addition to providing insight into the behavior of SVMs, the analysis of the bias–variance decomposition of the error can identify the situations in which ensemble methods might improve SVM performance. We present two possible ways of applying bias–variance analysis to develop SVM-based ensemble methods.

4.1   Bagged Ensemble of Selected Low-Biased SVM

We can schematically consider the following observations:

- We know that bagging lowers net–variance (in particular unbiased variance) but not bias [1].
- SVMs are strong, low-biased learners, but this property depends on the proper selection of the kernel and its parameters.
- If we can identify low-biased base learners with a relatively high unbiased variance, bagging can lower the error.
- Bias–variance analysis can identify SVMs with low bias.

Hence a basic high–level algorithm for a general *Bagged ensemble of selected low-bias SVMs* is the following: (a) select the SVM model with the lowest bias using bias–variance decomposition of the error; (b) perform bagging using as base learner the SVM with the estimated lowest bias. This approach combines the low bias properties of SVMs with the low unbiased variance properties of bagging and should produce ensembles with low overall error. Depending on the type of kernel and parameters considered, and on the way the bias is estimated for the different SVM models, different implementations can be given. Of course, we cannot expect high error reduction if the bias–variance analysis shows that the base learner has a high bias and a low unbiased variance.

4.2   Heterogeneous Ensembles of SVM

The analysis of bias–variance decomposition of error in SVM shows that the minimum of the overall error, bias, net–variance, unbiased and biased variance occur often in different SVM models. These different behaviors of different SVM models could be in principle exploited to produce diversity in ensembles of SVMs. Although the diversity of base learner itself does not assure the error of the ensemble will be reduced [12], the combination of accuracy and diversity in most cases does [3]. As a consequence, we could select different SVM models as base learners by evaluating their accuracy and diversity through the bias-variance decomposition of the error.

Our data show that the "optimal region" (low average loss region) is quite large in RBF-SVMs. This means that C and σ do not need to be tuned extremely carefully. From this point of view, we can avoid time-consuming model selection by combining RBF-SVMs trained with different σ values all chosen from within the "optimal region." For instance, if we know that the error curve looks like the one depicted in Fig. 3, we could try to fit a sigmoid-like curve using only few values to estimate where the stabilized region is located. Then we could train an heterogeneous ensemble of SVMs with different σ parameters (located in the low bias region) and average them according to their estimated accuracy. Bagging and boosting methods can also be combined with this approach to further improve diversity and accuracy of the base learners.

5   Conclusion and Future Works

We performed an analysis of the bias and variance of SVMs, considering gaussian, polynomial, and dot–product kernels. We discovered regular patterns in the behavior of the bias and variance, and we related those patterns to the parameters and kernel functions of the SVM.

The information supplied by bias-variance analysis suggests two promising approaches for designing ensembles of SVMs. One approach is to employ low-bias SVMs as base learners in a bagged ensemble. The other approach is to apply bias-variance analysis to construct a heterogeneous, diverse set of low-bias classifiers.

We plan to pursue both of these ensemble methods. We also plan to relate the bias and variance of SVMs to the geometrical and topological structure of the data [8].

Acknowledgments

This work has been partially funded by INFM and University of Genova.

References

[1] L. Breiman. Bias, variance and arcing classifiers. Technical Report TR 460, Statistics Department, University of California, Berkeley, CA, 1996.

[2] S. Cohen and N. Intrator. Automatic Model Selection in a Hybrid Peceptron/Radial Network. In In J. Kittler and F. Roli (eds.) *MCS 2001, Cambridge, UK*, pages 349–358, 2001.

[3] T.G. Dietterich. Ensemble methods in machine learning. In J. Kittler and F. Roli (eds.), *MCS 2000, Cagliari, Italy*, pages 1–15, 2000.

[4] P. Domingos. A Unified Bias-Variance Decomposition for Zero-One and Squared Loss. In *Proc. of the 17th National Conference on Artificial Intelligence*, pages 564–569, Austin, TX, 2000.

[5] P. Domingos. A Unified Bias-Variance Decomposition and its Applications. In *Proc. of the 17th ICML*, pages 231–238, Stanford, CA, 2000.

[6] J.H. Friedman. On bias, variance, 0/1 loss and the curse of dimensionality. *Data Mining and Knowledge Discovery*, 1:55–77, 1997.

[7] S. Geman, E. Bienenstock, and R. Doursat. Neural networks and the bias-variance dilemma. *Neural Computation*, 4(1):1–58, 1992.

[8] T.K. Ho. Data Complexity Analysis for Classifiers Combination. In J. Kittler and F. Roli (eds.), *MCS 2001, Cambridge, UK*, pages 53–67, 2001.

[9] T. Joachims. Making large scale SVM learning practical. In *Advances in Kernel Methods - Support Vector Learning*, pages 169–184. Cambridge, MA, 1999.

[10] R. Kohavi and D.H. Wolpert. Bias plus variance decomposition for zero-one loss functions. In *Proc. of the 13th ICML*, pages 275–283, Bari, Italy, 1996.

[11] E. Kong and T.G. Dietterich. Error - correcting output coding correct bias and variance. In *Proc. of the 12th ICML*, pages 313–321, San Francisco, CA, 1995.

[12] L.I. Kuncheva, F. Roli, G.L. Marcialis, and C.A. Shipp. Complexity od Data Subsets Generated by the Random Subspace Method: An Experimental Investigation. In J. Kittler and F. Roli (eds.), *MCS 2001, Cambridge, UK*, pages 349–358, 2001.

[13] C.J. Merz and P.M. Murphy. UCI repository of machine learning databases, 1998. http://www.ics.uci.edu/mlearn/MLRepository.html.

[14] R. Tibshirani. Bias, variance and prediction error for classification rules. Technical report, University of Toronto, Canada, 1996.

[15] G. Valentini and F. Masulli. NEURObjects: an object-oriented library for neural network development. *Neurocomputing*. (in press).

[16] V. Vapnik. *Statistical Learning Theory*. Wiley, New York, 1998.

An Experimental Comparison of Fixed and Trained Fusion Rules for Crisp Classifier Outputs

Fabio Roli[1], Šarūnas Raudys[2], and Gian Luca Marcialis[1]

[1]Dept. of Electrical and Electronic Engineering, University of Cagliari
Piazza d'Armi, I-09123 Cagliari, Italy
{roli,marcialis}@diee.unica.it
[2]Vilnius Gediminas Technical University, Saulėtekio 11, Vilnius, Lithuania
raudys@das.mii.lt

Abstract. At present, fixed rules for classifier combination are the most used and widely investigated ones, while the study and application of trained rules has received much less attention. Therefore, pros and cons of fixed and trained rules are only partially known even if one focuses on crisp classifier outputs. In this paper, we report the results of an experimental comparison of well-known fixed and trained rules for crisp classifier outputs. Reported experiments allow one draw some preliminary conclusions about comparative advantages of fixed and trained fusion rules.

1 Introduction

In general, the rules for combining multiple classifier decisions can be classified according to the types of information produced by the individual classifiers: abstract level or crisp classifiers outputs, ranked list of data classes, and measurement level outputs [1]. Abstract-level classifiers output a unique class label ("crisp" output) for each input pattern. For these classifiers with crisp outputs, several fixed (e.g., majority voting), adaptive (e.g., weighted majority voting), and trained fusion rules (e.g., Behavioural Knowledge Space [2]) have been proposed so far. At present, fixed rules are the most used and widely investigated ones, while the study and application of trained rules has received much less attention [3, 4]. Therefore, pros and cons of fixed and trained rules are only partially known even if one focuses on crisp classifier outputs. Some researchers remarked that trained rules can obviously outperform the fixed ones, provided you have a large enough and independent validation set for training them in an effective way [1-4]. Very recently, the problem of experts' "bias" in trained rules was discussed [5, 8]. Each expert is typically biased on the training data, so that the combiner cannot be trained on such data. A data set that is "independent" from the training set used for the individual classifiers should be used. In addition, the complexity of the fusion rule must be adapted to the size of such data set. Complex trained rules can be used only for large enough data set [5]. Duin et al. remarked that trained rules could be worthwhile in the case of individual classifiers with unbalanced performances, as fixed rules, like the majority voting, suffer the cases of unbalanced classifiers [3]. However, further work is necessary to produce clear guidelines for the choice between fixed and trained rules, and the practical use of trained combiners. In particular, the conditions under which trained rules can

F. Roli and J. Kittler (Eds.): MCS 2002, LNCS 2364, pp. 232–241, 2002.

significantly outperform the fixed ones should be investigated in detail, as the small sample size and bias problems can reduce to zero the potential advantages of trained rules.

In this paper, we report the results of an experimental comparison of well known fixed and trained rules for crisp classifier outputs, namely, the majority voting, the Bayesian rule (or "belief functions" method), and the Behavior-Knowledge Space (BKS) method [2]. In Section 2, we briefly discuss the main pros and cons of such rules. We focus the comparison on two aspects: the unbalance degree of individual classifier performances, and the size of the validation set available for trainable rules. These two aspects play an important role in many practical applications where classifiers with very different accuracy and limited data sets should be used. As an example, classifiers used in multimodal biometrics for identity verification are usually characterised by very different performances, and the validation set for training combination rules could be limited. Reported experiments allow one draw the two following, preliminary conclusions: i) majority voting usually works well for classifiers with similar accuracy, while the performances of the majority voting rule decrease when the unbalance degree of classifiers accuracy increases, ii) trained rules, like the Bayesian rule and the BKS method, can outperform majority voting for cases of unbalanced classifiers, provided the validation set at hand allows effective training of such rules. Finally, reported results highlight that k-nearest neighbour directed noise injection can help in creating validation sets that allow effective design of trainable rules.

2 Fixed and Trained Combination Rules for Crisp Classifier Outputs

2.1 Fixed Rules

With regard to fixed combination methods for abstract-level outputs, majority voting is the simplest rule to design and apply. In order to produce the final decision, the class voted by more than half of the experts is selected. Majority voting requires no prior training and it can be always used, as any type of classifier output can be easily converted to crisp output. Further details on majority voting can be found in [1, 9].

2.2 Trained Rules

In the following, we briefly describe two trained rules, namely, the Bayesian rule (or "belief functions" method), and the Behavior-Knowledge Space (BKS) method [1]. These trained rules follow the Bayesian approach. Both rules are aimed to estimate the posterior probabilities given the decisions of the individual classifiers.

Let S_i be the crisp output of the i-th classifier in a C-class problem, where $S_i \in \{\omega_1,...,\omega_C\}$ and $i = 1,...,N$. According to the Bayes rule, we assign the input pattern to the class ω_c if:

$$P(\omega_c \mid S_1,...,S_N) > P(\omega_j \mid S_1,...,S_N), \forall j = 1,...,C; j \neq c \qquad (1)$$

The posterior probability $P(\omega_c|S_1,...,S_N)$ can be directly estimated by computing how many patterns of the c-th class fall in each output's combination. This means that we have to estimate C^{N+1} probabilities from a validation set. Such method is called Behavior-Knowledge Space [2] or Multinomial rule [5].

Another way to calculate $P(\omega_c|S_1,...,S_N)$ is to assume the independence of the classifiers given the pattern class. We define the *belief value* that a pattern belongs to class ω_c as follows [1]:

$$bel(c) = P(\omega_c \mid S_1,...,S_N)$$ (2)

By applying the Bayes' formula under the hypothesis of conditional independence of the classifiers, we can write:

$$bel(c) = P(\omega_c \mid S_1,...,S_N) \approx \frac{\prod_i P(\omega_c \mid S_i)}{\sum_k \prod_i P(\omega_k \mid S_i)}$$ (3)

Each value $P(\omega_c|S_i)$ can be estimate from the confusion matrix of the individual classifier (this matrix should be computed by a validation set). If $m_{hk}^{(i)}$ is the number of patterns with "true" class ω_h and assigned class ω_k, and $m_k^{(i)}$ is the total number of patterns with assigned class ω_k:

$$P(\omega_h \mid S_i = \omega_k) = \frac{m_{hk}^{(i)}}{m_k^{(i)}}$$ (4)

The input pattern is assigned to the class that exhibits the maximum belief value. This method is commonly referred as Bayesian combination rule or Belief functions method [1].

2.3 Comparative Advantages

Many features can be considered for comparing fixed and trained combination rules. For example, the size of the data set (large data sets are necessary for using trainable rules), the size of the classifier ensemble (small ensembles should be preferred for trained rules), the degree of "balance" of classifier performances (fixed rules usually work well with balanced classifiers), etc. We refer to Duin et al. for an interesting discussion of the main features that should be considered [3]. In the following, we focus on the comparative advantages more related to this work.

A fundamental feature for choosing between fixed and trainable rules is surely the size and the "quality" of the validation set available. Although the same training set used for individual classifiers is sometimes used for designing trainable rules, it is clear that an independent validation set should be used in order to avoid "bias" of the fusion rule [5]. The size of the validation set is also very important. A trainable rule like BKS is asymptotically optimal. But a sort of "scissors" effect can happen for small validation sets [5]. Therefore, fixed rules, like majority voting, can outperform the trained ones for small validation sets. The complexity of the trained rule should be always adapted to the size of the validation set. Very complex rules like the BKS should be used only when very large validation sets are available. Simpler rules, like the belief functions, should be used for validation sets of limited size. It is worth noting that regularisation techniques (e.g., noise injection) and modelling (e.g., conditional independence in belief functions) can help with problems related to small sample size and complexity of fusion rule.

In our opinion, another feature that should be considered for choosing between fixed and trainable rules is the degree of balance of classifiers' performances. Theory and experiments suggest that fixed rules, like majority voting, work well for classifiers with similar accuracy. On the other hand, the accuracy of the majority-voting rule can be expected to decrease when the degree of classifiers' accuracy unbalance increases. Therefore, trained rules, like the Bayesian rule and the BKS method, should outperform majority voting for cases of unbalanced classifiers, provided the validation set at hand allows effective training of such rules. In the following, we report experiments aimed to investigate these issues.

3 Experimental Results

3.1 Data Sets

The following data sets were used in our experiments: Satellite and Feltwell.

- The Satellite data set consists of a set of remote-sensing optical images [5]. Each pixel is characterised by a 8-dimensional vector. The data set consists of 15878 patterns subdivided into training set (8626 patterns) and test set (7161 patterns). Patterns belong to two classes.
- The Feltwell data set consists of a set of multisensor remote-sensing images related to an agricultural area near the village of Feltwell (UK) [6]. Our experiments were carried out characterizing each pixel by a fifteen-element feature vector containing brightness values in six optical bands and over nine radar channels. We selected 10944 pixels belonging to five agricultural classes, and randomly subdivided them into training set (5124 pixels) and test set (5820 pixels).

3.2 Experiments Planning

Our experiments were aimed:

- to compare fixed and trained rules for different degrees of the unbalance of classifiers performances;
- to compare fixed and trained rules for different sizes of the validation set.

For each data set, we trained twenty multi-layer perceptrons (MLP) neural networks with the Levenberg-Marquardt learning method. Networks with one hidden layer were used. The following network architectures were used for the Satellite and Feltwell data sets, respectively: 8-30-1 and 15-20-5. All networks were trained on a sampled set of the original training set (around the tenth part of the original training set size was used – the other 9/10 of the training set was not used).

With regard to the first aim, for each data set, we created five classifier sets. These five ensembles are characterized by different degrees of the unbalance of classifier performances. A set of balanced classifiers was created by selecting the three MLPs out of twenty with the best accuracy on the test set. This set, called "best 3", is made up of networks whose accuracy differ much less than 4%. Other two sets of balanced classifiers were created by selecting the five and seven MLPs out of twenty with the best accuracy on the test set. These sets, called "best 5" and "best 7", also contain networks whose accuracy differ by less than 4%. The "best 3" ensemble obviously contains networks that are slightly more balanced than the "best 5" and "best 7" ensembles. An unbalanced ensemble made up of three networks (referred as "unbalanced" in the following Figures) was created by selecting networks whose accuracy differ around 4% or more. A strongly unbalanced ensemble made up of three networks (referred as "strongly unbalanced" in the following Figures) was created by selecting networks whose accuracy differ more than 8%.

With regard to the second aim, experiments were carried out with different sizes of the validation set. For each data set, we generated an "artificial validation set" from the subsampled training set by 2-nearest neighbors directed noise injection with $\sigma_n=1$ [7]. K-nearest neighbors directed noise injection is a "colored" noise injection that can be used to increase the size of the validation set. For each training pattern, the k-nearest neighbors belonging to the same class of the pattern are selected. Then, noise is added in the "subspace" identified by the training patterns and its k-nearest neighbors. This noise injection procedure is defined by three parameters: the number of neighbors (k), the number of new "artificial" patterns created around the training pattern (n_{nn}), and the noise variance (σ_n). Further details can be found in [7]. For each data set, the size of the artificial validation set was increased from 1 to fifteen times using the k-nearest neighbors directed noise injection. The reported error percentages (Figures 1-10) are averaged over 10 runs, that is, for each data set, ten groups of 20 MLPs were created.

3.3 Results

3.3.1 Results with the Satellite Data Set

Figures 1-5 show the results for the different classifier ensembles and for different sizes of the validation sets. Figures 1-3 show that the majority-voting rule outperforms the BKS method for balanced ensembles and small validation set sizes. BKS reaches the same accuracy of majority voting only for large validation sets. For this data set, the Belief functions method exhibits the same accuracy of majority voting, and no accuracy improvement is obtained by increasing the validation set size. This result obviously depends on the characteristics of the Satellite data set, and it cannot be claimed in general. Figures 1-3 suggest that Belief functions parameters are estimated well also in the case of small validation sets. It is worth noting that this fusion rule requires estimating a number of parameter smaller than the one of the BKS method. This can partially explain the superiority of Belief functions over BKS for small validation sizes.

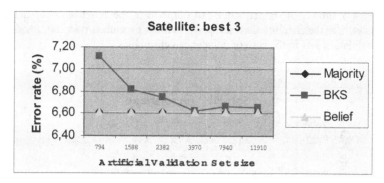

Figure 1: The percentage error rates of the trained and the fixed rules (i.e., the majority voting, the BKS method, and the Belief functions method) are shown for increasing values of the validation set. Results refer to the "best 3" ensemble.

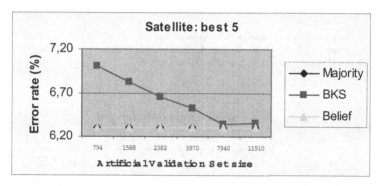

Figure 2: The percentage error rates of the trained and the fixed rules (i.e., the majority voting, the BKS method, and the Belief functions method) are shown for increasing values of the validation set. Results refer to the "best 5" ensemble.

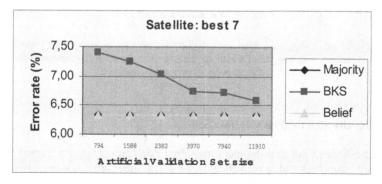

Figure 3: The percentage error rates of the trained and the fixed rules (i.e., the majority voting, the BKS method, and the Belief functions method) are shown for increasing values of the validation set. Results refer to the "best 7" ensemble.

Figures 4-5 show that trained rules can outperform the fixed ones for unbalanced ensembles. For the Satellite data set, performances of trained rules are good also for small validation sets in the case of unbalanced ensembles.

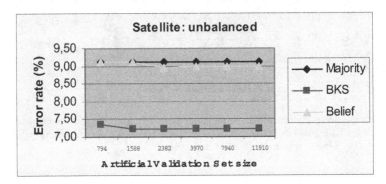

Figure 4: The percentage error rates of the trained and the fixed rules (i.e., the majority voting, the BKS method, and the Belief functions method) are shown for increasing values of the validation set. Results refer to the "unbalanced" ensemble.

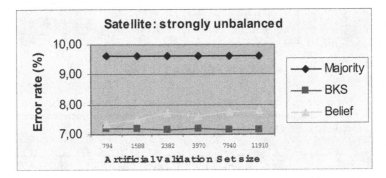

Figure 5: The percentage error rates of the trained and the fixed rules (i.e., the majority voting, the BKS method, and the Belief functions method) are shown for increasing values of the validation set. Results refer to the "strongly unbalanced" ensemble.

3.3.2 Results with the Feltwell Data Set

Figures 6-8 point out that the majority-voting rule can outperform trained rules for balanced ensembles and small validation sets. The superiority of trained rules comes out for large validation sets that allow effective design of such fusion rules. For the Feltwell data set, it is worth noting that the Belief functions method always outperform the BKS method. The superiority of Belief functions is likely due to the data set characteristics and to the smaller number of parameters that are to be estimated from the validation set. As for the Satellite data set, performances of trained rules improve for increasing sizes of validation set.

Figures 9-10 show that trained rules outperform the fixed ones for unbalanced ensembles. The superiority of trained rules slightly increases for large validation sets (Figure 9). It is worth noting the so-called "scissors" effect between majority voting and BKS (Figures 7 and 9), and between majority voting and Belief functions (Figure 8). Trained rules outperform majority voting when a large enough validation set is available.

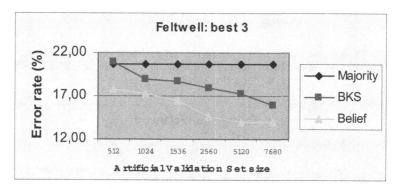

Figure 6: The percentage error rates of the trained and the fixed rules (i.e., the majority voting, the BKS method, and the Belief functions method) are shown for increasing values of the validation set. Results refer to the "best 3" ensemble.

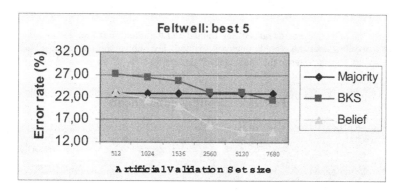

Figure 7: The percentage error rates of the trained and the fixed rules (i.e., the majority voting, the BKS method, and the Belief functions method) are shown for increasing values of the validation set. Results refer to the "best 5" ensemble.

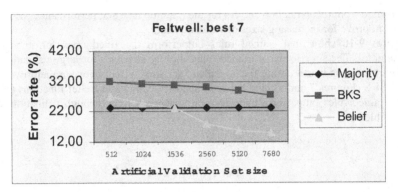

Figure 8: The percentage error rates of the trained and the fixed rules (i.e., the majority voting, the BKS method, and the Belief functions method) are shown for increasing values of the validation set. Results refer to the "best 7" ensemble.

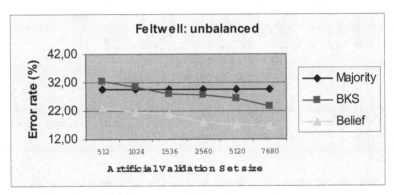

Figure 9: The percentage error rates of the trained and the fixed rules (i.e., the majority voting, the BKS method, and the Belief functions method) are shown for increasing values of the validation set. Results refer to the "unbalanced" ensemble.

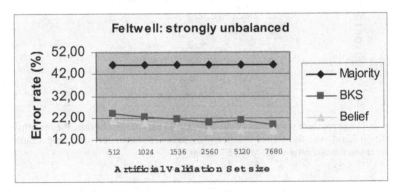

Figure 10: The percentage error rates of the trained and the fixed rules (i.e., the majority voting, the BKS method, and the Belief functions method) are shown for increasing values of the validation set. Results refer to the "strongly unbalanced" ensemble.

3 Conclusions

Although final conclusions cannot be drawn on the basis of the above limited set of experiments, the following observations can be made:

- majority voting usually works well for classifiers with similar accuracy, while the performances of the majority voting rule decreases when the degree of classifiers accuracy unbalance increases. It should be noted that performances of majority voting also depend on the error correlation among individual classifiers. The effect of correlation on majority voting performances should be investigated in detail [9, 10];

- trained rules, like the Bayesian rule and the BKS method, can outperform majority voting for the cases of unbalanced classifiers, provided the validation set at hand allows effective training of such rules;

- k-nearest neighbour directed noise injection can help in creating validation sets that allow effective design of trainable rules. To this end, other regularization and modelling techniques should be investigated [5, 8].

To sum up, further work is necessary to produce clear guidelines for the choice between fixed and trained rules, and the practical use of trained combiners. In particular, the conditions under which trained rules can significantly outperform the fixed ones should be investigated in detail, as the small sample size and bias problems can reduce to zero the potential advantages of trained rules.

References

[1] C.Y.Suen, L.Lam. Multiple classifier combination methodologies for different output levels, First International Workshop on Multiple Classifier Systems (MCS 2000). Springer-Verlag Pub., Lecture Notes in Computer Science, Vol. 1857, J.Kittler and F.Roli Eds., (2000) 52-66

[2] Huang, Y.S. and Suen, C.Y. A method of combining multiple experts for the recognition of unconstrained handwritten numerals. IEEE Trans. On Pattern Analysis and Machine Intelligence 17(1) (1995) 90-94.

[3] R.P.W. Duin, et al. A Discussion on Trained Combining of Classifiers. concept paper, January 2001, see: http://hades.ph.tn.tudelft.nl/~bob/papers/TrainedCombiners.pdf

[4] L.I.Kuncheva. Combinations of multiple classifiers using fuzzy sets. in Fuzzy Classifier Design (Chapter 8), Springer Verlag, May 2000, pp. 233-267

[5] S.Raudys. Combining the expert networks: a review. Proc. of the Int. Conference on Neural Networks and Artificial Intelligence, (R. Sadykhov Ed.), 2-5 October 2001, Minsk, Belorus, pp. 81-91

[6] G.Giacinto, F.Roli, and L.Bruzzone. Combination of Neural and Statistical Algorithms for Supervised Classification of Remote-Sensing Images. Pattern Recognition Letters, May 2000, vol. 21, no. 5, pp. 385-397

[7] M.Skurichina, S.Raudys, R.P.W. Duin. K-nearest neighbours directed noise injection in multilayer perceptron training. IEEE Trans. on Neural Networks, Vol. 11, 2000, pp. 504-511

[8] S.Raudys. Experts' bias in trainable fusion rules. submitted to IEEE Trans. on PAMI

[9] Lam, L., Suen, C.Y. Application of Majority Voting to Pattern Recognition: An Analysis of Its Behavior and Performance. IEEE Trans. on Systems, Man and Cybernetics-Part A 27(5), 1997, 553-568

[10] Kucheva, L.I., et al.. Is independence good for combining classifiers? Proc. of ICPR2000, 15th Int. Conference on Pattern Recognition, Barcelona, Spain, September 3-8, 2000, Vol. 2, pp. 168-171

Reduction of the Boasting Bias of Linear Experts

Arūnas Janeliūnas[1] and Šarūnas Raudys[2]

[1]Department of Mathematics and Computer Science, Naugarduko 24, Vilnius, Lithuania
arunas.janeliunas@verslas.com
[2]Vilnius Gediminas Technical University, Saulėtekio 11, Vilnius, Lithuania
raudys@das.mii.lt

Abstract. If no large design data set is available to design the Multiple classifier system, one typically uses the same data set to design both the expert classifiers and the fusion rule. In that case, the experts form an optimistically biased training data for a fusion rule designer. We consider standard Fisher linear and Euclidean distance classifiers used as experts and the single layer perceptron as a fusion rule. Original bias correction terms of experts' answers are derived for these two types of expert classifiers under assumptions of high-variate Gaussian distributions. In addition, noise injection as a more universal technique is presented. Experiments with specially designed artificial Gaussian and real-world medical data showed that the theoretical bias correction works well in the case of high-variate artificial data and the noise injection technique is more preferable in the real-world problems.

1 Introduction

In recent times ever more attention is being paid to the multiple classifier systems (MCS) [1-6]. To build the MCS, the designer often divides features into non-intersecting or intersecting subsets and uses each subset to design a corresponding simple classifier (expert). Then the individual decisions of the experts are combined by some fusion rule to arrive at a final decision. Another approach to designing experts is to divide the training data records into separate non-intersecting or intersecting subsets and then to use each subset to design simple experts in place of a complex one.

In experts design there arises the well-known tendency of classifiers to adapt to the specific learning data set. If the available data vectors are used both for designing experts and the fusion rule, then outputs of the experts form optimistically biased training data for the fusion rule designer [6-12]. We call this bias the „*expert boasting bias.*" Therefore, in order to design a reliable fusion rule, one needs to have an independent design data set, which differs from that of the experts' design data set. However, the researcher cannot always allow himself the luxury to split design data into two independent sets. Thus, special techniques should be applied during design of the fusion rule in order to reduce the influence of expert boasting bias.

The expert boasting bias is addressed very little in the pattern recognition literature. Kittler [7] proposes a theoretical framework for expert output correction („moderation"), which should reduce the risk of boasting bias. Bedworth [8] uses asymptotic results to derive boasting bias-corrected posterior class probabilities for

F. Roli and J. Kittler (Eds.): MCS 2002, LNCS 2364, pp. 242-251, 2002.

multilevel classifier fusion. Janeliūnas [12] derived expert boasting bias correction for the case when Fisher linear classifiers are used as experts and the fusion rule. Dramatic improvement of the MCS performance made by introducing boasting bias correction for k-NN experts [9] and the *Multinomial* classifier fusion rule [10] demonstrates the extremely important role that boasting bias correction can play in MCS design.

In our work we consider trainable classifier fusion rule realized by the means of single layer perceptron. Original theoretically-based boasting bias correction techniques for two types of linear expert classifiers, the standard Fisher linear classifier (FLC) and the Euclidean distance classifier (EDC), are presented under assumptions of multivariate Gaussian data. For non-Gaussian distributions we suggest noise injection as more universal technique for overcoming the experts' boasting bias.

The overall organization of the paper is as follows. In the second and third sections, we consider asymptotic and training data-based boasting bias correction techniques for the standard Fisher linear classifier. In the fourth section the bias correction transformation is given for the Euclidean distance classifier. The fifth section discusses a noise injection technique to overcome the experts' boasting bias. The sixth section is devoted to experimental analysis. The seventh section contains concluding remarks.

2   Boasting Bias Correction (BBC) for FLC-experts

Consider a situation where input feature space is divided into L feature sub-spaces or into L data regions and standard linear Fisher linear classifiers are used as experts in each feature sub-space or each data region. Let X_j^i be the training set vector (i is the number of classes $i = 1,2$ and j is a current number of the training vector, $j = 1,\dots, N_i$). Training vectors X_j^i are used to estimate mean vectors $\hat{M}_i$ and the common covariance matrix $\hat{\Sigma}$ of input pattern categories. Then the standard Fisher discriminant functions $g_s(X) = \hat{W}_s^{(F)\,T} X + \hat{w}_s$, ($s = 1, 2, \dots, L$) are produced. Here $\hat{W}_s^{(F)} = \hat{\Sigma}_s^{-1}(\hat{M}_1^{(s)} - \hat{M}_2^{(s)})$ and $\hat{w}_s = 1/2\,(\hat{M}_1^{(s)} + \hat{M}_2^{(s)})^T \hat{W}_s^{(F)}$.

Consider the asymptotic case, when following preconditions are met:
1) FLC-experts deal with two p-variate Gaussian pattern classes $N(\mu_i, \Sigma)$;
2) both classes are equally probable;
3) training set sizes are equal $N_2 = N_1 = N$;
4) both values, $p, N \to \infty$.

If we use input pattern vectors X, which are different from X_j^i, then the mean of sample-based Fisher discriminant function $g_s(X)$ is equal to [13, 12]:

$$Eg_s(X) \approx (-1)^i \frac{N\delta^2}{2N - p}, \tag{1}$$

and the standard deviation is the following:

$$Vg_s(X) \approx \frac{8N^2\left(N\delta^2 + 2p\right)}{(2N-p)^3}. \tag{2}$$

Here δ^2 is a standard squared Mahalanobis distance between two input pattern categories:

$$\delta^2 = (\mu_1 - \mu_2)^T \Sigma^{-1}(\mu_1 - \mu_2). \tag{3}$$

Note, that the values N, p, and δ^2 can differ for each of L FLC-experts.

However, inserting training vectors X_j^i into the discriminant function $g_s(X)$ we obtain the re-substitution estimates of the Fisher discriminant function $\hat{g}_s(X_j^i) = \hat{W}_s^{(F)T} X_j^i + \hat{w}_s$. The expected value of re-substitution estimate $\hat{g}_s(X_j^i)$ is equal to [12]:

$$E\hat{g}_s(X_j^i) \approx (-1)^i\left(\frac{N\delta^2}{2N-p} + \frac{2p}{2N-p}\right), \tag{4}$$

and the standard deviation can be expressed as

$$V\hat{g}_s(X_j^i) \approx \frac{2\left(N\delta^2 + 2p\right)}{2N-p}. \tag{5}$$

From the formulas (1), (2), (4) and (5) we see that compared to the true values of $g_s(X)$, the re-substitution values $\hat{g}_s(X_j^i)$ are biased. In small sample size and high dimensionality situations, the bias can be considerable. Therefore, if one uses the same data vectors X_j^i to design both the expert classifiers and the fusion rule, then in the fusion rule training the bias-corrected values (say $\hat{g}_s(X_j^i)_{\text{corrected}}$) of $\hat{g}_s(X_j^i)$ should be used.

In order to make the mean and the variance of $\hat{g}_s(X_j^i)_{\text{corrected}}$ to be equal to the mean and the variance of $g_s(X)$, from Equations (1), (2), (4) and (5) we derive following BBC transformation for the fusion rule training vectors:

$$\hat{g}_s(X_j^i)_{\text{corrected}} = \frac{2N}{2N-p}\,\hat{g}_s(X_j^i) + (-1)^i\,\frac{Np}{(2N-p)^2}\left(\delta^2 + 4\right). \tag{6}$$

To use the bias correction (6) practically, one needs to know Mahalanobis distance δ. The estimate $\hat{\delta}^2 = (\hat{\mu}_1 - \hat{\mu}_2)^T \hat{\Sigma}^{-1}(\hat{\mu}_1 - \hat{\mu}_2)$, obtained from the training vectors X_j^i, is optimistically biased [15]. The lesser is the number of training vectors N, the larger is the estimated value $\hat{\delta}$. Thus, if N is small, the estimate $\hat{\delta}$ can distort the boasting bias correction (6). Then the more suitable BBC rule may appear to be the one, which equalizes only the means of $\hat{g}_s(X_j^i)_{\text{corrected}}$ and $g_s(X)$:

$$\hat{g}_s(X_j^i)_{\text{corrected}} = \hat{g}_s(X_j^i) + (-1)^i \frac{2p}{2N - p}. \tag{7}$$

Here the Mahalanobis distance δ is ignored.

Note that in order to effectively utilize correction terms (6) and (7), expert classifiers must be built on training sets of different sizes and dimensionalities. Otherwise, we will have identical modification terms for all classifiers and the BBC will be insignificant.

3   Sample-Based Estimate of Mahalanobis Distance for FLC-experts

As we have mentioned before, the optimistically biased estimate $\hat{\delta}$ of Mahalanobis distance can distort the boasting bias correction (6). This situation can be improved by finding the unbiased estimate of Mahalanobis distance δ.

In the asymptotic case, the re-substitution classification error estimate of the FLC-expert is equal to [6, 15]:

$$\hat{P}_{RS}^F = \Phi \{ -\tfrac{1}{2} \delta_{\text{re-substitution}} \}. \tag{8}$$

Here the re-substitution estimate $\delta_{\text{re-substitution}}$ of Mahalanobis distance can be expressed as [6, 15]:

$$\delta_{\text{re-substitution}} = \delta \sqrt{T_\mu T_\Sigma}, \tag{9}$$

where $T_\mu = 1 + 2p/(\delta^2 N)$ and $T_\Sigma = 1 + p/(2N - p)$. Note that terms T_μ, T_Σ are individual for each expert.

When the re-substitution error $\hat{P}_{RS}^F$ of the expert is estimated, the unknown $\delta_{\text{re-substitution}}$ can be found by the means of the interpolation of Equation (8). Then the true Mahalanobis distance δ can be found from Equation (9).

4   Boasting Bias Correction for EDC-experts

If the training set size, N, is small and dimensionality p is large, instead of Fisher linear classifier experts, one ought to use simpler, Euclidean distance classifiers (EDC). However, EDC-experts also provide biased training data for the fusion rule designer. Therefore, the appropriate BBC technique must be applied.

The discriminant function of s-th EDC-expert is expressed as $h_s(X) = \hat{W}_s^{(E)T} X + \hat{w}_s$.
Here $\hat{W}_s^{(E)} = \hat{M}_1^{(s)} - \hat{M}_2^{(s)}$ and $\hat{w}_s = 1/2(\hat{M}_1^{(s)} + \hat{M}_2^{(s)})^T \hat{W}_s^{(E)}$. Like in [12] we derive for the asymptotic case that the mean of the Euclidean discriminant function $h_s(X)$ is equal to:

$$Eh_s(X) \approx (-1)^i \frac{1}{2}\delta^2, \tag{10}$$

and the standard deviation can be expressed as

$$Vh_s(X) \approx \left(1+\frac{1}{N}\right)\delta^2 + (-1)^i \frac{2p}{N}. \tag{11}$$

If we use the training vectors X_j^i, then we obtain the re-substitution estimates of the Euclidean discriminant function $\hat{h}_s(X_j^i) = \hat{W}_s^{(E)^T} X_j^i + \hat{w}_s$. In the asymptotic case the mean of $\hat{h}_s(X_j^i)$ is equal to

$$E\hat{h}_s(X_j^i) \approx (-1)^i \left(\frac{1}{2}\delta^2 + \frac{p}{N}\right), \tag{12}$$

while the standard deviation of $\hat{h}_s(X_j^i)$ remain the same as in Equation (11). Thus, the re-substitution estimates of Euclidean discriminant function $\hat{h}_s(X_j^i)$ are shifted by p/N in comparison with the true values of discriminant function $h_s(X)$. Therefore, the precise BBC transformation of EDC-experts' outputs is

$$h_s(X_j^i)_{\text{corrected}} = h_s(X_j^i) - (-1)^i \frac{p}{N}. \tag{13}$$

Note that in principle the sensitivity of the EDC-experts to the training set size greatly depends on the data. If input data vectors are situated in some linear subspace, then instead of formal dimensionality p, an effective dimensionality, $p^* = \left((\mu_1 - \mu_1)^T (\mu_1 - \mu_1)\right)^2 tr\left(\Sigma^2\right)/\left((\mu_1 - \mu_1)^T \Sigma(\mu_1 - \mu_1)\right)^2$, has to be used in Equation (13) (for more details, see e.g. [15]).

5   Noise Injection Technique to Reduce the Boasting Bias

The boasting bias corrections are useful if one operates with EDC or FLC experts and the data is high-variate uni-modal Gaussian. In other cases we cannot exploit this theoretically based opportunity. A very useful classification rule that can be used both as the experts and as the fusion rule is a non-linear single layer perceptron (SLP). In principle, training SLP in a whitened input feature space and optimal stopping allows us to obtain one of several different statistical classifiers [14,15]. Therefore one ought to use the asymptotic or sample-based BBC techniques derived above for SLP experts too. However, it is practically impossible to determine at which stage the SLP is after a number of training iterations and which BBC technique should be applied.

To train a SLP classifier one needs to determine an optimal number of iterations and use a validation data set. If an independent validation set is unavailable, one of possible ways to deal with this problem is to form pseudo-training or pseudo-validation sets by the means of noise injection. Often one injects a „white" Gaussian noise vectors, $N(0, \lambda I)$, where I is an identity matrix and λ is a positive scalar. Such an approach, however, can distort the geometry of the data. Further improvement is obtainable for high-dimensional problems, by adding k-NN-directed „colored" noise [10, 16]. We add noise to each single training vector repeatedly and in this way create a new data set that we call the „artificial validation set". We use this set to design the fusion rule. Noise injection is actually an introduction of additional information: the space between the nearest vectors of one pattern class is not empty, however, it is filled with vectors from the same category [15].

In principle, the roles of the artificial validation and the training sets can be interchanged. Assume that we can create as many noise vectors as we need. A k-NN-directed colored noise retains information about the data configuration. Thus, we can use it as non-biased training data for the fusion rule. Furthermore, we can use the real training data for a more reliable validation than is possible with the random noisy vectors.

However, in high dimensional space we meet difficulties with noise injection. The volume of the feature space becomes very large. Therefore, in high dimensions, we need to add noise more times. Also, a variance of the noise, σ_{noise}, has to be selected after several trials.

6   Experimental Results

We performed several experiments in order to show where the theoretical BBC transformation of the outputs of linear expert classifiers is effective and when the noise injection technique should be used.

6.1   Data Sets

Gaussian Data (GAD). The first data set is artificial 1000-variate Gaussian data with weakly correlated features ($\rho=0.1$) and symmetric means. The Mahalanobis distance between two classes is $\delta = 3.234$. Training set is composed of 100+100 vectors and the test set contains 2500+2500 vectors.

Medical-Gaussian Data (MGD). The second data were produced from 300-variate real-world medical data to be discussed later. From these biomedical data we estimated mean vectors and covariance matrices of two classes. Then the artificial Gaussian data was produced using obtained mean vectors and covariance matrices. The training set is composed of 100+100 vectors and the test set contains 2000+2000 vectors.

Medical Data (MED). The two classes of medical data comprise biofluids obtained from normal subjects and cancer patients. The data set consists of 140 samples with 300 spectral features (frequencies). There are 61 spectra for healthy patients and 79 for cancerous. For our experiments we used half of the data (30+39 vectors) for training and the other half of the data (31+40 vectors) for test.

6.2   Experiments

In all experiments linear classifiers (FLC or EDC) were used as experts. Classifier fusion was performed through the optimally stopped single layer perceptron. All results are averaged after 5 runs of the experiment with different randomly chosen training data sets.

The first experiment was designed to show the efficiency of derived theoretical BBC transformations. Here we used Gaussian data set and the dimensionalities of input vectors used by different experts varied substantially. Eleven competitive linear classifiers, working on non-overlapping feature subspaces, were used as experts. First of all we designed 2 good experts to work on 40-variate data. Then nine other "poor" experts dealt with 100-variate vectors. Results of the first experiment are presented in the first row of the Table 1.

The second experiment was intended to demonstrate the inefficiency of the theoretical BBC transformation even using Gaussian data, when not all preconditions for the asymptotic case are met. To produce linear experts, we randomly divided the 300-variate feature space of medical-Gaussian data into sixty 5-variate non-overlapping subspaces. Therefore, the data dimensionality for expert classifiers was not high. Also note that all classifiers were working on subspaces of the same dimensionality and with the same number of training vectors. Results of the second experiment are reported in the second row of the Table 1.

The third experiment shows that in principle the theoretical BBC can give a small gain even in low-dimensionality cases. We improved on the second experiment by randomly dividing features into 61 subspaces. Now 4 classifiers were working on 3-variate, 3 classifiers on 6-variate and 54 classifiers on 5-variate feature subspaces. The data dimensionality for expert classifiers remained low. However, in this cases the subspaces were now of a different dimensionality. The third row in the Table 1 reports results of the third experiment.

An objective of the fourth experiment was to show that theoretical BBC transformations are most effective when experts deal with the feature subspaces of substantially different size and when the training set is very small. We designed 8 expert classifiers on the medical-Gaussian data. Two of them were operating on 5-variate, five on 25-variate and one on 55-variate feature subspaces. We reduced the training set to 30+30 data vectors. Results of the fourth experiment are presented in the fourth row of the Table 1.

Table 1. Generalization errors in experiments with 1000-variate Gaussian data, 300-variate medical-Gaussian and 300-variate real-world medical data.

Experiment No.	Data	Non-corrected FLC	BBC (6) of FLC	BBC (7) of FLC	Noise injection for FLC	Non-corrected EDC	BBC (13) of EDC	Noise injection for EDC
1	GAD	0.3704	**0.2341**	0.2758	0.3637	0.3198	**0.3195**	0.3622
2	MGD	0.1423	0.1433	0.1425	**0.1408**	0.1558	0.1602	**0.1541**
3	MGD	0.1203	0.1191	**0.1182**	0.1189	0.1354	**0.1334**	0.1348
4	MGD	0.3658	**0.2741**	0.3621	0.3657	0.2229	**0.2215**	0.2229
5	MED	0.3431	0.2822	0.3144	**0.2645**	0.3072	0.3107	**0.2285**

The fifth experiment was aimed at showing which BBC technique, theoretical BBC transformations or a noise injection, should be preferred in solving real-world problems. For the fifth experiment we used the medical data. In order to produce linear classifiers on the medical data we used the same randomly selected feature subspaces as in the fourth experiment. Results of the fifth experiment are shown in the fourth row of Table 1.

6.3   Comments

In the case of the Gaussian data, the theoretical BBC both for Fisher linear and Euclidean distance classifiers leads to the improvement of classification performance. As one could expect, the precise BBC transformations (6) and (13) are the most effective. In the case of FLC classifiers the set of experts was specially designed to have 2 good and 9 poor FLC classifiers. Thus, asymptotic BBC transformations allowed the minimizing of boasting influence of poor FLC-experts and classification performance was improved dramatically. The sensitivity of simpler EDC-experts to the training data size, however, was rather low and the difference in quality between the 2 good and 9 poor EDC-experts was less significant. Therefore, the asymptotic BBC of EDC classifiers gave lower gain in generalization error. The same tendencies were demonstrated in the fourth experiment with the medical-Gaussian data. Also note that adding Gaussian noise to Gaussian and medical-Gaussian data helped very little to improve the classification performance of combined linear classifiers. Moreover, EDC classifiers are much more sensitive to the variance of injected noise. The large noise variance for Gaussian data (we added 3-NN directed noise with variance $\sigma_{noise} = 50$) distorted the distributions of the EDC-experts' outputs and noise injection for EDC-experts even had a significantly negative impact.

The second experiment with medical-Gaussian data show that certain deviations from asymptotic assumptions cause the asymptotic BBC transformations to be inapplicable even for artificial data. Here the noise injection technique can be applied.

Note that in the second experiment linear experts were produced on randomly selected feature subspaces of equal size. Therefore the difference in classifier performance was not significant and the impact of BBC transformations was slight. Also note that in the cases of both Gaussian data sets, the feature space was divided into separate subspaces *randomly*. A different set of feature subspaces may affect BBC transformations differently. Results of the third and fourth experiments are a good example of this. After randomly dividing feature space into subsets of different size, the theoretical BBC transformations outperformed the noise injection technique. Note also that the low dimensionality of feature subspaces for expert classifiers in the third experiment prevented the theoretical BBC transformations from obtaining a noticeable gain in the classification performance of the multiple classifier system.

The noise injection technique appears to be a more universal method to fight the experts' boasting bias. Noise injection with properly selected noise parameters (for medical-Gaussian and medical data we injected 3-NN directed noise with variance $\sigma_{noise} = 0.5$) works well in practically all circumstances. It outperforms the theoretical BBC transformations in the cases of real-world data and when the asymptotic preconditions are not met.

7   Concluding Remarks

In the MCS design we deal with a phenomenon that actually isn't addressed in the pattern recognition literature: if the same training data are used to design both the expert network classifiers and the fusion rule, the experts' outputs become optimistically biased. This reduces the overall performance of the multiple classification system.

If the underlying data model is known, one can use the theoretical results in the estimation of the rate of error in finite design set situations and design procedures that assist in reducing the experts' „self boasting" effect. We considered standard Fisher linear and Euclidean distance classifiers as experts and the single layer perceptron as a fusion rule. For these two types of linear classifier experts and for the underlying high-variate Gaussian data model we suggested original theoretically based boasting bias correction procedures. In principle, one can derive similar equations in instances where both types of expert classification rules, EDC and FLC, are used together. For Gaussian data the classification rules, such as the standard quadratic discriminant function and others, can be considered.

In designing ways to reduce the experts' boasting bias, it needs to be kept in mind that when using the theoretically based procedures one must know the parameters of the true data, and the real data should be similar to multivariate Gaussian data. Also, the effect of BBC is conditioned by the expert design stage. In order to have a gain from the theoretical BBC transformations, expert classifiers must be built on training sets of different sizes and dimensionalities.

A more universal method for correcting the experts' inherent boasting bias is noise injection. It can be used for standard statistical classifiers and artificial neural networks. However, like all statistical procedures, this approach has its limitations, such as the necessity to determine the variance of noise, the large number of noise injections and the large share of computer resources needed to do the math for multi-dimensional data.

Our analysis shows that, in principle, if the experts operate on high-variate Gaussian data, they differs in complexity and the sample size is small, then it is possible to develop theoretical BBC transformations that can dramatically improve the performance of MCS. For the real-world data and for the artificial data, which does not satisfy certain asymptotic preconditions, the noise injection approach is recommended.

Acknowledgments. The authors would like to thank Dr. Ray Samorjay and Dr. Richard Baumgartner of the Institute for Biodiagnostics of the National Research Council Canada in Winnipeg, Manitoba for providing the medical data set.

References

1. Kittler J. and Roli F. (eds): Multiple Classifier Systems. Springer Lecture Notes in Computer Science, Springer Vol. 1857 (2000), Vol. 2096 (2001).
2. Ho T.K.: Data complexity analysis for classifier combination. Multiple Classifier Systems. Lecture Notes in Computer Science. Springer Vol. 2096. (2001) 53-67.

3.   Kittler J., Hatef M., Duin R.P.W. and Matas J.: On combining classifiers. IEEE Transactions on Pattern Analysis and Machine Intelligence, Vol. 20 (1998) 226-239.

4.   Xu L., Krzyzak A. and Suen C.Y.: Methods for combining multiple classifiers and their applications in handwritten character recognition. IEEE Transactions on Systems, Man and Cybernetics, vol. 22 (1992) 418-435.

5.   Rastrigin L.A. and Erenstein R.Ch.: Method of Collective Recognition. Energoizdat, Moscow (1981) (in Russian).

6.   Raudys Š.: Combining the expert networks: a review. In: Sadykhov R.K. (ed.): Proc. of Int. Conference Neural Networks and Artificial Intelligence, ICNNAI'2001. BSU publication, Minsk (2001) 81-91.

7.   Kittler J.: A framework of classifier fusion: is still needed? In: F. Ferri, J.M. Inest, A. Amin and P. Pudil (eds), Advances in Pattern Recognition. Springer Lecture Notes in Computer Science 1876 (2000) 45-56.

8.   Bedworth M.: High Level Data Fusion. PhD Thesis, Aston Univ, UK (1999).

9.   Alkoot F.M., Kittler J.: Improving the performance of the product fusion strategy. In: Proc. 15th IAPR International Conference on Pattern Recognition, Barcelona, (2000).

10. Raudys Š.: Experts' Bias in Trainable Fusion Rules. In: IEEE transaction on Pattern Analysis and Machine Intelligence, (2001) (submitted).

11. Kahya Y.P., Güler E.C., Sankur B. and Raudys Š.: Hierarchical classification of respiratory sounds. In: Chang H.K. and Zhang U.T. (eds.): Proc. of 20th annual. Int. Conf. of IEEE Engineering in Medicine and Biology and Biology Society, Pts 1-6. Biomedical Engineering towards the year 2000 and beyond. Vol. 20 (2000) 1598-1601.

12. Janeliūnas A.: Bias correction of linear classifiers in the classifier combination scheme. In: Sadykhov R.K. (ed.): Proc. of Int. Conference Neural Networks and Artificial Intelligence, ICNNAI'2001. BSU publication, Minsk (2001) 92-99.

13. Raudys Š.: On the amount of a priori information in designing the classification algorithm. In: Technical. Cybernetics. Proc. Acad. of Sciences of the USSR. Nauka Moscow, N4 (1972) 168-174 (in Russian).

14. Raudys Š.: Evolution and generalization of a single neuron. I. SLP as seven statistical classifiers, In: Neural Networks 11 (1998) 283–96.

15. Raudys Š.: Statistical and Neural Classifiers: An integrated approach to design. Springer, London (2001).

16. Skurichina M., Raudys S. and Duin R.P.W.: K-nearest neighbors directed noise injection in multilayer perceptron training. In: IEEE Trans. on Neural Networks, 11 (2000) 504–511.

Analysis of Linear and Order Statistics Combiners for Fusion of Imbalanced Classifiers

Fabio Roli and Giorgio Fumera

Dept. of Electrical and Electronic Eng., University of Cagliari
Piazza d'Armi, 09123 Cagliari, Italy
{roli,fumera}@diee.unica.it

Abstract. So far few theoretical works investigated the conditions under which specific fusion rules can work well, and a unifying framework for comparing rules of different complexity is clearly beyond the state of the art. A clear theoretical comparison is lacking even if one focuses on specific classes of combiners (e.g., linear combiners). In this paper, we theoretically compare simple and weighted averaging rules for fusion of imbalanced classifiers. Continuing the work reported in [10], we get a deeper knowledge of classifiers' imbalance effects in linear combiners. In addition, we experimentally compare the performance of linear and order statistics combiners for ensembles with different degrees of classifiers imbalance.

1 Introduction

In the past decade, several rules for fusion of classifiers' outputs have been proposed [6]. Among the different features that can be used for classifying these rules (e.g., the type of classifiers' outputs [2]), herein we focus on the "complexity" of the fusion rule. Simple rules, like majority voting and simple averaging, are based on fixed combining schemes. Rules of intermediate complexity, like weighted averaging, are usually based on a set of parameters that should be tuned. Trained rules (e.g., Behavior Knowledge Space and Decision Templates [3,8]), require specific knowledge acquisitions that can impose heavy demands on quality and size of the training set. So far few theoretical works investigated the conditions under which specific fusion rules can work well, and a unifying framework for comparing rules of different complexity is clearly beyond the state of the art [6,11]. A clear theoretical comparison is lacking even if one focuses on specific classes of combiners (e.g., linear combiners). For example, theoretical and experimental results suggest that simple averaging of classifiers' outputs usually works well for classifiers with similar accuracy and zero or similar negative correlation ("balanced" classifiers), while weighted averaging should be used for imbalanced classifiers [1,4,7,10]. However, although classifiers' balance plays an important role in many practical applications (e.g., multimodal biometrics for identity verification [9]), the conditions of classifiers' imbalance under which weighted averaging can significantly outperform simple averaging are not completely clear. Ueda recently reported results that show small advantages of weighted averaging over simple averaging [4]. Tumer and Ghosh argued that weighted averaging could not outperform simple averaging even for

F. Roli and J. Kittler (Eds.): MCS 2002, LNCS 2364, pp. 252-261, 2002.
© Springer-Verlag Berlin Heidelberg 2002

imbalanced classifiers [1]. Since, in practical applications, the bad quality and the limited size of training sets can quickly cancel the theoretical advantages of weighted averaging, it is very important to assess clearly such ideal advantages. It is worth noting that the theoretical advantages of asymptotically optimal trained rules (e.g., the Behavior Knowledge Space rule) are also cancelled in the case of small data sets.

In this paper, we theoretically compare simple and weighted averaging of classifier outputs (Section 3). To this end, we used the framework developed by Tumer and Ghosh for simple averaging and order statistics combiners [1]. We extended such framework to the analysis of weighted averaging (Section 2). Continuing the work reported in [10], we got a deeper knowledge of classifiers' imbalance effects in linear combiners by further analysis and experiments (Sections 3.3 and 4). In addition, as Tumer and Ghosh argued that order statistics combiners could be effective with imbalanced classifiers [7], we experimentally compared the performance of linear and order statistics combiners for ensembles with different degrees of classifiers imbalance (Section 4).

2   An Analytical Framework for Linear and Order Statistics Combiners

Tumer and Ghosh developed a theoretical framework for analyzing the simple averaging rule and the order statistics combiners [1]. In the following, we briefly summarize this framework and its extension to the case of the weighted averaging rule. Further details can be found in [1, 10].

For a one-dimensional feature vector x, the outputs of an individual classifier approximating the a posteriori probabilities can be denoted as:

$$\hat{p}_i(x) = p_i(x) + \varepsilon_i(x) , \tag{1}$$

where $p_i(x)$ is the "true" posterior probability of the i-th class, and $\varepsilon_i(x)$ is the estimation error. The main hypothesis made in [1] is that class boundaries obtained from the approximated a posteriori probabilities are close to the optimal Bayesian boundaries. This allows focusing the analysis of classifier performance around the class boundaries. Assuming that the estimation errors $\varepsilon_i(x)$ on different classes are i.i.d. variables with zero mean and variance σ_ε^2, Tumer and Ghosh showed that the expected value of the added error (i.e., the error added to the Bayes one), E_{add}, can be expressed as:

$$E_{add} = \sigma_\varepsilon^2 / s , \tag{2}$$

where s is a constant term depending on the values of the probability density functions in the optimal decision boundary.

2.1   Linear Combiners

Now let us consider the weighted averaging of the outputs of an ensemble of N classifiers, with normalised weights w_k:

$$\sum\nolimits_{k=1}^{N} w_k = 1, \quad w_k \geq 0 \quad k = 1,...,N .$$ (3)

Using Eq. 1, the outputs of the weighted averaging combiner can be expressed as [10]:

$$\hat{p}_i^{ave}(x) = \sum\nolimits_{k=1}^{N} w_k \hat{p}_i^k(x) = p_i(x) + \sum\nolimits_{k=1}^{N} w_k \varepsilon_i^k(x) = p_i(x) + \bar{\varepsilon}_i(x) ,$$ (4)

where $\bar{\varepsilon}_i(x)$ denotes the estimation error of the combiner. We assume that, for any individual classifier, the estimation errors $\varepsilon_i^k(x)$ on different classes are i.i.d. variables with zero mean and variance $\sigma_{\varepsilon_k}^2$. We also assume that the errors $\varepsilon_i^m(x)$ and $\varepsilon_i^n(x)$ of different classifiers are correlated on the same class, with correlation coefficient ρ_i^{mn}, while they are uncorrelated on different classes [1,7]. Under these assumptions, we showed that the expected value, E_{add}^{ave}, of the added error of the weighted averaging combiner can be expressed as [10]:

$$E_{add}^{ave} = \frac{1}{s} \sum\nolimits_{k=1}^{N} \sigma_{\varepsilon_k}^2 w_k^2 + \frac{1}{s} \sum\nolimits_{m=1}^{N} \sum\nolimits_{n \neq m} \left(\rho_i^{mn} + \rho_j^{mn} \right) \sigma_{\varepsilon_m} \sigma_{\varepsilon_n} w_m w_n .$$ (5)

The above expression generalises to the case of weighted averaging the result obtained in [1] for simple averaging. For the purposes of our discussion, let us assume that the correlation coefficients of the different classes are equal: $\rho_i^{mn} = \rho_j^{mn} = \rho^{mn}$. It follows from Eqs. 2 and 5 that E_{add}^{ave} can be rewritten as follows:

$$E_{add}^{ave} = \sum\nolimits_{k=1}^{N} E_{add}^k w_k^2 + \sum\nolimits_{m=1}^{N} \sum\nolimits_{n \neq m} 2\rho^{mn} \sqrt{E_{add}^m E_{add}^n} w_m w_n .$$ (6)

Let us now first analyse the case of uncorrelated estimation errors (i.e., $\rho^{mn}=0$ for any $m \neq n$). In this case, Eq. 6 reduces to:

$$E_{add}^{ave} = \sum\nolimits_{k=1}^{N} E_{add}^k w_k^2 .$$ (7)

Taking into account Eq. 3, it is easy to see that the weights that minimise E_{add}^{ave} are:

$$w_k = \left(\sum\nolimits_{m=1}^{N} 1/E_{add}^m \right)^{-1} \left(1/E_{add}^k \right) .$$ (8)

Such optimal weights are inversely proportional to the expected added errors of the individual classifiers. For equal values of the expected added error, the optimal weights are $w_k=1/N$, that is, simple averaging is the optimal combining rule in the case of classifiers with equal performance ("balanced" classifiers). In such case, it can be shown that $E_{add}^{ave} = E_{add}^k / N$, that is, simple averaging reduces the expected added error of individual classifiers by a factor N [1,10].

Consider now the case of correlated estimation errors (Eq. 6). In this case, it is not easy to derive a general analytical expression for the optimal weights. However, it turns out from Eq. 6 that the optimal weights are $w_k=1/N$ if all the classifiers exhibit both equal performance and equal correlation coefficients. Otherwise, different weights are needed to minimise the expected added error E_{add}^{ave} of the combiner. It is worth noting that simple averaging is not the optimal rule if individual classifiers have the same accuracy but different pair-wise correlation. Weights are necessary also for compensating differences in correlation.

In Section 3, we use the above theoretical model for assessing the differences between the performance of simple and weighted averaging rules for imbalanced classifiers. Our aim is to investigate the conditions under which weighted averaging significantly outperforms simple averaging, and to provide a more formal definition of the concept of classifiers' imbalance.

2.2   Order Statistics Combiners

Let us now consider combining rules based on order statistics (OS) operators. As in [1,7], we consider the outputs of any of the N individual classifiers, for any class i, ordered as follows:

$$f_i^{1:N}(x) \le f_i^{2:N}(x) \le \ldots \le f_i^{N:N}(x) .$$ (9)

The well-known *max, min* and *med* combiners are defined as:

$$f_i^{\max}(x) = f_i^{N:N}(x), \quad f_i^{\min}(x) = f_i^{1:N}(x),$$ (10)

$$f_i^{\text{med}}(x) = \begin{cases} \left[f_i^{\frac{N}{2}:N}(x) + f_i^{\frac{N+1}{2}:N}(x) \right] \Big/ 2 & \text{if } N \text{ is even}, \\ f_i^{\frac{N+1}{2}:N}(x) & \text{if } N \text{ is odd}. \end{cases}$$

For unbiased estimation errors, Tumer and Ghosh analysed the case of i.i.d. errors. Note that in such case the individual classifiers exhibit equal performance and are uncorrelated. Therefore, the optimal rule is simple averaging. As shown above, simple averaging reduces the expected added error of individual classifiers by a factor N. Tumer and Ghosh found an analogous result for OS combiners [1,7]. They showed that the expected added error for OS combiners, E_{add}^{OS}, can be written as:

$$E_{add}^{OS} = \alpha E_{add}^k ,$$ (11)

where α depends on the order statistics and on the distribution of the estimation errors. This means that OS allow reducing the expected added error of individual classifiers by a factor α. In particular, it was shown that, for Gaussian estimation errors, the *med* combiner provides the best reduction factor. However, it turned out that $\alpha > 1/N$. This means that, for balanced classifiers exhibiting uncorrelated Gaussian errors, simple averaging is better than the OS combiners and weighted averaging.

It is worth noting that deriving the analytical expression of the added error E_{add}^{OS} for classifiers exhibiting different performance, or correlated estimation errors, is more difficult than for linear combiners. Our future work will address this issue. In section 4, we report an experimental comparison between linear and OS combiners for balanced and imbalanced classifiers.

3   Theoretical Comparison

In this section, we provide some quantitative evaluations of the theoretical improvements achievable by weighted averaging over simple averaging. To this end, we use the theoretical model that we outlined in Section 2. As remarked above, in this paper, only an experimental comparison between linear and OS combiners will be given (Section 4). In the following, we denote with ΔE_{add}^{ave} the difference between the expected added error achieved by simple averaging and the one achievable by weighted averaging using the optimal weights given in Eq. 8. Without loss of generality, we consider the N classifiers ordered for decreasing values of their expected added error E_{add}^k, so that $E_{add}^1 \geq E_{add}^2 \geq \ldots \geq E_{add}^N$.

3.1   Combining Uncorrelated Classifiers

For uncorrelated estimation errors (i.e., $\rho^{mn}=0$ for any $m \neq n$), we obtain from Eq. 6:

$$\Delta E_{add}^{ave} = \left(\sum\nolimits_{k=1}^{N} E_{add}^k \right) \Big/ N^2 - \left[\sum\nolimits_{k=1}^{N} \left(1 / E_{add}^k \right) \right]^1 . \tag{12}$$

Let us consider the behavior of ΔE_{add}^{ave} for fixed values of the difference $E_{add}^1 - E_{add}^N$ between the performance of the worst and the best individual classifier. A mathematical analysis of Eq. 12 shows that, for any given value of $E_{add}^1 - E_{add}^N$, ΔE_{add}^{ave} takes on the maximum value when the N-2 classifiers $(2,\ldots,N$-1$)$ exhibit the same performance of the worst individual classifier, that is, $E_{add}^1 = E_{add}^2 = \ldots = E_{add}^{N-1}$. For the sake of brevity, we omit this proof. This means that, according to our model, for a given value of the difference $E_{add}^1 - E_{add}^N$, the advantage of weighted averaging over simple averaging is maximum for an ensemble made up of N-1 classifiers with equal accuracy, and one classifier (E_{add}^N) much more accurate. Therefore, we can say that this is the condition under which, for any given value of $E_{add}^1 - E_{add}^N$, the degree of classifiers' imbalance should be considered maximum. Under this condition ($E_{add}^1 = E_{add}^2 = \ldots = E_{add}^{N-1}$), in Fig. 1 we report the values of ΔE_{add}^{ave} for values of $E_{add}^1 - E_{add}^N$ ranging from 0 to 25%. Three different values of E_{add}^N for the best individual classifier (1%, 5%, 10%) and two values of the ensemble size N=3,5 were considered. Fig. 1 shows that weighted averaging significantly outperforms simple averaging only for strongly imbalanced performance (i.e., for high values of $E_{add}^1 - E_{add}^N$), and if the performance of the best individual classifier is very good (i.e., for low values of E_{add}^N). Moreover, the advantage of weighted averaging decreases for increasing values of N (note that in practice it is unlikely to have many uncorrelated classifiers).

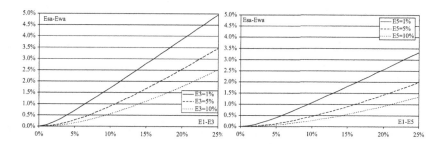

Fig. 1. Values of ΔE_{add}^{ave} (denoted as E^{sa}-E^{wa}) for uncorrelated classifiers. Results are reported for values of $E_{add}^{1} - E_{add}^{N}$ ranging from 0 to 25%. The results for N=3 (left) and N=5 (right) are shown. The values of E_{add}^{k} are denoted as E_k.

Let us now consider the optimal weights given in Eq. 8. It is easy to see that the highest weight is assigned to the best individual classifier. Moreover, the same weight (the minimum weight) is assigned to classifiers 1,...,N-1, as they have equal values of the expected added error. This minimum weight is reported in Figure 2, plotted against $E_{add}^{1} - E_{add}^{N}$, for the same values of E_{add}^{N} and N as in Fig. 1.

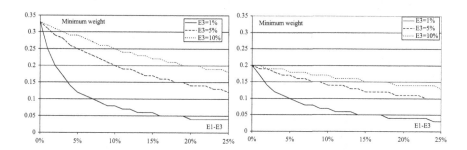

Fig. 2. Values of the minimum of the optimal weights, for N=3 (left) and N=5 (right). Results are reported for values of $E_{add}^{1} - E_{add}^{N}$ ranging from 0 to 25%.

Figures 1 and 2 show that high values of ΔE_{add}^{ave} correspond to low weights for classifiers 1,...,N-1. This means that weighted averaging significantly outperforms simple averaging when classifiers 1,...,N-1 exhibit errors much higher than the best individual classifier. In such case, low weights are assigned to classifiers 1,...,N-1. In particular, if the best individual classifier performs very well (i.e., if E_{add}^{N} is very small), a value of ΔE_{add}^{ave} higher than 1% can be achieved only by assigning to the other classifiers a weight lower than 0.1. This means that the performance of weighted averaging gets close to that of the best individual classifier, as the other classifiers are basically discarded.

3.2   Combining Correlated Classifiers

For correlated estimation errors (Eq. 6), we evaluated ΔE_{add}^{ave} by a numerical analysis of the optimal weights. In the following, we summarize the results that are useful for the purposes of our discussion. Details can be found in [10]. Analogously to Section 3.1, we analysed the behavior of ΔE_{add}^{ave} for different values of the difference $E_{add}^1 - E_{add}^N$. We considered the case of an ensemble made up of three classifiers (N=3), and the same values of $E_{add}^1 - E_{add}^N$ and E_{add}^N as in Section 3.1. Moreover, we considered values of the correlation coefficients ρ^{mn} in the range [-0.4, 0.8]. With regard to classifiers' imbalance, our analysis showed that, for any given value of $E_{add}^1 - E_{add}^N$, the maximum value of ΔE_{add}^{ave} is achieved for $E_{add}^1 = E_{add}^2 = \ldots = E_{add}^{N-1}$ (as in the case of uncorrelated errors). Such maximum value is achieved when the correlation between the best individual classifier and another classifier is minimum (in our case, the value of the correlation coefficient was -0.4), while all the other correlation coefficients must be as high as possible (in our case, 0.8). We then evaluated ΔE_{add}^{ave} for fixed values of the expected added errors of the individual classifiers, and for varying values of correlation imbalance. We found that imbalanced correlations significantly affect the performance of simple averaging only when the individual classifiers also exhibit imbalanced accuracy.

3.3   Classifiers' Imbalance for Linear Combiners

Our analysis pointed out the kind of classifiers' accuracy imbalance for which weighted averaging provides the maximum improvement over simple averaging. This allows us to quantify the concept of classifiers' imbalance for linear combiners. We showed that, for a given value of the difference $E_{add}^1 - E_{add}^N$ between the worst and the best individual classifier, the maximum value of ΔE_{add}^{ave} is achieved for $E_{add}^1 = E_{add}^2 = \ldots = E_{add}^{N-1}$. Accordingly, classifiers' imbalance can be characterized by $\Delta = E_{add}^1 - E_{add}^N$, and an additional feature related to the condition $E_{add}^1 = E_{add}^2 = \ldots = E_{add}^{N-1}$. To this end, a possible feature, denoted with δ_E, is the following:

$$\delta_E = \frac{\overline{E}_{add}^{2:N-1} - E_{add}^N}{E_{add}^1 - E_{add}^N} \, , \tag{13}$$

where $\overline{E}_{add}^{2:N-1} = \left(\sum_{k=2}^{N-1} E_{add}^k \right) / N - 2$. It is easy to see that δ_E takes on values in the range [0, 1], and is maximum if $E_{add}^1 = E_{add}^2 = \ldots = E_{add}^{N-1}$. The two features Δ and δ_E should be used for characterizing the degree of imbalance. It is worth noting that both such features play an important role. In particular, δ_E is aimed to evaluate how much the degree of imbalance, characterized by Δ, is favorable to weighted averaging. Weighted averaging can significantly outperform simple averaging only for ensembles with high values of δ_E and Δ. It is worth noting that our analysis pointed out the importance of the parameter δ_E for evaluating classifiers' imbalance in the case of linear combiners. The intuitive parameter Δ is not sufficient, as it does not take into account the condition that provides the maximum improvement of weighted averaging over simple averaging (i.e., $E_{add}^1 = E_{add}^2 = \ldots = E_{add}^{N-1}$).

4   Experimental Results

Our experiments were aimed at assessing some of the theoretical results described in the previous section. To this end, we compared the performance of linear and order statistics combiners for ensembles with different degrees of accuracy imbalance, and analysed the effects of imbalance. We used a data set of remote-sensing images related to an agricultural area near the village of Feltwell (U.K.) [5]. This data set consists of 10,944 pixels belonging to five agricultural classes. It was randomly subdivided into a training set of 5,820 pixels, and a test set of 5,124 pixels. Each pixel is characterised by fifteen features, corresponding to the brightness values in the six optical bands, and over the nine radar channels considered.

For our experiments, we used five ensembles made up of a k-nearest neighbours classifier (k-NN), with a k value of 15, and two multi-layer perceptron (MLP) neural networks with architectures 15-5-5 and 15-2-5. For each ensemble, the percentage error rates of the individual classifiers on the test set are shown in Table 1. Ensembles with different degrees of classifiers' imbalance were used. Table 1 shows the values of the features δ_E and Δ used to characterize the imbalance (Section 3.3). All the values were averaged over ten runs corresponding to ten training set / validation set pairs, obtained by sampling without replacement from the original training set. The validation set contained the 20% of patterns of the original training set. The training of MLPs was stopped as it reached the minimum error probability on the validation set.

According to the definition of classifiers' imbalance given in Section 3.3, ensemble 1 is balanced, while all the other ensembles are imbalanced. However, it should be noted that the imbalance of ensemble 1 is strictly due to the small range of classifiers accuracies ($\Delta=2.04$). The value of δ_E is quite high (0.81). This means that ensemble 1 would be potentially imbalanced (note that E_2 is closer to E_3 than E_1), but this potentiality cannot be exploited due to the small range of classifiers accuracies (Δ). Ensembles 4 and 5 were selected since both of them are imbalanced ($\Delta=16.22$), but only ensemble 4 is imbalanced in the sense that, according to our analysis, is useful for using weighted averaging (i.e., it also exhibits a high value of δ_E). For ensemble 5, MLP1 exhibits an accuracy that is much better than the one of the worst classifier. According to our theoretical analysis (Section 3.3), this is not the best case of imbalance for weighted averaging. Differently, the imbalance of ensemble 4 fits well with the case that our analysis predicts to be very good for weighted averaging (i.e., two classifiers with similar performance, and another classifier with performance that is much better). The same observations hold for the couple of ensembles 2 and 3. Therefore, we should expect that the advantage of weighted averaging over simple averaging for ensembles 2 and 4 should be greater than for ensembles 3 and 5, respectively.

Table 1. Percentage errors of the individual classifiers on the test set. With regard to classifiers imbalance, the values of δ_E and Δ are shown (Section 3.3).

	k-NN	MLP1	MLP2	δ_E	$\Delta=E_1-E_3$
ensemble 1	10.01	11.68	12.05	0.81	2.04
ensemble 2	10.01	18.20	18.00	0.97	8.19
ensemble 3	10.01	13.27	17.78	0.41	7.77
ensemble 4	10.01	25.97	26.23	0.98	16.22
ensemble 5	10.01	17.78	26.23	0.47	16.22

As in these experiments we were not interested in the problem of weight estimation, the optimal weights of the linear combination were computed on the test set by "exhaustive" search. The average performance of simple and weighted averaging, and of the order statistics combiners, are reported in Table 2, together with the values of the optimal weights for weighted averaging.

Table 2. Percentage errors of weighted averaging (E^{wa}), simple averaging (E^{sa}), and order statistics combiners (E^{min}, E^{med}, E^{max}) on the test set. The optimal weights of weighted averaging are also reported.

	combiner percentage error						optimal weights		
	E^{sa}	E^{wa}	E^{min}	E^{med}	E^{max}	$E^{sa}-E^{wa}$	k-NN	MLP1	MLP2
ens. 1	10.00	9.37	10.07	10.52	9.90	0.63	0.576	0.200	0.224
ens. 2	12.09	9.69	10.69	15.84	10.42	2.40	0.689	0.080	0.231
ens. 3	10.69	9.63	10.72	11.18	10.63	1.06	0.681	0.231	0.088
ens. 4	16.81	9.79	11.32	25.23	10.65	7.02	0.838	0.006	0.156
ens. 5	12.44	9.73	11.22	15.02	10.80	2.71	0.752	0.103	0.143

With regard to simple and weighted averaging, results in Table 2 are in agreement with the predictions of the theoretical model. The accuracy of simple and weighted averaging is quite similar for the balanced ensemble 1. The slight difference can be explained by observing that ensemble 1 exhibits a high value of δ_E. Weighted averaging outperforms simple averaging for the other ensembles. As predicted by our analysis, the advantage of weighted averaging over simple averaging is higher for ensembles 2 and 4 than for ensembles 3 and 5, respectively. This result confirms the importance of an appropriate definition of the concept of classifiers' imbalance. For linear combiners, both Δ and δ_E must be considered for evaluating the degree of imbalance. If one consider only the parameter Δ, ensembles 4 and 5 exhibit the same degree of imbalance ($\Delta=16.22$). However, our analysis showed that only ensemble 4 is imbalanced in the sense that makes weighted averaging very useful (i.e., it exhibits high values of Δ and δ_E). Table 2 also shows that the greater is the imbalance, the lower is the weight assigned to one of the worst individual classifiers. These results clearly point out that weighted averaging significantly outperforms simple averaging only for highly imbalanced classifiers, and only by discarding one of the worst classifiers.

Let us now consider order statistics combiners. Table 2 shows that the performance of the *min* and *max* combiners are pretty good. However, the *min* combiner performed not so well for ensembles 4 and 5, although such ensembles exhibited high values of Δ. The *med* combiner exhibited a quite surprising behavior. It seems very sensible to performance imbalance. This result demands for further investigations. With regard to the comparison of weighted averaging and order statistics combiners, weighted averaging always outperformed the best OS combiner. However, the accuracy difference is always smaller that 1%, even for highly imbalanced ensembles. Moreover, the best OS combiner always outperformed simple averaging. Since, in real applications, it can be difficult to estimate the optimal weights of the linear combination, this result suggests that OS combiners can be an effective combining rule for imbalanced classifiers, as argued by Tumer and Ghosh [7]. Finally, it should be noted that the imbalance conditions considered in our experiments were tailored for the comparison between simple and weighted averaging. The imbalance conditions that are most favorable to OS combiners will be investigated in our future work.

References

1. Tumer, K., Ghosh, J.: Linear and Order Statistics Combiners for Pattern Classification. In: Sharkey, A.J.C. (ed.): Combining Artificial Neural Nets. Springer (1999) 127-161
2. Xu, L., Krzyzak, A., Suen, C.Y.: Methods of Combining Multiple Classifiers and Their Applications to Handwriting Recognition. IEEE Trans. on Systems, Man, and Cybernetics 22 (1992) 418-435
3. Huang, Y.S., Suen, C.Y.: A Method of Combining Multiple Experts for the Recognition of Unconstrained Handwritten Numerals. IEEE Transactions on Pattern Analysis and Machine Intelligence 17 (1995) 90-94
4. Ueda, N.: Optimal Linear Combination of Neural Networks for Improving Classification Performance. IEEE Trans. on Pattern Analisys and Machine Int. 22 (2000) 207-215
5. Roli, F.: Multisensor Image Recognition by Neural Networks with Understandable Behaviour. Int. J. of Pattern Recognition and Artificial Intelligence 10 (1996) 887-917
6. Kittler, J., Roli, F. (eds.): Proc. of the 1st and 2nd Int. Workshop on Multiple Classifier Systems. Springer-Verlag, LNCS, Vol. 1857 (2000), and Vol. 2096 (2001)
7. K. Tumer, K., Ghosh, J.: Robust Combining of Disparate Classifiers through Order Statistics. To appear in: Pattern Analysis and Applications special issue on "Fusion of Multiple Classifiers"
8. Kuncheva, L., Bezdek, J.C., Duin, R.P.W.: Decision templates for multiple classifier fusion: an experimental comparison. Pattern Recognition, 34 (2001) 299-314
9. Roli, F., Kittler, J., Fumera, G., Muntoni, D.: An experimental comparison of classifier fusion methods for multimodal personal identity verification systems. Proc. of 3rd Int. Workshop on Multiple Classifier Systems (MCS 2002), in press
10. Fumera, G., Roli, F.: Performance analysis and comparison of linear combiners for classifier fusion. Proc. of IAPR Int. Workshop on Statistical Pattern Recognition (SPR 2002), in press
11. Kittler, J., Hatef, M., Duin, R.P.W.: On Combining Classifiers. IEEE Trans. on Pattern Analysis and Machine Intelligence 20 (1998) 226-239

Boosting and Classification
of Electronic Nose Data

Francesco Masulli[1,2], Matteo Pardo[3], Giorgio Sberveglieri[3], and
Giorgio Valentini[1,4]

[1] INFM, Istituto Nazionale per la Fisica della Materia
Via Dodecaneso 33, 16146 Genova, Italy
[2] Dipartimento di Informatica, Università di Pisa
Corso Italia 40, 56125, Pisa, Italy
`masulli@di.unipi.it`
[3] INFM and Dipartimento di Chimica e Fisica
Via Valotti 9-25123 Brescia, Italy
`pardo@tflab.ing.unibs.it, sbervegl@tflab.ing.unibs.it`
[4] DISI - Dipartimento di Informatica e Scienze dell'Informazione
Università di Genova, Via Dodecaneso 35, 16146 Genova, Italy
`valenti@disi.unige.it`

Abstract. Boosting methods are known to improve generalization performances of learning algorithms reducing both bias and variance or enlarging the margin of the resulting multi-classifier system. In this contribution we applied Adaboost to the discrimination of different types of coffee using data produced with an Electronic Nose. Two groups of coffees (blends and monovarieties), consisting of seven classes each, have been analyzed. The boosted ensemble of Multi-Layer Perceptrons was able to halve the classification error for the blends data and to diminish it from 21% to 18% for the more difficult monovarieties data set.

1 Introduction

Boosting methods have been successfully applied to many domains, ranging from text filtering, to natural language processing, classification of multisource remote sensing data, Geographical Information Systems, diagnosis of tumors and others [14, 15, 9, 7, 11, 1].

In this paper we present a novel application of boosting to electronic noses data. Electronic Noses (EN), in the broadest meaning, are instruments that analyze gaseous mixtures for discriminating between different (but similar) mixtures and, in the case of simple mixtures, quantify the concentration of the constituents.

Electronic nose data show typically a relatively small cardinality, as the experimental techniques are complex and time-consuming, and from this point of view resampling methods can help to improve the generalization capabilities of classifiers with small data sets.

In fact bagging and boosting are known to reduce variance [6]. Taking a weighted majority over many hypotheses, trained on different examples drawn

F. Roli and J. Kittler (Eds.): MCS 2002, LNCS 2364, pp. 262–271, 2002.

from the same data set, has the effect of reducing the random variability of the combined hypotheses: as a consequence, the variance is reduced. Boosting achieves bias reduction generating distributions that concentrate on harder examples, trying to generate diverse base learners specialized in different resampled data sets [5].

The generalization capabilities of boosting can also be explained in the framework of large margin classifiers theory, as it had been shown that boosting enlarges the margins of the training examples [17]. Recently Pedro Domingos showed the equivalence between the bias-variance interpretation and the margin-based explanation of the error reduction induced by boosting methods [4].

We applied boosted ensemble of Multi-Layer Perceptrons (MLP) to the classification of commercial coffees using electronic nose data. Commercial coffees are blends, which, for economic reasons, contain monovarietal coffees of various origins. For the producers the availability of analysis and control techniques is of great importance. There exists a rich literature on the characterization of coffee using the chemical profile of one of its fractions, such as the vapor of green or roasted beans or the phenolic fraction.

The usage of a single neural network (normally a Multi-Layer Perceptron, but Radial Basis Function Networks had also been investigated) as a classifier is a common solution to pattern recognition problems in EN odor analysis [8, 12]. We tried to improve the classification capabilities of single MLP using boosting methods.

The paper is organized as follows: the next section briefly introduces electronic noses and some pre-processing problems that characterize the applicative domain, then the experimental setup, results and discussion on the application of boosted MLP ensemble to electronic nose data are presented.

2   Electronic Noses

Electronic Noses (EN) consist of a sampling system (for a reproducible collection of the mixture), an array of sensors (which is the heart of the system) , electronic circuitry and data analysis software [8]. EN using arrays of chemical sensors can be divided into three categories according to the type of sensitive material used: inorganic crystalline materials (e.g. semiconductors, as in MOS-FET structures, and metal oxides); organic materials and polymers; biologically derived materials. Comparatively to classical techniques (e.g. the combination of gas chromatography and mass spectroscopy (GC-MS)), ENs are simpler, cheaper devices. They recognize a fingerprint, that is a global information, of the samples to be classified.

In particular for our experimentation we used the Pico-1 EN developed at the Gas Sensory Lab. in Brescia. The Pico-1 EN makes use of six thin film semiconductor sensors. For this experiment three SnO_2-based (one catalyzed with gold, one with palladium and one with platinum) and three $Ti - Fe$ sensors were employed. All of them were grown by sputtering with the RGTO technique [13].

The odor to be analyzed can be sampled either in a static way with a programmable autosampler comprising a syringe, or in a dynamic way letting the carrier flush through the headspace, or from stained steel canisters or nalophan bags through a pump. For this application the possibility of easily preparing the sample suggested the adoption of the more reproducible static headspace extraction with the autosampler.

Pico-1 precisely controls the sensor temperature via a feedback loop. Further, there is the possibility to steer the EN remotely via the TCP-IP interface. A simple user interface for the preliminary analysis of data (graphs of sensor responses, time development of extracted features, PCA score and loading plots) has also been implemented in *Matlab*.

The typical measurement consists of the exposure of the sensors to a concentration step, that is a change of odor concentration from zero to c (each component of the vector stands for a gas component) and back to zero again, and of the recording of the subsequent change in resistance. The classical feature extracted from the response curve is the relative change in resistance.

3   Experimental Setup

We used the the Pico-1 EN to analyze blended coffees (7 different blends) and 6 single varieties plus the Italian Certified Espresso (ICE). The *blended coffees* data set is composed by 187 samples and the *monovariety coffees* data set is composed by 225 samples. The data are six dimensional corresponding to the relative change in resistance achieved from the data registered by the six sensors.

For these experiments, 2 g of ground coffee are introduced into a vial with a volume of 20 cm^3 which is crimped with seal and septa. The vial is then left in an incubation oven at 50 C for 30 minutes in order to generate the aroma. Ten vials for every coffee type of the monovariety group and 12 vials for every coffee type of the blend group were prepared. Three successive extractions were performed from the same vial. While the data set is not big for machine learning standards, this is a considerable dataset to be collected with an E-Nose.

The first part of data analysis deals with signal processing (e.g. removal of spikes, noise filtering), the choice of the features to be considered in the subsequent analysis and data visualization stages. Drift correction is also considered as part of this processing of the data. This part of data is crucial for the quality of the final results, and requires a constant exchange with the experimental process, mainly to establish a sufficiently good and reliable measurement protocol.

The second part of the data analysis deals with inferring the relationships between the EN data and the corresponding class labels. We compared the results of a single Multi-Layer Perceptron (MLP) with the corresponding boosted MLP ensemble, using the *Adaboost.M1* algorithm introduced by Freund and Schapire [5, 6]. This boosting algorithm was originally designed for two-class classification problems, but it has been demonstrated that it is effective also for multiclass classification problems when the base learner is strong enough to achieve reasonably high accuracy [5]. In our implementation we used boosting by resampling, i.e. we chose a set of examples from the training set at random with replacement, according to the current probability distribution of the data. We randomly split the data in a training (70% of the data) and in a testing set (30%) and we repeated training of each learning machine six times using different pseudorandom initialization weights. The same series of pseudorandom initialization weights have been used both for single MLPs and boosted MLPs. In both cases we exploited MLPs with one hidden layer, using 5, 7 and 9 hidden units for the *blended coffees* and 20, 30 and 40 hidden units for the *monovariety coffees* data sets. All the experimentations have been performed developing applications using the C++ *NEURObjects* [1] library [19].

A global impression of the measurements can be gained from the PCA plots in Fig. 1. We note that:

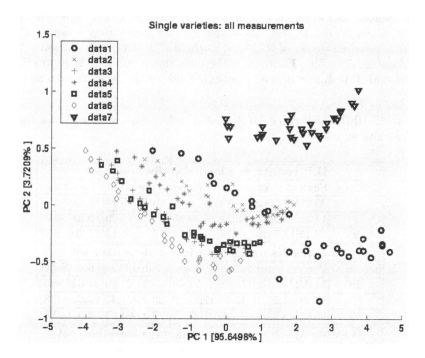

Fig. 1. PCA plot of the monovariety group of coffees. The values in square brackets refer to the percentage of the total variance for respectively the first and the second principal components.

1. Drift is present and it affects the first PC. Nonetheless the visual separation obtained with the 2nd and 3rd PCs wasn't seen to be any better.

---

[1] Download web site: http://www.disi.unige.it/person/ValentiniG/NEURObjects

2. Coffee #7 forms a distinct cluster: in fact this is a very roasted coffee and it is considered to be of the worst quality.
3. The ICE points (class #1) form two somewhat distinct clusters. The measurements of the cluster on the bottom right were made at different times: it is possible that the blend's headspace evolved differently with time with respect to that of the SVs (single varieties).
4. A third fact about the SV is that coffees #3 and #5 are mixed. This makes sense since the coffees are of the same type, both being washed arabic beans of good quality.

4   Results and Discussion

The results of our experimentation are summarized in Tab. 1. The table represents the results on the test sets of blended and monovariety coffee data sets, using boosted ensembles of MLP and single MLP trained with a classical backpropagation algorithm. Each row of the table shows results relative to MLP or boosted MLP with a predefined number of hidden units. The first column of the

Table 1. MLP and boosted MLP results on blended coffees and monovariety coffees data sets.

MLP results on blended coffees data set								
hidden #	Percent error rate on different runs					Best	Mean	Stdev
5	20.97	19.35	16.13	19.35	20.97	16.13	16.13	18.82	2.01
7	11.29	14.52	14.52	11.29	19.35	19.35	11.29	15.05	3.31
9	16.13	17.74	16.13	17.74	17.74	17.74	16.13	17.20	0.76

MLP results on monovariety coffees data set								
hidden #	Percent error rate on different runs					Best	Mean	Stdev
20	21.43	23.21	21.43	21.43	21.43	23.21	21.43	22.02	0.84
30	23.21	23.21	21.43	23.21	21.43	23.21	21.43	22.62	0.84
40	25.00	25.00	23.21	23.21	23.21	23.21	23.21	23.81	0.84

Boosted MLP results on blended coffees data set								
hidden #	Percent error rate on different runs					Best	Mean	Stdev
5	9.68	11.29	9.68	11.29	11.29	11.29	9.68	10.75	0.83
7	6.45	9.68	9.68	9.68	6.45	9.68	6.45	8.60	1.67
9	11.29	9.68	6.45	9.68	6.45	11.29	6.45	9.14	2.20

Boosted MLP results on monovariety coffees data set								
hidden #	Percent error rate on different runs					Best	Mean	Stdev
20	21.43	21.43	19.64	21.43	19.64	21.43	19.64	20.83	0.92
30	21.43	17.86	19.64	17.86	19.64	21.43	17.86	19.64	1.60
40	23.21	17.86	19.64	19.64	23.21	17.86	17.86	20.24	2.44

table refers to the number of hidden units of a single MLP or of a single MLP base learner of the boosted ensemble. The next 6 columns correspond to percent error rates obtained by different pseudorandom initialization of the weights of the MLP. The 8th column show the minimum error achieved (Best), while the next corresponds to the average error (Mean) and the last shows the standard deviation of the percent error rate (Stdev).

Comparing the overall results on the blended coffee data set between MLP and boosted MLP (Tab. 1), we can remark that the average error (Mean) is halved using boosted MLP ensembles: The percent error rate on the test set drops down from 15.05 to 8.60, using MLP with 7 hidden units as base learners, and similar results are obtained also using MLP with 5 and 9 hidden units. The minimum error, also, is reduced in a similar way, from 11.29 to 6.45 %.

A reduction of the percent error rate, both for the average and the minimum error can be observed also on the monovariety coffee data set, but with a remarkably lower decrement. In this case the average error decreases only from 22.02 to 19.64 and the minimum error from 21.43 to 17.86.

Fig. 2 and 3 show the error rates of the boosted MLP as a function of the number of base learners of the ensemble. The error rate on the training set drops to 0 after about 10 rounds of boosting on the blended coffee data set (Fig. 2), and after about 150 rounds on the monovariety coffee data set (Fig. 3). In both cases an exponential decrement of the error can be observed, according to Freund and Schapire's theorem stating that the training error exponentially falls to zero incrementing the number of base learners, given that the weighted error of each base learner is less than 0.5 [5].

The test error on the blended data set continues to decrease, even after the training error reaches zero. A similar trend can also be noted in the monovariety data set, even if the test error lowers more slowly. This fact has been observed also in other works [16, 18, 17] and has been explained in the framework of large margin classifiers, interpreting boosting as an algorithm that enlarges the margins of the training examples [17]: even if the training error reaches zero the boosting algorithm continues to enhance the margins, focusing on the hardest examples. As a consequence, the generalization capabilities of the boosted ensemble are improved [16].

Note that the spiky curves in Fig. 2 and 3 are due to the relative small number of examples in the testing set.

The test error error on the monovariety data set decreases slowly compared with the blended data set and using a less complex MLP as base learner the error remains unchanged at about 20% (Fig. 3 (a)). Moreover, the training error drops to zero only after more than 100 rounds of boosting. These results on the monovariety coffee data set can be explained considering three different but correlated items.

First, learning monovariety data could be an hard classification task: for instance, our results obtained using other ensemble methods such as Output Coding decomposition [2] show that it is difficult to shrink the error rate below 20% [10].

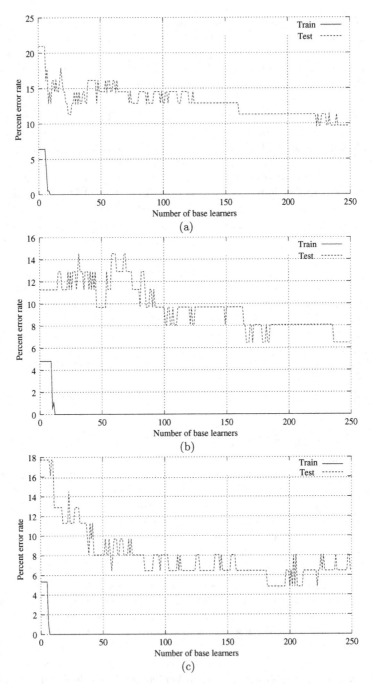

Fig. 2. Error curves for boosting MLP on the blended coffees data set. The base classifiers are MLP with 5 (a), 7 (b) and 9 (c) hidden units.

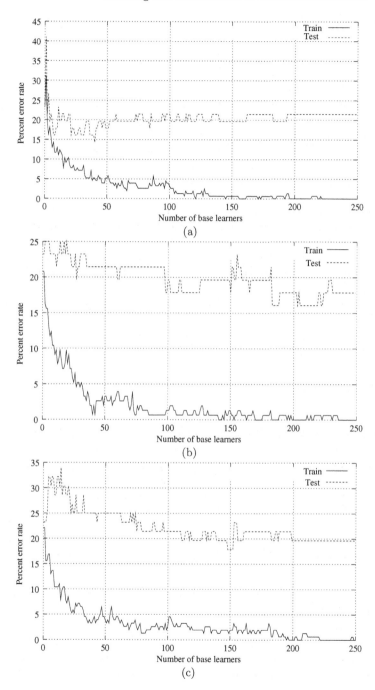

Fig. 3. Error curves for boosting MLP on the monovariety coffees data set. The base classifiers are MLP with 20 (a), 30 (b) and 40 (c) hidden units.

Second, outliers could be present in the data: the high values of the weights registered in subsets of the data could suggest that some data are difficult to learn, or that they are candidates to be outliers [6]. In fact the PCA plot in Fig. 1 shows that, for class one, a subset of the data is distinctly separated from the others, and this could be related to the fact that, for each class, three carousels of vials were analyzed: it is likely that for one of these carousels the autosampler settings have been changed.

Third, effectiveness of boosting fails when data are corrupted by noise [3]: During the sensitive analytic procedures involved in measurements performed through electronic noses, some noise can be added. The PCA plots in Fig. 1 show that drift phenomena are present.

Boosting enhances classification performances, but it requires training of ensembles of learning machines, with increasing computational costs. However, we need to perform an accurate model selection to achieve good results with a single MLP, and this requires an accurate and time consuming planning of the experimentation, while with boosting also a weak learner not accurately tuned for a particular problem can achieve good generalization results. For instance, in the presented experimentation, the worst boosted MLP achieves better result than the best single MLP, both for blended and monovariety data sets (Tab. 1). Moreover, we can also note that sometimes a remarkable reduction in the test error is reached even after few iterations of the boosting algorithm (Fig. 2), reducing in such a way the computational cost.

5   Conclusion

The Electronic Nose represents a new technique for the analysis of odorous mixtures, such as that emitted from coffee. Boosting improved classification performances of electronic noses, reducing in a significant way both the minimum and the average testing error on multiple runs of the boosted ensemble of MLP. Moreover a remarkable reduction of the error is reached even after few iterations of boosting. Even if boosting achieves its best performances with complex algorithms such as C4.5 or backpropagation when there is a reasonably large amount of data available [6], we have halved the testing error on the blended coffee data set, with only 187 training examples. On the other hand the moderate reduction of the test error achieved on the monovariety coffee data set can be explained considering that boosting is especially susceptible to noise and outliers.

Acknowledgments

This work has been partially funded by *Progetto Finalizzato* CNR-MADESS II, INFM and University of Genova. We thank Davide Della Casa for the implementation of the software applications used in this work.

References

[1] G.J. Briem, J.A. Benediktsson, and J.R. Sveinsson. Boosting. Bagging and Consensus Based Classification of Multisource Remote Sensing Data. In *MCS 2001, Cambridge, UK*, volume 2096 of *LNCS*, pages 279–288. Springer-Verlag, 2001.

[2] T.G. Dietterich. Ensemble methods in machine learning. In *MCS 2000, Cagliari, Italy*, volume 1857 of *LNCS*, pages 1–15. Springer-Verlag, 2000.

[3] T.G. Dietterich. An experimental comparison of three methods for constructing ensembles of decision tress: Bagging, boosting and randomization. *Machine Learning*, 40(2):139–158, 2000.

[4] P. Domingos. A Unified Bias-Variance Decomposition and its Applications. In *Proceedings of the 17th ICML*, pages 231–238, Stanford, CA, 2000. Morgan Kaufmann.

[5] Y. Freund and R. Schapire. A decision-theoretic generalization of on-line learning and an application to boosting. *Journal of Computer and Systems Sciences*, 55(1):119–139, 1997.

[6] Y. Freund and R.E. Schapire. Experiments with a new boosting algorithm. In *Proceedings of the 13th ICML*, pages 148–156. Morgan Kauffman, 1996.

[7] C. Furlanello and S. Merler. Boosting of Tree-based Classifiers for Predictive Risk Modeling in GIS. In *MCS 2000, Cagliari, Italy*, volume 1857 of *LNCS*, pages 220–229. Springer-Verlag, 2000.

[8] Gardner and Bartlett. *Electronic noses*. Oxford University Press, 1999.

[9] M. Haruno, S. Shirai, and Y. Ooyama. Using decision trees to construct a practical parser. *Machine Learning*, 34:131–149, 1999.

[10] F. Masulli, G. Valentini, M. Pardo, and G. Sberveglieri. Classification of sensor array data by Output Coding decomposition methods. In *International Workshop MATCHEMS 2001*, pages 169–172, Brescia, Italy, 2001.

[11] S. Merler, C. Furlanello, B. Larcher, and A. Sboner. Tuning Cost-Sensitive Boosting and its Application to Melanoma Diagnosis. In *MCS 2001, Cambridge, UK*, volume 2096 of *LNCS*, pages 32–42. Springer-Verlag, 2001.

[12] M. Pardo, G. Niederjaufner, G. Benussi, E. Comini, G. Faglia, G. Sberveglieri, M. Holmberg, and I. Lundstrom. Data preprocessing enhances the classification of different brands of espresso coffee with an electronic nose. *Sensors and Actuators B*, 69, 2000.

[13] G. Sberveglieri. *Sensors and Actuators B*, 6, 1992.

[14] R. Schapire and Y. Singer. Boostexter: A boosting-based system for text categorization. *Machine Learning*, 39(2/3):135–168, 2000.

[15] R. Schapire, Y. Singer, and A. Singhal. Boosting and Rocchio applied to text filtering. In *Proceedings of the 11th International Conference on Research and Development in Information Retrieval*, 1998.

[16] R.E. Schapire. A brief introduction to boosting. In 16th *IJCAI*, pages 1401–1406. Morgan Kauffman, 1999.

[17] R.E. Schapire, Y. Freund, P. Bartlett, and W. Lee. Boosting the margin: A new explanation for the effectiveness of voting methods. *The Annals of Statistics*, 26(5):1651–1686, 1998.

[18] H. Schwenk and Y. Bengio. Training methods for adaptive boosting of neural networks. In *Advances in Neural Information Processing Systems*, volume 10, pages 647–653. 1998.

[19] G. Valentini and F. Masulli. NEURObjects: an object-oriented library for neural network development. *Neurocomputing*. (in press).

Content-Based Classification of Digital Photos

R. Schettini°, C. Brambilla*, C. Cusano°

°ITC-TIM, *IMATI, Consiglio Nazionale delle Ricerche, Via Ampere 56, 20131 Milano,
Italy

Abstract. Annotating images with a description of the content can facilitate the
organization, storage and retrieval of image databases. It can also be useful in
processing images, by taking into account the scene depicted, in intelligent
scanners, digital cameras, photocopiers, and printers. We present here our
experimentation on indoor/outdoor/close-up content-based image classification.
More specifically, we show that it is possible to relate low-level visual features
to semantic photo categories, such as indoor, outdoor and close-up, using tree
classifiers. We have designed and experimentally compared several
classification strategies, producing a classifier that can provide a reasonably
good performance on a generic photograph database.

1 Introduction

The classification of photographs in semantic categories is an unresolved challenge in
multimedia and imaging communities. Annotating images with a description of the
content can facilitate the organization, storage and retrieval of image databases. It can
also be useful in processing images, by taking into account the scene depicted, in
intelligent scanners, digital cameras, photocopiers, and printers. The most appropriate
strategies of image enhancement, color processing, compression, and rendering
algorithms could be automatically adopted by the system (in a completely
unsupervised manner) if the image content were automatically and reliably inferred
by analyzing its low-level features, that is, features that can be computed without any
a-priori knowledge of the subject depicted. But there have been few efforts to
automate the classification of digital color documents to date. Athitsos and Swain [1]
and Gevers et al. [2] have faced the problem of distinguishing photographs and
graphics, Schettini et al. [3,4] the one of distinguishing photographs, graphics and
texts. As far as photographs classification is concerned, Szummer and Picard [5] have
performed indoor/outdoor classification by using k-nearest neighbors classifiers. To
classify an image, they classified subblocks of the image independently and then
combined the results in different ways. Vailaya et al. [6] have considered the
hierarchical classification of vacation images: at the highest level the images are
sorted into indoor/outdoor classes, outdoor images are then assigned to city/landscape
classes, and finally landscape images are classified in sunset, forest and mountain
categories. They used vector quantization to estimate the class-conditional densities of
the features and then derived a MAP (maximum a posteriori probability) criterion.

F. Roli and J. Kittler (Eds.): MCS 2002, LNCS 2364, pp. 272-281, 2002.

This work presents our experimentation on indoor/outdoor/close-up classification, which is based on the use of tree classifiers. Besides the use of different classification methods, we think that the key difference between our approach and those described in [5] and [6] is that, by using trees, we have been allowed to consider many features at the same time and handle the possible nonhomogeneity of the feature space. Section 2 of the work outlines the classification strategy we adopted, while Section 3 lists and describes the features used to index the images. In Section 4 we report the results obtained.

2   Image Classification

To perform the classification we used tree classifiers constructed according to the CART methodology [7]. Briefly, tree classfiers are classifiers produced by recursively partitioning the predictors space, each split being formed by conditions related to the predictors values. In tree terminology subsets are called nodes: the predictors space is the root node, terminal subsets are terminal nodes, and so on. Once a tree has been constructed, a class is assigned to each of the terminal nodes, and when a new case is processed by the tree, its predicted class is the class associated with the terminal node into which the case finally moves on the basis of its predictors values. The construction process is based on training sets of cases of known class. In the two experiments described here the predictors are the features indexing the whole image and those indexing its subblocks, and the training sets are composed of images whose semantic class is known.

Tree classifiers compare well with other consolidated classifiers. Many simulation studies have shown their accuracy to be very good, often close to the achievable optimum [7]. Moreover, they provide a clear understanding of the conditions that drive the classification process. Finally, they imply no distributional assumptions for the predictors, and can handle both quantitative and qualitative predictors in a very natural way. Since in high dimensional and very complex problems, as is the case here, it is practically impossible to obtain in one step good results in terms of accuracy, no matter how powerful the chosen class of classifiers is, we decided to perform the classification by also using what is called a 'perturbing and combining' method [8,9]. Methods of this kind, which generate in various ways multiple versions of a base classifier and use these to derive an aggregate classifier, have proved very successful in improving accuracy. We used bagging (bootstrap aggregating), since it is particularly effective when the classifiers are unstable, as trees are, that is, when small perturbations in the training sets, or in the construction process of the classifiers, may result in significant changes in the resulting prediction. With bagging the multiple versions of the base classifier are formed by making bootstrap replicates of the training set and using them as new training sets. The aggregation is made by majority vote. In any particular bootstrap replicate each element of the training set may appear repeated times, or not at all, since the replicates are obtained by resampling with replacement. Figure 1 shows how the resulting classifier, called the bagged classifier, is obtained.

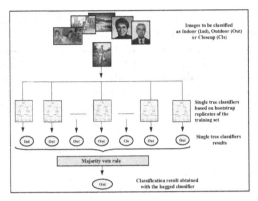

Fig. 1. The scheme of the baggede classifier.

To provide a measure of confidence in the classification results and, still, greater accuracy, we applied an ambiguity rejection rule [10] to the bagged classifier: the classification obtained by means of the majority vote is rejected if the percentage of trees that contribute to it is lower than a given threshold. In this way only those results to which the classifier assigns a given confidence, as set by the threshold, are accepted. The rule is 'global' in the sense that it is constant over the feature space.

3 Image Description Using Pictorial Features

We have used the following features to index the whole images and the subblocks identified by a 4 X 4 equally spaced grid:

Color distribution, described in terms of the moments of inertia (i.e. the mean, variance, skewness and kurtosis) of the distribution of hue, saturation and value [11];

Edge distribution, the statistical information on image edges extracted by Canny's algorithm: i) the percentages of low, medium, and high contrast edge pixels in the image; ii) the parametric thresholds on the gradient strength corresponding to medium and high contrast edges; iii) the number of connected regions identified by closed high contrast contours; iv) the percentage of medium contrast edge pixels connected to high contrast edges [12], v) the histogram of edge directions quantized in 18 bins;

Wavelets. Multiresolution wavelet analysis provides representations of the image data in which both spatial and frequency information are present. In multiresolution wavelet analysis we have four bands for each level of resolution: a low-pass filtered version of the processed image, and three bands of details. Each band corresponds to a coefficient matrix one forth the size of the processed image. In our procedure the features are extracted from the luminance image using a three-step Daubechies multiresolution wavelet expansion producing ten sub-bands [13]. Two energy features, the mean and variance, are then computed for each subband;

Texture. The estimate of texture features was based on the Neighborhood GrayTone Difference Matrix (NGTDM), i.e. coarseness, contrast, busyness, complexity, and strength [14, 15];

Image composition. The HSV color space was partitioned into eleven color zones corresponding to basic color names. This partition was defined and validated empirically by different groups of examiners. The spatial composition of the color regions identified by the process of quantization was described in terms of: fragmentation (the number of color regions), ditribution of the color regions with respect to the center of the image, and distribution of the color regions with respect to the x axis, and with respect to the y axis [16];

Skin Pixels, the percentage of skin pixels. We used a statistical skin color detector based on the r, g chromaticities of the pixel; a training set of 30,000 color skin data was used to model the probability distribution of skin color [17].

4 Experimental Results

As said, the problem was to classify a digital photo as indoor, outdoor, and close-up. The indoor class included photographs of rooms, groups of persons, and details in which the context also indicated that they were taken inside. The outdoor class included natural landscapes, buildings, city shots and details in which the context concurred to indicate that the photographs were taken outside. The close-up class included portraits and photos of objects in which the context supplied no information of where the photo was taken. The image database used in our experiments contained over 9215 images collected from various sources, such as images downloaded from the web, or acquired by scanner. It included some 1750 indoor images, 5000 outdoor images, and 2400 close-ups. All this material varied in size (ranging from 150x150 pixels to 900x900 pixels), resolution, and tonal depth.

In the first experiment we used as predictors the features listed in Section 3, computed on the whole image. Tables 1 and 2 show the classification accuracy achieved using a single tree classifier on the training and test sets respectively. The training set was equally distributed among the typologies present in the three classes, and contained about 5100 images (1200 indoor, 2300 outdoor and 1500 close-up). The test set contained some 4100 photos (550 indoor, 2700 outdoor and 900 close-up) which had not been utilized in the training set.

		Predicted class		
		Indoor	Outdoor	Closeup
True class	Indoor	0.99	0.00	0.01
	OutDoor	0.01	0.98	0.01
	Closeup	0.00	0.01	0.99

Single tree/Training set/no subblock

Table 1. Classification accuracy obtained on the training set using a single tree.

		Predicted class		
		Indoor	Outdoor	Closeup
True class	Indoor	0.76	0.14	0.11
	OutDoor	0.08	0.79	0.12
	Closeup	0.12	0.11	0.78

Single tree/Test set/no subblock

Table 2. Classification accuracy obtained on the test set using a single tree.

Tables 3 and 4 show, instead, the classification accuracy achieved on the training and test sets respectively, using a bagged classifier obtained by aggregating the trees based on 25 bootstrap replicates of the training set. As expected, the use of the bagged classifier produced a marked improvement in classification accuracy: by 12%, 12% and 9% in the test set, for the indoor, outdoor and close-up classes respectively. The aggregation of a larger number of trees brought no significant improvement.

		Predicted class		
		Indoor	Outdoor	Closeup
True class	Indoor	0.99	0.00	0.01
	OutDoor	0.01	0.99	0.00
	Closeup	0.00	0.00	1.00

Bagged classifier/Training set/no subblock

Table 3. Classification accuracy obtained on the training set using the bagged classifier.

		Predicted class		
		Indoor	Outdoor	Closeup
True class	Indoor	0.88	0.07	0.05
	OutDoor	0.05	0.91	0.04
	Closeup	0.07	0.06	0.87

Bagged classifier/Test set/no subblock

Table 4. Classification accuracy obtained on the test set using the bagged classifier.

The misclassified images are generally photographs that are either overexposed or underexposed, or with a background that provide little information about the class to which the images belong. Indoor images misclassified as outdoor often show a window, while outdoor images misclassified as indoor are images of building details, with little outdoor background. We consider acceptable the misclassification of close-up images as indoor or outdoor and viceversa: it simply reveals the overlapping between the close-up and the other categories. We then performed a second experiment to extract the local inter-class differences, using as predictors the same features computed on 4X4 subblocks of the image. The images of the training and test sets are those used in the previous experiment. Tables 5 and 6 show the classification accuracy achieved using a single classifier.

		Predicted class		
		Indoor	Outdoor	Closeup
True class	Indoor	0.98	0.00	0.02
	OutDoor	0.01	0.97	0.02
	Closeup	0.00	0.01	0.99

Single tree/Training set/Subblock

Table 5. Classification accuracy obtained on the training set using a single tree, trained with subblock indexing.

		Predicted class		
		Indoor	Outdoor	Closeup
True class	Indoor	0.79	0.10	0.11
	OutDoor	0.11	0.80	0.09
	Closeup	0.12	0.10	0.78

Single tree/Test set/Subblock

Table 6. Classification accuracy obtained on the test set using a single tree, trained with subblock indexing.

Tables 7 and 8, instead, register the accuracy reached on the training and test sets, respectively, using the bagged classifier.

		Predicted class		
		Indoor	Outdoor	Closeup
True class	Indoor	1.00	0.00	0.00
	OutDoor	0.00	0.99	0.01
	Closeup	0.00	0.01	0.99

Bagged classifier/Training set/Subblock

Table 7. Classification accuracy obtained on the training set using the bagged classifier, in the case of subblock indexing.

		Predicted class		
		Indoor	Outdoor	Closeup
True class	Indoor	0.92	0.05	0.03
	OutDoor	0.07	0.87	0.06
	Closeup	0.06	0.04	0.90

Bagged classifier/Test set/Subblock

Table 8. Classification accuracy obtained on the test set using the bagged classifier, in the case of subblock indexing.

In this experiment as well the application of the bagged classifier improved remarkably the classification accuracy. With respect to the whole image indexing, the 4x4 subblock indexing improved the classification accuracy for the indoor and close-up classes, but not for the outdoor class, for which, in fact, it got worse. In general the subblock indexing experiment presented the same misclassification problems as the whole image indexing experiment.

Figures 2, 3 and 4 show the effects of the application of the rejection rule in the accuracy-rejected plane, with varying rejection thresholds, for the indoor, outdoor and close-up classes respectively. Each figure shows the experimental results, for both the whole (W) and the subblock (SBLK) indexing, for the test set. On the whole, the above figures reflect the better performance of the classifiers based on the 4X4 subblock indexing.

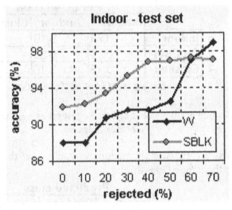

Fig. 2. Accuracy-rejection trade-offs for the indoor class test set.

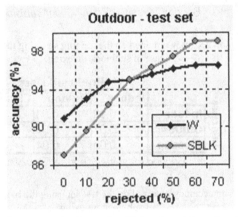

Fig. 3. Accuracy-rejection trade-offs for the outdoor class test set.

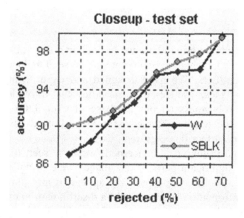

Fig. 4. Accuracy-rejection trade-offs for the close-up class test set.

Table 9 is a summary of the experiments performed in terms of classification accuracy evaluated on particular image typologies of the three classes involved. The percentages refer to the test set. The typologies we considered are *people* and *not people* for the indoor class, *building, landscape, people* and *zoom* for the outdoor class, *people* and *object* for the *close-up* class. For each typology the table reports the classification accuracy obtained by the single classifier (SC), by the bagged classifier (BC) and by the application of the rejection rule (RJ) to the bagged classifier, with the rejection rule threshold *t* set at the intermediate values of 55% and 60%. For each of these classification strategies the results of the experiments with the whole image and with subblock indexing are compared. For the rejection rule experiments, both the classification accuracy of the cases not rejected and the percentage of rejected cases are given.

Image typology	SC		BC		RJ, t=0.55				RJ, t=0.60			
					W		Sblk		W		Sblk	
	W	Sblk	W	Sblk	accur.	reject.	accur.	reject.	accur.	reject.	accur.	reject.
Indoor - people	73	77	88	91	87	4	92	4	88	11	93	12
Indoor - not people	80	83	90	93	90	2	93	2	90	8	94	9
Outdoor - building	80	86	94	92	93	2	94	4	95	4	96	9
Outdoor - landscape	88	94	98	96	98	1	96	3	98	2	98	7
Outdoor - people	70	65	83	74	83	10	77	12	86	19	81	28
Outdoor - zoom	83	78	95	89	95	3	92	7	95	6	95	15
Closeup - object	81	83	89	91	89	4	91	4	92	8	93	11
Closeup - people	73	68	83	87	83	2	87	7	88	22	90	20

Table 9. Comparison of the classification accuracy (in percentage) of the experiments, evaluated on particular image typologies in the test set.

5 Conclusions

With the experiments described here we have shown that it is possible to relate low-level visual features to semantic photo categories, such as indoor, outdoor and close-up, using tree classifiers. We have designed and experimentally compared several classification strategies, producing a classifier that provided a reasonably good performance and robustness on our database of over 9200 images collected from various sources. The results obtained have also allowed us to identify points that would benefit from further investigation.

As far as **image indexing** is concerned, we have seen that classification results were worst when significant parts of the images were occupied by skin regions, .i.e. by people (see Table 9). As people may appear in any photograph of the classes considered, this information is not actually a discriminant in establishing the category to which a photo belongs. We are now refining the skin/people detector in order to make it much more stable (still assuming uncontrolled lighting conditions). We should then like to use significant skin regions to drive adaptive image partitions and then classify the parts of image that are not "occupied" by people. In fact, it is the context in which the subject is depicted that guides our interpretation of the scene.

With regard to the **classification strategy**, the experiments performed have proved the feasibility of using the bagging method and the rejection rule to boost classification accuracy. These tools, however, could be further refined. In particular, we should like to create a more robust rejection rule by incorporating, together with the global measure proposed here, feature space-dependent information, such as the accuracy inside the terminal nodes. An online version of our system is available at the address: http://quicklook.itim.mi.cnr.it/qclass/quickclass.html.

Acknowledgement

This investigation was performed as a part of a ST Microelectronics research contract. The authors thank ST Microelectronics for permission to present this paper.

References

1. V. Athitsos, M. Swain, Distinguishing photographs and graphics on the World Wide, Web. Proc. Workshop in Content-based Access to Image and Video Libraries, 10-17 (1997).
2. T. Gevers, AWM Smeulders, PicTo Seek: combining color and shape invarinat features for image retrieval, IEEE Trans. On Image Processing, **19**(1), 102-120 (2000).
3. R. Schettini, C. Brambilla, A. Valsasna, M. De Ponti, Content-based image classification, Proc. Internet Imaging Conference, Proceedings of SPIE 3964 (G.B. Beretta, R. Schettini eds.), 28-33 (2000).
4. R. Schettini, C. Brambilla, A. Valsasna, M. De Ponti, Automatic image classification using pictorial featres, Proc. VIII Color Imaging Conference: Scottsdale (Arizona), 184-188 (2000).
5. M Szummer, R. Picard, Indoor-outdoor image classification, Proc. Int. Workshop on Content-Based Access of Image and Video databases, 42-51 (1998).

6. A. Vailaya, M. Figueiredo, A. K. Jain, and H.-J. Zhang, Image classification for content-based indexing, IEEE Transactions on Image Processing, **10**(1) ,117-130 (2001).
7. L. Breiman, J.H. Friedman, R.A. Olshen, C.J. Stone, Classification and Regression Trees, Wadsworth and Brooks/Cole, 1984.
8. L. Breiman, Bagging predictors, Machine learning, **26**, 123-140 (1996).
9. L. Breiman, Arcing classifiers, Annals of Statistics, **26**, 801-849 (1998).
10. Vailaya and A. Jain, Reject option for VQ-based bayesian classification, Proc. 15th International Conference on Pattern Recognition, Barcelona, Spain, September, 2000.
11. M.A Stricker, M. Orengo, Similarity of color images, SPIE Storage and Retrieval for Image and Video Databases III Conference, (1995).
12. J. Canny, A computational approach to edge detection, IEEE Trans. On Pattern Analysis and Machine Intelligence, IEEE-**8,** 679-698 (1986).
13. P. Scheunders , S. Livens, G. Van de Wouwer, P. Vautrot, D. Van Dyck, Wavelet-based texture analysis, International Journal Computer Science and Information management. wcc.ruca.ua.ac.be/~livens/WTA/, (1997).
14. M. Amadasun, R. King, Textural features corresponding to textural properties, IEEE Transaction on System, Man and Cybernetics, **19**(5), 1264-1274 (1989).
15. H. Tamura, S. Mori, T. Yamawaki, Textural features corresponding to visual perception, IEEE Transaction on System, Man and Cybernetics, **8**, 460-473 (1978).
16. P. Ciocca, R. Schettini, A relevance feedback mechanism for content-based retrieval, Information Processing and Management, **35**, 605-632 (1999).
17. Y. Miyake, H. Saitoh, H. Yaguchi, and N. TsukadaFacial Pattern detection and color correction from television picture for newspaper printing, Journal of Imaging Technology, **16**, 165-169 (1990).

Classifier Combination for *In Vivo* Magnetic Resonance Spectra of Brain Tumours

Julià Minguillón[1], Anne Rosemary Tate[2,4], Carles Arús[3], and
John R. Griffiths[2]

[1] Unitat de Combinatòria i Comunicació Digital, Escola Tècnica i Superior
d'Enginyeries, Universitat Autònoma de Barcelona, 08193 Bellaterra, Spain
jminguillon@ccd.uab.es
[2] CRC Biomedical MR Research Group, St George's Hospital Medical School,
University of London, Cranmer Terrace, London, SW17 0RE, UK
[3] Departament de Bioquímica i Biologia Molecular, Universitat Autònoma de
Barcelona, 08193 Bellaterra, Spain
[4] School of Cognitive and Computing Sciences, University of Sussex, Falmer,
Brighton, UK.

Abstract. In this paper we present a multi-stage classifier for magnetic
resonance spectra of human brain tumours which is being developed as
part of a decision support system for radiologists. The basic idea is to
decompose a complex classification scheme into a sequence of classifiers,
each specialising in different classes of tumours and trying to reproduce
part of the WHO classification hierarchy. Each stage uses a particular
set of classification features, which are selected using a combination of
classical statistical analysis, splitting performance and previous knowledge. Classifiers with different behaviour are combined using a simple
voting scheme in order to extract different error patterns: LDA, decision
trees and the k-NN classifier. A special label named "unknown" is used
when the outcomes of the different classifiers disagree. Cascading is also
used to incorporate class distances computed using LDA into decision
trees. Both cascading and voting are effective tools to improve classification accuracy. Experiments also show that it is possible to extract
useful information from the classification process itself in order to help
users (clinicians and radiologists) to make more accurate predictions and
reduce the number of possible classification mistakes.

1 Introduction

[1]H Magnetic Resonance Spectroscopy (MRS) [1] is attracting much attention for
non-invasive diagnosis of brain tumours. These tumours currently present a difficult clinical problem: the oncologist needs to know the type of cell from which the
cancer originates, as well as the "grade", or degree of malignancy, before choosing appropriate therapy. Some benign tumours respond well to surgery, whereas
more aggressive types that are essentially incurable may respond temporarily
to palliative treatment. Radiological examination by MRI does not usually give

F. Roli and J. Kittler (Eds.): MCS 2002, LNCS 2364, pp. 282–292, 2002.

conclusive diagnoses, and an incorrect diagnosis could result in the patient failing to receive life-saving treatment. Consequently, the current "gold standard" is stereotactic biopsy followed by histopathology. Biopsy of the brain is expensive, unpleasant for the patient and sometimes has severe side effects, with even occasional deaths. There is thus much interest in MRS, which is a totally non-invasive method - nothing is injected or biopsied. ^{1}H MRS of brain tumours can be performed with many hospital MRI instruments, after slight modification. It gives a spectrum in which the peaks represent signals from hydrogen atoms in chemicals within the tumour. Different tumour types contain characteristic patterns of chemicals, and there are also patterns associated with greater or lesser degrees of malignancy. However, visual interpretation of these spectra is difficult, with many ambiguous cases, and few doctors are trained in it. Consequently, clinical MRS is little used at present, and there have been many attempts to develop automated classification procedures. Hitherto, these have only worked with artificial datasets in which the spectra are drawn from a few well-characterised tumour types [2, 3, 4]. Our study is the first, to our knowledge, to tackle the "real world" problem in which an unknown brain tumour can represent any possible tumour type or grade, and to make classifications according to the standard WHO categories.

There are some fundamental problems when developing an automatic procedure for classifying brain tumour spectra. There is a long list of tumour types [5], some of which are very rare. In addition, some diagnostic criteria are of fundamental importance (e.g. "is it benign or malignant?") whereas others are of merely academic significance. Furthermore, some spectra are less satisfactory than others, either for technical reasons or because the tumour itself contains areas of cyst or haemorrhage. Developing a classifier that can take a spectrum from any undiagnosed tumour and assign it unequivocally to the appropriate class, may therefore not be possible. But this is not necessarily an important goal as in most cases there will be much useful evidence from factors such as the clinical presentation or the anatomical MRI that narrow down the diagnostic possibilities. We have therefore approached this as a multi-stage problem. Ideally, the system would: reproduce the WHO classification grading structure: perform well when the number of samples is low; use previous knowledge about the problem; be robust when the training data might contain errors, since the "gold standard" pathology classification is not always 100% accurate; and finally, help the users to extract relevant information from the classifier, rather than provide (possibly more accurate) "black box" classifiers that they cannot understand. In addition we need a method for selecting the best points or regions of the spectra for classification, since an MR spectrum is a vector of between 512 and 4096 spectral intensities.

Decision trees [6] allow us to build classifiers that partially fulfil all these requirements. Previous experiments [7] with MR spectra show that different classifiers make different mistakes. This can be exploited using a simple voting scheme which labels as "unknown" those samples where different classifiers disagree. An advantage of combining several classifiers in a multi-stage scheme is that different features (i.e. points or regions of the spectra) may be used at different levels. Several classifiers may be used to establish a minimum threshold to ensure class, or "unknown" and, when two classifiers disagree, this fact may be used to find (or indicate the possibility of) mixtures of two or more classes.

This paper is organised as follows: Section 2 describes the structure of the tumour classification problem and the available data sets and pre-processing. Section 3 describes the classifiers used and the multi-stage scheme. Section 4 describes the experiments and Section 5 summarises the conclusions and proposes future work.

2   Classification of MR Spectra

2.1   Data

The spectra were acquired at three clinical centres: Institut de Diagnòstic per la Imatge (IDI) Bellvitge, Spain, Centre Diagnostic Pedralbes (CDP) Barcelona, Spain, and St. George's Hospital (SGH), London, U.K. One short echo ^{1}H (20 or 30 ms) spectrum was acquired for each patient. Prior to entering the spectra into the analysis, strict quality control and validation procedures were applied to all the data. Following biopsy, the pathology slides for each case was examined by a panel of neuro-pathologists to provide a consensus diagnosis (see http://carbon.uab.es/INTERPRET/cdap.html). Only those tumour classes for which we had at least 4 representatives were used. This resulted in the following classes of spectra: 81 astrocytomas (18 grade II, 6 grade III, and 57 grade IV), 32 metastases, 37 meningiomas, 6 oligodendrogliomas, 6 lymphomas, 5 primitive neuroectodermal tumour (pnets), 4 schwannomas, 4 haemangioblastomas and 14 samples from normal volunteers. Figure 1 shows a plot of a typical spectrum.

2.2   Pre-processing

All spectral processing (from raw signal to processed spectrum) was carried out automatically using a set of stand-alone programs developed (in C) for the decision support tool. The intensities in frequency region known to represent the major peaks was extracted from each spectrum and the resulting vector (of 512 intensity values) was then normalised to have norm $L_2 = 1$. We do not use all 512 points, because only those in range [0.5, 4.2] ppm^1 are considered to have relevant information for tumour classification, giving a total of 195 variables, from v_{151} (4.2 ppm) to v_{345} (0.5 ppm).

3   Combining Classifiers

Combining classifiers with different bias-variance decomposition behaviour, can reduce both bias and variance and thus improve classification error [8]. In this

---

^{1} the ppm scale defines the positions of the peaks with respect to a predefined reference.

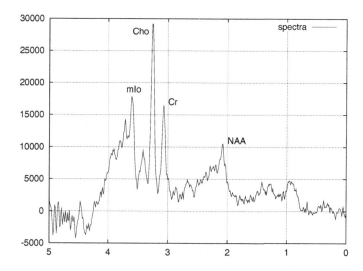

Fig. 1. A typical spectrum from a grade II astrocytoma, showing the position of the peaks representing myoinositol (mIo), choline (Cho), creatine (Cr) and N-acetylaspartate (NAA).

paper we describe how we build a sequence of classifiers each specialising in a concrete problem, and combine them in a way that allows the extraction of different information about the samples being classified. We decided to develop a multi-stage classification system that reproduces the hierarchical structure of the WHO tumour classification that is used by clinicians. Three different types of classifiers are used: linear discriminant analysis (LDA) [9], decision trees [6] and the nearest neighbour classifier (k-NN) [10]. These classifiers were chosen because LDA is simple and interpretable (it is easy to show results and reasons), and good for small sample set sizes. Nevertheless, it may not be very accurate depending on the complexity of the boundaries defined by the different tumour classes and whether or not these overlap, or are mixtures. Decision trees are also simple and interpretable (when using orthogonal splits). They have a good generalisation performance and may include *a priori* knowledge about the problem being solved. Finally, the k-NN classifier is very simple and fast when the number of samples and data dimensionality are small. No training is needed, and as the number of samples is small, no special techniques for reducing nearest neighbour cost are required. Experiments show that the optimal value for k is very sensitive to the number of samples available for each class, so we try several values for k choosing the smallest k yielding a good generalisation error. Other methods (support vector machines or neural networks, for example) generally require more samples than we have available or do not allow the users to interpret results easily.

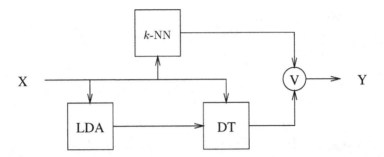

Fig. 2. Cascading and voting architecture for each classification stage. The LDA classifier and the decision tree (DT) are cascaded and then combined with the k-NN classifier using a simple voting scheme (V).

At each stage, two classifiers are built: a k-NN classifier and a decision tree. The results of both classifiers are combined using a voting scheme with a very simple rule: if both outcomes agree, the label will be the outcome of the voting scheme, otherwise, generate "unknown". The basic idea of combining k-NN and decision trees is to exploit their different behaviour to improve classification performance. Since they try to solve the same problem using different approaches, they may make different mistakes. When enough data is available, LDA is used with decision trees as the first stage of a cascading ensemble [11]; the latter uses the class distances and transformed points computed by LDA. Figure 2 shows the combined cascading and voting scheme used at each stage of the classification system. Cascading can be thought of as the process of asking a sequence of experts to give a decision. The cheapest (simplest) expert is consulted first and then the information that it provides is passed to the next expert in the sequence, and so on. The second expert decides whether to use this additional information or not.

3.1   Feature Selection

It is known that different points from the spectra provide plausible biochemical explanations for discriminating between tumour classes. We use this "prior" knowledge to select the points used as classification features. Trying to build a classification system using LDA or the k-NN classifier using the 195 input variables is pointless: data dimensionality is too high and the number of samples for several classes is too small. It is important to include only those variables which are relevant to the classification problem. A classical correlation analysis may be used to find the points with higher discriminating properties. A decision tree can also be used to find other classification variables that remain hidden using correlation analysis: at each stage we take the data set containing the samples from the classes being classified, and a limited depth decision tree (three or four levels is enough for such small data sets) is built without any pruning. For each split we rank classification features according to its splitting performance, and (depending on the stage and data set being considered), the first or the two first classification features are selected. Then, all these variables that have statistical significance for classification purposes are checked with an expert spectroscopist and those that cannot represent known metabolites are discarded. This approach has been successfully used previously [4, 7].

3.2   The "Unknown" Class

As described in the previous section, when the two classifiers of the same stage disagree, the outcome of the classifier is "unknown". This value may also be used to label those predictions made by a decision tree with a small margin. This margin is defined for each leaf as the probability of making a right prediction minus the probability of making a mistake. Therefore, the new labelling rule for a leaf i is

$$l'_i(t) = \begin{cases} l_i(t) & \text{if } P\{t_i(x) = y\} - P\{t_i(x) \neq y\} > \epsilon \\ \text{"unknown"} & \text{otherwise.} \end{cases}$$

where $t_i(x)$ is the computed label using majority voting. This allows us to discard those samples that fall in leaves which contain elements from several classes. The value for ϵ depends on the number of classes and it is determined empirically. A similar approach has been successfully used in [12].

4   Experimental Results

The classification system was split into four stages: 1) discriminates between tumour and normal samples, 2) tries to classify tumour samples as benign or malignant, 3) tries to separate malignant tumours according to their malignancy grade and in 4) several classifiers are built for each malignancy grade in order to discriminate between WHO tumour classes. Each experiment was carried as follows: at each stage, the original data set containing all samples related to such stage is split using N-fold cross-validation (NFCV) with $N = 10$ following the recommendations of [9] for small size data sets. This process is repeated five times and all results are averaged, resulting in a total of 50 experiments at each stage. Decision trees were built using entropy as the splitting criterion and pruned back using tree size and misclassification error as complexity measures.

4.1   Stage 1: Tumour Vs. Normal

Separating tumours from normal samples is the easiest stage. It is well known that, unless the voxel (volume from which the spectra is acquired) has been placed in a region where an aggressive infiltrating tumour is mixed with brain parenquima, tumour samples have little or no N-Acetylaspartate (NAA) which is shown by a peak at 2.0 ppm. In addition, tumours have much higher choline levels (shown by a peak at 3.22 ppm). When a decision tree was used for feature selection, two regions were detected as the most important for separating the two groups: the NAA peak and the Creatine peak (around 3.03 ppm). Thus, we selected variables v_{200} (Choline), v_{210} (Creatine), and v_{263} (NAA). Using a k-NN classifier with $k = 1$, a 99.3% classification accuracy is achieved, showing that this first stage can be fully automated with almost no intervention by the radiologist. Two of the samples were misclassified: S1 and S2. When the spectra were visually inspected it appeared that this may have been due to the fact that the voxel from which the spectra were obtained included a large proportion of normal brain parenquima (due to voxel mispositioning). A decision tree was also built using the same points. In this case, classification accuracy is 99.2%, and two samples are misclassified: S1 again, and a normal sample misclassified as tumor (S3). Decision trees always use v_{263} to separate tumors from normal samples. If we combine the outcomes of the two classifiers, only one sample remains unclassified, S1. For the other two samples, the generated label is "unknown", as both outcomes disagree. This fact can be used to alert the spectroscopist to place the voxel in another position.

4.2   Stage 2: Malignant Vs. Benign Tumours

All samples labelled as tumour by the previous classifier are used to build a new classifier which tries to determine whether a tumour is malignant or not. Meningiomas and schwannomas are benign tumors, the rest are malignant or have malignant potential. We also have several tumors which are in the borderline (haemangioblastomas), and it would be useful to identify them. However, there are only four samples of these. Since haemangioblastomas are considered benign tumors, but with uncertain malignant potential, we decided to treat them as benign and delay final classification to an optional third stage. Six points were used as classification features: v_{244} (2.36 ppm, glutamate, glutamine and macromolecules), v_{172} (3.74 ppm, glutamate, glutamine, alanine), v_{210} (2.98 ppm, creatine), v_{191} (3.38 ppm), v_{159} (3.99 ppm) and v_{304} (1.22 ppm, lipid/lactate). We tested several values for k, and $k = 3$ produced the best classification performance. LDA and decision trees were tested alone but also in a cascading ensemble. Table 1 shows the results for this stage. Notice that cascading reduces decision tree misclassification error noticeably.

4.3   Stage 3: Malignancy Grade

The third stage tries to establish the malignancy grade for those samples classified as malignant tumours by the previous stage. We do not try to separate benign tumours into meningiomas, schwannomas and haemangioblastomas because we only have 4 samples of the two last tumour classes as compared with the 37 meningiomas, and the results we obtain are completely biased towards accurately classifying meningiomas, even if we force equal *a priori* probabilities. This will be accomplished when new samples are available. Determining the degree of malignancy is important, because it gives an indication of the

Table 1. Left table: classification accuracy for each classifier, the cascading ensemble and the resulting voting scheme. P is the percentage of samples not classified as "unknown", and E is the misclassification error. Right table: confusion matrix for the voting scheme. β is the percentage of tumours classified as a class that really belong to such class.

classifier	P	E
LDA	—	0.1682
k-NN ($k = 3$)	—	0.1235
Tree	—	0.0894
LDA + Tree	—	0.0788
Voting scheme	89.9%	0.0563

class	benign	malignant	unknown	total
benign	139	31	48	218
malignant	12	582	38	632
total	151	163	86	850
β	92.1%	94.9%	—	—

patient outcome, and may determine the treatment prescribed. We use three malignancy grades commonly accepted, labelled low, medium and high. Low grade (WHO grade II) consists of low-grade astrocytomas, oligo-astrocytomas and oligo-dendrogliomas. Medium grade (WHO grade III) consists of astrocytomas (and anaplastic oligoastrocytoma, but we do not have enough samples to include them in our experiments). Finally, high grade (WHO grade IV) includes metastasis, glioblastomas, pnets and lymphomas. Results are shown in Table 2. The variables selected for this stage are v_{181}, v_{201}, v_{309}, v_{317}, v_{264} and v_{197}.

Table 2. Left table: classification accuracy for each classifier, the cascading ensemble and the resulting voting scheme (no cascading). Right table: confusion matrix for the voting scheme (no cascading).

classifier	P	E
LDA	—	0.2154
k-NN ($k = 5$)	—	0.1815
Tree	—	0.1108
LDA + Tree	—	0.1231
Voting scheme	83.8%	0.0679

class	low	medium	high	unknown	total
low	57	0	8	55	120
medium	4	0	17	9	30
high	8	0	451	41	500
total	69	0	476	105	650
β	82.6%	—	94.7%	—	—

Notice that in this case cascading does not improve tree performance. The reason is that we only have 6 samples for medium grade tumours and LDA performs poorly. Furthermore, those samples do not form a cluster, so k-NN makes also a lot of mistakes, and therefore, not any sample is labeled as medium grade. Because grade III is an intermediate stage, classifying medium grade tumours is often a problem even for the pathologists.

4.4 Stage 4: Tumour Class

The last stage of our classifier consists of two different classifiers. The first one tries to separate low-grade tumours into oligos (both oligo-astrocytomas and oligo-dendrogliomas) and astrocytomas. The second classifier tries to separate high-grade tumours in primary tumours and metastasis, and then primary tumours in glioblastomas, lymphomas and pnets.

Low grade malignant tumours A very simple classifier for separating low-grade astrocytomas and oligodendrogliomas was built using v_{227}, v_{172} and v_{181}. Table 3 shows the results for this classifier. Using only these three points, results are very good. Cascading drops misclassification error of the decision tree from 0.12 to 0.08, even with a high misclassification error of the LDA classifier.

Table 3. Left table: Classification accuracy for each classifier, the cascading ensemble and the resulting voting scheme. Right table: confusion matrix for the voting scheme.

classifier	P	E
LDA	—	0.21
k-NN (k = 3)	—	0.16
Tree	—	0.12
LDA + Tree	—	0.08
Voting scheme	84.0%	0.0476

class	astro	oligo	unknown	total
astro	64	0	8	72
oligo	4	16	8	28
total	68	16	16	100
β	94.1%	100.0%	—	—

High grade malignant tumours This is probably the most difficult question nowadays related to tumour classification, since this is the most common tumour group, and the different tumour types within it are those the radiologists most easily confuse when using MRI. This classifier is in fact a two-stage classifier: the first one tries to separate primary tumours from the rest (metastasis). The second one tries to identify each one of the primary tumour classes (glioblastomas, lymphomas and pnets). Due to the lack of space, we only show results for the first classifier, which is in fact the hardest problem to solve. Furthermore, we only have a few lymphomas and pnets, so our results are biased towards glioblastomas. We used v_{317}, v_{304}, v_{242}, v_{236}, v_{215} and v_{220}. Table 4 shows the results for this classifier. We decided to include the cascading ensemble into the voting scheme results because β values are more balanced. Notice that these results are the worst, as they correspond to the hardest problem we try to solve in this paper.

Table 4. Left table: Classification accuracy for each classifier, the cascading ensemble and the resulting voting scheme. Right table: confusion matrix for the voting scheme.

classifier	P	E
LDA	—	0.392
k-NN (k = 5)	—	0.326
Tree	—	0.188
LDA + Tree	—	0.218
Voting scheme	75.0%	0.1733

class	primary	secondary	unknown	total
primary	278	3	59	340
secondary	62	32	66	160
total	340	35	125	500
β	81.8%	91.4%	—	—

5   Conclusions and Future Work

In this paper we have presented a multi-stage classifier for classification of ^{1}H MR spectra from brain samples. Our goal was to build a classification system which may help clinicians to take decisions and learn from the classification process itself. Several conclusions may be drawn:

- The inherent hierarchical structure of the tumour classification problem is well described using a sequential combination of classifiers.
- Each stage uses its own set of classification features reducing classification cost and learning algorithm resilience.
- When the number of samples for each class is large enough, cascading improves decision tree performance, using LDA as a first classifier.
- Combining several classifiers with different bias-variance behaviour under a voting scheme allows us to have partial classification and a more robust classification system.

Further work is in progress to improve the classification results, but also to learn more about the classification process itself: which tumor classes are misclassified more often, which stage is more critical, system response to rare tumors, and so. Cascading not only at each stage but also between stages is also an interesting subject of study. A completely independent test set is being prepared to test the performance of the classification path developed, so we will be able to check our classification system in a real scenario.

Acknowledgements

This paper was partially supported by Spanish government grant TIC2000-0739-C04-01, and EU grant INTERPRET IST-199-10310. We thank the IDI, CDP and SGH centres for providing the validated data set used in this paper.

References

[1] Danielsen, E.R., Ross, B.: MRS Diagnosis of Neurological Diseases. Marcel Dekker, Inc, NY (1999)
[2] Preul, M.C., et al.: Accurate, noninvasive diagnosis of human brain tumors by using proton magnetic resonance spectroscopy. Nature Medicine **2** (1996) 323–325
[3] Hagberg, G., et al.: *In vivo* proton MR spectroscopy of human gliomas: Definition of metabolic coordinates for multi-dimensional classification. Magnetic Resonance in Medicine **34** (1995) 242–252
[4] Tate, A.R., et al.: Towards a method for automated classification of 1H MRS spectra from brain tumours. NMR in Biomedicine **11** (1998) 177–191
[5] Kleihues, P., Sobin, L.H.: WHO classification of tumors. Cancer **88** (2000) 2887
[6] Breiman, L., Friedman, J.H., Olshen, R.A., Stone, C.J.: Classification and Regression Trees. Wadsworth International Group (1984)

[7] Tate, A.R., Ladroue, C., Minguillón, J.: Developing classifiers for single-voxel ^{1}H brain tumour *in vivo* spectra for the INTERPRET decision support tool. Technical Report CSRP543, U. of Sussex, Cognitive and Comp. Sciences (2002)

[8] Domingos, P.: A unified bias-variance decomposition and its applications. In: Proc. of the 17th Int. Conf. on ML, Stanford, CA, USA (2000) 231–238

[9] Hastie, T., Tibshirani, R., Friedman, J.: The elements of statistical learning. Data mining, inference and prediction. Springer series in statistics. Springer (2001)

[10] Dasarathy, B.: Nearest Neighbor Pattern Classification Techniques. IEEE Computer Society Press, Los Alamitos, CA, USA (1991)

[11] Gama, J., Brazdil, P.: Cascade generalization. ML **41** (2000) 315–343

[12] Minguillón, J., Pujol, J., Zeger, K.: Progressive classification scheme for document layout recognition. In: SPIE Proc., Volume 3816, Denver, CO (1999) 241–250

Combining Classifiers of Pesticides Toxicity through a Neuro-fuzzy Approach

Emilio Benfenati[1], Paolo Mazzatorta[1], Daniel Neagu[2], and Giuseppina Gini[2]

[1] Istituto di Ricerche Farmacologiche "Mario Negri" Milano,
Via Eritrea, 62, 20157 Milano, Italy
{Benfenati, Mazzatorta}@ marionegri.it
[2] Dipartimento di Elettronica e Informazione, Politecnico di Milano,
Piazza L. da Vinci 32, 20133 Milano, Italy
Neagu@fusberta.elet.polimi.it, Gini@elet.polimi.it
http://airlab.elet.polimi.it/imagetox

Abstract. The increasing amount and complexity of data in toxicity prediction calls for new approaches based on hybrid intelligent methods for mining the data. This focus is required even more in the context of increasing number of different classifiers applied in toxicity prediction. Consequently, there exist a need to develop tools to integrate various approaches. The goal of this research is to apply neuro-fuzzy networks to provide an improvement in combining the results of five classifiers applied in toxicity of pesticides. Nevertheless, fuzzy rules extracted from the trained developed networks can be used to perform useful comparisons between the performances of the involved classifiers. Our results suggest that the neuro-fuzzy approach of combining classifiers has the potential to significantly improve common classification methods for the use in toxicity of pesticides characterization, and knowledge discovery.

1 Introduction

Quantitative structure–activity relationships (QSARs) correlate chemical structure to a wide variety of physical, chemical, biological (including biomedical, toxicological, ecotoxicological) and technological (glass transition temperatures of polymers, critical micelle concentrations of surfactants, rubber vulcanization rates) properties. Suitable correlations, once established and validated, can be used to predict properties for compounds as yet unmeasured or even unknown.

Classification systems for QSAR studies are quite usual for carcinogenicity [8], because in this case carcinogenicity classes are defined by regulatory bodies such as IARC and EPA. For ecotoxicity, most of the QSAR models are regressions, referring to the dose giving the toxic effect in 50% of the animals (for instance LC_{50}: lethal concentration for 50% of the test animals). This dose is a continuous value and regression seems the most appropriate algorithm. However, classification affords some advantages. Indeed, i) the regulatory values are indicated as toxicity classes and ii) classification can allow a better management of noisy data. For this reason we investigated classification in the past [7], [8] and also in this study. No general rule exists to define

F. Roli and J. Kittler (Eds.): MCS 2002, LNCS 2364, pp. 293-303, 2002.
© Springer-Verlag Berlin Heidelberg 2002

an approach suitable to solve a specific classification problem. In several cases, a selection of descriptors is the only essential condition to develop a general system. The next step consists in defining the best computational method to develop robust structure–activity models.

Artificial neural networks (ANNs) represent a suitable tool that have been used to develop a wide range of real-world applications, especially when other solving methods fail [3]. They exhibit advantages such as learning ability from data, classification capabilities and generalization, computationally fastness once trained due to parallel processing, and noise tolerance. The major shortcoming of neural networks is represented by their low degree of comprehensibility (characterized as "black boxes"). More transparency is offered by fuzzy neural networks FNN [13], [15], [17], which represent a paradigm combining the comprehensibility and capabilities of fuzzy reasoning to handle uncertainty, and the capabilities to learn from examples.

The paper is organized as follows. Section 2 presents the aspects of data preparation, the chemical descriptors, some of the most used classification techniques and shows how they behave for toxicology modeling, with a emphasis to pesticides task. Section 3 proposes the neuro-fuzzy approach in order to manage the integration of all the studied classifiers, based on the structure of Implicit Knowledge Module (IKM-FNN) of the hybrid intelligent system NIKE (Neural explicit&Implicit Knowledge inference system [16]) developed in Matlab[1]. Preliminary results indicate that combination of several classifiers may lead to the improved performance [5], [10], [11]. The extracted fuzzy rules give new insights about the applicability domain of the implied classifiers. Conclusions of the paper are summarized in the last section.

2   Materials and Methods

2.1   Data Set

For this paper a data set constituted of 57 common organophosphorous compounds has been investigated. The main objective is to propose a good benchmark for the classification studies developed in this area. The toxicity values are the result of a wide bibliographic research mainly from "*the Pesticide Manual*", ECOTOX database system, RTECS and HSDB [1]. An important problem that we faced is connected with the variability that the toxicity data presents [2]. Indeed, it is possible to find different fonts showing for the same compound and the same end–point LC_{50} different for about two orders of magnitude. Such variability is due to different factors, as the different individual reactions of organisms tested, the different laboratory procedures, or is due to different experimental conditions or accidental errors.

The toxicity value was expressed as $Log_{10}(1/LC_{50})$. Then the values were scaled in the interval [-1..1]. Four classes were defined: Class 1 [-1..-0.5), Class 2 [-0.5..0), Class 3 [0..0.5), Class 4 [0.5..1] (Table 2).

---

[1] The MathWorks, Inc.

2.2 Descriptors

A set of 150 descriptors were calculated by different software: Hyperchem 5.0[2], CODESSA 2.2.1[3], Pallas 2.1[4]. They are split into six categories: Constitutional (34), Geometrical (14), Topological (38), Electrostatic (57), Quantum–chemicals (6), and Physico–chemicals (4). A selection of the variables, to better describe the molecules, is necessary to obtain a good model. There is the risk that some descriptors does not add information, increase the noise, and make more complex the result analysis. Furthermore, using a relatively low number of variables, the risk of overfitting is reduced. The descriptors selection (Table 1) was obtained by Principal Components Analysis (PCA), with the Principal Components Eigenvalue (Scree) Plot method, using SCAN[5]:

Table 1. Names of the chemical descriptors involved in the classification task.

	Cat.	Cod.
Moment of inertia A	G	D1
Relative number of N atoms	C	D2
Binding energy (Kcal/mol)	Q	D3
DPSA-3 Difference in CPSAs (PPSA3-PNSA3) [Zefirov's PC]	E	D4
Max partial charge (Qmax) [Zefirov's PC]	E	D5
ZX Shadow / ZX Rectangle	G	D6
Number of atoms	C	D7
Moment of inertia C	G	D8
PNSA-3 Atomic charge weighted PNSA [Zefirov's PC]	E	D9
HOMO (eV)	E	D10
LUMO (eV)	Q	D11
Kier&Hall index (order 3)	T	D12

2.3 Classification Algorithms

The classification algorithms used for this work are five: LDA (Linear Discriminant Analysis), RDA (Regularized Discriminant Analysis), SIMCA (Soft Independent Modeling of Class Analogy), KNN (K Nearest Neighbors classification), CART (Classification And Regression Tree). The first two are parametric statistical systems based on the Fisher's discriminant analysis, the third and fourth are not parametrical statistical methods, the last one is a classification tree.

LDA: the Fischer's linear discrimination is an empirical method based on p–dimensional vectors of attributes. Thus the separation between classes occurs by an hyperplane, which divides the p–dimensional space of attributes.

RDA: The variations introduced in this model have the aim to obviate the principal problems that afflict both the linear and quadratic discrimination. The regulation more efficient was carried out by Friedman, who proposed a compromise between the two previous techniques using a biparametrical method for the estimation (λ and γ).

---

[2] Hypercube Inc., Gainsville, Florida, USA
[3] SemiChem Inc., Shawnee, Kansas, USA
[4] CompuDrug; Budapest, Hungary
[5] SCAN (Software for Chemometric Analysis) v.1.1, from Minitab: http://www.minitab.com

SIMCA: the model is one of the first used in chemometry for modeling classes and, contrarily to the techniques before described, is not parametrical. The idea is to consider separately each class and to look for a representation using the principal components. An object is assigned to a class on the basis of the residual distance, rsd^2, that it has from the model which represent the class itself:

$$r_{ijg}^2 = \left(\hat{x}_{ijg} - x_{ijg}\right)^2, \quad rsd_{ig}^2 = \left(\sum_j r_{ijg}^2\right)/(p - M_g) \tag{1}$$

where $\hat{x}_{igj}$ = co–ordinates of the object's projections on the inner space of the mathematical model for the class, x_{igj} = object's co–ordinates, p = number of variables, M_g = number of the principal components significant for the g class, $i = 1,..,n$ = number of objects, $j = 1,..,p$ = number of variables.

KNN: this technique classifies each record in a data set based on a combination of the classes of the k record(s) most similar to it in a historical data set (where $k = 1$).

CART is a tree–shaped structure that represents sets of decisions. These decisions generate rules for the classification of a data set. CART provides a set of rules that can be applied to a new (unclassified) data set to predict which records will have a given outcome. It segments a data set by creating two–way splits.

The classification obtained using these algorithms is shown in Table 2.

Table 2. True class and class assigned by the algorithms for each compound (the 40 molecules with a blank background were used to train the neuro-fuzzy classifier).

[1]	True Class [2]	CART [3]	LDA [4]	KNN [5]	SIMCA [6]	RDA [7]
Anilofos	2	2	2	1	2	2
Chlorpyrifos	1	2	2	1	2	2
Chlorpyryfos-methyl	2	2	2	1	2	2
Isazofos	1	1	1	2	1	1
Phosalone	2	2	2	2	2	2
Profenofos	1	2	2	1	2	2
Prothiofos	2	2	2	2	2	2
Azamethiphos	2	2	2	1	4	2
Azinphos methyl	1	1	1	2	1	1
Diazinon	3	3	1	1	4	1
Phosmet	2	2	2	1	2	2
Pirimiphos ethyl	1	1	1	1	1	1
Pirimiphos methyl	2	3	1	2	1	1
Pyrazophos	2	2	1	4	2	1
Quinalphos	1	1	1	2	1	1
Azinphos-ethyl	1	1	1	1	2	1
Etrimfos	1	1	1	3	3	1
Fosthiazate	4	2	2	2	4	2
Methidathion	1	1	1	1	1	1
Piperophos	3	3	3	2	2	3
Tebupirimfos	4	1	1	3	4	1
Triazophos	1	1	1	2	1	1
Dichlorvos	2	4	2	2	2	2
Disulfoton	3	3	3	1	3	3
Ethephon	4	4	4	4	4	4
Fenamiphos	1	1	3	2	1	1
Fenthion	2	2	3	2	2	3

	[1]	[2]	[3]	[4]	[5]	[6]	[7]
Fonofos		1	1	3	2	1	3
Glyphosate		4	4	4	4	4	4
Isofenphos		3	3	3	1	3	3
Methamidophos		4	4	4	3	4	4
Omethoate		3	3	3	3	3	3
Oxydemeton-methyl		3	3	3	3	3	3
Parathion ethyl		2	2	2	3	-1	3
Parathion methyl		3	3	3	3	3	3
Phoxim		2	2	1	1	1	1
Sulfotep		1	1	3	2	2	2
Tribufos		2	2	2	2	2	2
Trichlorfon		2	2	1	1	2	4
Acephate		4	4	1	3	4	4
Cadusafos		2	2	3	3	2	2
Chlorethoxyfos		2	2	2	3	2	2
Demeton-S-methyl		3	3	3	3	3	3
Dimethoate		3	3	1	1	3	3
Edifenphos		2	2	3	1	2	2
EPN		2	2	2	2	2	2
Ethion		2	2	2	2	2	2
Ethoprophos		3	3	3	2	2	3
Fenitrothion		3	2	3	3	3	3
Formothion		3	3	2	3	3	3
Methacrifos		2	2	2	2	2	3
Phorate		1	1	3	2	1	3
Propetamphos		3	3	3	4	2	3
Sulprofos		3	3	3	2	3	3
Temephos		3	3	2	1	3	2
Terbufos		1	1	3	2	3	3
Thiometon		3	3	3	3	3	3

Table 3. Performances of the classification algorithms.

	NER% fitting	NER%validation	Descriptors
LDA	64.91	61.40	D1,D2, D3, D4
RDA	84.21	71.93	D1, D2, D3, D4, D6, D7, D8, D11, D12, D13
SIMCA	92.98	77.19	D1, D2, D3, D4, D5, D6, D7, D8, D10, D11, D12
KNN	-	61.40	D1, D12
CART	85.96	77.19	D1, D2, D3, D4, D5, D9

2.4 Validation for the Classification Algorithms

The more common methods for validation in our approach are: i) Leave–one–out (LOO); ii) Leave–more–out (LMO); iii) Train & Test; iv) Bootstrap. We used LOO, since it is considered the best working on small dimension data sets [9]. According to LOO, given n objects, n models are computed. For each model, the training set consists of $n-1$ objects; the evaluation set consists of the object left.

The Non Error Rate percentage (NER%, Table 3) represents the ability of the algorithm in modeling the problem (fitting) and predicting his value (validation, using LOO). To estimate the predictive ability, we considered the gap between the experimental (fitting) and predicted value (cross–validation) for the n objects left, one by one, out from the model.

3 The Neuro-fuzzy Combination of the Classifiers

3.1 Motivations and Architecture

Combining multiple classifiers could be considered as a direction for the development of highly reliable pattern recognition systems, coming from the hybrid intelligent systems (HIS) approach. Combination of several classifiers may result in improved performances [4], [5]. The necessity of combining multiple classifiers is arising from the main demand of increasing quality and reliability of the final models. There are different classification algorithms in almost all the current pattern recognition application areas, each one having certain degrees of success, but none of them being as good as expected in applications. The proposed combination technique for the toxicity classification is a neuro-fuzzy gating the output of implied classifiers, trained against real classification values. This approach allows multiple classifiers to work together.

The hybrid intelligent system NIKE (developed by the third author) was used to automate the process, from data representation for toxicity measurements, to predicting the toxicity for a new input. It also suggests how the fuzzy inference produced the result [16], using the effect measure method [6] to combine the weights between the layers of the network and to select the strongest I/O dependencies. For NIKE, we defined the *implicit knowledge* (IK) as acquired through learning by fuzzy neural nets.

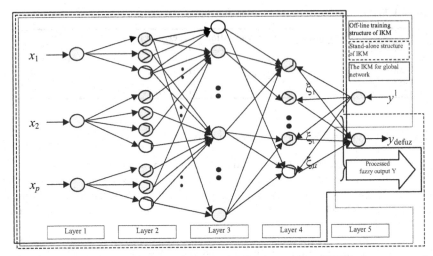

Fig. 1. Implicit Knowledge Module implemented as FNN2.

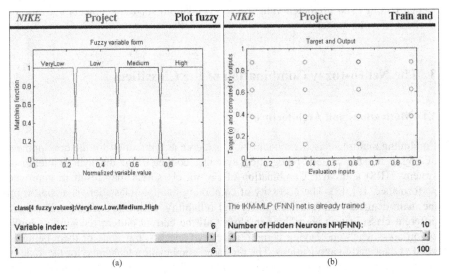

Fig. 2. NIKE: (a)The fuzzy terms of the generic linguistic variable Class; (b) the FNN model.

The IKM-FNN is a multilayered neural structure with the input layer performing the membership degrees of the variables, a fully connected three-layered FNN2 [15], and a defuzzification layer [16] (Fig.1). The weights of the connections between layer 1 and layer 2 are set to one. A linguistic variable X_i is described by m_i fuzzy sets, A_{ij}, having the degrees of membership performed by the functions $\mu_{ij}(x_i)$, $j=1,2,..,m_i$, $i=1,2,..,p.$, (in our case, $p=5$, all $m_i=4$, on the classes of the prediction result of the classifiers, as inputs, and on the classes of the toxicity values, as the output y_{defuz}). Layers 1 and 5 are used in fuzzification for training and prediction, and layers 2-4 define a feedforward network [18] to represent rules through FNN training [14].

3.2 Results

Since NIKE modules process only data scaled into the interval [0..1], every class was represented by the centroid of each of the four classes in which the available domain was split: 0.135 (class 1), 0.375 (class 2), 0.625 (class 3), and 0.875 (class 4). The inputs and the output followed a trapezoidal (de)fuzzification (Fig. 2): *VeryLow* (0..0.25), *Low* (0.25..0.5), *Medium* (0.5..0.75), *High* (0.75..1).

Table 4. Confusion matrix of the neuro-fuzzy combination of classifiers.

		Assigned Class				N° of objects
		1	2	3	4	
True Class	**1**	13	2			15
	2		20			20
	3		1	15		16
	4				6	6

Table 5. True and assigned class for the wrong predictions of the neuro-fuzzy combination of classifiers.

	True Class	CART	LDA	KNN	SIMCA	RDA	FNN
Chlorpyrifos	1	2	2	1	2	2	2
Profenofos	1	2	2	1	2	2	2
Fenitrothion	3	2	3	3	3	3	2

For the FNN described in Fig. 1 and implemented using NIKE shell, the $p = 5$ inputs represent the classification of the above described algorithms for a given compound: x_1=output$_{CART}$, x_2=output$_{LDA}$, x_3=output$_{KNN}$, x_4=output$_{SIMCA}$, x_5=output$_{RDA}$.

The neuro-fuzzy network was trained on a training set of 40 cases (70% of the entire set, as depicted in Table 2). The training set was used for the adjustment of the connections of the FNN with backpropagation (*traingdx*) algorithm, that updates weight and bias values according to gradient descent momentum and an adaptive learning rate. The neuro-fuzzy network was a multi-layered structure with the 5x4 above described fuzzy inputs and 4 fuzzy output neurons, the toxicity class linguistic variable (Fig. 2.a). Since different models (5 to 50 hidden units) were built, the best processing modules were the IKM-FNN with 10, 12, 19 neurons (Fig. 3).

A momentum term of 0.95 was used (to prevent too many oscillations of the error function). The nets were trained up to 5000 epochs, giving an error about 0.015. The recognition error for the above models is 5.26% (Table 4, 5, Fig. 3). Table 5 shows the three wrong predictions of the best trained versions of the system, used to calculate the accuracy: two of them are identical, as input values (Chlorpyrifos and Profenofos).

The confusion matrix shows the ability in prediction of our approach. The best performance was obtained by SIMCA (Table 3), which could correctly classify almost 93% of the molecules. This encouraging result was obtained with whole data set involved in developing the model. If we take a look to the NER% validated with LOO, we can notice that we loss a lot of the reliability of the model when we predict the toxicity of an external object. Such a behavior proves the ability in modeling of these algorithms, but shows also their incapacity in generalization. The neuro-fuzzy approach seems to overcome this problem, succeeding in voting for the best opinion and underling all the considered classification algorithms (Fig. 3).

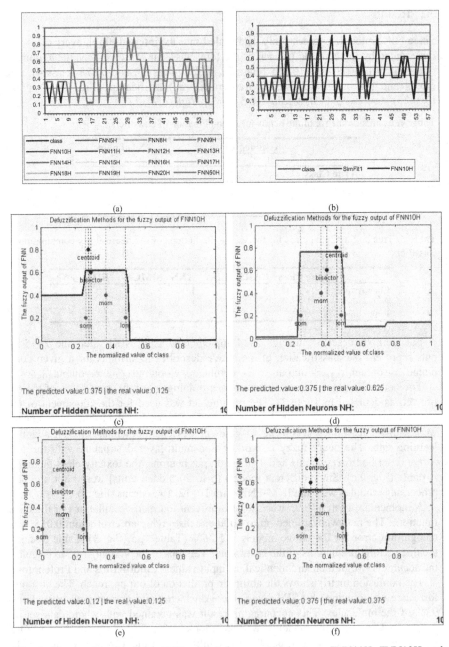

Fig. 3. The results of training FNNs: (a) 3-5 errors, the best are FNN10H, FNN12H and FNN19H; (b) the chosen model, FNN10H, against the SIMCA results and the real ones; (c) the bad fuzzy inference prediction for 2 cases in class 1 (Chlorpyrifos and Profenofos); (d) the bad fuzzy inference prediction for the case in class 3 (Fenitrothion); two samples of good prediction for test cases: (e) a class 1 sample (Phorate); (f) a class 2 sample (Edinfenphos).

3.3   Interpreting the Results of the Neuro-fuzzy Combination of the Classifiers

The most relevant fuzzy rules were extracted from the IKM-FNN structures using Effect Measure Method (EMM) [6][12]. The EMM combines the weights between the layers of the proposed structure (Fig. 1) in order to select the strongest dependencies between the fuzzy output and the inputs. This approach takes advantage of predictive capabilities of FNN and gives reasons to explain the output and the patterns discovered by the IKM part of the proposed system, as well as highlights and adjusts some explicit rules given by human experts.

A pre-processing step to delete the contradictory rules was done. We considered as contradictory the rules: (1) those having different output predictions than the same input class, and a relative small coefficient of trust:

```
IF RdaFit1 is:Medium  THEN class is:VeryLow (47.79%)
IF RdaFit1 is:Medium  THEN class is:High    (47.62%)
```

or (2) rules showing big differences between the value of the input (the classification) and the output of the system (the inputs and the outputs must be in similar domains):

```
IF KnnXFi1 is:VeryLow THEN class is:Low     (54.98%)
IF KnnXFi1 is:Low     THEN class is:VeryLow (55.99%)
IF KnnXFi1 is:High    THEN class is:Low     (78.70%)
```

Finally, the following list of the most trusty fuzzy rules was considered for the chosen net (IKM-FNN10H):

```
IF CarFit1 is:VeryLow THEN class is:High    (39.22%)
IF CarFit1 is:Low     THEN class is:High    (82.30%)
IF CarFit1 is:Medium  THEN class is:High    (48.74%)
IF CarFit1 is:High    THEN class is:High    (39.04%)

IF SimFit1 is:VeryLow THEN class is:Medium  (61.25%)
IF SimFit1 is:Low     THEN class is:Medium  (36.04%)
IF SimFit1 is:High    THEN class is:Medium  (43.72%)

IF RdaFit1 is:VeryLow THEN class is:Low     (75.65%)
IF RdaFit1 is:Low     THEN class is:Low     (100.00%)
IF RdaFit1 is:High    THEN class is:High    (76.39%)
```

Three types of fuzzy rules were obtained: (1) some could be grouped by the same output, or (2) by having the same fuzzy term in the premise and conclusion, and, finally, (3) rules with mixed terms in premises and conclusion parts. From the first two groups of fuzzy rules (in italics), we could conclude that, the opinion of the specific entry classifier is not important for the given output. More precisely, CART prediction for values *High* of toxicity (class 4) is better to not be taken in consideration comparing with the other approaches.

```
IF (CarFit1 is:VeryLow) OR (CarFit1 is:Low) OR (CarFit1 is:Medium) OR
(CarFit1 is:High) THEN class is:High
```

Similarly, SIMCA outputs are not so important for predicting class 3 (*Medium* values of toxicity: the second group of fuzzy rules). From the last group of rules (in bold), we could find the best classifier from the involved systems. In our case, to predict class 2 (*Low* toxicity) is better to consider the opinion coming from RDA. The same opinion is very important for predicting the class 4 (*High* toxicity) cases too.

4 Conclusions

Classification of the toxicity requires a high degree of experience from computational chemistry experts. Several approaches were described to generate suitable classifiers for the considered patterns. We investigated five different classifiers and a neuro-fuzzy correlation of them, to organize and classify toxicity data sets. Our approach shown an improved behaviour as a combination of classifiers. The method is viewed as a specific part of a hybrid intelligent system, in which different knowledge representation approaches could improve the final model. Some results on fuzzy rules extraction, and the possibility to interpret particular inferences, suggest the neuro-fuzzy approach has the potential to significantly improve classification methods used for toxicity characterization.

Acknowledgment: the work is partially funded by E.U. HPRN-CT-1999-00015.

References

1. Benfenati, E., Pelagatti, S., Grasso, P., Gini, G.: COMET: the approach of a project in evaluating toxicity. Gini, G. C.; Katritzky, A. R. (eds.): Predictive Toxicology of Chemicals: Experiences and Impact of AI Tools. AAAI 1999 Spring Symposium Series. AAAI Press, Menlo Park, CA (1999) 40-43
2. Benfenati, E., Piclin, N., Roncaglioni, A., Varì, M.R.: Factors Influencing Predictive Models For Toxicology. SAR and QSAR in environmental research, 12 (2001) 593-603
3. Bishop, C.M.: Neural networks for pattern recognition. Clarendon Press, Oxford (1995)
4. Chen, K., Chi, H.: A method of combining multiple probabilistic classifiers through soft competition on different feature sets. Neurocomputing 20 (1998) 227-252
5. Duin, R.P.W., Tax, D.M.J.: Experiments with Classifier Combining Rules. Lecture Notes in Computer Science, Vol. 1857. Springer-Verlag, Berlin (2000) 16-29
6. Enbutsu, I., Baba, K., Hara, N.: Fuzzy Rule Extraction from a Multilayered Network. Procs. of IJCNN'91, Seattle (1991) 461-465
7. Gini, G., Benfenati, E., Boley, D.: Clustering and Classification Techniques to Assess Aquatic Toxicity. Procs. of the Fourth Int'l Conf. KES2000, Brighton, UK, Vol. 1 (2000) 166-172
8. Gini, G., Lorenzini, M., Benfenati, E., Brambilla, R., Malvé, L.: Mixing a Symbolic and a Subsymbolic Expert to Improve Carcinogenicity Prediction of Aromatic Compounds. Kittler,J., Roli,F. (eds.): *Multiple Classifier Systems.* Springler-Verlag, Berlin (2001) 126-135
9. Helma, C., Gottmann, E., Kramer, S.: Knowledge discovery and data mining in toxicology. Statistical methods in medical research, 9 (2000) 131-135
10. Ho, T., Hull, J., Srihari, S.: Decision combination in multiple classifier systems. IEEE Trans. Pattern Anal. Machine Intelligence 16/1 (1994) 66-75
11. Jacobs, R.A.: Methods for combining experts' probability assessments. Neur. Comp. 7/5(1995)867-888
12. Jagielska, I., Matthews, C., Whitfort, T.: An investigation into the application of ANN, FL, GA, and rough sets to automated knowledge acquisition for classification problems. Neurocomp,24(1999)37-54
13. Kosko, B.: Neural Networks and Fuzzy System. Prentice-Hall, Englewood Cliffs (1992)
14. Lin, C.T., George Lee, C.S.: Neural - Network Based Fuzzy Logic Control and Decision System. IEEE Transactions on Computers, 40/12 (1991) 1320-1336

15. Nauck, D., Kruse, R.: NEFCLASS-X: A Neuro-Fuzzy Tool to Build Readable Fuzzy Classifiers. BT Tech. J. 16/3 (1998) 180-192
16. Neagu, C.-D., Avouris, N.M., Kalapanidas, E., Palade, V.: Neural and Neuro-fuzzy Integration in a Knowledge-based System for Air Quality Prediction. App Intell. J. (2001 accepted)
17. Palade, V., Neagu, C.-D., Patton, R.J.: Interpretation of Trained Neural Networks by Rule Extraction, Procs. of Int'l Conf. 7th Fuzzy Days in Dortmund (2001) 152-161
18. Rumelhart, D.E., McClelland, J.L.: Parallel Distributed Processing, Explanations in the Microstructure of Cognition. MIT Press (1986)

A Multi-expert System for Movie Segmentation

L.P. Cordella[1], M. De Santo[2], G. Percannella[2], C. Sansone[1], M. Vento[2]

([1]) Dipartimento di Informatica e Sistemistica
Università di Napoli "Federico II"- Via Claudio, 21 I-80125 Napoli, Italy.
{cordel,carlosan}@unina.it
([2]) Dipartimento di Ingegneria dell'Informazione e di Ingegneria Elettrica
Università di Salerno - Via P.te Don Melillo,1 I-84084, Fisciano (SA), Italy.
{desanto,pergen,mvento}@unisa.it

Abstract. In this paper we present a system for movie segmentation based on the automatic detection of dialogue scenes.
The proposed system processes the video stream directly in the MPEG domain: it starts with the segmentation of the video footage in shots. Then, a characterization of each shot between dialogue and not-dialogue according to a Multi-Expert System (MES) is performed. Finally, the individuated sequences of shots are aggregated in dialogue scenes by means of a suitable algorithm. The MES integrates three experts, which classifies a given shot on the basis of very complementary descriptions; in particular an audio classifier, a face detector and a camera motion estimator have been built up and employed.
The performance of the system have been tested on a huge MPEG movie database made up of more than 15000 shots and 200 scenes, giving rise to encouraging results.

1. Introduction

More and more videos are generated every day, mostly produced and stored in analog form. In spite of this, the trend is toward the total digitization of movies and video products given that the effective use of them is hindered by the difficulty of efficiently classifying and managing video data in the traditional analog format.

In the past few years, several algorithms have been presented in the scientific literature to allow an effective filtering, browsing, searching and retrieval of information in video databases. It is generally accepted that the first step toward an effective organization of the information in video databases consists in the segmentation of the video footage in shots that are defined as the set of frames obtained through a continuous camera recording. Anyway, even if the individuation of shots represents a fundamental step, it is clear that this approach does not allow an effective non linear access to the video information. This is evident from at least two points of view: firstly, humans usually remember different events after they watched a movie, and hence they also think in terms of events during the retrieval process; secondly, a modern movie contains more than 2000 shots on average, which means that an intelligent video analysis program needs to process 2000 frames per movie to give a coherent representation.

F. Roli and J. Kittler (Eds.): MCS 2002, LNCS 2364, pp. 304-313, 2002.
© Springer-Verlag Berlin Heidelberg 2002

Consequently, it is necessary to define units for accessing the video footage obtained by grouping semantically correlated shots. *Scene* is the term most used in the scientific literature to call this semantic unit. First approaches for detecting scenes (see for example [1, 2]) operate by simply clustering the shots according to the visual content of the most representative frames (also called key-frames). Anyway the quoted techniques do not take into account any model for the scene, so the results are not always semantically coherent. In fact, it is worth noting that the way the shots are grouped in a scene generally depends on the type of scene under analysis as well as on the video genre. The scenes of a TV-news program are different from the scenes of a talk-show, of a documentary, of a movie. Hence, it is important to aggregate shots also considering a model for the scene. Several recent papers try to define models for scene detection, mainly in the field of TV-news, where effective and simple models can be defined. For example, in [3] a method based on a Hidden Markov Model to segment TV-news at various semantic levels it is presented, while in [4], Bertini et al. describe the use of multiple features for content-based indexing and retrieval of TV-news.

The same problem is much more complex when the movies domain is faced: there are much more different scene types and for each kind of scene different styles can be adopted depending on the Movie Director. Interestingly enough, although scene analysis can be very useful for several purposes (think for example to video abstraction and automatic classification of the video genre) only few papers have been presented on the problem of detection and characterization of scenes in movies. Among those few, an interesting one is [5] where Saraceno et al. define some simple rules to group the shots of a movie according to some semantic types.

In this paper we present a system for video segmentation based on the automatic detection of dialogue scenes within movies. The detection of dialogue scenes is a task of particular interest given the special semantic role played by dialogue based scenes in the most part of movies. The proposed system starts with the segmentation of the video footage in shots. Then, it operates a characterization of each shot as dialogue or not-dialogue according to a multi-expert approach, where each decision system (expert, hereinafter) classifies a given shot on the basis of a particular description while employing the most appropriate decision technique. The final result is obtained by combining the single decisions through suitable rules [6]. In this way, if the utilized experts consider different and complementary aspects of the same decision problem, the combination of the single decisions provides a performance that is better than that of any single expert. Finally, the individuated sequences of shots are aggregated in dialogue scenes by means of an appropriate algorithm.

In order to improve the computational efficiency of the whole process, we analyze the video footage directly in the MPEG coded domain.

While the general approach of multiple experts is not new (see for example [7, 8]), its application to this specific problem is interesting and quite novel, and the obtained results on a huge MPEG movie database are encouraging.

2. The Proposed System

As stated in the introduction, the proposed method starts with the segmentation of the video footage in shots. Then, a characterization of each shot between dialogue and not-dialogue according to a Multi-Expert System (MES) is performed. Finally, the individuated sequences of shots are aggregated in dialogue scenes by means of a suitable algorithm. This approach can be justified on the basis of the following considerations: *i*) a scene is a group of semantically correlated shots; *ii*) *almost all* the shots belonging to a dialogue scene can be characterized as dialogue shots; and *iii*) the shots belonging to the same dialogue scene are temporally adjacent.

Therefore, it follows that the proposed system can be structured according to three successive stages, as depicted in Fig.1:

Stage 1 - shot boundaries detection
Stage 2 - dialogue / not-dialogue shot classification
Stage 3 - shot grouping

A short description of each of the quoted stages is given in the following.

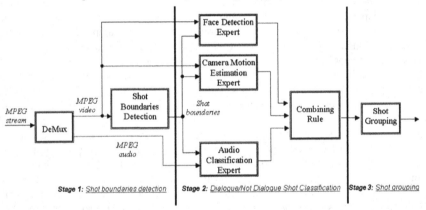

Fig. 1. Block diagram of the system for automatic detection of dialogue scene.

Shot boundaries detection: the problem of automatic detection of shot boundaries has been widely investigated in the recent years; hence, the scientific literature is rich of papers discussing approaches which allow us to reliably segment videos in shots both in the uncompressed and in the MPEG coded domain. For the purposes of this paper, we have implemented the technique described in [9] that is characterized by good performances both in terms of correct detection and of low computational requirements, since it operates directly on the compressed stream.

Dialogue/not-dialogue shot characterization: this classification is performed through the use of a multi-expert system. The rationale lies in the assumption that, by suitably combining the results of a set of experts according to a rule (combining rule), the performance obtained can be better than that of any single expert. The successful implementation of a multi-expert system (MES) implies the use of the most complementary experts as possible, and the definition of a combining rule for determining the most likely class a sample should be attributed to, given the class to which it is attributed by each single expert.

Therefore, for the purpose of shot classification as dialogue or not, we introduce the following set of experts:

1. Face detection,
2. Camera motion estimation,
3. Audio classification

which are integrated within the whole system as shown in Fig.1.

Each expert can be viewed as constituted by a sensor and a classifier. Each expert of the system has two inputs: the MPEG video or audio stream and the complete list of the shots boundaries. The latter information is used by the sensor to access and characterize the MPEG data at shot level. The output of the sensor is used by the classifier to perform the dialogue / not-dialogue shot classification. In our system we have integrated three experts whose sensors implement the algorithms described in [10] for face detection, in [11] for camera motion estimation and in [12] for audio stream classification, all working directly in the video/audio coded domain. It is worth noting that the output of the first sensor is correlated in a simple way to the output of the corresponding expert; in fact, the presence (absence) of a face implies a dialogue (not dialogue) shot. On the contrary, the sensor for camera motion estimation provides three estimates respectively for the zoom, tilt and pan rate for each P frame. Then, the average and the standard deviation of the zoom, tilt and pan rate over each shot constitute the features vector used by a neural network to perform the shot classification. Finally, the sensor for audio classification uses the same feature vector defined in [12], but in our case the classification is realized through a neural network trained to recognize only the dialogue and not-dialogue shot classes.

Then, the outputs of the single experts are combined according to a suitable combining rule (for a review of the most common used rules see [6]).

Shot grouping: the final stage of our approach provides to group in dialogue scenes the shots classified in the previous stage. The rationale of the algorithm for shot grouping derives from the consideration that the shots belonging to a dialogue scene are temporally adjacent. However, the shot grouping algorithm has to properly handle also the possible classification errors generated at stage 2. In fact:

− a **false alarm** (i.e. a not dialogue shot classified as dialogue) might cause the declaration of an inexistent short dialogue scene, and

− a **missed detection** (i.e. a dialogue shot classified as not dialogue) might cause the partitioning of a dialogue scenes in two scenes.

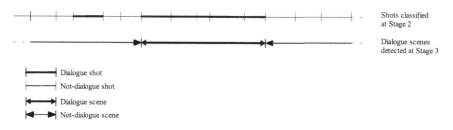

Fig. 2. Examples of scene transitions in case of $N = 3$ are depicted.

Thus the shot grouping algorithm implements the following rule: a transition from a *dialogue scene* to a *not-dialogue scene* (and vice versa) is declared when a sequence of at least *N not-dialogue* (*dialogue*) shots occurs. In Fig. 2, there are depicted examples of scene transitions in case of $N = 3$.

3. Experimental Results

In order to assess the performance of the proposed system we used a large and significant database of video footages obtained from 10 movies. It results in about 20 hours, corresponding to more than 15000 shots and 228 dialogue scenes. In the construction of this movie database particular care was taken to include a representative of the major movie genres (action, comedy, drama, science fiction, fantasy, etc) so that to reproduce the high variability of the video characteristics over the different genres. More details on the chosen movies are given in [13].

In order to set-up the proposed system and to assess its performance, we extracted two disjoint sets of samples from the database: a training set (henceforth **TRS**) and a test set (**TS**). The **TS** has been built by choosing continuous sequences of *L* shots from each movie, where *L* was obtained as approximately the 30% of the total number of shots in that movie. The choice of using temporally adjacent shots is motivated by the fact that such sequences have to be used to test the Stage 3 of the system in the detection of dialogue scenes. The **TRS** were built by randomly choosing among the remaining part of the database a number of samples corresponding to the 50% of the whole dataset. Note that the remaining 20% of samples of the database were used for building the validation set (**VS**); this set was required for training the neural classifiers of the 2nd stage, as it will be clarified in the next subsections.

3.1 Performance Evaluation of the Stage 1

This stage provides the segmentation of the video stream in shots, by mean of the technique described in [9]. In order to assess the performance of this algorithm we carried out a comparison between the algorithm output and the ground truth. Such a comparison consists in the evaluation of the numbers of missed detections (MD, i.e. cut frames which were not detected by the algorithm) and false alarms (FA, i.e. non-cut frames which were declared as cuts from the algorithm). Then the overall performance is usually expressed in terms of *Recall* and *Precision*, which represent the fraction of correctly detected cuts with respect to the true cuts and the total number of detected cuts, respectively. They are defined as it follows:

$$Re\,call = \frac{CD}{CD + MD} \quad \text{and} \quad Pr\,ecision = \frac{CD}{CD + FA} \tag{1}$$

where *CD* is the number of correctly detected cuts.

The algorithm implemented in this stage of our system required a tuning phase in order to select a suitable threshold that maximized the performance. In order to take into account both *Precision* and the *Recall*, we used a unique performance index defined as the sum of the preceding indexes; in this way we are able to weight equally both indexes. The tuning phase required us to select the value of the threshold that maximized the performance on the **TRS**. Once completed the tuning phase, we tested the algorithm on the **TS**, obtaining the following performance: *Recall* = 0.96 and *Precision* = 0.94. These results confirms how the selected algorithm is able to perform very accurately, even if it is interesting noting that the performance of the implemented cut detection algorithm is lower with respect to what the authors declare in [9]. In fact, they report no missed detections and only one false alarm on their test set composed of only 27000 frames and 269 cuts.

3.2 Performance Evaluation of Stage 2

The camera motion expert and the audio expert are built by using a neural network - namely, a Multi-Layer Perceptron (MLP) - for their classification modules.

The architecture of the neural classifier of the audio and the camera motion experts has been chosen after a preliminary optimization phase on the **TRS**. In particular, the MLP net adopted for the audio expert is made up of 35 hidden neurons, while the net for the camera motion expert has 25 neurons in the hidden layer.

In Table 1 there are the *confusion matrices* obtained on the **TS** by the best audio, camera motion and face experts.

	Audio		Camera Motion		Face	
	ND	**D**	**ND**	**D**	**ND**	**D**
ND	**77.57%**	22.43%	**58.43%**	41.57%	**76.43%**	23.57%
D	20.01%	**79.99%**	23.59%	**76.41%**	30.45%	**69.55%**

Table 1. The confusion matrix obtained on the **TS** by the best audio, camera motion and face expert, where **ND** and **D** stand for *Not-dialogue* and *Dialogue shot*, respectively.

The face expert required a different experimentation since it employs a naive classifier. It simply associates the presence/absence of a face in the central I-frame of the shot to a dialogue/not-dialogue shot. Anyway, this expert also required a training phase in order to set-up some parameters of the face detection algorithm [10], with particular reference to the skin color module. In this case we used the same training, validation and test set defined for the other two experts.

After having assessed the performance of each expert, their results have to be fused together in the combiner. In Table 2, it is represented the *Coverage Table* evaluated on the **TS**, which reports the joint behavior of the three experts with respect to the shot classification task. In particular, the rows of this table represent the percentage of samples in the test set for which respectively three, two, one or zero experts performed the correct classification.

From Table 2 it is readily available the recognition rate achievable by employing a majority voting rule: it is given by the sum of the recognition rates of the first two rows of the quoted table. Hence, by using this simple rule it is possible to achieve a recognition rate of 83.97% (not-dialogue shots) and 86.2% (dialogue shots) for the 2nd stage of the system.

# Correct classification	Not-Dialogue	Dialogue
3	32.18%	45.17%
2	51.79%	41.03%
1	12.31%	8.38%
0	3.72%	5.42%

Table 2. The coverage table evaluated on the **TS** by considering the outputs of the three experts.

It is worth noting that the multi-expert approach allows to obtain a relative overall improvement of about 8% with respect to the best single expert (the Audio one – about 79% correct classification). In Table 3, we have reported the relative improvements obtained by using the MES with respect to each single expert.

	Not-Dialogue	Dialogue
Audio	8.3%	7.8%
Camera motion	43.7%	12.8%
Face	9.9%	23.9%

Table 3. The relative improvements obtained by using the MES with respect to each single expert in the dialogue/not-dialogue classification of the shots.

3.3 Performance Evaluation of Stage 3

In the 3rd stage of the system the shots, classified in the 2nd stage, are aggregated in dialogue and not-dialogue scenes. This is realized by the simple shot grouping algorithm described in Section 2.

Before going into the details of the tests that we carried out in order to assess the performances of this stage, it is worthwhile to dwell upon the set of indexes which we are going to estimate. It is important that such set is able to give a correct representation of the actual performances of the system.

We decided to provide a description of the overall performance of our technique in terms of **Correct Detection** (**CD**) and **False Alarms** (**FA**), which respectively account for the actual dialogue scenes which were detected and the dialogue scenes which were detected without being actually present in the movie.

These two parameters are defined as follows:

$$CD = \frac{CDS}{DS}\% \quad \text{and} \quad FA = \frac{FDS}{NDS}\% \tag{2}$$

where:
- CDS is the number of actual dialogue scenes, which were detected;
- FDS is the number of dialogue scenes which were detected, but not actually present in the movie;
- DS is the number of actual dialogue scenes;
- NDS is the number of actual not-dialogue scenes.

To this aim, we declare that an actual dialogue scene has been correctly detected if at least one of its shots is present in a detected dialogue scene. Anyway, it can be simply devised how the indexes introduced before provide only a rough description of the real performances of the system: no information about the "quality" of the detection is given. In fact, such indexes do not account for scenes which are only partially detected and/or split and/or merged. In order to cope with such a problem we introduce two other sets of indexes: *overlap percentages* and *split/merged scenes percentages*.

The first set of indexes has been introduced in order to give a condensed view of how much the detected dialogue scenes coincide with the actual dialogue scenes. Hence, we define the **percentage of correct overlap (*CO*)** and the **percentage of false overlap (*FO*)**, given by:

$$CO = \frac{DSF}{ADSF}\% \quad \text{and} \quad FO = \frac{NDSF}{ADSF}\% \tag{3}$$

where:
- *DSF* is the number of frames of the detected dialogue scenes which overlap to the real dialogue scenes;
- *NDSF* is the number of frames of the detected dialogue scenes which do not overlap to the real dialogue scenes;
- *ADSF* is the number of frames of the actual dialogue scenes which have been detected by the system. The rationale inspiring the choice of excluding the undetected actual dialogue scenes relies on the fact that with such set of parameters we want to give a measure only of the quality of the detected scenes.

The set of indexes about split/merged scenes has been introduced in order to take into account the errors occurring when an actual dialogue scene is split into two or more dialogue scenes or vice versa when two or more dialogue scenes are merged together. To this aim we define the **percentage of merged dialogue scenes (*MS*)** and the **percentage of the split dialogue scenes (*SS*)** as it follows:

$$MS = \frac{AS}{DDS}\% \quad \text{and} \quad SS = \frac{DiS}{DDS}\% \tag{4}$$

where:
- *AS* is the number of the detected dialogue scenes, which were merged into a single scene;
- *DiS* is the number of the detected dialogue scenes, which were divided into two or more scenes;
- *DDS* is the number of the detected dialogue scenes.

Note that according to the previous definitions it might occur also the situation of a detected dialogue scene that is both merged and divided. In such case this scene is considered for the computation of both *MS* and *SS*.

After the definition of these indexes, we can evaluate the results of the experimental campaign carried out on the video sequences of the **TS**. It is worth recalling that the **TS** has been built by considering a continuous sequence of *L* shots from each movie, where *L* was obtained as approximately the 30% of the total number of shots in that movie.

The experimentation of the 3rd stage of the system required to set only the parameter *N* that was defined in Section 2, representing the minimum number of adjacent shots that allows switching among the two different types of scenes. We tested the system for different values of the parameter *N*. In Table 4, there are reported the experimental results obtained by setting *N* = 3 and 4.

The first conclusion which can be drawn is that the dialogue scene segmentation is significant only in the cases of $N = 3$ and 4. In fact, a higher value gives rise to under-segmentation: many scenes are merged together; conversely with $N = 2$ over-segmentation occurs.

	N = 3	N = 4
Correct Detections (CD)	**90.83%**	**88.78%**
False Alarms (FA)	7.89%	6.88%
Split Scenes (SS)	16.32%	13.39%
Merged Scenes (MS)	14.68%	17.89%
Correct overlap (CO)	82.64%	76.80%
False overlap (FO)	11.54%	6.67%

Table 4. There are reported the experimental results obtained by setting $N = 3$ and 4.

The experimental results are very appealing as in both cases we obtained about 90% in the detection of the dialogue scenes. Furthermore also the results about over-lap are quite good with about 80% of correct overlap and only 10% of false overlap. The results about scene overlap are important since they represent an index of the quality of the detection. Low values of *CO* accompanied by high values of *FO* would be misleading, in the sense that they could not allow a user to perceive the true se-mantic content of the scene.

In order to evaluate the improvement in the overall performance introduced by the use of sensor fusion approach with respect to the case of a single expert, we have tested our system using in the 2nd stage only the best expert (audio). We have reported in Table 5 the experimental results obtained with this expert in case $N = 3$ together with the relative improvement introduced by the use of the MES.

	Audio	Relative improvement
Correct Detections (CD)	*81.27%*	*11.8%*
False Alarms (FA)	*19.38%*	*59.3%*
Split Scenes (SS)	*23.31%*	*30.0%*
Merged Scenes (MS)	*21.34%*	*31.2%*
Correct overlap (CO)	*75.70%*	*9.2%*
False overlap (FO)	*17.72%*	*34.9%*

Table 5. The experimental results obtained by using the audio expert in the 2nd stage of the system with $N=3$; the relative improvement introduced by the use of the MES are also reported.

From the experimental results reported in Table 5 it is evident the improvement yielded by the employment of a MES. The advantages are considerable not only in the percentage of correct detection, but also for the other indexes. The use of information about face presence and camera motion allows improving the overall quality of the segmentation.

4. Conclusions and Perspectives

In this work we have faced the problem of movie segmentation. The proposed approach is based on the detection of dialogue scene by means of a Multi-Expert System (MES). The MES is constituted by three different experts which analyze the video and audio tracks of the movie directly in the MPEG coded domain. Although each expert is not characterized by optimal performances in the classification of the shots (this is due both to the errors of the sensor and of the classifier which constitute each expert), their combined use gives good performances even when a very simple combining rule is used. This confirms our initial hypothesis that the utilized experts consider different and complementary aspects of the same decision problem. Current research is focused on improving the overall performance of the system by implementing the experts as classifiers able to yield also some information about the reliability of the classification, and by using more sophisticated combining rules. Actually, we are also exploring the possibility to extend the proposed approach to detect action scenes within movies.

References

[1]   M. M. Yeung, B. Liu, "Efficient matching and clustering of video shots", in Proc. IEEE ICIP'95, vol II, pp. 260-263.

[2]   A. Hanjalic, R. Lagendijk, J. Biemond, "Automated high-level movie segmentation for advanced video-retrieval systems", in IEEE Trans. on Circuits and Systems for Video Technology, vol. 9, No. 4, June 1999, pp. 580-588.

[3]   S. Boykin, A. Merlino, "Machine learning of event segmentation for news on demand", in Communications of the ACM, Feb. 2000, vol. 43, No. 2, pp. 35-41.

[4]   M. Bertini, A. Del Bimbo, P. Pala, "Content-based Indexing and Retrieval of TV-news", in Pattern Recognition Letters, 22, (2001), 503-516.

[5]   C. Saraceno, R. Leopardi, "Identification of Story Units in Audio-Visual Sequences by Joint Audio and Video Processing", in Proc. ICIP'98, pp. 363-367, 1998.

[6]   L. P. Cordella, P. Foggia, C. Sansone, F. Tortorella and M. Vento, Reliability Parameters to Improve Combination Strategies in Multi-Expert Systems, Pattern Analysis & Applications, Springer-Verlag, vol. 2, pp. 205–214, 1999.

[7]   T.K. Ho, J.J. Hull, S.N. Srihari, "Decision Combination in Multiple Classifier Systems", IEEE Transactions on Pattern Analysis and Machine Intelligence 1994; 16(1): 66-75.

[8]   J. Kittler , J. Hatef, R.P.W. Duin, J. Matas, "On Combining Classifiers", IEEE Trans. on PAMI, vol 20 n.3 March 1998.

[9]   S.C. Pei, Y.Z. Chou, "Efficient MPEG compressed video analysis using macroblock type information", in IEEE Trans. on Multimedia, pp. 321 – 333, Dec. 1999, Vol. 1, Issue: 4.

[10] H. Wang, S.F. Chang, "A Highly Efficient System for Automatic Face Region Detection in MPEG Video", IEEE Trans. on Circuits and Systems for Video Technology, vol. 7, no. 4, August 1997, pp. 615-628.

[11] Y.P. Tan, D.D. Saur, S.R. Kulkarni, P.J. Ramadge, "Rapid Estimation of Camera Motion from Compressed Video with Application to Video Annotation", IEEE Trans. on Circuits and Systems for Video Technology, vol. 10, no. 1, February 2000, pp. 133-146.

[12] M. De Santo, G. Percannella, C. Sansone, M. Vento, "Classifying Audio of Movies by a Multi-Expert System", Proc. of the 11th ICIAP, pp. 386-391, 2001.

[13] M. De Santo, G. Percannella, C. Sansone, M. Vento, "Dialogue Scenes Detection in Mpeg Movies: a Multi-Expert Approach", LNCS, vol. 2184, pp. 192-201, Sept. 2001.

Decision Level Fusion of Intramodal Personal Identity Verification Experts

J. Kittler[1], M. Ballette[2], J. Czyz[3], F. Roli[2], and L. Vandendorpe[3]

[1] Centre for Vision, Speech and Signal Processing,
University of Surrey, Guildford, Surrey GU2 7XH, UK
J.Kittler@eim.surrey.ac.uk
[2] Communications and Remote Sensing Lab.,
Université catholique de Louvain, B-1348 Belgium
[3] Department of Electrical Engineering, University of Cagliari, Italy

Abstract. We investigate the Behavior Knowledge Space [4] and Decision Templates [7] methods of classifier fusion in the context of personal identity verification involving six intramodal experts exploiting frontal face biometrics.

The results of extensive experiments on the XM2VTS database show the Behavioural Knowledge Space fusion strategy achieves consistently better results than the Decision Templates method. Most importantly, it exhibits quasi monotonic behaviour as the number of experts combined increases.

1 Introduction

Personal identity verification based on biometrics is a commercially very important problem. It arises in security and surveillance applications where access to services, buildings or files should be restricted to authorised individuals. Many low risk applications of the technology also exist, such as the retrieval of faces from video and image databases, video annotation, face identity aide memoir, biometric based automatic car driver settings customisation (stereo, seat, heating), computer logging, mobile phone security and countless others.

Although many different biometric sensors have been developed, there is a particular interest in face based verification. This modality has a wide range of applications because of its noncontact nature of sensing. It is often also the only biometric available when searching through large image and video databases for a particular individual. Although a considerable progress has been made in enhancing the performance of face based verification algorithms, many applications require further reduction of error rates before they become commercially viable.

In this paper we investigate the merits of combining multiple face experts. The general issues of multiple classifier fusion have been the subject of discussion at a series of workshop on this topic [5]. The main objective is to establish whether the beneficial effects of classifier fusion extend also to the scenario of combining multiple biometric experts of the same modality, even if their individual performance rates are significantly different. It is then pertinent to ask

F. Roli and J. Kittler (Eds.): MCS 2002, LNCS 2364, pp. 314–324, 2002.

under what circumstances a poorly performing expert can still provide useful information that leads to an overall improvement in the system error rates. These issues have been addressed by several authors (see e.g. [8]).

The aim of this paper is to investigate decision level fusion methods in the context of combining multiple frontal face personal identity verification experts. The fusion task is difficult as the experts are not only correlated, but also their performance levels differ by as much as a factor of three. Earlier comparative studies of multiple expert systems in the personal identity verification scenario demonstrated that while simple fusion strategies such as combination by averaging or decision by majority vote, which do not require any training, improve the verification performance, they do not measure up to trainable strategies such as Decision Templates [7] or the Behavior Knowledge Space [4] method. The goal of the comparison here is to establish whether these fusion techniques are also effective in intramodal fusion.

Through extensive experiments on the XM2VTS database using the Lausanne protocol we find that the Behavior Knowledge Space fusion rule works well even in the intramodal multiple expert fusion setting. First of all, it achieves the best results as compared to the Decision Template method. Most importantly, it exhibits monotonic behavior as the number of experts combined increases. This is a very important conclusion of the study, as it means that by adding experts, the performance of the multiple expert system will not be degraded. We also demonstrate that for a sufficient number of experts combined the optimal configuration selected on the evaluation set is also aposteriori optimal on the test set.

The paper is organised as follows. In the next section we describe the individual face verification experts involved in the study. In Section 3 we outline the two decision level fusion methods investigated. In Section 4 we define the experimental set up. The results of the comparative study and the findings are presented in Section 5. Finally, in Section 6 the paper is drawn to conclusion.

2   Frontal Face Verification Experts

Six frontal face verification experts were deployed in the study. All six methods use manually registered face images which are then photometrically normalised.

Three of the six face experts were designed at the University of Surrey. They confirm or reject the claimed identity in the Fisher subspace derived using the Linear Discriminant Analysis. The LDA projection maximises the ratio of between class and within class scatters. In the face recognition or face verification application scenarios the within class covariance matrix is invariably rank deficient, as the number of training images is normally lower than the dimensionality of the image data. For this reason the Linear Discriminant Analysis is performed in a Principal Component Analysis (PCA) subspace associated with the nonzero eigenvalues of the mixture covariance matrix. In this subspace the LDA axes are known to perform pre-whitening of the within class covariances. In other words, the within class covariance matrix becomes an identity matrix.

Although in this situation the Euclidean metric should be an ideal criterion for measuring the similarity between probe and model images, we found that normalised correlation yielded better results [6]. The normalised correlation projects the probe vector onto the mean vector of the claimed client identity, emanating from the origin. The magnitude of projection is normalised by the length of the mean and probe vectors. However, the best performance in the Fisher subspace was achieved using a data dependent gradient metric which adapts the direction in which the distance between the probe and the template is measured according to the local configuration of other clients. These clients are considered as representatives of potential impostors and therefore they can be viewed as samples of the impostor distribution [6].

In all three cases the claimed personal identity is accepted if the appropriate score (distance or correlation coefficient) is within a prespecified threshold. The threshold is determined experimental by computing the Receiver Operating Characteristics (ROC) curve on the evaluation set and selecting the equal error rate operating point (equal false rejection and false acceptance rates).

In summary, the three University of Surrey experts make decisions about the claimed identity of the probe face image in the LDA space. **Unis-eucl** measures the distance between the probe vector and the clients template using the Euclidean metric. **Unis-gdm** performs the comparison between the projected probe and template images in the one dimensional subspace of the LDA space defined by the gradient direction. Finally, **UniS-noc** computed the normalised correlation between the two vectors.

The other three face experts were implemented by the Université catholique of Louvain la Neuve. One of the experts implemented the *normalised correlation* method. Although the algorithm is essentially the same, minor variations in the way the geometric and photometric normalisations were performed and in the computation of the LDA subspace resulted in slight differences in performance between this **UCL-noc** implementation and **Unis-noc**. The other two experts are based on the probabilistic matching method of Moghaddam et al [3]. The method models the difference between a probe and the client template by a combined intrapersonal and imposter distributions with the former defined in the PCA space and the latter in the PCA space complement. The two implementations, **UCL-pm1** and **UCL-pm2**, differ by the photonormalisation technique employed at the preprocessing stage.

3   Fusion Methods

In order to describe the fusion methods which we experimented with let us first introduce the necessary notation. We consider the task of personal identity verification as a two class pattern recognition problem where pattern Z (face image input) is to be assigned to one of the 2 possible classes ω_i $i = 1, 2$. Let us assume that we have L classifiers, each representing the given pattern by some measurement vector. Denote the measurement vector used by the jth classifier $\mathbf{x}_j$. Each classifier computes the respective aposteriori probabilities for the two hypotheses that an identity claim is either true or false. The aposteriori probability for the claim being true computed by expert j will be denoted $P(\omega_1|\mathbf{x}_j)$. The probability that the claim is false $P(\omega_2|\mathbf{x}_j)$ is given by $1 - P(\omega_1|\mathbf{x}_j)$.

3.1 Decision Templates

In the *Decision Templates* approach proposed in [7] the support of all the experts for all the classes jointly is taken into account in making the final decision. This joint representation of expert outputs is captured by the *Decision Profile* matrix

$$D(Z) = \begin{bmatrix} \theta_{11} \dots \theta_{1j} \dots \theta_{1c} \\ \dots \dots \dots \dots \dots \dots \\ \theta_{i1} \dots \theta_{ij} \dots \theta_{ic} \\ \dots \dots \dots \dots \dots \dots \\ \theta_{L1} \dots \theta_{Lj} \dots \theta_{Lc} \end{bmatrix} \tag{1}$$

Each entry θ_{ij} of the decision profile matrix represents the 'degree' of support given by the classifier i to the hypothesis that Z comes form class ω_j. This support can be expressed in terms of the class aposteriori probability $P(\omega_j|\mathbf{x}_i)$, its hardened equivalent Δ_{ij} or a score value of a classifier confined to the range $[0,1]$. Note that the matrix elements along each row should sum up to one.

For an unknown pattern Z the fusion rule then compares the *Decision Profile* $D(Z)$ with class specific templates D_{T_i}, $\forall i$ each of which defines a representative target matrix for the respective class. For non overlapping classes the ideal template for class j would theoretically be a matrix of all zeros everywhere apart from the jth column, the elements of which should be set to one, i.e.

$$D_{T_i} = \begin{bmatrix} 0 \dots 0 \ 1 \ 0 \dots 0 \\ \dots \dots \dots \dots \dots \\ 0 \dots 0 \ 1 \ 0 \dots 0 \\ \dots \dots \dots \dots \dots \\ 0 \dots 0 \ 1 \ 0 \dots 0 \end{bmatrix} \tag{2}$$

However, in practice better results can be obtained by defining the decision template D_{T_i} by the means of training, based on a representative data set $\Xi = \{\mathbf{x}_k(j), \ k = 1,..,L, \ j = 1,..,N\}$ of cardinality N. In our study the training is performed using an evaluation set which is distinct from the set used for the training of the individual experts. Let β_{ji} an indicator of the class membership of pattern $\mathbf{x}_k(j)$ taking values

$$\beta_{ji} = \begin{cases} 1 \ if \ \mathbf{x}_k(j)\epsilon\omega_i \\ 0 \ if \ \mathbf{x}_k(j)\epsilon\omega_l, \ l \neq i \end{cases} \tag{3}$$

Then the trained decision template $D_{T_i}(\Xi) = [d_{ks}^i]$ for class i can be defined in terms of its matrix elements d_{ks}^i as

$$d_{ks}^i = \frac{\sum_{j=1}^N \beta_{ji}\theta_{ks}[\mathbf{x}_k(j)]}{\sum_{j=1}^N \beta_{ji}} \tag{4}$$

Thus the decision template D_{T_i} for class ω_i is the average of the decision profiles of the elements of the training set Ξ from class i. When pattern Z is submitted for classification the Decision Template scheme matches the decision profile $D(Z)$ to D_{T_i}, $i = 1 \ldots c$ and produces the soft class labels:

$$\mu_i(Z) = \mathcal{S}(D_{T_i}, D(Z)) \tag{5}$$

where $\mathcal{S}$ is interpreted as a *similarity measure*. The higher the similarity between the decision profile of pattern Z and the decision template for class i, the higher the support for i. Since the general idea is to compare the matrix $D(Z)$ to c template matrices $D_{T_1} \ldots D_{T_c}$, any measure that does this might be appropriate. In our experiments we used only the *Euclidean distance* between the decision profile and decision template matrices,

$$\mu_D^i(\mathbf{x}) = 1 - \frac{1}{Lc} \sum_{k=1}^{L} \sum_{s=1}^{c} (d_{ks}^i - \theta_{ks}(\mathbf{x}))^2 \tag{6}$$

but there is no reason to stop at this choice and any norm can be used.

3.2   Behavior Knowledge Space

The *Behavior-Knowledge Space* (BKS) method proposed by Huang et al [4] also considers the support from all the experts to all the classes jointly. However, the degree of support is quantified differently than in the Decision Templates approach. Here the decisions Δ_{ji} of experts $i = 1, ..., L$ regarding the class membership ω_j, $j = 1, ..., c$ of pattern Z are mapped into an L dimensional discrete space and the BKS fusion rule is defined in this space. In order to be more specific, let us designate the decision of the jth expert about pattern Z by $\delta_j(Z)$ which can be expressed as

$$\delta_j(Z) = argmax_{i=1}^c P(\omega_i | \mathbf{x}_j) \tag{7}$$

Thus $\delta_j(Z)$ assumes integer values from the interval $[1, c]$. The combination of the decision outputs $\delta_j(Z)$, $j = 1, ..., L$ defines a point in the L-dimensional discrete space, referred to as the Behavior Knowledge Space (BKS). We can consider each point in this space to index a bin (cell). The BKS fusion rule then associates a separate consensus decision with each of the bins in the BKS space.

Let us denote by $h_i(d_1, .., d_L)$ the histogram of the patterns from a set Ξ which belong to class ω_i and fall into the bin $(d_1, .., d_L)$ by virtue of the indexation process defined in (7). The BKS fusion rule then assigns a new pattern Z as follows

$$\delta(Z) = \begin{cases} argmax_{i=1}^c h_i(\delta_1(Z), .., \delta_L(Z)) & if \quad \sum_{k=1}^c h_k(\delta_1(Z), .., \delta_L(Z)) > 0 \\ & and \quad \frac{h_{\delta(Z)}(\delta_1(Z), ..., \delta_L(Z))}{\sum_{k=1}^c h_k(\delta_1(Z), ..., \delta_L(Z))} \geq \lambda \\ \delta_0(Z) & otherwise \end{cases} \tag{8}$$

where $\delta_0(Z)$ denotes a rejection or a decision by an alternative fusion process such as the majority *Vote*, or the fusion strategies suggested in [9] and [4]. Thus a special line of action is taken when the indexed bin of the BKS histogram is zero, or if the proportional vote held by the most representative class in the bin is below threshold λ. In our two class experiments the above conditions were always satisfied. However, a number of studies on how to find the value of the threshold have been reported (see for instance Huang and Suen [4]).

In summary, the class with the greatest number of votes in each bin is chosen by the BKS method. In our experiments we considered different weights for the two different classes based on the class a priori probabilities. Thus for each combination of classifiers we divided the number of occurrences of each class by the respective numbers of samples in set Ξ.

4   Experimental Set Up

We conducted our experiments in decision level fusion of multiple face modality experts in personal identity verification on the XM2VTS database. It consists of recordings of 295 subjects at one month intervals. The database contains 4 sessions. During each session two head rotation and speaking shots were taken. The Lausanne protocol splits randomly all 295 subjects into 200 clients, 25 evaluation impostors and 70 test impostors. Two different evaluation configurations were defined. They differ in the distribution of client training and client evaluation data. Configuration I takes the first shot from the first 3 sessions as training data, while the second shots are taken for evaluation. Configuration II takes sessions 1 and 2 as training data and session 3 as evaluation data. Our experiments are based on configuration I for which the evaluation set contains 600 client shots (200 clients x three shots), and 40000 imposter cases(25 impostors x 8 shots x 200 clients). The test set contains 400 client shots (200 clients x 2 shots) and 112000 imposter cases (70 impostors x 8 shots x 200 clients).

Table 1. Average success rates of individual experts on the Evaluation set and Test set

EXPERT	EVALUTION SET	TEST SET
UniS-gdm	97.83	97.15
UniS-noc	96.46	96.90
UniS-eucl	88.80	91.15
UCL-noc	96.11	96.68
UCL-pm1	94.43	95.34
UCL-pm2	95.29	96.14

The strength of the individual experts can be gleaned from the single expert results in table **Table 1**. They are expressed as the average success rates (ASR) of client acceptance and impostor rejection. We note that Unis-gdm is the best expert overall. The test set results confirm the superiority in performance of this expert. It is also interesting to note that the test set error rate using expert Unis-gdm (100-ASR) is about 3 times better than the error rate achieved by the worst expert, Unis-eucl.

Table 2. Client correlation matrices of UniS experts

	UniS-noc		UniS-gdm	
UniS-eucl	549	0	549	0
	31	19	38	13
UniS-noc			581	0
			6	13

Table 3. Impostor correlation matrices of UniS experts

	UniS-noc		UniS-gdm	
UniS-eucl	35729	876	36091	559
	3034	336	3069	331
UniS-noc			38491	267
			619	623

The choice of these experts is interesting because of the strong correlations between some of them as it is evident from **Table 2, Table 3, Table 4, Table 5**. In these tables the top-left element of each matrix represents the number of shared correct decisions (acceptance/rejection for client/impostor respectively) of the pair of experts. The bottom-right element shows the number of shared false rejections/acceptances (client/impostor) of the two experts. The top-right figure gives the number of client/impostor claims accepted/rejected by the expert on the left and rejected/accepted by the expert at the top. It is evident, that for some of them, the set of false acceptances and false rejections is a subset of the set of another expert errors. In combining them we want to explore how the Decision Templates and BKS methods behave in an intramodal fusion scenario.

Note that there is a strong correlation between the errors committed in recognising clients by the UniS experts. In **Table 2** we can see that all the errors committed by UniS-gdm and UniS-noc are committed by UniS-eucl, while the other errors committed by UniS-eucl are not committed by the others. In other words, the errors (in recognising the clients) committed by UniS-gdm and UniS-noc are a subset of those committed by UniS-eucl.

Table 4. Client correlation matrices of UCL experts

	UCL-pm1		UCL-pm2	
UCL-noc	567	15	573	9
	5	13	7	11
UCL-pm1			563	9
			17	11

Table 5. Impostor correlation matrices of UCL experts

	UCL-pm1		UCL-pm2	
UCL-noc	37524	1305	37996	833
	599	572	600	1571
UCL-pm1			37399	724
			1197	680

When fusing the available experts we have the choice of combining any subset of them. The number of experts combined, L, could range from 2 up to 6. For each value of L we find the set of experts that performs best on the evaluation set and record the winning combination of experts. The same combination is then evaluated on the test set. We repeat this experiment for the two fusion rules described in Section 3. The results of the experiments are presented and discussed in the next section.

5   Experimental Results

In **Table 6 and Table 7** we can see the evaluation set results achieved using the Decision Template and the BKS method. Note that on the evaluation set the *Decision Templates* combination is never better than the best single expert. With the number of experts increasing, the performance of the combined systems peaks at 3 experts and then starts decreasing, dropping below the best single expert level significantly. This applies also to the performance of *Decision Templates* on the test set, with the combined rate exceeding that of the single best expert only for the combinations of 3 and 4 experts respectively. The improvement of the best combination over the single best expert is not significant. The performance on the test set is shadowed by the aposteriori best performance which shows that the selection of combinations on the evaluation set is reliable.

In contrast the *Behavior Knowledge Space* method delivered excellent performance in all respects. On both the evaluation and test set the error rates for the best combinations of experts were better than that for the best single expert

Table 6. DT and BKS: Performance on the Evaluation set

N. experts	DT	BKS
2	97.02	97.92
3	97.51	98.15
4	96.46	98.21
5	96.12	98.34
6	95.81	98.43

in all cases. Most importantly, the improvements, as a function of the number of experts fused, are monotonic, with one exception only. Thus the best performance is obtained by the highest number of experts combined. In the case of the evaluation set the improvements are flat. However, the performance gains on the test set is worth while even when adding the last to the set of five. This brings the best combined system error rate down to 1.51%. For any number of experts the best combined system performance is mirrored by the best aposteriori performance which confirms that we achieved the best designs possible.

Table 7. DT and BKS : Performance on the Test set

N. experts	DT	BKS
2	87.79	97.39
A POSTERIORI	87.79	97.39
3	97.7	97.78
A POSTERIORI	97.7	97.78
4	97.28	97.68
A POSTERIORI	97.8	98.05
5	96.60	98.08
A POSTERIORI	96.60	98.19
6	96.24	98.49
A POSTERIORI	96.33	98.49

One of the most important findings is the quasi monotonicity behaviour of the BKS method. This is quite surprising for a number of reasons. First of all we know that some of our experts are highly correlated. Second, the average error rates of the experts differ by a considerable margin. It appears the the BKS classifier combination method is coping very well with both difficulties. This is consistent with the theoretical analysis of the decision level fusion rules reported in [2] which showed that the improved performance of multiple classifiers derived from the increased resolution of the combined decision output space of the fused component classifiers.

6   Conclusions

In this study we investigated the Behavior Knowledge Space [10] and Decision Templates [7] methods of classifier fusion in the context of personal identity verification. The study involved six experts exploiting the frontal face biometrics The experts are not only correlated, but also their performance levels differ by as much as a factor of three.

Through extensive experiments on the XM2VTS data base using the Lausanne protocol we found that the Behavior Knowledge Space fusion strategy achieved consistently better results than the Decision Templates method. Most importantly, it exhibited quasi monotonic behaviour as the number of experts combined increased. This is a very important conclusion of the study, as it means that by adding experts, the performance of the multimodal system will not be degraded. This avoids the need to select a subset of experts to optimise performance. We also demonstrated that for a sufficient number of experts combined the optimal configuration selected on the evaluation set was also aposteriori optimal on the test set.

7   Acknowledgement

This work was supported by the European Union Project Banca.

References

[1] The extended m2vts database.   http://www.ee.surrey.ac.uk/Research/VSSP/ xm2vtsdb/, 9 2000.
[2] J Grim, J Kittler, P Pudil, and P Somol. Information analysis of multiple classifier fusion. In J Kittler and F Roli, editors, *Multiple Classifier Systems 2001*, pages 168–177, 2001.
[3] B.Moghaddam and A.Pentland, "Probabilistic visual learning for object representation," In S.K. Nayer and T. Poggio,editors, *Early Visual learning*, pp. 99-130, 1997.
[4] Y. Huang and C. Suen. A method of combining multiple experts for the recognition of unconstrained handwritten numerals. *IEEE Transaction on Pattern Analysis and Machine Intelligence*, 17(1), 1 1995.
[5] J. Kittler and Eds. F. Roli. *Multiple classifier systems*. Springer, 2000, 2001.
[6] J Kittler, Y P Li, and J Matas. On matching scores for lda-based face verification. In M Mirmehdi and B Thomas, editors, *Proceedings of British Machine Vision Conference 2000*, pages 42–51, 2000.
[7] L. Kuncheva, J.C. Bezdek, and R.P.W. Duin. Decision templates for multiple classifier fusion : an experimental comparison. *Pattern Recognition*, 34:299–314, 2001.
[8] L.I. Kuncheva and C.J.Whitaker. Feature subsets for classifier combination: An enumerative experiment. In *Proceedings of the International Workshop on Multiple Classifier Systems*, volume LNCS2096, pages 228–237. Springer, 2001.
[9] K-D. Wernecke. A coupling procedure for the discrimination of mixed data. *Biometrics*, 48:497–506, 6 1992.

[10] L. Xu, A. Krzyzak, and C.Y. Suen. Methods of combining multiple classifiers and their applications to handwriting recognition. *IEEE Transaction. SMC*, 22(3):418–435, 1992.

An Experimental Comparison of Classifier Fusion Rules for Multimodal Personal Identity Verification Systems

Fabio Roli[1], Josef Kittler[2], Giorgio Fumera[1] and Daniele Muntoni[1]

[1] Dept. of Electrical and Electronic Eng., University of Cagliari
Piazza d'Armi, 09123 Cagliari, Italy
{roli, fumera}@diee.unica.it
[2] Centre for Vision, Speech and Signal Processing
School of Electronics, Computing and Mathematics, University of Surrey
Guildford GU2 7XH, U.K.
J.Kittler@eim.surrey.ac.uk

Abstract. In this paper, an experimental comparison between fixed and trained fusion rules for multimodal personal identity verification is reported. We focused on the behaviour of the considered fusion methods for ensembles of classifiers exhibiting significantly different performance, as this is one of the main characteristics of multimodal biometrics systems. The experiments were carried out on the XM2VTS database, using eight experts based on speech and face data. As fixed fusion methods, we considered the sum, majority voting, and order statistics based rules. The considered trained methods are the Behaviour Knowledge Space and the weighted averaging of classifiers outputs.

1   Introduction

Automatic personal-identity verification systems based on biometrics data can play an important role in several applications. Typical examples are access control, surveillance applications, and retrieval of faces from video databases. Several sensing modalities have been developed, based on the different biometrics characteristics which allow to distinguish individuals from each other. Relatively simple modalities are fingerprint, face and voice, while more sophisticated ones include, for instance, the iris pattern or the thermal signature of the human face acquired by a infrared camera. However, although individual modalities have proven to be reliable in ideal environments, they can be very sensitive to real environmental conditions. For instance, speaker verification degrades rapidly in noisy environments. Similarly, the effectiveness of face recognition and verification strongly depends on lighting conditions and on variations in the subject's pose in front of the camera. Therefore, in the last years, interest has been growing in using multiple modalities. Even if each individual modality can be weak, different modalities can provide complementary information. This can allow increasing the robustness of the resulting system to environmental conditions, as shown in [1,2,3,15].

The design of a personal identity verification system capable to effectively exploit the information coming from multiple modalities requires a suitable decision-level fusion method [4,5,6,7,8]. Several decision-level fusion rules have been developed

F. Roli and J. Kittler (Eds.): MCS 2002, LNCS 2364, pp. 325–335, 2002.
© Springer-Verlag Berlin Heidelberg 2002

over the last ten years [9]. For the purposes of our discussion, such rules can be subdivided into two main categories: fixed rules, like the majority voting and the sum rule [3,9,10,11], and trained rules, like the weighted averaging of classifiers outputs and the Behaviour Knowledge Space method [9, 10,12]. According to theoretical and experimental results, researchers agree that fixed rules usually perform well for ensembles of classifiers exhibiting similar performance [13,20]. On the other hand, trained rules should handle more effectively classifiers exhibiting different accuracy or different pair-wise correlation [20]. One of the main problems that appears in fusing multiple biometrics modalities is that individual biometrics subsystems often exhibit significantly different performance [15]. Therefore, the fusion of different biometrics modalities is a task for which trained rules should perform better than fixed rules. However, the conditions of performance imbalance under which trained rules can significantly outperform fixed rules are not completely clear [20,21]. Moreover, in real applications like multimodal biometrics, the bad quality and/or the limited size of training sets can quickly cancel the theoretical advantages of asymptotically optimal trained rules like the Behavior Knowledge Space [21].

In this paper, we compare some fixed and trained fusion rules on a multimodal personal-identity verification task, involving two basic biometrics modalities: speaker voice and frontal face image. Five fixed fusion rules (sum, majority vote, and three rules based on order statistics operators), and two trained rules (the Behaviour Knowldge Space and the weighted averaging of classifier outputs) were considered. These rules are described in Section 2. In Section 3, we describe the XM2VTS data base and the classifiers used for our experiments. Experimental results are then reported. Conclusions are drawn in Section 4.

2   Fixed and Trained Fusion Rules

In this paper, we considered the task of personal identity verification as a two-class pattern recognition problem. The two classes, ω_1 and ω_2, are related to the hypotheses that an identity claim is either true or false. Multiple experts, based on different biometrics modalities, are fused to estimate the a posteriori probabilities $P(\omega_1|x_i)$ and $P(\omega_2|x_i)$ of the two classes. The i-th expert represents an input pattern by a measurement vector x_i. The measurement vectors are distinct for the two speech experts, while they are the same for the three elastic graph-matching experts and for the two Fisher face experts. Further details on these experts are given in Section 3.1.

We considered five fixed and two trained fusion rules. The first fixed rule is the *Sum* rule [3,11], which consists in assigning an input pattern to the class ω_j for which:

$$\sum_{i=1}^{N} P(\omega_j \mid x_i) = \max_{k=1}^{N} \sum_{i=1}^{N} P(\omega_k \mid x_i), \tag{1}$$

where N is the number of experts. The second fixed rule is the *Majority vote*, and it is defined in terms of hard decisions Δ_{ki} reached for each class ω_k by the i-th expert. It consists in assigning an input pattern to the class ω_j for which:

$$\sum_{i=1}^{N} \Delta_{ji} = \max_{k=1}^{c} \sum_{i=1}^{N} \Delta_{ki}, \tag{2}$$

where:

$$\Delta_{ki} = \begin{cases} 1 & if\ P(\omega_k\ |\ \mathbf{x}_i) = \max_{j=1}^c P(\omega_j\ |\ \mathbf{x}_i), \\ 0 & otherwise, \end{cases} \tag{3}$$

and c denotes the number of classes. The main advantage of these rules is their simplicity, and the fact that they do not require any training. In addition, they have proven to be effective in many applications. The other fixed rules are based on Order Statistics (OS) operators applied to the experts' outputs [13]. We used the well-known *Min*, *Med* and *Max* operators. Let us consider the a posteriori probabilities estimated by the N individual experts ordered as follows:

$$P(\omega_j\ |\ \mathbf{x}_{1:N}) \le P(\omega_j\ |\ \mathbf{x}_{2:N}) \le \ldots \le P(\omega_j\ |\ \mathbf{x}_{N:N}). \tag{4}$$

For a given input pattern $\mathbf{x}$, the outputs of the rules based on the *Min*, *Med* and *Max* OS operators, $P^{os}(\omega_j|\mathbf{x})$, are defined as follows:

$$P^{\max}(\omega_j\ |\ \mathbf{x}) = P(\omega_j\ |\ \mathbf{x}_{N:N}), \quad P^{\min}(\omega_j\ |\ \mathbf{x}) = P(\omega_j\ |\ \mathbf{x}_{1:N}), \tag{5}$$

$$P^{\mathrm{med}}(\omega_j\ |\ \mathbf{x}) = \begin{cases} \dfrac{P(\omega_j\ |\ \mathbf{x}_{N/2:N}) + P(\omega_j\ |\ \mathbf{x}_{(N+1)/2:N})}{2} & if\ N\ is\ even, \\ P(\omega_j\ |\ \mathbf{x}_{(N+1)/2:N}) & if\ N\ is\ odd. \end{cases}$$

The corresponding decision rules simply consist in assigning an input pattern to the class ω_j for which $P^{os}(\omega_j|\mathbf{x})$ is maximum. Even if OS-based rules are fixed rules, they can provide more flexibility with respect to other fixed rules like Sum and Majority vote. As pointed out in [13,20], this can make OS-based rules an intermediate solution between fixed and trained rules.

The first trained rule we considered is the *Weighted average* rule. It is basically a variant of the *Sum* rule. It consists in assigning an input pattern to the class ω_j for which:

$$\sum_{i=1}^N w_i P(\omega_j\ |\ \mathbf{x}_i) = \max_{k=1}^N \sum_{i=1}^N w_i P(\omega_k\ |\ \mathbf{x}_i), \tag{6}$$

where w_i is the weight assigned to the i-th expert. We used normalised weights:

$$\sum_{k=1}^N w_k = 1, \quad w_k \ge 0 \quad k = 1, \ldots, N. \tag{7}$$

In principle, weighted averaging of classifiers' outputs should handle the imbalance of classifiers' accuracy better than the Sum rule. However, it has been found experimentally that weighted averaging could fail to outperform the Sum rule even for ensembles of classifiers exhibiting different accuracy [13]. In particular, it has been argued that OS combiners could be more effective and robust than weighted average, as, in real applications, it can be difficult to estimate the optimal weights [13,20].

The other trained rule we used is the *Behaviour Knowledge Space* (BKS) method [10,12]. Let us denote the decision of the k-th classifier for the input pattern $\mathbf{x}$ as $\delta_k(\mathbf{x})$. For a c-class problem, $\delta_k(\mathbf{x})$ can take on values $1, \ldots, c$. The vector of the classifiers' decisions, $(\delta_1(\mathbf{x}),\ldots,\delta_N(\mathbf{x}))$, defines a point in a c-dimensional discrete space, which is called Behaviour Knowledge Space (BKS). Each point of the BKS can be considered as indexing a bin (cell). For each cell (i.e., for each value of the classifiers' decision vector $\delta_k(\mathbf{x})$, $k = 1, ..., N$), the class with the highest number of patterns is estimated from a validation set. The BKS rule assigns the input pattern $\mathbf{x}$ to such class. It is easy to see that the BKS can be regarded as a look-up table that maps the classifiers' decision vector into a class. With respect to the original formulation of this fusion method, in our experiments, we weighted the two classes according to their prior probabilities.

3   Experimental Comparison

3.1   The XM2VTS Database and the Experts Used

Two biometrics modalities were considered in this work: speaker voice and frontal face image. For our experiments, we used the XM2VTS database. It is a multimodal database consisting of face images, video sequences and speech recordings taken on 295 subjects at one-month intervals. The database contains four sessions. During each session two head rotation and speaking shots were taken. According to the Lausanne protocol [14], the 295 subjects were subdivided into 200 clients, 25 evaluation impostors and 70 test impostors. Two different configurations were defined. They differ in the distribution of clients into the training and evaluation sets. We used the configuration that takes the first shot from the first three sessions as training data, and the second shot as evaluation data. Hence, the evaluation set contains 600 clients shot and 40,000 impostor cases. The test set contains 400 client shots and 112,000 impostor cases.

Several experts were designed for each modality, using different representations of the biometrics data and distinct matching procedures. For our experiments, we used two speech experts and six frontal face experts. The members of the European project M2VTS have developed them, with the exception of one of the face experts that was developed by the University of Sydney. In the following, we briefly summarise the main characteristics of the eight experts. Further details can be found in [15].

The two speech experts have been developed at IDIAP in Switzerland. The first one (denoted hereafter as *Expert 3*) is based on second order statistical moments computed on the speech signal. For this expert, a text-independent verification process was used. The second speech expert (*Expert 4*) is based on the Hidden Markov Model approach [16]. The text independent verification process was used for this expert.

The six face experts are based on three different approaches to face image representation. The same method is used for the initial approximated face detection, which exploits the cromaticity of the face skin. The experts differ in the techniques used for the subsequent accurate geometric registration. Two experts (*Expert 1* and *2*) were designed at the University of Surrey [17]. They confirm or reject the claimed identity in the Fisher subspace derived by the Linear Discriminant Analysis. The only difference is that Expert 1 processes automatically registered images, while Expert 2 uses semi-automatic registration. Three experts (*Expert 5, 6* and *7*) were designed at the Aristotle University of Thessaloniki [18]. They are based on elastic graph matching. They differ in their internal threshold values setting, used to control the degree of elasticity of the graph. One expert (*Expert 8*) was developed at the University of Sydney, and is based on the concept of fractal neighbour distance.

The expert scores on the XM2VTS database are available from [19]. The thresholds for each expert were computed on the evaluation set using the Receiver Operating Curve (ROC), so that the false acceptance and false rejection error rates were equal. Next, using these threshold values, the client and impostor error rates were measured on the test set. The overall error rate was also computed as the average of client and impostor error rates. These values are reported in Table 1.

Table 1. Percentage error rates of the eight experts on the evaluation and test sets.

	Error rate	Expert 1	Expert 2	Expert 3	Expert 4	Expert 5	Expert 6	Expert 7	Expert 8
Eval. set	Average	5.366	3.500	0.615	0.090	7.995	8.165	8.170	12.925
	Client	5.367	3.500	0.830	0.170	8.000	8.170	8.170	13.000
	Impostor	5.365	3.500	0.400	0.010	7.990	8.160	8.170	21.850
Test set	Average	7.185	3.105	4.205	0.740	7.055	7.510	7.310	12.940
	Client	6.750	2.750	7.000	0.000	6.000	7.250	6.500	12.250
	Impostor	7.620	3.460	1.410	1.480	8.110	7.770	8.120	13.630

Table 1 points out the performance "imbalance" of the experts considered. In particular, the average test set error rate of the worst expert, Expert 8, is about 18 times greater than that of the best one, Expert 4. The absolute difference is 12.2%. Moreover, the average error rate of Expert 4 is about 4 and 6 times better than the ones of the next two best experts, Expert 2 and 3, with absolute differences of about 2.4% and 3.5%, respectively.

3.2   Experimental Results

Our experiments were aimed at:
- comparing the performance of the fusion rules for ensembles with increasing numbers of experts;
- comparing the performance of the fusion rules for ensembles with different degrees of classifiers' performance imbalance.

With regard to the first aim, we considered the combination of any subset of the available experts. The number of experts to combine, N, ranges from 2 up to 8. For each value of N, we found the set of experts that performed best on the evaluation set, and then we evaluated the same combination on the test set. This was repeated for all the fusion rules described in Sect. 2. For the weighted average rule, values of the weights proportional to the average recognition rates of the corresponding experts on the evaluation set were used. For each rule and all the considered numbers of experts, the average test-set error rates are reported in Table 2.

Table 2. For each rule, the average test set error rates of the best mixtures of experts selected on the evaluation set are reported. For each value of N, the row named *Experts* indicates the experts considered by their numbers (e.g., 14 refers to the set made up of Expert 1 and Expert 4).

				Sum			
N	2	3	4	5	6	7	8
Experts	14	134	1348	12348	123468	1234568	all
Av. Error	0.69	0.62	0.56	0.56	0.57	0.60	0.82

				Vote			
N	2	3	4	5	6	7	8
Experts	34	134	1348	12348	123478	1234678	all
Av. Error	2.66	0.79	0.45	0.45	0.71	0.83	2.82

				Min			
N	2	3	4	5	6	7	8
Experts	34	134	1234	12348	123458	1234578	all
Av. Error	2.417	2.417	2.417	0.552	0.722	0.724	50.000

				Med			
N	2	3	4	5	6	7	8
Experts	46	247	1347	12467	123467	1234678	all
Av. Error	0.663	0.614	0.532	0.643	0.494	1.147	2.640

				Max			
N	2	3	4	5	6	7	8
Experts	45	456	4567	24567	245678	2345678	all
Av. Error	0.573	0.573	0.573	0.573	0.573	0.573	0.574

				Weighted average			
N	2	3	4	5	6	7	8
Experts	46	246	1246	12346	123468	1234568	all
Av. Error	0.671	0.658	0.658	0.650	0.669	0.691	0.809

				Behaviour Knowledge Space			
N	2	3	4	5	6	7	8
Experts	34	134	1348	12348	123478	1234678	all
Av. Error	0.740	0.740	0.680	0.610	0.740	0.740	1.400

Let us first consider the performance of the fixed fusion methods. The Sum and Vote rules performed quite similarly, except for sets made up of two and eight experts. In such cases, the error rate of the Sum rule was lower of about 2%. For $N < 5$, it is worth noting that both rules selected Expert 1 instead of Expert 2, although the first one exhibited a higher error rate on the evaluation set. Moreover, for $N > 3$, the Sum and Vote rules always selected Expert 8, which is the worst individual expert. This result points out that it is better to combine the most complementary experts rather than the best performing ones.

Fixed fusion rules based on OS operators exhibited very different performance. The Max rule provided a nearly uniform error rate for any value of N. It outperformed Sum and Vote, except for $N = 4, 5$. The Med rule exhibited similar error rates for $N < 7$, but its performance degraded significantly for $N = 7, 8$. The Min rule seems instead very unreliable. It exhibited error rates higher than Med and Max for $N = 2, 3, 4$. In particular, it exhibited an error rate equal to 50% when all the available experts were combined. It should be noted that the error rate increased from 0.724% to 50% when Expert 6 was added to the others. Also note that the average test set error rate of

Expert 6 was 7.51%. This result could be due to the different distributions of the output values exhibited by different experts with respect to clients and impostors. As a consequence, when, for different patterns, the combiner outputs are selected from different experts, as happens for OS based rules, there can be cases in which it is not possible to find a suitable decision threshold.Consider now the trained rules, namely Weighted averaging and BKS. Weighted averaging performed slightly better than the BKS method, in particular for $N = 8$. However, the Max rule always outperformed both the Weighted average and the BKS rules. Moreover, the performance of these two rules are comparable to those of the Sum rule. The Vote rule outperformed the BKS rule for $N = 4, 5, 6$, although the two rules selected the same combinations of experts. Analogously, the Sum rule performed better than the Weighted average rule for values of N from 3 to 7. For $N = 6, 7$, it should be noted that these two rules selected the same combinations of experts. To sum up, results in Table 2 do not show a clear superiority of trained rules over the fixed ones.

It is worth noting that fixed and trained rules exhibited error rates that do not decrease monotonically as the number of experts increases. However, some rules exhibited quasi mononotic behaviors, that is, their error rates decrease if one consider a limited range of the N parameter. Although definitive conclusions cannot be drawn on the basis of these experiments, such results raise a serious methodological question of how to decide when the fusion of more experts starts being counterproductive.

With regard to the second goal of our experiments, we used ensembles of experts exhibiting different degrees of performance imbalance. In particular, four ensembles made up of three experts were selected. The difference (denoted with Δ) between the error rates of the worst and the best expert was used as a measure of performance imbalance. The experts of each ensemble and the corresponding test set average error rates are reported in Table 3.

Table 3. Test set average error rates for the four ensembles made up of three experts. The difference (denoted with Δ) between the error rates of the worst and the best expert was used as a measure of performance imbalance.

	Experts	Average Error Rates			Δ
Ensemble 1	5,1,7	7.055	7.185	7.310	0.255
Ensemble 2	2,7,6	3.105	7.310	7.510	4.405
Ensemble 3	2,3,6	3.105	4.205	7.510	4.405
Ensemble 4	2,6,8	3.105	7.510	12.940	9.835

According to the values of parameter Δ, Ensemble 1 is balanced, while the other ensembles are relatively imbalanced. In particular, Ensembles 2 and 3 are characterized by the same value of Δ, but different error rates of the "intermediate" expert. Ensemble 4 exhibits the highest value of the parameter Δ.

In this experiment, we were interested in comparing the performance of fixed and trained rules for ensembles with different degrees of classifiers' performance imbalance, disregarding the problems due to the bad quality and/or the limited size of training set. In other words, we were interested in the ideal behavior of the trained fusion rules. Therefore, we computed the optimal values of the weights for the Weighted average rule by "exhaustive" search on the test set. Analogously, the BKS rule was trained on the test set. The average test-set error rates of the considered fusion rules are reported in Table 4.

Table 4. For each ensemble, the test set average error rates of the different fusion methods are reported.

	Sum	Vote	OS min	OS med	OS max	W.A.	BKS
Ens. 1	6.014	5.696	6.465	6.725	9.049	3.205	4.909
Ens. 2	5.739	5.836	7.475	6.465	5.325	2.184	4.246
Ens. 3	4.420	1.035	7.470	1.587	5.325	0.351	0.474
Ens. 4	5.509	3.895	7.474	11.980	5.325	2.150	3.487

Let us consider first the fixed fusion rules. Table 4 shows that the Sum rule outperformed the best individual expert only for the balanced Ensemble 1. The performance of the Vote rule was quite good. In particular, it exhibited an excellent performance for Ensemble 3. The performance of the three combining rules based on OS operators were often significantly worse than the ones of the Sum and the Vote rules. The only exception is the Med combiner for Ensemble 3. However, the Med combiner exhibited an error rate very similar to that of the worst expert for Ensemble 4. The Max rule performed worse than all the individual experts for the balanced Ensemble 1.

Let us now consider the performance of the trained rules. Note that the Weighted average rule always outperformed both the best individual expert and all the other combining rules. In particular, the error rate improvements over the Sum rule are reported in Table 4. We point out that the Weighted average rule significantly outperformed the Sum rule even for the balanced Ensemble 1. However, the corresponding improvement is comparable to that achieved for the imbalanced ensembles, in particular for Ensemble 4. Moreover, looking at the optimal weights, which are reported in Table 6, it is possible to note that a very low weight is assigned to one of the worst experts. This points out that Weighted average can significantly outperform Sum only by discarding one or more of the worst experts [20]. Consider now the BKS rule. It outperformed the best individual expert only for Ensembles 1 and 3. Moreover, it is worth noting that its performance was quite similar to those of the Vote rule. The difference between the error rates is greater than 1% only for Ensemble 2. The BKS rule achieved very good performance for Ensemble 3, like Weighted average, Vote and Med.

To sum up, Tables 4 and 5 show that trained rules can significantly outperform the fixed ones in the ideal case (i.e., when they are trained on the test set). Such theoretical advantage can obviously be cancelled, or strongly reduced, in real cases, as Table 2 points out. It is worth noting that trained rules handle more effectively the cases of imbalanced classifiers (Table 4).

To analyze further the above performance, we computed the correlation coefficients among the outputs of the experts of each ensemble. They are reported in Table 7. For Ensemble 3, the outputs of each pair of experts exhibited very low correlation, except for the outputs of experts 2 and 6 corresponding to clients. It should be noted that Ensemble 3 is made up of experts using two different sensing modalities. The correlations of the other ensembles are significantly greater, at least for some pairs of experts. This can explain the good performance achieved by the most of the rules for Ensemble 3. However, it is interesting to note that the Sum rule failed to take advantage of low correlated experts, as can be seen from Table 4.

Table 5. Difference between the error rates of Sum and Weighted average for the four ensembles.

Ensembles	1	2	3	4
E^{sa}-E^{wa}	2.809	3.555	4.069	3.359

Table 6. Optimal weights of Weighted average for the four ensembles.

Ens. 1	5	1	7	Ens. 3	2	3	6
	0.010	0.780	0.210		0.030	0.140	0.830
Ens. 2	2	7	6	Ens. 4	2	6	8
	0.850	0.000	0.150		0.080	0.870	0.050

Table 7. Correlation coefficients between the outputs of each pair of experts belonging to the four ensembles. The correlations have been computed separately for the two classes of clients and impostors.

Ensemble 1	(1,5)	(1,7)	(5,7)	Ensemble 2	(2,6)	(2,7)	(6,7)
Clients	0.440	0.424	0.975	Clients	0.421	0.452	0.977
Impostors	0.091	0.026	0.960	Impostors	-0.050	0.041	0.964
Ensemble 3	(2,3)	(2,6)	(3,6)	Ensemble 4	(2,6)	(2,8)	(6,8)
Clients	0.036	0.421	0.067	Clients	0.421	0.363	0.548
Impostors	0.013	-0.050	0.057	Impostors	-0.050	0.068	0.505

4 Conclusions

In this paper, we compared by experiments several rules for fusing multi-modal personal-identity verification experts. We focused on the fusion of imbalanced experts, that is, experts exhibiting very different performance, as this is the typical condition in this application.

According to theoretical and experimental results, researchers agree that fixed rules usually perform well for ensembles of classifiers exhibiting similar performance, while trained rules should handle more effectively classifiers exhibiting different accuracy or different pair-wise correlation [20,21]. However, the conditions of performance imbalance under which trained rules can significantly outperform fixed rules are not completely clear [20,21]. Moreover, in real applications like multimodal biometrics, the bad quality and/or the limited size of training sets can quickly cancel the theoretical advantages of trained rules.

The reported results showed that trained rules, in particular Weighted averaging, can provide significant improvements over fixed rules in the ideal case (i.e., when they are trained on the test set). In other words, the advantages of trained rules strongly depend on the quality and the size of the training set. On the other hand, our experiments showed no clear advantage of the trained rules over the fixed ones when they were trained on the evaluation set.

Our results also showed that the correlation between the outputs of the different experts could significantly affect the performance of both fixed and trained rules. In particular, it seems that the Vote rule can exploit low correlation between the combined experts as effectively as trained rules. However, under the same conditions, the Sum rule did not exhibit this behaviour. Among trained rules, the Weighted average outperformed slightly the BKS rule. Among fixed rules, the Vote rule exhibited good performance, comparable to those of the BKS rule. In contrast, the effectiveness of OS based rules appeared to be poor for the considered application.

To sum up, the reported results demand a further investigation of the conditions, in terms of performance and correlation imbalance, under which trained rules can significantly outperform fixed rules. Such conditions seem to depend strongly on the particular fusion rules considered.

References

1. Ben-Yacoub, S., Abdeljaoued, Y., Mayoraz, E.: Fusion of face and speech data for personal identity verification. IEEE Trans. on Neural Networks 10 (1999) 1065-1074
2. Ben-Yacoub, S., Luettin, J., Jonsson, K., Matas, J., Kittler, J.: Audio-visual person verification. In: Computer Vision and Pattern Recognition. IEEE Computer Society, Los Alamitos, California (1999) 580-585
3. Kittler, J., Hatef, M., Duin, R., Matas, J.: On combining classifiers. IEEE Trans. on Pattern Analysis and Machine Intelligence 20 (1998) 226-239
4. Bigun, J., Borgerforce, G., Sanniti di Baja, G. (Eds.): Audio- and Video-Based Biometric Person Authentication. Springer (1997)
5. Proc. of Int. Conf. on Audio- and Video-Based Biometric Person Authentication, Springer (1999)
6. Bigun, J., Smeraldi, F. (Eds.): Audio- and Video-Based Biometric Person Authentication. Springer (2001)
7. Poh, N., Korczak, J.: Hybrid biometric person authentication using face and voice features. Proc. of 3rd Int. Conf. on Audio- and Video-Based Biometric Person Authentication (2001) 348-351
8. Ross, A., Jain, A.K., Qian, J.Z.: Information fusion in biometrics. Proc. of 3rd Int. Conf. on Audio- and Video-Based Biometric Person Authentication (2001) 354-359
9. Kittler, J., Roli, F. (Eds.): Multiple Classifier Systems. Springer-Verlag, LNCS, Vol. 1857 (2000), and Vol. 2096 (2001)
10. Xu, L., Krzyzak, A., Suen, C.Y.: Methods of Combining Multiple Classifiers and Their Applications to Handwriting Recognition. IEEE Trans. on Systems, Man, and Cybernetics 22 (1992) 418-435
11. Kittler, J.: Combining Classifiers. Pattern Analysis and Applications 1 (1998) 18-27
12. Huang, Y.S., Suen, C.Y.: A Method of Combining Multiple Experts for the Recognition of Unconstrained Handwritten Numerals. IEEE Transactions on Pattern Analysis and Machine Intelligence 17 (1995) 90-94
13. Tumer, K., Ghosh, J.: Linear and Order Statistics Combiners for Pattern Classification. In: Sharkey, A.J.C. (ed.): Combining Artificial Neural Nets. Springer (1999) 127-161
14. Luettin, J., Matre, G.: Evaluation protocol for the extended m2vts database (xm2vtsdb). Technical Report IDIAP-COM 98-05, Dalle Mole Institute for Perceptual Artificial Intelligence, http://www.idiap.ch (1998)

15. Kittler, J., Ballette, M., Roli, F.: Decision level fusion in multimodal personal identity verification systems. Submitted to the Information Fusion journal, special issue on Fusion of Multiple Classifiers.
16. Duc, B., Maitre, G., Fisher, S., Bigun, J.: Person authentication by fusing face and speech information. Proc. 1st Int. Conf. on Audio- and Video-based Biometric Person Authentication (1997) 311-318
17. Kittler, J., Li, Y.P., Matas, J.: On matching scores for Ida-based face verification. Proc. of British Machine Vision Conference (2000) 42-51
18. Tefas, A., Koutrpoulos, C., Pitas, I.: Morphological elastic graph matching applied to frontal face authentication under well controlled and real conditions. Proc. of IEEE ICASSP (1999)
19. The extended m2vts database. http://www.ee.surrey.ac.uk/Research/VSSP/xm2vtsdb/ (2000)
20. Roli, F., Fumera, G.: Analysis of linear and order statistics combiners for fusion of imbalanced classifiers. 3rd Int. Workshop on Multiple Classifier Systems (MCS 2002), Cagliari, Italy, June 2002, Springer-Verlag, LNCS, in press.
21. Roli, F., Raudys, S., Marcialis, G.L.: An experimental comparison of fixed and trained fusion rules for crisp classifier outputs. 3rd Int. Workshop on Multiple Classifier Systems (MCS 2002), Cagliari, Italy, June 2002, Springer-Verlag, LNCS, in press.

Author Index

Lecture Notes in Computer Science

For information about Vols. 1–2287
please contact your bookseller or Springer-Verlag